China's Emerging Tec[...]

In less than thirty years, China has become a major force in the global economy. One feature of its rapid ascent has been an enormous expansion of the country's science and technology (S&T) capabilities, thanks to the emergence of a large and increasingly well-educated talent pool. Yet China finds itself faced with a number of major challenges as to whether its full S&T potential may be realized. At the heart of these challenges lie a number of uncertainties surrounding the quality, quantity, and effective utilization of China's S&T workforce. Written by two leading experts in the field, this book is the first in forty years to address these critical issues. Building on exciting new research and a plethora of comprehensive statistical materials, its findings will have significant policy implications both for China and the international community, especially in terms of issues relating to national competitiveness and innovation potential.

DENIS FRED SIMON is Professor of International Affairs and Director of the Program on US–China Technology, Economic, and Business Relations, Pennsylvania State University.

CONG CAO is Senior Research Associate at the Neil D. Levin Graduate Institute of International Relations and Commerce, State University of New York.

China's Emerging Technological Edge

Assessing the Role of High-End Talent

DENIS FRED SIMON AND CONG CAO

CAMBRIDGE
UNIVERSITY PRESS

CAMBRIDGE UNIVERSITY PRESS
Cambridge, New York, Melbourne, Madrid, Cape Town, Singapore, São Paulo, Delhi

Cambridge University Press
The Edinburgh Building, Cambridge CB2 8RU, UK

Published in the United States of America by Cambridge University Press, New York

www.cambridge.org
Information on this title: www.cambridge.org/9780521885133

First published 2009

Printed in the United Kingdom at the University Press, Cambridge

A catalogue record for this publication is available from the British Library

Library of Congress Cataloguing in Publication data
Simon, Denis Fred.
  China's emerging technological edge : assessing the role of high-end talent /
Denis Fred Simon, Cong Cao.
    p.   cm.
  Includes bibliographical references and index.
  ISBN 978-0-521-88513-3 (hardback) 1. Technology–China. 2. Technological
innovations–China. 3. Technology transfer–China. 4. Technology and
state–China. 5. Globalization–China. I. Cao, Cong, 1959– II. Title.
  T27.C5S62 2009
  338.951′06–dc22
  2008053259

ISBN 978-0-521-88513-3 hardback
ISBN 978-0-521-71233-0 paperback

Contents

List of Figures and tables	*page* vi
Acknowledgements	xi
Abbreviations	xvi
Introduction	xviii
1	Human resources, technological innovation, and economic growth	1
2	China's talent challenge	22
3	Human resources in science and technology, and their structure and characteristics in China	57
4	Higher education and scientists and engineers in the pipeline	110
5	Utilization of scientists and engineers in China	166
6	"Brain drain," "brain gain," and "brain circulation"	212
7	Supply and demand of science and technology talent in China: key drivers	254
8	China's talent in key emerging technologies	284
9	Whither China's talent pool?	333
Appendix: Understanding Chinese science and technology human resources statistics	347
References	376
Index	397

Figures and Tables

Figures

3.1 Definition of human resources in science and
technology (HRST)   *page* 60
3.2 Relations between professionals, human
resources in science and technology (HRST),
science and technology (S&T) personnel, and
research and development (R&D) personnel
in China   69
6.1 Rates of return of overseas Chinese students   229
7.1 China's population change by age groups   268
7.2 Analytical models and variables   270
7.3 From official data to reality: "estimated" size
of China's engineering graduate pool   275
8.1 Demand for undergraduates in economics and
business administration (2004) (%)   328
A.1 China's science and technology (S&T) statistics system   357

Tables

2.1 New entrants, total enrollment, and graduates at
China's regular institutions of higher education   26
2.2 Foreign corporate research and development
(R&D) centers in China   32
2.3 Gross enrollment rate of higher education for
18–22-year-olds (%)   35
2.4 Per college student expenditure and share
of public source   37
2.5 Universities identified by the 211 Program and
the 985 Program of the Ministry of Education   46
3.1 Category and distribution of Chinese talent
(*rencai*) (2000 and 2003) (million persons)   67

3.2 Tertiary education system: a comparison 70
3.3 China's human resources in science and
     technology (HRST) (million persons) 72
3.4 Professionals – total and in state-owned enterprises
     and institutions (1000 persons) 73
3.5 Science and technology (S&T) personnel, research
     and development (R&D) personnel, and scientists
     and engineers in China (1000 persons) 75
3.6 (a) Institutional distribution of science and
     technology (S&T) personnel (1000 persons); 79
     (b) Institutional distribution of S&T personnel (%); 79
     (c) Institutional distribution of scientists and engineers
         involved in S&T activities (1000 persons); 80
     (d) Institutional distribution of scientists and engineers
         involved in S&T activities (%) 80
3.7 (a) Institutional distribution of research and
         development (R&D) personnel (full-time
         equivalent [FTE], 1000 persons–year); 81
     (b) Institutional distribution of R&D personnel (full-time
         equivalent [FTE], %) 82
3.8 Science and technology (S&T) personnel scientists
     and engineers in large- and medium-sized
     foreign-invested enterprises (FIEs) 84
3.9 (a) Geographical distribution of China's science
         and technology (S&T) personnel (1000 persons); 85
     (b) Geographical distribution of China's scientists and
         engineers engaged in S&T activities (1000 persons) 87
3.10 Female professionals (1000 persons) 91
3.11 Females among advisors of graduate students 91
3.12 Distribution of professionals, by age and rank, in
     independent research and development (R&D)
     institutes (%) 93
3.13 (a) Age profile of advisors for graduate
         students (persons); 94
     (b) Age profile of advisors for graduate students (%); 95
     (c) Age profile of advisors for doctoral students
         (persons); 96
     (d) Age profile of advisors for doctoral students (%) 97

3.14 Scientists and engineers with advanced degrees in China's
civilian research and development (R&D) institutes (%)   97
3.15 Educational attainment of faculty members at
Chinese universities   98
3.16 Educational attainment of Chinese research
and development (R&D) personnel, by types of
danwei and disciplines (2000)   100
3.17 China's science and technology (S&T) papers,
cataloged by the *Science Citation Index* (SCI),
Engineering Index (EI), and the *Index of Science
and Technology Proceedings* (ISTP) and their
respective shares and ranks in the world   102
3.18 Scientists and engineers (S&Es) in the Chinese
population and workforce   106
3.19 International comparison of human resources
in science and technology (HRST)   107
4.1 Cheung Kong scholars at universities identified
by the 985 Program (persons)   123
4.2 Top Chinese baccalaureate-origin institutions
of United States' doctorate recipients (1999–2003)
(persons)   125
4.3 Undergraduate admissions (persons)   131
4.4 Admissions, enrollment, and graduation in favored
specialties at the bachelor's degree level (persons)   134
4.5 Undergraduate engineering admissions, by
specialties (persons)   139
4.6 Admissions of graduate students, by fields of
study (persons)   143
4.7 Admissions into graduate programs, by level of
degree (persons, %)   144
4.8 Graduates of undergraduate programs at regular
institutions of higher education, by field of study
(persons, %)   146
4.9 Distribution of graduates at postgraduate level, by
field of study (persons, %)   153
5.1 Mobility structure at China's research and
development (R&D) institutes (1998–2005) (%)   181
5.2 (a) Age profile of recipients of general programs at
the National Natural Science Foundation of China   188

(b) Age profile of recipients of key programs at the
National Natural Science Foundation of China 189
5.3 (a) Average wage of Chinese employees, by sector
(RMB, 1978–2002) 196
(b) Average wage of Chinese employees, by sector
(RMB, 2003–2006) 198
5.4 Average wage in the information and research
sectors, by ownership (RMB, 2003–2006) 202
5.5 Average wage of Chinese employees, by region
and select sectors (RMB, 2006) 205
6.1 Chinese students leaving for and returning from
overseas destinations each year, 1978–2006 223
6.2 Cumulative totals of Chinese students overseas
and back in China each year, 1985–2007 224
6.3 Chinese students and scholars in the USA 226
6.4 Chinese students going overseas and returning,
by type of support (persons) 228
6.5 Programs targeting returnees or attracting the
return of overseas Chinese talent 235
6.6 Effectiveness of the programs attracting the
return of high-quality overseas Chinese talent 240
6.7 Chinese students and scholars who returned from
overseas, by level of the education received overseas 241
7.1 China's gross domestic product (GDP) and its
growth 257
7.2 Foreign direct investment (FDI) (US $ billion) 258
7.3 Level of informatization 261
7.4 China's gross expenditure on research and
development (GERD), government expenditure on
education, and their percentages of gross domestic
product (GDP) 262
7.5 China's high-technology trade (US $ billion) 264
7.6 Demand forecasting scenarios (2007–2010) 272
7.7 Forecast of the supply and demand of scientists
and engineers in China (1000 persons) 273
8.1 (a) Science and technology (S&T) personnel in
high-technology industry, by sector (persons) 287
(b) Scientists and engineers in high-technology
industry, by sector (persons) 287

(c) Percentage of scientists and engineers among
    science and technology (S&T) personnel (%)   288
8.2 (a) Science and technology (S&T) personnel
        in high-technology foreign-invested enterprises (FIEs),
        by sector (persons)   291
    (b) Scientists and engineers in high-technology
        foreign-invested enterprises (FIEs), by sector
        (persons)   291
    (c) Percentage of scientists and engineers among science
        and technology (S&T) personnel in high-technology
        foreign-invested enterprises (FIEs) (%)   292
8.3 Geographical distribution of China's scientists
    and engineers in high-technology industry
    (persons)   294
8.4 Geographical distribution of scientists and
    engineers in high-technology industry, by sector
    (2006) (persons)   297
8.5 Chinese software professionals and supply and
    demand (1000 persons)   300
8.6 Pilot software engineering schools and
    affiliated universities   303
8.7 Graduates and enrollment in software and
    software-related specialties (2006) (persons)   307
8.8 Chinese software companies with
    CMM/CMMI certification (2000–2006)   310
8.9 Geographical distribution and educational
    background of China's software professionals
    (2002) (persons)   313
8.10 Enrollment in economics and business
     administration programs and total enrollment at
     bachelor's degree level (1999–2003) (persons)   328
A.1 Major publications on China's science and
    technology (S&T) and related statistics   360
A.2 Postgraduates in academic and calendar
    years (persons)   373

Acknowledgements

Tackling a problem as complex and challenging as assessing the scientific, engineering, and managerial talent-base of a country as complicated and dynamic as the People's Republic of China requires a great deal of patience and persistence as well as a strong collaborative effort. Gaining a real operational understanding of the workings of the overall Chinese statistical system as well as the science and technology (S&T) data system, including the collection, processing, and classification approaches, is not a small task by any measure. This undertaking is made even more daunting by the fact that the Chinese system, generally speaking, lacks the same degree of openness and transparency concerning access to very detailed information about the workings of the Chinese economy and research and development (R&D) system. Nonetheless, we decided to persevere and embarked upon what often proved to be a very taxing and demanding research project. We are happy to report that the strength of our commitment and fortitude has yielded very positive results, including the production and publication of what we hope will be viewed as an important contribution to understanding contemporary China.

Both authors have been studying China's human resources in science and technology (HRST) for many years. Simon wrote his master's thesis at the University of California, Berkeley on "manpower planning in China" in 1975, while Cao studied the elite members of the Chinese Academy of Sciences (CAS) for his doctoral dissertation, the situation among young Chinese scientists with Richard P. Suttmeier, and China's "brain drain" phenomenon later on. Having some grounding in this often complicated field of study helped us to gain traction and find our direction during the early stages of the project.

In writing this book, we benefited from various types and sources of support. The effort actually began in 2005, as a research project focussed on studying the supply, demand, and quality of China's scientific and engineering talent; the specific results from this component of our research are presented and discussed in Chapter 7. That aspect of our research was supported by a grant graciously provided by the International Business Machines Corporation (IBM). In particular, Nicholas M. Donofrio, recently retired from his position as IBM's executive vice president of innovation and technology, served as the champion of the initial project, which has now evolved into a larger study entitled, "The Global Talent Index™." This more comprehensive project has witnessed the continuation of the collaboration between the Neil D. Levin Graduate Institute of International Relations and Commerce under the State University of New York, and IBM. Michael Bazigos has been coordinator on the IBM side, and along with his colleagues – Phil Swan, Martin Fleming, Doug Handler, Seth Hollander, and David Yaun – who not only have lent their help when needed, but also challenged as well as stimulated us. Our interactions with our IBM colleagues were always intellectually intense and frequently yielded new and valuable insights that we believe have found their way into this book.

Many scholars in the China studies field have encouraged our endeavors as they too have recognized the need for a serious stocktaking of China's S&T human capital. These include Richard P. Suttmeier, Jon Sigurdson, William Fischer, Adam Segal, Erik Baark, Yifei Sun, Linda Jakobson, Ding Jingping, and Zhou Yuan, among others. Cao's field research in China was, in part, supported by a grant from the US National Science Foundation to Dr. Suttmeier (OISE-0440422).

The Levin Graduate Institute in New York City provided us with a wonderful environment to carry out our research and study the problems of innovation in China as a whole. President Garrick Utley's support for the idea of creating an actual "Global Talent Index" dovetailed very nicely with the authors' common interest in China's scientific and engineering contingency. Garrick's reference point for turning out an authoritative, useful, and convenient tool for understanding the talent pool in technologically developed and emerging economies was derived from the *Military Balance*, an annual publication produced by the International Institute for Strategic Studies. Other Levin staff members have also been extremely encouraging and supportive, including Michael DiGiacomo, Thomas Moebus, Lin Wei, Christine Li, Leydi Zapata, and Jason Zheng Ye. With Levin's strong institutional support, we have been able to build a first-rate Chinese materials library focussed on S&T policy and innovation in China, including large numbers of important statistical yearbooks, monographs, and other research materials. We are proud of having created perhaps the most comprehensive collection of such Chinese materials outside, if not inside, of mainland China. Having these materials readily available has helped to facilitate the completion of this book and, we hope, helped to enhance its value.

Bilguun Ginjbaata and Howard Harrington helped us analyze the supply and demand data. A huge amount of credit and gratitude goes to Bojan Angelou, who worked tirelessly with the entire team to help build the underlying statistical model and produce the accompanying regression analyses. We are extremely grateful for his valuable contributions.

Joseph Chamie, director of research at the Center for Migration Studies, called our attention to the United Nations population projection, which is greatly appreciated.

We also want to acknowledge the many colleagues and friends in China who have provided valuable guidance, access to sources of data, and their own critical insights. In particular, we would like to mention the following individuals: Fang Xin and her team who did the strategic study on talent for the "Medium- to Long-Term Plan for the Development of Science and Technology" (MLP); Zhou Yuan, then at the National Research Center for Science and Technology for Development (NRCSTD), renamed recently as the Chinese Academy of Science and Technology for Development (CASTED) – a policy think-tank under the Ministry of Science and Technology (MOST); Gao Changlin, and especially Song Weiguo, at the CASTED Division for S&T Statistical Analysis; Wang Yali at the Center for S&T Statistics and Information at the Huazhong University of Science and Technology; Zhao Yuhai of the National Bureau of Statistics; and Jin Xiaoming and Li Xin from the Department of International Cooperation within the MOST. Pan Chengguang and Li Qun, the Chinese Academy of Social Sciences; Hu Ruiwen with the Shanghai Academy of Educational Science; Li Jianjun of the Chinese Academy of Personnel Science at the Ministry of Personnel; Zhao Lanxiang of the Institute of Policy and Management at the Chinese Academy of Sciences (CAS) shared with us their own work on China's talent. We would like to thank Linda Jakobson of the Finnish Institute of International Affairs, who shared with us the information she obtained from the US National Science Foundation on Chinese-origin PhDs in the American workforce, and Jin Bihui of the National Science Library of the CAS, who shared with us the data on international collaboration of Chinese scientists. Liu Xiaoying, director of the S&T Bureau in Dalian, along with her colleague Wan Jiuwen, willingly discussed a broad range of local talent issues with us. Vice-President Zhang Rong at Nanjing University exchanged ideas with us about the skills and placement challenges facing Chinese undergraduate students. Ding Jingping, then principal consultant with Watson Wyatt Beijing, and Guo Xin, managing director for Great China for Mercer Human Resource Consulting readily took time out of their own busy days to share their knowledge and insights on human resources management practice in China. Fan Houming, Levin's first in-residence visiting scholar, shared his first-hand knowledge of Chinese higher education with us while on leave from Dalian Maritime University. Liu Fengchao, of the Dalian University of Technology, and his doctoral student Sun Yutao, quickly located materials on Chinese software talent at our last-minute request. We also have learned a great deal from the managers working within both Chinese companies and multinational corporations (MNCs) about their experience dealing with talent in China. We especially want to thank Jiang Hongbo, president of the Zhonglian Computer Company in Dalian, for his helpfulness in explaining the challenges of building an outsourcing talent base in China. Last, but not least, we have benefited from our numerous conversations with the dozens of Chinese policymakers, enterprise executives, software engineers, and scholars from across China who have come to Levin over the last few years for advanced training in leadership, management, and the commercialization of R&D.

At Cambridge University Press, Paula M. Parish, commissioning editor of business and management, recognized the significance of the topic and graciously agreed to work with us when the book was still only a proposal.

In various forms and at various stages, Chapter 7 has been presented at various conferences, including the Qinghua–Stanford Conference Workshop on Greater China's Innovative Capacities: Progress and Challenges, Beijing, 2006; the Conference on Operation, Performance, and Prospects for China's Industrial Innovation System: Impact of Reform and Globalization, New York, 2006; the

INFORMS annual meeting, Pittsburgh, 2006; the Conference on Education for Innovation in India, China, and America, Atlanta, 2007, and so on. Comments from participants at these conferences helped us to improve the chapter as well as the book as a whole.

Finally, but most important, the two of us made many prolonged trips to China to collect data and conduct field research for this book. We truly appreciate the love, understanding, and support we receive every day from our respective families; Denis would like to acknowledge and express his deep gratitude to his wife Fredda, his daughter Melissa, and his son Mitchell, while Cong is greatly indebted to his wife Xiaozuo and his son Yiyang.

Abbreviations

AAAS	American Association for the Advancement of Science
AACSB	Association to Advance Collegiate Schools of Business
BRIC	Brazil, Russia, India, and China
CAE	Chinese Academy of Engineers
CAS	Chinese Academy of Sciences
CASS	Chinese Academy of Social Sciences
CAST	China Association for Science and Technology
CCP	Chinese Communist Party
CEO	chief executive officer
COSTIND	Commission of Science, Technology, and Industry for National Defense
CSIA	China Software Industry Association
FDI	foreign direct investment
FIE	foreign-invested enterprises
FTE	full-time equivalent
GDP	gross domestic product
GERD	gross expenditure on research and development
GPCR	Great Proletariat Cultural Revolution
HHMI	Howard Hughes Medical Institute
HRST	human resources in science and technology
ICT	information and communications technology
IPR	intellectual property right
ISCED	International Standard Classification of Education
MBA	Master of Business Administration
MII	Ministry of Information Industry
MIT	Massachusetts Institute of Technology
MLP	China's Medium- to Long-Term Plan for the Development of Science and Technology (2006–2020)
MNC	multinational corporation
MOEd	Ministry of Education

MOF	Ministry of Finance
MOFCOM	Ministry of Commerce
MOLSS	Ministry of Labor and Social Security
MOP	Ministry of Personnel
MOPS	Ministry of Public Security
MOST	Ministry of Science and Technology
NBS	National Bureau of Statistics
NDRC	National Development and Reform Commission
NIBS	National Institute of Biological Science
NPC	National People's Congress
NRCSTD	National Research Center for Science and Technology for Development
NSF	National Science Foundation, USA
NSFC	National Natural Science Foundation of China
OECD	Organization for Economic Co-operation and Development
PPP	purchasing power parity
R&D	research and development
SCI	Science Citation Index
SEC	State Education Commission, the predecessor of the Ministry of Education
S&T	science and technology
UNESCO	United Nations Educational, Scientific, and Cultural Organization
USTC	University of Science and Technology of China
WTO	World Trade Organization

Introduction

In the span of less than three decades, China has evolved from a peripheral player to become the most potent engine in the global economy. Along with its rapid economic progress, and the many improvements in the quality of life for large numbers of the Chinese population, a variety of indicators suggest that China's science and technology (S&T) capabilities also are on a sharply rising trajectory. Since the early 1990s, spending on S&T by the Chinese government has been increasing at a rate approximately twice that of overall economic growth. In 2007, China spent RMB (*reminbi*) 366 billion (US $50 billion) on research and development (R&D), or 1.49 percent of its increasing gross domestic product (GDP), highest among countries with similar economic development level, though the percentage is still lower than that of most of the major developed economies (NBS, 2008).[1] Chinese institutions of higher education have been turning out an increasing number of well-prepared graduates. In 2006, China graduated some 159 000 students with masters and doctoral degrees in science and technology, on top of 1.34 million engineering undergraduates as well as 197 000 science undergraduates (NBS, 2007: 794). Unequivocally, this represents the world's highest output in terms of overall numbers.

In recent years, there also has been a steady increase in the number of international papers published by Chinese scientists. Measured by the number of papers included into the *Science Citation Index* (SCI), a

---

[1] According to the Organization for Economic Co-operation and Development (OECD), using the purchasing power parity (PPP) measure, however, in 2006 China became the world's second-largest spender on R&D (US $136 billion), ranking only behind the USA (US $330 billion) (OECD, 2006). Of course, it should be noted that attempts to measure China's economic output in PPP terms are subject to discussion, as its gross domestic product (GDP) based on that was reduced by 40 percent in a recent recalibration (Porter, 2007). It should also be recognized that the gap in spending between China and the USA remains substantial, with the USA spending being more than twice that of Chinese spending.

bibliometric database published by the Thompson Scientific, part of Thompson Reuters, in 2006 China ranked fifth in the world. Notable achievements have been recorded in a number of emerging scientific fields such as genomics and nanotechnology.[2] Foreign investment, as well as imported technology and equipment, continues to pour into China, making it one of the largest recipients of foreign capital and know-how in the world. While most attention has been focussed on the rapidly expanding export side of China's foreign trade, it must also be remembered that China has become one of the world's largest importers. And, most recently, many of the world's technologically most innovative companies have decided to move beyond setting up manufacturing facilities in China to establishing advanced R&D centers to develop new products and services for global markets as well as the Chinese domestic market. By the end of 2007, there were well over 1000 foreign R&D centers operating in the People's Republic of China.

In early 2006, with a great deal of fanfare, China's leadership issued a new "Medium- to Long-Term Plan for the Development of Science and Technology (2006–2020)" (MLP). In addition to setting ambitious national priorities and formalizing the leadership's commitment to allocate substantial financial and people resources to meet the announced goals, the MLP specifically defines enhancing indigenous innovation capability (*zizhu chuangxin*), leapfrogging in key scientific disciplines, and utilizing S&T to support and lead future economic growth as the major objectives (Cao *et al.*, 2006). In a word, once considered one of the more backward developing countries, China today stands as one of the world's most robust and dynamic economic forces. These trends have led many observers to ask, in a similar vein, whether China also is poised to become a superpower in science and technology (see, for example, Keely & Wilsdon, 2007; Sigurdson, 2006).[3]

Underlying the massive transitions taking place in the Chinese economy and S&T system is the emergence of a very large, increasingly

---

[2] China is one of the six countries, the others being developed ones, participating in the decoding of the human genome at the turn of the century. On China's achievement in nanotechnology, see Zhou and Leydesdorff (2006).

[3] In fact, according to a recent assessment by the Georgia Institute of Technology, China already tops the USA on the Technological Standing reading, which combines four indicators – National Orientation, Socio-economic Infrastructure, Technological Infrastructure, and Productive Capacity (Porter *et al.*, 2008).

well-educated talent pool. The term "talent" (*rencai*)[4] is a concept that has gained increasing popularity and importance in China over the last few years; specifically, it denotes those Chinese with higher-caliber abilities and skills of strategic significance to the country's modernization and national wealth creation.[5] Leveraging the significant investments that heretofore have been made to modernize and upgrade the country's higher education system and R&D infrastructure, China hopes to capture and harness the country's most strategic resource – its talented people – to embark on a quest to close appreciably the prevailing technological gap between itself and the West in fields ranging from biotechnology to nanotechnology. The launch of the MLP reflects a commitment to rely more on "brains" rather than "brawn" to bring China into a strong, leadership position during the early part of the twenty-first century.

At the heart of the debate about whether China's potential can be realized, however, lie a number of critical issues all touching upon, or dealing directly with, lingering uncertainties surrounding the quantity, quality, and effective utilization of China's current and future scientific and technical workforce. Will China have sufficient talent to compete head-on with the USA and the world's other leading technological nations? Is China's indigenous talent qualified to meet the needs of the country's economic, scientific, and education enterprises? How will demographic trends in China affect the supply of college-age candidates for university enrollment? What has been the impact of Chinese scientists and engineers who have been trained abroad and have returned to the People's Republic of China? Is China still facing a "brain drain" problem, and if so, how serious is it? And last but not least, what factors with regard to the changing complexion of the Chinese economy and foreign investment will affect the supply and demand for high-end talent?

Building on some very exciting original field research as well as a plethora of comprehensive statistical materials and analysis dealing with

---

[4] Originally, "talent" means "currency." In the Bible, the parable of the talents tells how three servants approach the different amount of talents given by their master in accordance with each servant's ability – invest or keep it – and end up with different outcome, which, according to Stringer and Rueff (2006: xviii–xix), "helped shape out understanding of the concept of talent, and subsequently, how the word itself acquired its modern meaning."

[5] In Chinese terms, *rencai* can also mean "treasures."

the structure, size, and composition of the scientific and engineering talent pool in China, this book tries to answer these critically important questions. The analysis offered in this book has significant policy implications for both China and many other countries, such as the USA, especially in terms of such issues as national competitiveness and innovation potential.

From the perspective of both contemporary China studies and the literature on competitiveness, the book is long overdue in that it is the first comprehensive look at China's human resources in science and technology (HRST) in over four decades – since the publication in the 1960s of *Professional Manpower and Education in Communist China* by Leo Orleans (1961) and *Scientific and Engineering Manpower in Communist China* by Chu-yuan Cheng (1965). Although breaking new ground at the time, both books were constrained by serious data availability and quality issues. Ironically, both books appeared around the time of China's successful testing of its first atomic weapon in 1964; this somewhat unexpected development reinforced the need to monitor S&T developments in the People's Republic of China. Fortunately, Orleans continued his work in this field, taking advantage of the opening up of China's relations with the outside world and the expanded availability of statistical data from China. Orleans contributed several, more detailed monographs in the 1980s on China's scientific workforce (Orleans, 1980, 1983) and Chinese students in the USA (Orleans, 1988, 1992). Between then and now, however, while such organizations as the Organization for Economic Co-operation and Development (OECD) and the US National Science Foundation (NSF) periodically provide quantitative updates and analyses of China's scientific and technical workforce in the context of international comparisons of graduate education around the world and the global mobility of talent, there has been virtually no detailed scholarly book-length work devoted to the topic, even though the topic has become steadily more important as China's expanded prominence in international and regional S&T affairs has generated a growing need for a deeper, more sophisticated understanding of its present and future S&T talent pool. While Chinese academics have published some work on the topic in recent years – most notably: *Stride from a Country of Tremendous Population to a Country of Profound Human Resources* (Research Group on China's Education and Human Resources, 2003); *Report on China's Talent 2005* (Chinese Academy of Personnel Science, 2005); *China Education and Human Resource Development Report 2005–2006* (Min & Wang, 2006); and *Report on the Development of Chinese Talent* series (Pan, various years), most have been more descriptive and qualitative in nature, and have not taken both the supply and demand aspects of S&T talent into consideration.[6]

In addition to much scholarly attention paid to the relations between Chinese intellectuals, including scientists and engineers, and the state (see, for example, Goldman *et al.*, 1987; Goldman & Gu, 2004; Hamrin & Cheek, 1986; Miller, 1996), there have been studies written in the West about China's HRST from other perspectives. One of the most interesting was *Thread of the Silkworm*, by Iris Chang (1996), which is the story of the life of one individual Chinese scientist, Qian Xuesen, often seen as the father of the Chinese missile program. Chang's story about Dr. Qian is especially relevant to the present book because she documents the experiences of an individual who, under some pressure, returned to China after building what seemed to be a successful career as a defense scientist at Cal Tech in the USA. Lueck's (1997) study of Chinese intellectuals during and after the Tiananmen Square incident on June 4, 1989 also tries to bring into focus the challenges of working in the R&D profession in a rapidly changing Chinese environment. And recently Cao has systematically examined the characteristics of the leading academicians (*yuanshi*) of the Chinese Academy of Sciences (CAS), and to a less extent, the *yuanshi* of the Chinese Academy of Engineering (CAE), and the process through which Chinese scientists have been elected into the elite (Cao, 2004a; Cao & Suttmeier, 1999), and China's emerging scientific elite (Cao & Suttmeier, 2001).

All of these works provide some degree of understanding about the world of the Chinese scientist and engineer, but few attempts have been made to conduct the type of overall stocktaking of high-end S&T talent resources that was produced in the early 1960s. This book, in its own way, attempts to fill the prevailing gap by bringing together a significant volume of new statistical data and interview information about the scientific and engineering community in China. It represents

---

[6] While copy-editing this book we learned that the China Academy of Science and Technology (CAST) just released a report on China's HRST (CAST, 2008), but we are unable to incorporate it into the book as we have not had chance to read it.

the first of its kind in terms of incorporating a statistically based supply and demand approach and model to forecast the growth and availability of China's S&T talent over the next five years and to analyze the massive new availability of original policy documents and statistical materials on Chinese S&T talent. Compared with the raw materials that Orleans and Cheng, respectively, had to work with, we have clearly had some major advantages, stemming in no small way, from the premium that Chinese officials have placed on cooperation with the West and providing increased access to foreign researchers. This availability and increased access for foreign researchers affords observers of the Chinese scene a greater ability to determine where China's scientists and engineers stand when compared with their counterparts elsewhere.

The book also offers a timely assessment of the strength and weakness of China's S&T talent pool. Because of the relative scarcity of accurate information on the subject as well as the misrepresentation of the information, there have been growing political concerns in the USA and other developed countries about the increasing size of the Chinese scientific and engineering talent pool and its implications for the economic and technical future of OECD countries and beyond. Many of these concerns reflect an incomplete, and sometimes exaggerated and distorted, picture of the Chinese talent situation and education system. For example, the source of the figure of 1.6 million Chinese engineers used in a McKinsey study on global outsourcing seems to be derived more from popular perceptions or anecdotes rather than actual statistical analysis (McKinsey Global Institute, 2005) and a most recent study of the Chinese health biotechnology sector introduces an absurdly higher number of Chinese scientific and technological personnel – 55.75 million – from a Chinese source but does not clarify what this number means (Frew *et al.*, 2008: 52).[7] As a recent study from Duke University correctly points out – and in fact, as Chinese education statistics also indicate – not every so-called "engineer" graduating from a Chinese university is equal (Wadhwa & Gereffi, 2005). Of the 1.34 million "engineering students" graduated from Chinese colleges in 2006, for example, more than half – 57 percent – were in the short-cycle, two- to three-year abbreviated programs (*zhuanke*); that is, the level of education and formal training that these

---

[7] We could not find this number in any official S&T statistics.

graduates received is much lower than that obtained from a certified program conferring a more traditional bachelor's degree. Further, if we exclude those who entered domestic and foreign graduate schools after their bachelor's degree as well as those with low quality and mismatched skills, and those who chose a non-technical profession, the number of qualified, available job candidates in engineering would fall to around 200 000 (see Chapter 7). While still large, this number represents only 35 percent of those with an engineering bachelor's degree or much smaller percentage of the total pool of engineering graduates. The surge of Chinese college graduates since the late 1990s has further disturbed the debate about whether China has raised the quality of its graduates at the same time as it has increased enrollments. This book will help demystify the size and composition questions surrounding China's talent pool, leading to a deeper, more thorough understanding of China's current and future human resources in the S&T pipeline.

Objectives and organization of the book

In making a substantial investment in the data collection efforts that form this book's underpinning, we were driven by three main objectives. First, simply and succinctly stated, our goal has been to enhance overall understanding of the supply, demand, and utilization of scientific and engineering talent in China. In this regard, we strongly believe that it is important to differentiate fact from fiction with respect to the formal statistical and popular media-driven data coming out of China and other parts of the world about the Chinese talent pool. As suggested, there is a considerable amount of hyperbole and exaggeration in the air that simply needs to be corrected or debunked. If government, enterprise, and university decision-makers in China and abroad do not have appropriate data and analysis to support their policy decisions, the chances of critical mistakes and blunders occurring are enhanced.

Second, we wanted to connect the Chinese case with the larger discussions about global talent so that we may all better understand how China's emergence as a more prominent player in the global innovation system will affect and influence the shape and nature of that system in the years ahead. Whether we accept the idea of a global talent *pool* or the existence of *pools* of talent, the fact remains that

China's S&T personnel are playing a more active and productive role in world science and technology affairs. Thus, we are interested not only in what role Chinese scientists have played and will play in their own S&T community at home, but also in the role they have played and will play on the larger international stage.

And, third, we wanted to encourage others, including our counterparts in China, to build on this work. As part of the preparatory work for its new MLP, which was launched in January 2006, the government assigned to one of 20 strategic research teams responsibility for addressing China's high-end talent needs for the coming 15 years. Unfortunately, this study was not made available to us, but from what we understand, it was heavily driven by a supply model without ample consideration of the changing nature of the demand side – the only demand variable is R&D expenditure.[8] This has led some observers to suggest that while the Japanese may have developed the "just in time" philosophy, in the realm of talent development, Chinese thinking is apparently characterized by a "just in case" mentality! We believe that the type of approach used in drafting the MLP requires reconsideration. Our hope is that more study will be done in China on this important topic, and that other foreign scholars will be given a chance to collaborate with their Chinese counterparts. It is our ambition to build one more cooperative bridge between China and the West so that the integration of the People's Republic of China into the world S&T community may continue in a constructive and harmonious manner.

In this regard, this book should also be viewed as a link connecting together existing research, statistical information, and analytic models and methodologies regarding the study of science, engineering, and management talent in other countries with the Chinese case. The analysis offered in the book tests the applicability and validity of the prevailing literature about talent development and utilization at the national level.

With all these in mind, the book, which is composed of nine chapters plus an appendix, is divided into three parts. The first part,

---

[8] At least we knew that the team working on HRST based its analysis on the data published in China's statistical yearbooks, and the result was disclosed in a paper published in a Chinese journal (Li & Yu, 2004).

which includes the initial two chapters, reviews the literature on the relations between human capital and economic development and discusses the dilemmas and challenges that China faces as it seeks to move beyond its role as a "factory to the world." The next five chapters constitute the second part of the book. Chapter 3 introduces the concept of HRST, an internationally used definition, and discusses its applicability to the study of Chinese S&T talent. The chapter then provides a stock-take of China's overall S&T talent pool, including its structure and characteristics. As part of a broad examination of the development of the higher education system in post-1978 China, Chapter 4 analyzes the pipeline through which China produces undergraduate and graduate students, especially in science, engineering, and management, and identifies the problems and issues faced by China in turning out a larger volume of such students. Chapter 5 examines how Chinese S&T talent has been utilized from the perspective of prevailing policy goals versus and the real-world situation. Chapter 6 discusses the impact of the "brain drain" problem on China's ambition to become an innovation-oriented nation.

The second part of the book ends with Chapter 7, a forecast of the demand and supply of scientific and engineering talent in China in the years to come.

The last part consists of two chapters. Chapter 8 surveys the talent situation in key technology fields, highlighting China's relative strengths and weaknesses, and Chapter 9 contains a discussion of the changing role of scientists and engineers in Chinese society and political economy, as well as offering an examination of the potential impact that China's S&T talent will have on global technological competition and international scientific advances during the first part of the twenty-first century.

Data sources used in this book

The data used in this book were drawn mainly from open-source primary Chinese language materials along with statistical data published in China by the National Bureau of Statistics (NBS) through the China Statistical Press. We also collected substantial amounts of data and information from other Chinese government agencies, including the Ministries of Science and Technology, Education, Labor and

Social Security, Personnel,[9] and Information Industry. In addition, useful materials were secured from the CAS, the CAE, the Chinese Academy of Social Sciences (CASS), and the China Association for Science and Technology (CAST). Many hours and days over the course of more than a year were spent in Beijing and Shanghai tracking down and rummaging through piles of old, but sometimes relevant, Chinese ministerial yearbooks, statistical data books, magazines, and scholarly books. Overall, we tried to go back as far as the available statistical materials would allow us to highlight more precisely in our statistical model growth trends and changes in the talent stock over time; as we quickly discovered, however, the reliability of the existing data became progressively suspect. These problems were compounded by the impact of the Dengist-led program of reform and structural change, launched in 1978 and especially after 1992: the entire complexion of the Chinese economy has undergone a substantial transformation, especially in terms of the role of markets and the design of S&T organizations.

That said, it also is the case that China has made tremendous improvements over the last 10–15 years in pushing its S&T statistical system to be more accurate, open, and transparent. Unfortunately, as will be discussed later in the book, the available S&T data in China still remain plagued by quality problems, especially when compared with similar types of data from the OECD countries. In reviewing the data used in our analysis, we try to highlight in the text and the Appendix where we believe that existing data is simply off the mark and where possible, why (see also Gao *et al.*, 2006 for a discussion on the progress and problems of China's S&T statistical system). While throughout our research the problems associated with the data situation created multiple challenges, the only saving grace, if there is one, is that Chinese researchers and scholars must depend on the same sets of statistical materials and data that were made available to us, as they did for the MLP. In this sense, we feel confident in both the integrity and the completeness of the data contained in this book, even if it is not ideal from the perspective of our overall research goals and objectives.

---

[9] The Ministry of Personnel and the Ministry of Labor and Social Security were merged into the Ministry of Human Resources and Social Security in 2008, but the book uses all their original names unless to specify the impacts of the change.

Early on, we made the strategic decision that we could work within the framework of the current data problems and shortcomings; we did not believe there was much utility in trying to wait until such time as Chinese data may "catch up" with international standards to support the study of China's S&T system in general and HRST in particular. Instead, after multiple discussions with Chinese policymakers and researchers working in this issue area, we decided that we could "scrub" the reported data where necessary, filter and correct aberrant data points, and adjust for obvious inconsistencies to improve the quality of the overall dataset. Our conversations with an array of Chinese S&T policy analysts, academics, and government officials from the Ministry of Education, Ministry of Science and Technology, and Ministry of Personnel, as well as with the NBS, the CAS, and the CASS, among others, helped us to better understand not only the statistics themselves but also the actual trends and patterns of supply and demand, quality, location, and utilization of S&T talent in China.

In the final analysis, utilizing various Chinese statistical yearbooks and other open documents, we constructed a comprehensive working dataset on the scientific and engineering talent pool of the People's Republic of China, which yielded a broad range of information about the evolving Chinese S&T system, higher education system, and personnel situation. To further ensure the integrity of the data and analysis, we also carefully cross-checked all information and tried to provide useful interpretations to make the data as internationally comparable as possible. At the risk of exaggeration and claiming too much credit, as presented in this book, we believe that the final dataset used to produce this book and the associated analysis is the most comprehensive, most systematic, and best available inside and outside of China at present.

1 | Human resources, technological innovation, and economic growth

It has become a well established fact that a nation's economic growth depends heavily upon its overall talent base. The size, quality, and utilization of a country's human resources determine, to a great degree, its prevailing level of technological sophistication as well as its future technological trajectory. Under the broad umbrella of human resources, the role of scientific and technical personnel probably is the most critical; accordingly, the term – "human resources in science and technology" (HRST) – has become accepted internationally as one of the key metrics for assessing a nation's real and potential technological strength(s). In the aftermath of the Cultural Revolution (1966–1976) and the debilitating impact of that movement on China's innovative capabilities, Chinese leaders have come to understand and appreciate the need to develop and harness a large pool of highly skilled human resources to promote, support, and sustain the country's technological progress, economic growth, social development, and national security. It is this drive to create and deploy a well-trained, highly competent scientific and technical talent pool that stands out not only as one of the hallmarks of China's modernization program, but, in all likelihood, also the key variable that will determine the nature of China's competitive positioning in the coming years.

This book examines the contribution – real and potential – of China's talent pool to the enhancement of that nation's science and technology (S&T) capabilities. Our approach begins with a review of relevant schools of thought regarding the role of high-end talent across three dimensions. The first dimension addresses the relationship between human resources and economic growth. Treating human resources as form of "capital" and through careful economic analysis (though this is not the place to go into great detail about pertinent economic theory and associated econometric models), this perspective highlights the fact that human capital has a positive impact on economic growth through productivity gains for a society and economy as well as wage increases for individuals. Since the end of the Second World War, if not earlier, in the economic history of the world, developing as well as developed economies have been left with no choice but to follow a path of human resources-reinforced economic growth.

The second dimension looks at the pivotal role that talent plays in supporting rapid technological innovation. As Schumpeter and others have shown convincingly, innovation is an important engine of economic growth. Even more important, innovation has the potential to reshape the prevailing global economic and technological landscape. This is especially true for late-comer economies which seek to catch up and perhaps even leapfrog ahead. Without an ample-sized cohort of well-trained scientists and engineers who can carry out research and development (R&D) activities and turn research into new, commercially viable products and services, their future prospects may be quite limited.

The third dimension, still unfolding, relates human resources and globalization. The emergence of a so-called "global talent pool," if there is one, is the direct consequence of the "flat" world in which large numbers of highly mobile talented people are able to choose where they want to work and live as traditional notions of employment give way to more footloose, virtual models of job definition, job responsibilities, and performance expectations. In a globally flat world, employment is less and less tied to a fixed national or local space (Friedman, 2005). As the number of highly trained college graduates, especially in engineering and technology disciplines, has been growing significantly in the emerging economies such as China and India, an important transformation has been occurring, spurred on by adoption of more open, liberal economic and trade policies. In parallel with the changes in domestic policy that have been taking place in these emerging markets, an increasing number of multinational corporations (MNCs) have decided, for both strategic and cost reasons, to relocate their operations abroad for improved access to the growing number of skilled individuals as well as to rapidly expanding markets with large and increasingly affluent populations. By so doing, MNCs are hoping to capture the growing availability of talent on a worldwide basis and leverage those human resources globally to not merely maximize their financial returns but also strengthen their innovation capacity. The growing availability of these types of jobs may have helped to reverse the traditional problems of "brain drain" faced by countries such as China and India (Saxenian, 2006). However, in the meantime, ironically, there now is a growing apprehension about an "internal" brain drain problem that derives from the increasingly apparent tendency of "returnees" and domestic professionals to seek positions within the newly established R&D and engineering centers set up by MNCs in these countries and to forgo opportunities with domestic firms, universities, or R&D establishments. Thus, instead of a so-called "brain gain," there actually still may be problems for domestic organizations to attract "the best and the brightest." The growing intensity of the competition for talent is one of the defining features the globalized world of the twenty-first century.

This chapter will review the main core of intellectual thought surrounding each of the three areas. Each is important in helping us to better understand the Chinese case and to place the People's Republic of China situation in an appropriate global context. Of all China's vast resources, the talent factor may be the most strategically important to its overall development. Through our examination of current thinking on the role of talent, we also hope to highlight where the Chinese case may depart from the existing studies. In a word, we hope to bring about a better understanding of the logic of human resources development in China and lay a foundation for the discussions in the chapters to come.

Human resources and economic growth

A substantial body of scholarly and policy research has established the positive relationship between human resources or human capital[1] and economic growth. The use of the term "human capital" dates back to the American economist Jacob Mincer in the late 1950s (Mincer, 1958),[2] though the best-known application of the concept has been attributed to Theodore Schultz and Gary Becker, both Nobel Prize-winning economists who argued that "much of the unexplained

---

[1] For our purpose in the book, "human capital" and "human resources" are interchangeable.

[2] It is worthwhile to note that as early as 1890, Alfred Marshall noted that "the most valuable of all capital is that invested in human beings" (cited in Becker, 1993: 27; 1964/1994).

increase in productivity, wages, and economic growth recognized by economists could be explained by investments in human capital" (Brown, 2001: 5). Schultz, an agricultural economist, viewed human capital as a way of showing the advantages of investing in education to improve agricultural output, and by extension, to improve productivity and nation's wealth. According to him, there has been a "decline in the economic importance of farmland and a rise in that of human capital – skills and knowledge" (Schultz, 1980: 642). Schultz also demonstrated that the yield on human capital in the US economy was larger than that based on physical capital (Schultz, 1961).

The term "human capital" was coined by Becker (1993) because "people cannot be separated from their knowledge, skills, health or values in the way they can be separated from their financial and physical assets." Becker's seminal book, *Human Capital*, laid the foundation for the study of this subject area, whose importance has become more and more significant over the years (Becker, 1964/ 1994). In his view, "expenditures on education, training, medical care, and so on can be considered as investments in human capital," which, though intangible, may be further used to significantly enhance the economic prospects of a nation and the welfare of individuals (Becker, 1993). Though not replacing land, labor, or capital totally, human capital can be substituted for them to various degrees and be included in production.

In the 1980s, human capital, or more accurately, *the skills and knowledge that make labor forces productive*, along with technological change or innovation, were incorporated into economic growth theory. According to Robert Solow's (1956) neoclassical model of exogenous economic growth, output growth depends upon the growth of two factors of production – capital and labor – and upon exogenous changes in technology. This theory was quite useful in describing the growth experience of the USA and other industrialized nations, and helped economists to rule out some popular misconceptions about the causes of sustained disparities in growth rates, such as differences in tax codes and trade barriers. But for Robert Lucas (2003), also an economic growth theorist, technology, knowledge, and human capital – "all just different terms for the same thing" – hold the key to endogenous economic growth. He distinguishes the *internal* effects of human capital through schooling and the *external* ones, including on-the-job training or learning-by-doing, by pointing out that the latter is at least as important as the former in the formation of human capital and "even an important element in the growth of knowledge," because they "have to do with the influences people have on the productivity of others." According to him, a rise in human capital leads to a rise in national income with the level of income highly correlated to that of human capital (Lucas, 1988: 37–8).

It is Paul Romer (1986), however, who argues explicitly that knowledge is the basic form of capital and that economic growth is driven by knowledge accumulation. His model, also an endogenous growth one, includes four basic inputs – capital and labor, the two in Solow's theory, human capital, and technology – with the key being an adequate stock of human capital. He finds that "what is important for growth is integration not into an economy with a large number of people but rather one with a large amount of human capital" (Romer, 1990: S98). The development of new knowledge also follows the law of diminishing returns in production; that is, when a fixed input is combined in production with a variable input, say capital and labor, using a given technology, each additional unit of variable input yields less and less additional output, but investment in knowledge leads to increasing returns in marginal products. In other words, because of the spillover effects, or the *external* effects in Lucas's model, the stock of knowledge and embodied human capital determine the growth rate, and continuous investment into them can sustain the long-term growth of a firm as well as a nation. Indeed, in essence, Romer's research foresees the key drivers underlying the onset of the knowledge economy and the demand for talent in this new form of economy.

There is an extensive and rather detailed literature on rates of increasing return on education and training, primarily based on the human capital theory, beginning with the classical growth models developed in the 1950s and including the so-called endogenous growth models that are still widely applied in many current empirical studies. This literature mainly explores the direct quantitative relationship between investment in education and training *and* the level and growth in terms of per capita gross domestic product (GDP).

There is no doubt that investment in education is an individual's decision, as labor market earnings increase for individuals with more education as a result of gaining productive skills through schooling (Becker, 1993). Indeed, the human capital theory has been used to explain why individuals decide to make investment in education and on-the-job training. In particular, according to Becker (1993), high school and college education in the USA "greatly raise a person's income, even after netting out direct and indirect costs of schooling, and after adjusting for the better family backgrounds and greater abilities of more educated people." Such a claim, together with the assumption that school changes a student's life and perspective, suggest that independent of socioeconomic status, family dynamics, or the skills and knowledge that students possess prior to schooling, it is largely what takes place inside the classroom that contributes to increased earnings once students enter the labor market. Econometric estimates and quantitative analyses at the micro-level further explain a large portion of an individual's annual or monthly income by their level of education and work experience, and consistently show a statistically significant and positive financial gain of an individual's average years of education – even after controlling for other factors such as the parent's level of income or education. And, the economic payoff of higher education, in terms of the increased wages over lifetimes, is enormous. In the USA, for example, a college graduate earns about two-thirds more than a high school graduate in their lifetime (US Census Bureau, 2006).

However, "human capital accumulation is a *social* activity, involving *groups* of people in a way that has no counterpart in the accumulation of physical capital" (Lucas, 1988: 19). Further, returns to society and the economy as a whole may be even higher than those to the investing individuals if their colleagues are inspired by the new knowledge. This is because schooling that improves productivity and earnings at the individual level can plausibly be translated to increased growth at the national level. Consequently, *external* effects can lead to total returns exceeding the sum of the returns to those individuals who spent more time studying. In fact, it is the rapid accumulation of human capital that has driven rapid economic growth, and empirical evidence confirms this linkage. Not only has almost one-fifth of the increase in GDP between 1948 and 1973 in the USA been attributed to the expansion and enhancement of the American education system, the contribution of education to productivity rose from 25 percent to more than 30 percent between 1973 and 1981, even when productivity growth began to falter (Brown, 2001).

Moreover, it has become a recognized global phenomenon that accumulation of human capital leads to sustained economic development.

Robert Barro, for example, uses educational attainment as proxy for human capital to explain cross-country differences in economic growth rates.[3] He finds that the educational attainment of a country's adult population is significantly and positively related to that country's subsequent growth rate of per capita GDP. In particular, his findings imply that human capital and physical capital investment tend to work together, both being associated with faster national growth conditional on initial income. The channels of effects involve the positive effect of human capital on physical investment, the negative effect of human capital on fertility, and an additional positive effect on growth for given values of investment and fertility (Barro, 1991). In a similar manner, Benhabib and Spigel (1994) present cross-country evidence that the growth rate of total factor productivity depends on a nation's human capital stock.

The success of economic "catch-up" by the USA, Japan, and newly industrialized economies further illustrates the importance of human capital development. The East Asian economic miracle is largely attributed, among other things, to the region's sustained levels of investment in human capital over a long period. We can identify an "education miracle" behind the economic miracle (Haq & Haq, 1998) or describe economic development in East Asia as human resource-led development (Behrman, 1990). For example, to catch up with the advanced economies in the West, Japan, as a latecomer to industrialization and modern economic growth, invested heavily in education, especially in its early development stage. During the one hundred years between 1890 and 1990, Japan witnessed an increase in its citizens' average schooling from 1.3 years to 11.5 years with an annual increase of 2.2%, but most dramatic increase occurred between 1890 and 1940 when the annual increase reached 3.3%, while the annual

---

[3] The average years of education of the population aged 25–64 is a proxy for the measurement of human capital. Apparently, all countries increase their average years of school over time. Enrolment rate, attainment rate, and quality also are important, though difficult to measure. Experience and further training will certainly also raise human capital. "Years of schooling" as a measure of human capital could be misleading as it treats years of schooling at different levels and different disciplines within the same level of education as the same. Other possible measures include attainment rates and enrolment rates. Quality of human capital is also difficult to measure. For a discussion on the measurement issue around human capital, see Bergheim (2005).

increase between 1890 and 1910 in particular was 4.4% (Godo & Hayami, 2002).

Massive development in the human capital stock through investment in education also has contributed to the economic take-off in South Korea. As a result of emphasizing education for decades and acting accordingly, Koreans raised their average years of education from 7 years in the early 1970s to around 13 years in 2003, faster than the rate of economic growth (Bergheim, 2005: 14). Singapore's industrial training system, under government's guidance, is now considered one of the best in the world for high-tech production (Lall, 2001: 159–61). In general, in these types of vibrant economic settings, a 10 percent rise in human capital leads to a 9 percent rise in GDP per capita over the long run (Bergheim, 2005: 9).[4]

However, Jones (1995b) finds that over a period of time the growth rate of the United States' economy has not responded to the steady increase in the number of scientists engaged in R&D and other measures of research intensity. To explain this, he proposes the economy's growth rate is proportional to the rate of growth of population, that is, increasing the size of the talent pool has a scale effect on the level, but not the growth rate, of per capita GDP (Jones, 1995a). This accommodation to the more broadly held view about the synergies between growth and human resources development only serves to highlight the fact that a country's talent base becomes increasingly important over time and that importance does not recede even as industrialization proceeds ahead or the transition to a knowledge economy begins.

Talent and technological innovation

There is little doubt that the combined imperatives of competition and wealth creation in the knowledge-economy era demands a well-trained and highly skilled labor force, and, in particular, innovative scientific and technical personnel. Indeed, research has been

---

[4] The region also benefited from rapid accumulation of physical capital, an increasingly sophisticated internal and international division of labor, rapid demographic transition, and endogenous growth factors, including institutions and values. Nevertheless, investments in education seem to be central to the economic success of the East Asian economies (Wood & Berge, 1997).

conducted on the role of talent in creating, disseminating, and using knowledge and in driving and sustaining technological innovation.

In his Nobel Lecture, Schultz (1980: 648) points out, "it is important not to overlook the increase in the stock of physicians, other medical personnel, engineers, administrators, accountants, and various classes of research scientists and technicians." In particular, it was engineers and scientists and other highly skilled workers, not raw labor, who performed high-end R&D and innovative activities (Romer, 1990). And scientists tend to speed up the rate of innovation, reduce the cost of innovation in leading economies, and help latecomers to be more adaptive to technologies that were discovered elsewhere (Nelson & Phelps, 1966). In a word, S&T talent can effectively raise the growth rate in leaders as well as followers in economic development by way of technological innovation.

Technological innovation starts with an undertaking of R&D activities. If in the time of Isaac Newton scientific research was just a hobby of amateurs, and still was so in the era of Thomas Edison, nowadays it has become embedded in the behavior of successful organizations, be they universities, research institutes, or corporations. Therefore R&D often requires huge sustainable investment and support from both government and society. Moreover, the world of innovative activities is a domain that generally requires participants to possess higher educational credentials (doctorates in many cases), expertise, and years of experience. In other words, innovation requires skilled talent. The dominance of the USA in science and technology since the Second World War has, to large extent, been associated with its possession of a high-caliber talent base.

At the turn of the twentieth century, graduate education to train high-quality scientists and engineers started to flourish in the USA. During the Second World War, the USA benefited greatly from the influx of scientific talent such as Albert Einstein and Enrico Fermi, who fled Fascist governments in Nazi Germany and Italy; their contributions literally helped the Allies to win the war, especially their contribution to the development of nuclear weapons. After the war, American and European scientists and engineers gave birth to such high-tech industries as information technology and biotechnology, which today have become the pillars of the knowledge economy. Immigrants from India, China, and other countries with a strong tradition of prioritizing education, along with America's locally schooled and trained scientific workforce, have contributed greatly to US technological advance and strong economic growth (Wadhwa *et al.*, 2007).

Looking from the vantage point of the twenty-first century, it has become evident that competition within and across a global know-ledge-based economy is essentially competition about innovation capability, which, in turn, is underscored by the growing competition for talent between firms, regions, and nations. One of the key meas-ures of innovative strength is embedded in R&D activities, which may be viewed as a proxy for education and training in higher-level skills. While it is true that there can be no research without talent, and not much innovation without research, it is equally true that expenditure on R&D tends to be higher in countries with a high concentration of scientific and technical talent. Thus, Romer (1990) includes in his model of "endogenous economic growth" an R&D sector which uses valuable resources to produce more new ideas and bring about tech-nical change. Simply stated, using the analytic lens provided by this class of endogenous growth models we can see that an increase in the stock of resources – financial and human – engaged in R&D activity is directly related to a permanent increase in the economy's growth rate.

Expenditure on R&D, however, also tends to be higher in countries which strive to catch up with the advanced economies. The "catching-up" and leapfrogging process requires a capacity to create new tech-nology as well as a capacity for absorbing and adapting technology created elsewhere. This absorptive capacity is considered directly related to the human capital stock present in the catching-up country, which tends to be the product of an enhanced higher education and research system established through enormous investment and sup-port – both public and private.

Because of the importance of human resources in driving the exponential increase in scientific and technological knowledge, the size of the talent pool in each country is explicitly linked to its indi-genous technology level. In this regard, the higher education system shoulders the main responsibility for preparing and supplying the qualified technical, professional, and managerial workforce that is required to support national as well as regional and local innovation systems within each country. Of course, it is the quality, rather than just the quantity, of human resources that stands at the heart of innovation. In East Asia, a high level of human resource development focused on scientists and engineers has given rise to the rapid and sustained pace of technological progress that the region has experienced since Japan and the four Asian tigers – Taiwan, South Korea, Hong Kong, and Singapore – began their concerted efforts to move beyond low-cost manufacturing as the basis for their continued economic growth (Simon, 1997).

In the era of the knowledge economy, scientific talent is more likely to comprise knowledge workers. A term coined by Peter Drucker (1959), "knowledge worker" originally meant skilled and educated people who made their living manipulating information. Nowadays, the core of knowledge workers comprises scientists and engineers as well as managerial personnel. According to Richard Florida (2002), most recently, scientists and engineers engaged in the production of new ideas and knowledge mainly solve problems in a wide range of knowledge-intensive industries such as high-technology sectors, financial services, the legal and healthcare professions, and business management; they and other professionals constitute the core of the "creative class." The creativity of the new class, in Florida's terms, also is associated with other two factors – technology and tolerance. Talented people always try to find places to live and work where there are not only knowledge-intensive jobs, many being high-technology, but also tolerance of different ideas and values which sustain the economic growth through attracting talented people. It is the combined effect of these three Ts – talent, technology, and tolerance – that contributes to the economic prosperity of a region and a nation, such as Silicon Valley, Boston's Route 128, Austin, and the "Research Triangle" in North Carolina. It is this same synergy between talent and location that defines the new industrial "cluster" geographies and agglomeration dynamics which increasingly dominate the economic landscape of the twenty-first century global economy.

Globalization and mobility of talent

As we forge deeper into the twenty-first century, the effects of globalization continue to be ubiquitous. The dynamics of global economic and technological development are producing dramatic, indeed revolutionary, changes in the cross-border movement of goods, capital, and, most importantly, talent; the associated innovation and intellectual property are serving as "a major engine of economic growth" (ILO, 1998: 203). Globalization has engendered a pronounced restructuring of the global workplace; prevailing assumptions about the nature of international competition and the process of economic development are undergoing a fundamental rethinking in many quarters. While the exact shape and configuration of the new global economic order and technology system remains to be seen, it is clear that the role of high-end scientific, engineering, and managerial talent – the supply and demand as well as quality and utilization – will be a pivotal issue for both public and private sector actors.

In this new, highly fluid, and sometimes turbulent period in world history, competition will revolve around the ability to access, manage, and coordinate specialized trans-border knowledge networks structured around both R&D and educational systems. With MNCs searching the world for pockets of high-quality talent, many nations, especially among the newly industrialized economies, have come to recognize that their attractiveness to foreign investors and global companies strategically lies in the ranks of their available scientific and engineering personnel. Moreover, in an era when innovation capability is a major competitive factor, these nations also recognize that their current and future negotiating power and competitive leverage will derive increasingly from their sustained ability to drive indigenous innovation. As a result, policymakers have placed a new premium on the education of high-quality scientific and engineering talent that can create new knowledge and thus fuel the capacity for product and services innovation in consumer and industrial sectors.

Under such circumstances, countries seeking to promote their economic development or maintain and enhance their competitive positioning must have in place a high-end human talent pool that will be their "ticket" to participate in the types of innovation-related activities and networks required for success by the steadily demanding conditions of the global economy. Countries such as India and China already have made substantial progress in this regard and already have achieved a comparatively much higher level of integration into the mainstream of global economic and technology affairs (McKinsey Global Institute, 2005).

The issues surrounding the global talent pool are multifaceted. Three issues in particular seem to stand out. First, there are the supply-side issues, which revolve around the degree to which governments have been able to put in place effective and efficient systems of higher education to prepare sufficient numbers of qualified individuals to handle the ever more demanding job requirements of the knowledge economy. To illustrate the rapidity of the changes occurring, we just have to look at the USA versus the Indian and Chinese education systems. According to a Duke study of engineering education, whereas American universities graduated 70 000 engineers in 2004, China and India together graduated five times as many (Wadhwa & Gereffi, 2005). Moreover, quality differences in higher education which were seemingly unassailable 20 years ago are steadily disappearing as the investments made by the Indian and Chinese governments have started to pay off in terms of faculty, facilities, and curriculum, although it is clear that the quality of education varies from school to school in both countries *and* they have a long way to go to really catch up with the West in instilling students with creativity.

Of course, the simple availability of talent does not ensure its effective utilization. Nor does it ensure that the structure and composition of the talent pool is well-matched to the evolving needs of the economy – both global and local. This is true for domestic enterprises and governments as well as for MNCs seeking to harness the new "pools" of skilled talent available around the globe. Although concerns continue to be expressed about talent shortages, even in China and India where there appears to be an abundance of graduates (McKinsey Global Institute, 2005), one burning question is: Why is there such poor utilization of existing talent? Or, is enough being done to nurture existing talented individuals, and have employers found the right combination of material and affective rewards to motivate people to take on challenging assignments? This is an especially relevant question as the imperatives of competition and growth combine to place increased pressures on enterprise leaders to produce more in the way of new, innovative products and services.

The second issue deserving critical attention deals with the demand side of the global talent question. Companies such as Microsoft, Intel, CISCO, IBM, and Siemens – to name just a few – increasingly see the world as a series of differentiated talent pools; to service global markets as well as local ones, it has become necessary to have almost on-demand access to these hubs of talented individuals. Corporate patterns of innovation are indeed changing as evidenced by the fact that more overseas R&D activities are taking place by American, European, and Japanese firms outside their headquarters' locations, especially in the Asia-Pacific region. The consequences are potentially far-reaching; we may be witnessing the end of "national systems of innovation" and a move toward more globally integrated systems of innovation (see, for example, Ernst, 2006).

With competition for talent intensifying on a global scale and traditional models of technology creation and commercialization undergoing a significant transformation, the role of government in the talent arena is the third area of importance. Some nations have decidedly attempted to develop a national talent strategy, based on the belief that domestic governments are not yet ready to accede their domains to the demands of global markets and corporations, and on concerns about "brain drain," the loss of talented people, especially in developing countries. Therefore, the countries of the European Union, under the umbrella of the Lisbon Agenda, are pushing for a revitalization of R&D, with the hope that some of the scientists and engineers who may seek to migrate to the USA might have their minds changed as a result of the new, innovative environment being created across the continent (Ertl, 2006). China, as this book reveals, has instituted major reforms to revitalize its S&T system and enhance it own innovation potential. Toward that end, it also is attempting to liberalize its human resources systems to attract more talent, including those who have been trained abroad but remain reluctant to return home, by strengthening its cooperation with international educational and research institutions, and by encouraging temporary returnees in the form of technology spin-offs and project advisors (Saxenian, 2006).

Most recently, another dimension has been added to the supply and demand equation for scientists and engineers – namely, the growth in outsourcing has become an important vehicle affecting the cost structure and utilization patterns of talent at home in the USA and around the world as well (Gereffi, 2006). The search for talent overseas is clearly driving a new sensitivity to the "global dimensions" of the talent pool, but there is a growing sense that even with overseas expansion and talent acquisition there remains a perceived, if not real, shortage of desired talent irrespective of location. The pool of professionals targeted by MNCs in such talent "rich" nations as China and India are not endless. The problem that these nations have been facing is not the production of graduates in science, engineering, and other professions, but the production of *qualified* graduates. These nations also face the challenge of becoming innovative societies through indigenous efforts, which means they, too, have placed a premium on the cultivation and retention of talent for their own economic and technological objectives. It is in this sense that the twenty-first century will find companies and governments engaged in a "talent war" as they compete for the hearts and minds of the best qualified individuals with all sorts of financial and nationalistic appeals.

Tangible assets and even intellectual property rights become only as important as the talent pool with the capability to create new innovations. The world appears to be in the midst of a shift in thinking, from a world-view focussed on the prevailing "distribution of rents" to one emphasizing "the creation of new rents" (Hagel & Brown, 2005: 2). While in the past century, policymakers have generally crafted economic agendas around "overarching goals defined as natural resource development, industrial development, or development of robust financial markets," entering the twenty-first century, economic policy agendas must instead focus more aggressively on "talent development." Moreover, the value of these conventional resources and markets, which continues to be important, will increasingly be shaped and enhanced by "the relative success in building comparative advantage in talent markets" (Hagel & Brown, 2005: 164).

In a world of globalization and trans-border innovation networks, MNCs do not show signs of being willing to retreat from their prevailing interests in accessing talent any time and any place. To the surprise of some, however, the existence of a high-end knowledge workforce shortage has become steadily more apparent, leading many international companies and universities to look even further afield to meet their scientific and engineering labor needs. Previous studies continue to support and reinforce the idea that present and future investments in talent will yield economic value. In fact, the positive correlation between the quality and size of a country's labor market and GDP growth seems to be getting even stronger (Cohen & Zaidi, 2002). Yet, looks may also be deceptive. As this book will show, even China faces a gap with respect to the number of scientists and engineers who can readily be deployed, let alone *qualified* ones. Consequently, while having an ample supply of talent is a necessary requirement for future competitiveness, it is not sufficient. How a nation actually nurtures and sustains its high-end talent pool will have an even more direct impact on its competitiveness and also attractiveness as a site for overseas R&D, outsourcing, and advanced manufacturing (Brown *et al.*, 2001). This is especially true for China. Viewed from this perspective, although the simple availability of talent can be an important instrument for moving up the value chain in the globalized economy of the twenty-first century, it is also the case that the ability to establish a more cohesive balance regarding the supply–demand equation for talent rests on a much more complex set of variables which must be addressed in a rather holistic manner.

Strategic importance of talent in China's development

Although the bulk of the research – the relations between human capital or human resources and economic development, between talent and technological innovation, and the globalization of talent – has largely been focussed on developed countries, the same findings seemingly are applicable to the developing world as well (Brown, 2001: 7). In fact, Schultz's interests were on low-income countries, mainly India; for him, human capital is as important as, if not more than, material capital in India's economic growth story. As a whole, "the research capacity of a considerable number of low income countries is impressive" (Schultz, 1980: 648). The human capital theory also is highly relevant in the case of China, an equally large and economically vibrant country.

Chinese culture always has embodied a deep appreciation for the critical impact of education on individuals as well as society. Indeed, China has had a long tradition linking education with proper conduct as well as education with higher income; as one Chinese saying indicates that "One finds a house of gold in books." Education also is a vehicle for moving into positions with higher social status and privilege; in pre-modern China, scholar-officials were those who followed Confucius' instruction to achieve excellence in education and subsequently passed the civil service examinations (*keju kaoshi*). Of course, it is difficult to rationalize this strong cultural and historical interest in education with the events that transpired during the heyday of China's destructive Cultural Revolution. The Chinese education system was turned asunder as universities were closed, professors were vilified, and scientific and technical learning were discarded in favor of political education. At the time, it is probably fair to say that China's leadership did not appreciate the long-term damage being wrought by the Cultural Revolution. The timing could not have been worse as China closed its doors to the outside and foreign ideas at a time when the basic underpinnings of the information and electronics revolutions were taking place in the West. It was only in the late 1970s with the re-opening of the country after the downfall of the Gang of Four and the re-emergence of Deng Xiaoping as the de facto Chinese leader that the huge technological gap between China and the West was recognized and the larger strategic implications understood. Unfortunately, the consequences of "ten lost years" between 1966 and 1976 would continue to reverberate for many decades to come, especially in terms of the huge vacuum that was created regarding the decimated ranks of scientific, engineering, and managerial personnel as well as university faculty and teachers.

Recent studies of urban Chinese have reinforced the notion that China has benefited from the current renewed interest and investment in education at all levels. While one study, based on a survey of 20 cities, finds a modest rise in the economic rate of returns to education from 2.8% in 1978 to 3.6% in 1993 (Zhao & Zhou, 2002); another study using nationally representative data found that the net returns to education almost doubled between 1988 and 1995, from 2.1% to 4.4% for males and from 4.4% to 8.1% for females (Hauser & Xie, 2005). In still another study, the returns to education rose from 2.76% in 1991 to 8.21% in 2000 (Yue, 2004). In addition, survey data of urban works between 1999 and 2000 indicate that the more education a worker had, the less likely she was to be laid off and the better her chances of finding new employment if laid off (Maurer-Fazio, 2006). For many Chinese, higher education still represents a potentially life-changing mechanism, especially in conjunction with the possibility of studying abroad. This is especially true in the era of the one-child policy.

On the surface, the Chinese leadership is as familiar as its counterparts elsewhere in realizing the strategic importance of talent in its modernization endeavor. For example, Mao Zedong indicated in the 1940s that people are the most important of all things in the world, but the People's Republic of China under his leadership saw intellectuals – those with education and knowledge – treated horrendously. Deng Xiaoping, when he returned to the leadership position in the reform and open-door era, once again advocated respecting both knowledge and talent. Quite clearly, and to their credit, China's current leaders, many of whom have received higher education in science and engineering themselves, have a much better understanding than their revolutionary predecessors of the strategic role played by advanced science and technology as well as competent talent. And, even in the midst of continued lethargy about larger political reform in China, it has become easier for Chinese scientists and engineers to have dialogue with their leaders and to express a range of opinions about the economic and technical merits of various projects, initiatives, and policies. The gradual, albeit still incomplete, emergence of a more "pluralistic" polity in which various ideas and opinions may be expressed more openly and without the ever-present fear of political retribution is one of the hallmarks of change in the nature of the regime in so far as scientific and engineering talent is concerned.

In recent years, talent development has become a mandate from the central to local governments, especially as the Chinese leadership under President Hu Jintao and Premier Wen Jiabao has sought to make China into a so-called "innovation-oriented nation." At this critical juncture of its economic development and scientific and technological advance, China requires not simply sufficient numbers of qualified scientists and engineers, but also a group of talented individuals who are innovative thinkers, risk-takers, and technological entrepreneurs who can drive the frontier of new knowledge-creation. Because of this need the government has significantly increased its investment in education and science and technology. There is a growing understanding that the percentage of investment allocated for the education and S&T sectors must be enlarged, especially as the sources of growth inside the economy change, and environmental as well as energy considerations are forcing a shift to a cleaner, innovation-driven economic model. China's human resources in S&T also are important because its cadre of scientists and engineers have become involved in the growing search for pockets of talent around the world, thanks to a globalization process that has made the cross-border flow of goods, capital, and talent significantly easier. In fact, China has become fully integrated into the world knowledge-creation system in terms of its talent pool; it is now increasingly commonplace to find Chinese scientists and engineering talent as full-fledged participants in large and small multi-country S&T projects as its talent looks for opportunities globally as well. Of course, as suggested earlier, one of the major challenges facing China as well as India and several other countries centers on its ability to harness and retain its own talent, especially after providing improved learning conditions and more modernized facilities. A number of major cultural, economic, and political hurdles, however, stand in the way of accomplishing this goal; everything from compensation levels to the learning environment for the children of this talent seem to provide ample obstacles as things currently stand. This also explains why many Chinese students who were trained abroad, especially the best and the brightest, have not returned upon finishing their studies.

Moreover, as Nobel Laureate in Economics James J. Heckman (2005) points out, China's policies during the reform period have favored physical investment over human capital investment, although the latter as measured by the rate to education and skill formation is very high. In fact, as discussed in this book, despite recent increases in overall investment in the education sector, China's government budgetary expenditure on education as a percentage of GDP has been significantly lower than that in many countries and has not reached the 4 percent target set up for the year 2000. On top of that, investment in education has been more focused on the construction of buildings and facilities than on the hiring of world-class faculty. Unlike China's more open, market-oriented economy where wage rates for many high-tech jobs, e.g. telecommunications, seem to be increasingly responsive to supply and demand factors, the education sector has not been as quick to address compensation issues, and even some of the quality and credential questions which need to be resolved if improvements are to become real in the near future.

Conclusion

There is little doubt that the effective and efficient development and deployment of scientific and technical talent provides both challenges and opportunities for China as well as the rest of the world. The prevailing literature on the role of human resources as a key factor in development as well as competitiveness reflects the existence of a strong causal link in both cases. In the current era of globalization, however, the new salience attached to talent cultivation and utilization stems from a new imperative – the rising demands and requirements of the global innovation system. With the added impetus being given to building research, design, and engineering capabilities on a national and local level by governments *and* on a global level by multinational corporations, the talent factor quickly has risen to the top as the "make or break" factor in determining current and future innovation performance. As this chapter has tried to highlight, having enough bodies, simply stated, is not sufficient. What is required in today's world of increasing pressures for more innovative outputs is having a stock of creative, dynamic, entrepreneurial thinkers and doers who can make the difference between those who win and those who lose the innovation race. Chinese officials, like their counterparts among the Organization for Economic Co-operation and Development (OECD) countries and their Asian neighbors, understand this equation very well. And, like their counterparts, they are determined to meet the evolving talent needs of the Chinese economy through added investment as well as qualitative enhancements in the learning and working environment inside Chinese organizations – enterprises, research institutes, and universities.

To a large extent, since the onset of the reform and open-door era, China has developed its economy by harnessing imported equipment, technology, and managerial "*know*-how." In many ways, however, China has steadily moved away from relying on foreign "*show*-how" and has made the transition to capturing foreign know-how to advance its economy and technological capabilities. Currently, Chinese leaders are seeking to push the country to a new stage, one where indigenous innovation is the watchword. Coincidentally, as Chinese leaders continue to stress the strengthening of the domestic innovation system and the build-up of China's domestic talent base, many MNCs – which have largely been the main providers of technology transfer to China – also have actively expanded R&D operations in the People's Republic of China. Initially, the R&D investments of the global technology leaders were primarily attracted by the huge Chinese market with a population of 1.3 billion and the rationale of being in close proximity to their operations. Today, their thinking seems to have evolved. The new strategic thrust of these firms is to harness Chinese "brain power" and to gain access to new sources of knowledge embedded in China-based centers of innovation. Driven by the imperatives of globalization, these MNCs want to integrate China into their trans-national innovation systems. Although China possesses highly capable and talented scientists and engineers who have a solid technical foundation, strong research credentials, and a hard-working attitude, especially returnees who have come back to the People's Republic of China after their foreign studies, an appreciable number of these high-value technical personnel do not have the opportunity to bring their knowledge and talents into full play inside their respective domestic institutions. Low tolerance for risk-taking and "failure" remain major inhibitors to innovational. Therefore, it has become fashionable, as well as desirable, for these high-quality researchers to seek employment with foreign companies in China.

China, however, as a large continental economy with a huge population and stated ambitions to play on a global stage seeks to build its talent pool, driven as much by the imperatives of "techno-nationalism" as well as "techno-globalism." China's talent pool, in this respect, may be very much an instrument in helping to enhance China's national leverage on the global stage in everything from international standards-setting to intellectual property rights protection. There also are obvious national security considerations that are operative in this context as well. Quite possibly, a surge in Chinese "techno-nationalism" could create some tensions from both operational and strategic perspectives between various Chinese entities and global companies. It raises major questions about which forces will have the strongest pull on China's talent in the future – short- and long-term. Although conflicts are not inevitable, the potential for dissension is very real and remains ever present. This makes it imperative to ensure that prevailing uncertainties about the size, use, location, and quality of the country's talent pool are reduced. It is hoped that the data and analysis in this book will make a contribution in this regard.

2 | *China's talent challenge*

Ironically, even as the numbers concerning China's production of new scientists and engineers have continued to rise in a dramatic fashion, there have been conflicting perceptions about the actual talent situation in China. On one hand, as noted in the Introduction, as spending on science and technology (S&T), research and development (R&D), and education has been growing at an accelerated rate, not surprisingly, large increases in the size of the country's overall talent pool have occurred as well. At present, China's overall S&T talent pool is the largest in the world, and the number of scientists and engineers in China is the world's second largest. Moreover, the evolving pipeline seemingly remains full as Chinese universities graduate the world's largest number of students. On the other hand, complaints continue to proliferate from multiple segments of the economy and society – from Chinese government officials to enterprise chief executive officers (CEOs), including the country heads of most multinational corporations (MNCs) that operate in China – about the problems that plague the local talent pool: demand seems to be exceeding supply; quality problems are rampant; and the talent already in place remains difficult to manage and retain.

Indeed, China faces a serious talent challenge as it seeks to sustain domestic economic growth and technological advance. The active members of its professional community are young when compared with their counterparts in the West – many being fresh out of school – so that they lack the concomitant experience of their peers abroad, especially in many leadership positions in the Chinese research system. According to the McKinsey Global Institute (2005), the well-recognized global management consultancy, only 10 percent of 9.6 million young Chinese engineers, finance workers, accountants, quantitative analysts, generalists, life-science researchers, doctors, nurses, and support staff with up to seven years' work experience are "employable" by MNCs. China's lack of talent is most serious in the

50–60-year-old age group, and especially at the high end of the talent spectrum. In fields as well as geographies where there is an apparent surplus of professionals many problems limit their value and impact. In some instances there is a gap between the knowledge students acquired in school and the precise skills required for their jobs; in other cases, the structure and distribution of the talent pool at senior, middle, and junior levels is misaligned or does not match up well in terms of disciplines with the evolving skill needs of the immediate region.

This chapter discusses the origins and derivation of the various challenges facing China in the talent domain. The analysis also focuses on the major efforts that the Chinese leadership has taken to address and overcome the country's problems concerning talent development and utilization.

The origins of China's talent problems

The impact of the Cultural Revolution

Unlike many countries, such as Japan and those within the European Union (EU), which face a talent dilemma largely attributed to changing demographic factors and population dynamics, the sources and origins of China's talent problems stem from a complex array of ideological and political factors that are unique and extremely complex. First and foremost, China's talent problems are the consequence of the lingering effects of the Great Proletarian Cultural Revolution, a disastrous and highly damaging political movement which lasted for 10 tumultuous years from 1966 to 1976. It was launched by the then Chinese Communist Party (CCP) leader, Mao Zedong, to regain the power that he had lost to his rivals within the party and government bureaucracy – the so-called "persons in power taking the capitalist road" ("capitalist roaders" for short, *zouzipai*). Traumatizing and embittering practically all Chinese, its negative effects extend far beyond the realm of the Chinese political system – the Cultural Revolution continues to see its most deleterious effects on the higher education system concerning the infrastructure and capacity for training of the talent that is needed to support China's current and future modernization drive. It is hard to imagine, but even today – more than three decades after the end of the Cultural

Revolution – the legacy of the turbulence wrought by the so-called "ten lost years" continues to be felt in terms of numbers, skills, and experience (or lack of it) among the ranks of the talent pool.

Of course, the Cultural Revolution is not the first political campaign in the history of the People's Republic of China that has left its imprint on the Chinese higher education system. The Anti-Rightist Campaign in 1957 was also extremely detrimental from the perspective of talent development and deployment. In the early 1950s, just after the success of the communist revolution, the mood across the Chinese scientific and educational communities seemed very high, and, in a show of great patriotic zeal, many scientists trained and working abroad returned home to support the building of a "new China." At the time, the CCP promoted a policy of "letting a hundred flowers bloom, and letting a hundred schools of thought contend" with the apparent practical aim of giving intellectuals a greater sense of participation and thus simulating, directly or indirectly, a fresh flow of ideas that would hasten the progress of socialist construction.[1] After repeated requests from the CCP, intellectuals finally aired their views in large numbers. Among other things, they advocated for more freedom and autonomy in scientific research and higher education administration, hinting that the CCP had interfered and controlled too much in these areas. The CCP, however, saw these comments and others as a threat to its continued leadership and retaliated immediately and harshly by labeling some half a million intellectuals and even college students "rightists," with the implication being that they did not support the socialist goals of the CCP and Mao Zedong. Intellectuals as a whole were deliberately humiliated, purged, became the target of virulent attacks, were dismissed from their jobs, and sent to the countryside or frontier areas for "labor reform."

In a sense, the Cultural Revolution was an extension of the political radicalism of 1957, though it went to an even further extreme. While attacking so-called "bourgeois, reactionary academic authorities," namely high-ranking intellectuals such as senior researchers working in places such as the Chinese Academy of Sciences (CAS) and

---

[1] The first half of the slogan was first used by Mao Zedong in 1951 to characterize party policy for theoretical and literary reform, and the second half was a phrase describing the situation of academic freedom during the "Warring States" period of Chinese society (475–221 BC).

university professors who were accused of aiding and abetting the capitalist roaders, the Cultural Revolution had a particularly devastating influence on Chinese science and education. The decade from 1966 to 1976 became a true nightmare for Chinese intellectuals, who, as a social group, were denounced as "stinking number nine" (*chou laojiu*) at the bottom of the barrel as social outcasts after landlords, rich peasants, counter-revolutionaries, bad elements, rightists, traitors, spies, and capitalist roaders. Many of them were attacked personally in big-character wall posters (*dazibao*), criticized and humiliated at public meetings, and investigated and interrogated by radicals. Sometimes, their most virulent attackers were their own students, who had assumed the garb and role of the Red Guard (*hongweibing*) – the groups of radical, ultra-leftist Chinese youth who became one of the principle tools of Mao Zedong to attack those who, seemingly, opposed him in the political realm. The homes of many intellectuals were ransacked and their properties confiscated, and they were abused and tortured physically and psychologically. University professors were accused of "poisoning young students" through their teaching, and if they happened to have studied overseas they were often labeled American or Soviet "spies." Many were deprived of their rights to teach and engage in research; some even lost their lives to political persecution.

With its assault on intellectualism, the Cultural Revolution totally paralyzed China's education system as many campuses became a battleground for playing out conflicts between rival political factions. Some campuses, such as Qinghua University in Beijing, actually became a site for armed conflict as the tensions of the Cultural Revolution took on a life of their own (Hinton, 1972). Formal higher education, denounced as an institution for cultivating revisionist and bourgeois seedlings, was halted completely in 1966. No new students were admitted between 1966 and 1969 (Table 2.1). And most existing students were forced to discontinue their studies and were sent to factories, the rural countryside, or army camps to atone for the sins of their minds; the same types of treatment were meted out to faculty members and staff.

China's colleges and universities reopened their doors in 1970, as Mao Zedong proclaimed in 1968 that "it is still necessary to have universities; here I refer mainly to those of science and engineering" (graduate education was not restored until 1977). Few students were

Table 2.1 *New entrants, total enrollment, and graduates at China's regular institutions of higher education*

Year	Undergraduate (1000 persons)			Graduate (persons)		
	Entrants	Enrollees	Graduates	Entrants	Enrollees	Graduates
1949	31	117	21	242	629	107
1950	58	137	18	874	1 261	159
1951	52	153	19	1 273	2 186	166
1952	79	191	32	1 785	2 763	627
1953	81	212	48	2 887	4 249	1 177
1954	92	253	47	1 155	4 753	660
1955	98	288	55	1 751	4 822	1 730
1956	185	403	63	2 235	4 841	2 349
1957	106	441	56	334	3 178	1 723
1958	265	660	72	275	1 635	1 113
1959	274	812	70	1 345	2 171	727
1960	323	962	136	2 275	3 635	589
1961	169	947	151	2 198	6 009	179
1962	107	830	177	1 287	6 130	1 019
1963	133	750	199	781	4 938	1 512
1964	147	685	204	1 240	4 881	895
1965	164	674	186	1 456	4 546	1 665
1966		534	141		3 409	1 137
1967		409	125		2 557	852
1968		259	150		1 317	1 240
1969		109	150			1 317
1970	42	48	103			
1971	42	83	6			
1972	134	194	17			
1973	150	314	30			
1974	165	430	43			
1975	191	501	119			
1976	217	565	149			
1977	273	625	194		226	
1978	402	856	165	10 708	10 934	9
1979	275	1 020	85	8 110	18 830	140
1980	281	1 144	147	3 616	21 604	476
1981	279	1 279	140	9 363	18 848	11 669
1982	315	1 154	457	11 080	25 847	4 058
1983	391	1 207	335	15 642	37 166	4 497

Table 2.1 (*cont.*)

Year	Undergraduate (1000 persons)			Graduate (persons)		
	Entrants	Enrollees	Graduates	Entrants	Enrollees	Graduates
1984	475	1 396	287	23 181	57 566	2 756
1985	619	1 703	316	48 671	87 331	17 004
1986	572	1 880	393	41 310	110 371	16 950
1987	617	1 959	532	39 017	120 191	27 603
1988	670	2 066	553	35 645	112 776	40 838
1989	597	2 082	576	28 569	101 339	37 232
1990	609	2 063	614	29 649	93 018	35 440
1991	620	2 044	614	29 679	88 128	32 537
1992	754	2 184	604	33 439	94 164	25 692
1993	924	2 536	571	42 145	106 771	28 214
1994	900	2 799	637	50 864	127 935	28 047
1995	926	2 906	805	51 053	145 443	31 877
1996	966	3 021	839	59 398	163 322	39 652
1997	1 000	3 174	829	63 749	176 353	46 539
1998	1 084	3 409	830	72 508	198 885	47 077
1999	1 597	4 134	848	92 225	233 513	54 670
2000	2 206	5 561	950	128 484	301 239	58 767
2001	2 683	7 191	1 036	165 197	393 256	67 809
2002	3 205	9 034	1 337	202 611	500 980	80 841
2003	3 822	11 086	1 877	268 925	651 260	111 091
2004	4 473	13 335	2 391	326 286	819 896	150 777
2005	5 045	15 618	3 068	364 831	978 610	189 728
2006	5 461	17 388	3 775	397 925	1 104 653	255 902
2007	5 660	18 850	4 480	420 000	1 200 000	310 000

Sources: National Bureau of Statistics Bureau of Comprehensive Statistics on National Economy, 2005: 78–83; NBS, 2007: 789–790; National Bureau of Statistics, 2008.

admitted for a couple of years before admissions picked up. However, the total enrollment never reached the levels in place before the Cultural Revolution. Moreover, radical politics colored the academic atmosphere and learning environment inside the higher education system. The academic world may have seemed to have been granted a respite, but still it was quite clear once the doors reopened that "politics was in command."

Mao Zedong ordered that the period of schooling must be short-ened, and so the standard course of undergraduate study was reduced from the traditional four and five years, depending upon disciplines (programs in medicine and architecture and at some prestigious schools, for example, usually had lasted for five years before the Cultural Revolution); the "new" Maoist curriculum was for only two to three years. The negative effects of this reduction in classroom learning were compounded by a cut in the length of the junior and senior high school education from six to four years. Because Mao Zedong instructed that the admissions process for college students should give preference to those from the families of workers, peasants, and sol-diers, and to workers, peasants, and soldiers themselves with practical experience, all high school graduates had to go to factories or the countryside or join the army for several years, before being given possible consideration for admission to higher education. Admissions criteria shifted away from academic performance and became focussed on recommendations from the factories, communes, or military camps with which the future students were affiliated. The official college entrance examinations carried much less significance. For example, in 1973, while sitting for a college entrance examination, Zhang Tiesheng, one of the recommended applicants, knew that he would fail the examination. Instead of answering the formal questions, he wrote a complaint claiming that he was unfairly tested against his peers as he had had no time to prepare for the examination. His complaint was pulled out by the radicals, who not only supported his admissions, but also used the opportunity to attack college entrance examinations (Pan, 2003: 121). Consequently, when "worker–peasant–soldier stu-dents (*gongnongbing xueyuan*)," as the cohort of college students admitted between 1970 and 1977 is known, arrived at a college campus, many of them had not even finished a high school education, so that they had to take some time to refresh their elementary know-ledge. A peasant-origin female student, for example, who studied automation control at Qinghua University, China's equivalent to the Massachusetts Institute of Technology (MIT) in the US higher engin-eering and technology education hierarchy, told visiting Americans in 1973 that when she entered the university she had only been through one year of junior middle school (Science for the People, 1974: 185).

And finally, because Mao Zedong stressed that education should serve so-called "proletarian politics" and be combined with production, the "approved" academic curriculum became less professional and more political and practical. Qinghua University was no longer so much a center of learning, but functioned as a liaison office, where science and engineering majors spent 80 percent of their time learning practical subjects and working in factories, 15 percent of their time studying Marxism–Leninism–Mao Zedong Thought and 5 percent of their time doing farm work and "learning from the People's Liberation Army." In the meantime, professors and students often made extensive visits to factories and communes to study and help solve practical problems (Hinton, 1972: 14; Science for the People, 1974: 182). Interestingly, China's attempts to respond to the needs of the rural areas was not inconsistent with the prevailing views of organizations such as the World Bank and United Nations, which at the time were advocating less concentration on building a so-called academic "ivory tower" that was generally insensitive to the broader needs of society. Yet, although in a developing country there is indeed something to be said about the need to avoid an excessive focus simply on the needs of the urban centers and the relatively well-off segments of the populace, the quality of Chinese education itself during this period was so diminished that even the knowledge and expertise needed to respond to the vast needs of rural China was undermined by a continued excessive emphasis on politics and correct ideology.

Obviously, these conditions and arrangements did not provide circumstances conducive to training the next generation of scientists, engineers, and other professionals. It is estimated that China lost at least one million undergraduates and 100 000 graduate students to the Cultural Revolution (Qu, 1993: 648). Some of the students admitted before and during the Cultural Revolution persevered against the odds and furthered their studies in domestic and overseas graduate schools after the Cultural Revolution; ever since, many of them have been playing important roles in China's educational and scientific enterprise and economic sector. For example, Bai Chunli, a "*gongnongbing xueyuan*" from Beijing University entered the CAS in 1978 as a graduate student and went on to be a post-doctoral fellow at the California Institute of Technology, thereafter becoming the first Chinese worker at the famous Jet Propulsion Laboratory since China's renowned aerodynamicist Qian Xuesen was expelled from the USA in the 1950s. To his great credit, Bai Chunli is now executive vice president of the academy; he also is one of China's most noted specialists in nanotechnology.

Wan Gang, the recently appointed minister of science and technology, is also a *"gongnongbing xueyuan"* who graduated from Tongji University in Shanghai and eventually received his doctorate in engineering from the Technical University of Clausthal, in Germany. He is a specialist in clean-engine technology, and, prior to returning to China, spent over 10 years working for Audi in Germany. Along with Bai Chunli, several other *"gongnongbing xueyuan"* have become prestigious members (*yuanshi*) of the Chinese Academy of Sciences and the Chinese Academy of Engineering. Nonetheless, as a whole, given the low quality of their real education, the *"gongnongbing xueyuan"* cohort was largely quite ill-prepared for helping to drive China's economic, social, and techno-logical development, especially in terms of shouldering the type and level of leadership responsibility required in today's highly competitive, innovation-driven world.[2]

"Brain drain"

China's talent challenge has been made even more complicated and onerous by the fact that some of the best talent has been attracted away – not only to foreign countries in conjunction with China's decision to "open its doors" in the late 1970s after the Cultural Revolution (an external "brain drain") but also to the growing number of MNCs operating in China in such fields as manufacturing, sales, distribution, professional services, and, lately, R&D (an internal "brain drain"). In the same way that the Cultural Revolution con-tributed to China's talent gap in the 50 plus age group, and across the leadership echelon, the overall "brain drain" phenomenon has further lowered the qualifications hurdle for senior assignments in the research system and universities. It is not simply the relative youth of the emerging leadership cohort in China's S&T system that is of principal concern, but rather the lack of a more experienced cadre of directors and supervisors in science, engineering, and management to guide the next generation and transfer knowledge about critical aspects of technology as well as research, project, and people management.

---

[2] Nevertheless, the CCP Central Committee Politburo members elected in the 17th CCP National Congress in October 2007 include *"gongnongbing xueyuan"* Ji Jinping, Wang Qishan, Li Yuanchao, and Zhang Dejiang.

According to China's official statistics, between 1978 and the end of 2007, 1.21 million Chinese went abroad for study and research, of whom only 320 000 individuals have returned while some 657 000 are still pursuing their education (MOEd, 2008).[3] Given the large number of students graduated by Chinese institutions of learning – tens of millions of undergraduates and close to one million with postgraduate degrees in recent years – we may say that China has not lost many talented students to overseas study. Yet we also must acknowledge that among those who have not returned are most likely the best and brightest, and many in the age group in which China is currently experiencing a substantial shortage. In the USA, for example, in the very dynamic, innovative field of life science, it is estimated that several thousands of scientists of Chinese origin are running independent laboratories. Unfortunately, among the returned life scientists thus far, based on a variety of performance metrics, only a very small number appear to be of the same caliber. Overall, most of the Chinese scholars have remained in the USA after receiving a PhD in science and engineering. More accurately, as of 2003, there were 62 500 China-born holders of science and engineering doctorates working in the USA with 75 percent with American degrees (National Science Board, 2006: Table A3–18). Large numbers of Chinese graduates of high quality presumably remain in other technologically advanced countries as well. Of course, this is not a zero-sum issue as many of these same Chinese act as bridges between the Chinese scientific community on the mainland and their international counterparts abroad, helping to promote cooperation and collaboration. Moreover, some of the non-returned scholars assist China's educational and research organizations as well as enterprises in a variety of other ways, such as facilitating communication about S&T developments or investment opportunities (see Chapter 6 for a full discussion on the "brain drain" issue).

As noted above, the open-door policy initiated in the late 1970s has also attracted a very large volume of foreign investment to China over the last 20-plus years. First came the companies run by businessmen from Hong Kong, Macau, and Taiwan, and those of Chinese origin, focussing on labor-intensive manufacturing activities in toys, fashions, and other low-end products. With the steady improvement and

---

[3] Some estimate that the numbers of both those who have gone overseas and returnees are higher than official statistics.

Table 2.2 *Foreign corporate research and development (R&D) centers in China*

Year	Number of R&D centers
1997	24
2001	124
2002	150
2003	300
2004	400
2005	750
2006	980
2007	1 140

Source: Authors' research.

normalization of the Chinese investment environment, especially after Deng Xiaoping's tour to southern China in 1992, MNCs have gradually moved their higher value-added operations to China. This is particularly true with respect to the period since China became a member of the World Trade Organization (WTO). Not only has penetrating a huge Chinese market with increasingly affluent consumers been a high priority, but, so too, has been the opportunity to take advantage of the relatively higher-quality but less-expensive labor force. Since the late 1990s, many foreign corporations have expanded their R&D presence in China by opening independent R&D centers, some of which are actively collaborating with Chinese researchers or research organizations. According to statistics from China's Ministry of Commerce, there were 1140 foreign corporate R&D centers in China as of the end of 2007 (Table 2.2).

This number is probably somewhat overstated. In reality, a sizable number of the so-called foreign R&D centers are not truly independent units but largely are affiliated with the Chinese operations of their parent firms, mainly performing adaptive R&D activities – mostly development – and their registration with China's Ministry of Commerce is designed to take advantage of the preferable tax and import treatment that the Chinese government has made available. Some observers have suggested that such R&D efforts by foreign-invested enterprises (FIEs) in China are part of the global development strategy of the parent companies – being close to their Chinese operations and localizing technology developed in the "local base"

(Serger, 2006; Sun *et al.*, 2007). In this regard, the mere presence of these R&D centers should not be taken as firm evidence that these companies are making a concrete contribution to China's national innovation system; the full benefits to China are yet to be fully realized and thus in the short term should probably not be exaggerated. Looked at from a longer-term perspective, however, and with the comparative experiences of places such as Taiwan and Singapore in mind, when at least 30-plus large MNCs, including Microsoft, IBM, Intel, GE, Motorola, Nokia, Unilever, Procter & Gamble, AstraZeneca, and others have set up 60-plus facilities engaging in innovative research in China, there is a very high likelihood that in tapping into the domestic high-quality pool, there will be some significant spillover in terms of the diffusion of knowledge, especially from among those who eventually leave this type of employment to start their own companies and develop their own new commercially viable products and services.

Unfortunately, while such spillover may indeed turn out to be appreciable, the prevailing talent situation remains problematic. It is clear that the MNCs are seeking to hire the best available high-quality researchers, even poaching from domestic enterprises, research institutes, and universities, to enable them to advance beyond the use of cheap labor in relatively standardized manufacturing operations in China. The data on S&T personnel in large- and medium-sized FIEs appear to confirm such a shift (see Table 3.8).

Therefore, as has been demonstrated, the combined impact of the Cultural Revolution and the "brain drain" – the overseas study and the attraction of Chinese scientific and engineering talent to MNCs – has created a significant gap among the ranks of scientists, engineers, and other professionals in the 50–60-year-old age group. That is, even though there is relative abundance among those in the younger age, there remains a real and significant shortage across the leadership group that is needed, and expected, to take on and overcome China's innovation bottlenecks.

Quality problems also abound

The problems that revolve around the age structure of the talent pool, as well as the impact of the "brain drain," have been exacerbated by some very notable, well recognized quality issues. Because of the current talent shortage, especially at the high end, the younger generation has been prematurely placed, utilized, and even promoted, especially in fields where there are apparent shortages and in those regions where fewer scientists, engineers, and other professionals are willing to work.[4] Some of these "younger" individuals have been moved into significant leadership roles, although their credentials, knowledge, and skills do not seem to command such responsibilities. It is questionable whether these less-qualified individuals are prepared to assume their positions and associated job responsibilities; frequently, as heretofore has been the case, the fact that such people have been given this authority has served as a real deterrent to attracting the more-qualified individuals who are being asked to return from abroad or who are being recruited to join these types of organizations.

The good news appears to be that China's leaders, at both the national level and within the scientific establishment, seem to recognize inherent problems and limitations in the current system. Along with stepping up the recruitment among those Chinese who have remained abroad, a notable development in tackling the talent problem has been the dramatic expansion of higher education, although "water far away could not help extinguish the fire nearby," as a Chinese proverb would suggest. Since 1999, China has witnessed a new "Great Leap Forward" in higher education with millions of new students being admitted to regular institutions of higher education. In 2007, the new intake at China's regular institutions of higher education reached 5.66 million, more than five times that of 1998, the year prior to the admissions enlargement (see Table 2.1). It took China eight years to increase its total enrollment in higher education from one million (1980) to more than two million (1988), and another 11 years to double enrollment to more than four million (1999); in 2007, however, total enrollment rose to close to 19 million at regular institutions of higher education. If those in various adult higher education programs are counted, higher education is no longer something offered only to the elite in China. The enrollment rate for the 18–22-year-old group reached 15 percent in 2002 and is postulated to reach at least 25 percent of all high school graduates by 2020 (Table 2.3).

---

[4] This situation has appreciably deteriorated with the demise of the old-style job assignment (*fenpei*) system; nowadays, in China's more market-driven economy, most college graduates seem to have more job choices.

Table 2.3 *Gross enrollment rate of higher education for 18–22-year-olds*

Year	Gross enrollment rate (%)
1991	3.5
1992	3.9
1993	5.0
1994	6.0
1995	7.2
1996	8.3
1997	9.1
1998	9.8
1999	10.5
2000	12.5
2001	13.3
2002	15.0
2003	17.0
2004	19.0
2005	21.0
2006	22.0

Source: Ministry of Education Bureau of Development and Planning, 2007: 15.

It also seems to support the notion that there is a growing perception that higher education in China is becoming more necessary for quality employment and career development.

At the same time, the ambitious decision to increase enrollments has had many ramifications. In addition to raising questions about the ability of Chinese universities to absorb the new admissions increase in terms of facilities and staffing, and about the employment opportunities available for graduates, there has been concern about the possibility that rapid growth in enrollment might lead to reductions in the quality of education. Unfortunately, this concern has been crystallized. The quality of higher education has not been able to keep pace with the huge enrollment growth. For example, one frequently heard complaint is that the quality of many new faculty members is disappointing. Despite some real improvements in this regard, with enhancements of salaries and new research money, the overall quality of the academic ranks has not been upgraded fast enough to be in alignment with the quantitative expansion of higher education. While the problem remains quite real, it is one that the Chinese educational leadership is familiar with and considers inevitable for the time being. As of 2006, approximately 39% of faculty members in Chinese universities had received postgraduate education, with only 10% of them possessing a doctoral degree (those without a doctoral degree are now required to study for one while performing teaching and research), although at the very prestigious Beijing and Qinghua universities, professors with doctoral credentials hover around the 50% mark (see Table 3.15 and further discussion in Chapter 4). Consequently, many of those in college teaching positions actually are not well prepared for the task of training the next generation of professionals, thus lowering the overall quality of graduates and negatively affecting the career prospects of these young people.

To some extent, the quality problem of Chinese higher education may also be attributed to a lack of adequate funding. Expansion in higher education is supposed to be accompanied by real increases in higher education expenditures so that Chinese universities can upgrade their facilities, equipment, and instrumentation, and, most importantly, recruit new and better qualified faculty members. Although the Chinese economy has grown continuously and rapidly over the last 20 years, investment in education has constituted less than 3 percent of the government budgetary expenditures – among the lowest in the world. Since 1999, China has seen its per-college-student expenditure decreasing year after year as a result of the rapid expansion of enrollments; in essence, the growth rate of higher education expenditure has been slower than that of education enrollment (Table 2.4). In particular, higher education has lost its aura as a public good as the contribution of public funds to per-student expenditure has been around 40 percent.

Even more problematic is the fact that the government's new spending on higher education has been mainly used to support the 211 Program and the 985 Program at key (*zhongdian*), or China's most prestigious universities (to be discussed), thus ignoring the need for broader-quality improvements throughout Chinese universities as a whole. That is, although higher education in China is becoming a "mass education" phenomenon as measured by the rate of high school seniors attending colleges, looked at from the financial perspective, and measured by per-student expenditure, it is not so.

Table 2.4 *Per college student expenditure and share of public source*

Year	Per student expenditure (RMB)	Public source (RMB)	Share of public source (%)
1992	4091.94	2086.24	50.98
1993	4102.30	2040.55	49.74
1994	5047.61	2063.36	40.88
1995	5442.09	2339.73	42.99
1996	5956.70	2604.36	43.72
1997	6522.91	2865.60	43.93
1998	6775.19	2892.65	42.69
1999	7201.24	2962.37	41.14
2000	7309.58	2921.23	39.96
2001	6816.23	2613.56	38.34
2002	6177.96	2453.47	39.71
2003	5772.58	2352.36	40.75
2004	5552.50	2298.41	41.39
2005	5375.94	2237.57	41.62
2006	5868.53	2513.33	42.83

RMB, *reminbi*.
Source: Ministry of Education, National Bureau of Statistics, and Ministry of Finance, various years.

Curriculum issues also have contributed to some serious quality problems. It is often common to discover that the active curriculum in many programs is obsolete as some faculty members themselves do not understand the need for up-to-date knowledge. There also do not seem to be pressures, mechanisms, or incentives to promote individual faculty investments of time and effort in this regard. Curricula as a whole tend to be narrowly designed and delivered, a legacy of the Soviet-inspired higher education influence in the 1950s, rather than covering a wide spectrum of knowledge or interdisciplinary approaches to prepare students with the ability to jump easily and quickly to something new and different. The possibility of introducing a more flexible curriculum that promotes strong skills development and innovative thinking has not been finalized (Julius, 1997). There is a wide variation in terms of what to teach and how much to teach, which leads to uneven quality as well as content across institutions. This may seem ironic in view of the continued role of the Ministry of Education as an overseeing body in the realm of curriculum and course delivery, and quality control and assessment, but it remains the case simply because the rate of growth has outstripped the ability to monitor and evaluate what actually is happening on the ground in many programs. Finally, college students still have to devote a significant portion of their freshman and sophomore years to studying political ideology, a topic in which they appear to be less and less interested.

The quality issues embedded within China's higher education have become a serious source of concern to actual and potential employers, who in many instances must thoroughly retrain many new graduates once they are hired. And, because of high turnover rates, many employers are not willing to invest heavily in more than on-the-job training versus continuous education that is necessary for employees to update their knowledge and learn new skills as part of their career development and human capital accumulation, as suggested in Chapter 1. Not surprisingly, given the cloud that has emerged concerning the performance capabilities of new graduates, many face tremendous challenges finding their first jobs. Among those students who graduated from college in 2006, well over 25 percent were unable to secure acceptable jobs within the first six months after graduation; the situation actually deteriorated from that of 2005. The situation in 2007 and 2008 was just as serious.

Population getting old

Finally, looked at from a demographics perspective, China's talent problems may persist or even worsen as its population gets older. Since 1979, when China introduced a family planning policy which limits most urban residents to one child, irrespective of one's feelings about the ethics or religious aspects of the policy, the fact is that the nation has successfully and effectively controlled its population explosion and kept its natural population growth rate very low – around 0.1 percent – for many years. The good news is that China has moved from a population reproduction pattern of "high birth-rate, low death-rate, and high natural growth rate" to one characterized by "low birth-rate, low death-rate, and low natural growth rate," which is quite a remarkable achievement for the world's most populous country (Research Group on China's Education and Human Resources, 2003: 39–40). Chinese leaders also have come to appreciate more fully the latent wealth represented by the country's huge population – a sort of "demographic dividend," or the real benefits that have come from hundreds of millions of people born between the 1950s and the 1970s being employed as part of a relatively young, but increasingly skilled workforce. They have accounted for 27 percent of China's economic growth in the reform and open-door era (*Twenty-First Century Economic Herald* September 18, 2007).

The bad news, however, is that at the same time as the government has achieved its goal of tight population control, China has experienced important changes in the country's population structure with the age of its workforce steadily climbing and the size of its evolving college-eligible population beginning a gradual decline in recent years. In other words, the "demographic dividend" will not last for much longer. In the 1990s, China's working population – the age group composed of those aged 16–59 years – hovered around 60 percent of the total population. This trend will be maintained until such time that the pace of population aging accelerates, and thereafter, the proportion of the working-age population will tend to decline. In fact, according to predictions by some demographers, China will face a labor shortage as early as 2009, though the aging trend will pick up even faster after that time (*Twenty-First Century Economic Herald* September 18, 2007). With changes in Chinese society, in terms of nutrition and housing, and the many issues surrounding care for the elderly, this has generated global concern as to whether China will grow old before it grows rich. Therefore, the period from now until around 2015 represents an important period in which China must necessarily increase its investment in human resources, consolidate and restructure its existing talent pool, and, most importantly, prepare for the coming of an aging society. If China misses this narrow window of opportunity to address its current and future talent issues in a cohesive and concerted fashion, the pressure from the aging society, plus the legacy of problems across the higher education system, could slow down the process of China's modernization and the construction of a harmonious and comprehensive well-off society.

The leadership weighing in

In a word, China's talent problem – compounded by an aggregation of various factors – is so strategic and critical that it is related not only to

China's general economic development, but also to its ambition to become a more competitive, innovation-oriented society and play a more important role in the global affairs. It is against such a backdrop that the ruling CCP and government have made a strong commitment to ameliorate the current talent problems as well as those on the horizon.

In fact, this is not the first time in the history of the People's Republic of China that the talent problem has been taken so seriously. Emerging from the Cultural Revolution, for example, China almost immediately restored formal higher education by starting to admit new high school graduates at the same time as enrolling those who had been unable to attend higher education because of the Cultural Revolution. A nationwide college entrance examination was administered in late 1977 and first new undergraduate cohort was on college campuses in early 1978. The fall of 1978 saw the admission of another cohort of students (see Table 2.1). China's higher education situation in the late 1970s and early 1980s revealed an interesting phenomenon, previously unseen in the history of higher education in the world, in terms of the age distribution of students. At that time, students who had been denied the opportunity to go to college or had been turned down for non-academic reasons during the Cultural Revolution were some 30 years old, whereas those fresh out of high school were around 18, and there were many who were aged in between. Graduate education was also restored, with some of the students having graduated from universities ten years earlier and others not even having finished their formal undergraduate education.

To catch up with the global information and high-technology revolution that China missed while experiencing domestic chaos from 1966 to 1976, the nation dispatched a significant number of existing members of the technical community for overseas training to make up for their lack of formal graduate education in some cases, and to update their knowledge and skills in others. A new, revitalized cadre of scientists, engineers, and other professionals was thus reborne. Realizing the need to fill in the age gap across the technical community, China also sent newly admitted college students to study abroad. Suffice to say, the impact of the overseas study movement has had some very positive results with respect to China's higher education and scientific enterprise, even taking into account the impact of the "brain drain." Those who were privileged to have such an opportunity to study abroad are now actively engaged in China's political, economic, educational, and scientific affairs.[5]

Deng Xiaoping, then China's paramount leader, apparently was the main force behind all of these efforts. He pointed out that science and technology is the most important productive force, and that China should respect talent and knowledge, which are pivotal to the country's modernization drive. Scientists and engineers who had been sent to the countryside were called back for duty, and Deng Xiaoping even volunteered to take care of the logistics issues so that professionals did not have to waste their precious time on things that could divert their attention away from their research. Professional titles were no longer associated with the so-called "bourgeois right," as was the case before and during the Cultural Revolution. The future, indeed, did seem quite promising and the same spirit that prevailed during the early 1950s seemed once again to exist among the ranks of China's scientific community.

Since the onset of the so-called "four modernizations" program, even though there has periodically been some retreat, China's leadership has viewed talent as a strategic resource. Today, even more so than in the 1980s and 1990s, talent, along with S&T and education, are seen as the key to building a harmonious and comprehensive well-off society, and to solving the nation's problems in environment, energy, urban–rural, and regional development disparity, social inequality, aging population, industrial competitiveness, and national security. In the mid-1990s "rejuvenating the nation with science, technology, and education" (*kejiao xingguo*) became China's new development strategy, and the government initiated various programs that aimed to implement that strategy. Investment in higher education has become one of the most essential measures. Although the enlargement of higher education admissions, starting from 1999, has yielded various unintended consequences, it not only has accommodated the interest of Chinese in their children's education, but also has resulted in a tremendous enhancement in the facilities found at Chinese institutions of higher education. In many respects, this "Great Leap Forward" of the 1990s, in retrospect, was an investment hedge against

---

[5] In fact, an increasing number of the leadership cohort at national and local levels in China have had some form of overseas training, short- and long-term, during this early period (Li, C., 2005a).

the coming of an aging society and a decline in the college-bound population around 2015.

Just as the "*kejiao xingguo*" strategy emphasized the role of science, technology, and education in China's modernization endeavor, "empowering the nation through talent" (*rencai qiangguo*) is an inevitable follow-up, especially for China to turn itself into an innovative society. At the turn of the twenty-first century, China deliberately seems to have changed its S&T development strategy from "master imitator" to indigenous innovation (*zizhu chuangxin*) with an emphasis on domestic-based, innovation-driven technological capability-building and enhancement. The core of the new strategy is to develop Chinese intellectual property rights with domestic content, including patents and technical standards, as well as talent which could lead the creation of such intellectual property rights. The new strategy was initiated because the political and scientific leadership realized that, given the growing role of knowledge in the globalized economy of the twenty-first century, China does not possess enough domestic intellectual property rights, nor does it have a talent pool of high-enough caliber at the present time able to shoulder the full responsibility assigned by the leadership for a comprehensive national innovation drive.

Thus, in May 2002, the General Office of the CCP Central Committee and the General Office of the State Council (2002) approved an outline for building-up of China's talent pool in a concerted fashion between 2002 and 2005. On May 23, 2003, the Politburo of the CCP Central Committee convened a meeting to decide on the strengthening of the "party administers talent" (*gang guan rencai*) principle, by which it established the principle that the CCP has the final say on the talent issue (*People's Daily* May 24, 2003: 1). On June 9, the CCP Central Committee approved the establishment of a national level talent work coordination group. This group is responsible for the following areas.

- The macro-guidance and comprehensive coordination of the talent situation and talent build-up in the entire country.
- Learning and grasping the nation's talent situation and making policy recommendations to the CCP Central Committee on the talent work based on the demands of social and economic development.
- Evaluating and coordinating the implementation of the talent development plan.

- Coordinating and advising on talent-related policies, rules, laws, and regulations.
- Providing coordination and advice on the training, attracting, and utilization of talent and talent mobility, stimulation, and security.
- Implementation of important talent initiatives.

The coordination group convened its first meeting on June 12, and engaged an array of Chinese researchers on the topic some ten days later (*People's Daily* June 13, 2003: 4). At the same time, the CCP Central Committee's Department of Organization dispatched several groups to conduct field investigation into the talent situation in various regions.

All these activities led to a major national talent conference, held between December 19 and 20 of that year, which called for the creation of a more skilled professional labor force. This is the first time since the establishment of the People's Republic of China that the CCP Central Committee and the State Council convened a special conference on talent. The conference confirmed the "party administers talent" principle; most significantly, Hu Jintao, the CPP General Secretary and Chinese President, indicated at the conference that the talent issue is at a strategic level in the party and national agenda on development. He emphasized that "today, the heightened international competition boils down to a competition of human resources" (*People's Daily* December 21, 2003: 1). Afterwards, the central leadership issued a series of talent development-related policy documents on areas within which the party sought to establish its prerogative and exert its influence. For example, the CCP Central Committee and the State Council issued a circular on further strengthening talent work, while the party's Department of Organization and the government's Ministry of Personnel started to take stock of the nation's talent by surveying China's talent situation.

Also, in 2003 China started the preparatory work tied to the formulation of the 15-year "Medium- to Long-Term Plan for the Development of Science and Technology (2006–2020)" (MLP). The MLP, which was released in January 2006 by China's State Council, makes it clear that China intends to become an innovative society by 2020, and includes such commitments as an investment of 2.5 percent of its increasing GDP into R&D; the contribution to economic growth from technological advance reaching over 60 percent; decreasing dependence on imported technology to less than 30 percent of new technology adoption; and becoming one of the top five countries in the world in terms of the number of invention patents granted to its citizens as well as Chinese-authored scientific papers becoming among the world's most often cited. In particular, the MLP calls for a more strategic role for China's domestic talent pool; the strategic positioning of the talent is confirmed by the fact that it was one of the 20 key strategic research areas as part of the MLP initial background work (Cao *et al.*, 2006).[6] In proposing to leapfrog ahead in S&T achievements and become an innovative nation, the MLP suggests that China should focus on the structural adjustment of its talent pool, raising talent's innovation capability, and better utilizing the current stock of talent, while maintaining a suitable quantitative growth.

Dedicated programs for nurturing and attracting talent

China's emphasis on talent nurturing and cultivation is not just lip service. This is most evident in so far as almost all of the government programs in science, technology, and education initiated since the mid-1990s have had a substantial talent component. These programs include:

- the 211 Program, 985 Program, the Cheung Kong Scholars Program, and High Level Talent Program at the Ministry of Education.
- the Knowledge Innovation Program and the One-Hundred Talents Program at the CAS.
- the National Science Fund for Distinguished Young Scholars at the National Natural Science Foundation of China (NSFC).
- One Hundred, One Thousand, and Ten Thousands of Talent Program administered by the Ministry of Personnel.

---

[6] Strategic research, which is sometimes a confusing and misleading term, was the research on 20 critical topics or areas of long-term strategic importance through assessing China's strengths, weaknesses, opportunities, and threats (SWOT) in S&T development. The 20 topics ranged from S&T management system reform and the formation of a national innovation system, regional S&T development, basic science, and high-technology industrialization to manufacturing, agriculture, and energy, each directed by a leading scientific personality.

The Ministry of Education programs

The 211 Program was launched in 1993 to help position some 100 of China's universities as world-class distinguished academic institutions by the early twenty-first century. To that end, 107 leading universities and approximately 600 disciplines have been identified as key targets. In his speeches on the occasion of the centennial anniversary of the founding of Beijing University in May 1998, the then CCP General Secretary and PRC President, Jiang Zemin, reaffirmed such a goal. The 985 Program, so named to commemorate Jiang's May 1998 speech, chose Beijing, Qinghua, Zhejiang, Nanjing, Fudan, and Shanghai Jiaotong universities, the University of Science and Technology of China, Xi'an Jiaotong University, the Harbin Institute of Technology, and the Beijing Institute of Technology, the so-called "keys" among keys (*zhongdian zhong de zhongdian*) to potentially become "world-class universities," as well as 29 others (Table 2.5).[7]

While the 211 Program, and especially the 985 Program, have upgraded the infrastructure of China's leading universities, the Cheung Kong Scholars Program aims to build an army of leading scholars active at the international research frontier. Launched in August 1998 with an initial donation of HK $70 million (US $9.5 million) from Hong Kong billionaire Li Kai-shing's Cheung Kong Holdings, and supported with matching funds from the Ministry of Education, the program provides money to endow a series of professorships for outstanding young and middle-aged scientists (usually aged under 45) residing either in China or abroad. Each professorship carries an annual stipend of RMB (*renminbi*) 100 000 (US $12 000), which was quite significant at the turn of the century, on top of the appointee's regular salary and benefits from a university. To accommodate the interest of expatriate Chinese and their desire to contribute to the

---

[7] It is interesting to notice that four of the seven universities under the direct administration of the Commission of Science, Technology, and Industry for National Defense (COSTIND), the government agency in charge of China's national defense-related S&T activities and personnel training – the Beijing Institute of Technology (key among keys), the Beijing University of Aeronautics and Astronautics, the Harbin Institute of Technology, and the Northwestern Polytechnical University – have been selected into both the 211 Program and the 985 Program, while the other three – Harbin Engineering University, the Nanjing University of Science and Technology, and the Nanjing University of Aeronautics and Astronautics – are the 211 Program institutions.

Table 2.5 *Universities identified by the 211 Program and the 985 Program of the Ministry of Education*

Region	University
Beijing –211 Program: 23 –985 Program: 8	Qinghua University* Beijing University* Renmin University of China* Beijing Jiaotong University Beijing University of Technology Beijing University of Aeronautics and Astronautics* Beijing University of Science and Technology Beijing Institute of Technology* Beijing University of Chemical Engineering Beijing University of Posts and Telecommunications China Agricultural University* Beijing University of Forestry Communication University of China Central University for Nationalities* Beijing Normal University* Central Conservatory of Music University of International Business and Economics Beijing University of Chinese Medicine Beijing Foreign Studies University Peking Union Medical College Chinese University of Political Science and Law Central University of Finance and Economics North China Electric Power University
Shanghai – 211 Program: 10 – 985 Program: 4	Shanghai International Studies University Fudan University* East China Normal University* Shanghai University Donghua University Shanghai University of Finance and Economics East China University of Science and Technology Tongji University* Shanghai Jiaotong University* Second Military Medical University
Tianjin – 211 Program: 3 – 985 Program: 2	Nankai University* Tianjin University* Tianjin Medical University

Table 2.5 (*cont.*)

Region	University
Chongqing – 211 Program: 2 – 985 Program: 1	Chongqing University* Southwest University
Hebei – 211 Program: 1	Hebei University of Technology
Shanxi – 211 Program: 1	Taiyuan University of Technology
Inner Mongolia – 211 Program: 1	Inner Mongolia University
Liaoning – 211 Program: 4 – 985 Program: 2	Dalian University of Technology* Northeastern University* Liaoning University Dalian Maritime University
Jilin – 211 Program: 3 – 985 Program: 1	Jilin University* Northeast Normal University Yanbian University
Heilongjiang – 211 Program: 4 – 985 Program: 1	Harbin Institute of Technology* Harbin Engineering University Northeast Agricultural University Northeast Forestry University
Jiangsu – 211 Program: 11 – 985 Program: 2	Nanjing University* Southeast University* Suzhou University Nanjing Normal University China University of Mining and Technology China Pharmaceutical University Hohai University Nanjing University of Science and Technology Southern Yangtze University Nanjing Agricultural University Nanjing University of Aeronautics and Astronautics
Zhejiang – 211 Program: 1 – 985 Program: 1	Zhejiang University*
Anhui – 211 Program: 3 – 985 Program: 1	University of Science and Technology of China* Anhui University Hefei University of Technology

Table 2.5 (*cont.*)

Region	University
Fujian – 211 Program: 2 – 985 Program: 1	Xiamen University* Fuzhou University
Jiangxi – 211 Program: 1	Nanchang University
Shandong – 211 Program: 3 – 985 Program: 1	Shandong University* Ocean University of China* China University of Petroleum
Henan – 211 Program: 1	Zhengzhou University
Hubei – 211 Program: 7 – 985 Program: 2	Wuhan University* Huazhong University of Science and Technology* China University of Geosciences Wuhan University of Technology Huazhong Normal University Huazhong Agricultural University Zhongnan University and Economics and Law
Hunan – 211 Program: 4 – 985 Program: 3	Hunan University* Central South University* Hunan Normal University National University of Defense Technology*
Guangdong – 211 Program: 5 – 985 Program: 2	Sun Yat-sen University (Zhongshan University)* Jinan University South China University of Technology* South China Normal University Guangzhou University of Traditional Chinese Medicine
Guangxi – 211 Program: 1	Guangxi University
Sichuan – 211 Program: 5 – 985 Program: 2	Sichuan University* Southwest Jiaotong University University of Electronic Science and Technology of China* Sichuan Agricultural University Southwest University of Finance and Economics
Yunnan – 211 Program: 1	Yunnan University

Table 2.5 (*cont.*)

Region	University
Guizhou – 211 Program: 1	Guizhou University
Shaanxi – 211 Program: 7 – 985 Program: 4	Northwest University Xi'an Jiaotong University* Northwestern Polytechnic University* Chang'an University Northwest Agriculture and Forestry University* University of Electronic Science and Technology of China* Fourth Military Medical University
Gansu – 211 Program: 1 – 985 Program: 1	Lanzhou University*
Xinjiang – 211 Program: 1	Xinjiang University

*A university is identified by the Ministry of Education as both a 211 Program and a 985 Program university.
Source: Authors' research.

so-called motherland *and* even that of foreign scholars, the program has set up a special professorship whose holders do not have to work full-time, but just for a total of three to four months annually, in Chinese universities. Cheung Kong Scholars with distinguished achievements will be given a Cheung Kong Scholar Achievement Award, with prize money reaching as high as RMB1 million (US $120 000).

Initially, the Ministry of Education intended to appoint 500–1000 Cheung Kong Scholars during the first three- to five-year period, first in the fields of natural sciences and engineering. The program was later extended to the social sciences and humanities as well. Through a vigorous review process, including a final approval by a committee comprising Chinese scholars from home and abroad, a total of 813 professors and 308 special professors have been appointed at one hundred universities; most of them have been recruited directly from overseas or have had overseas study and research experience. Fourteen professors have been given the Cheung Kong Scholar Achievement Award.

In 2004, the Ministry of Education renewed the Cheung Kong Scholars Program with the Cheung Kong Holdings. Now, the new Cheung Kong Scholar Achievement Award includes scientists from the CAS who are not Cheung Kong Scholars and scientists from Hong Kong and Macau.

Also in 2004, the Ministry of Education decided to combine all talent-seeking programs under its administration into one. The High-Level Innovative Talent Development Program now has three levels of programs, with specific targets and goals for each of them. The Cheung Kong Scholar and Innovation Team Building Program, at the highest level, selects 200 Cheung Kong Scholars and 60 innovation teams every year; the New Century Outstanding Talent Support Program aims at supporting some 1000 scholars annually with the potential to become the first-rate talent in the natural and social sciences; and the Nurturing Young Core Faculty Member Program targets 10 000 core young faculty members each year so as to raise the over level of teaching and research in higher education. The Ministry of Education has also specified that some of the funds for the 211 Program and 985 Program distributed to universities should be used for talent recruitment and nurturing.

The Ministry of Education programs have activated the enthusiasm of provincial and municipal governments and various ministries that have allocated more money from their budgets for higher education and talent development. For example, regional governments and ministries have committed funds to the institutions chosen by the 211 Program and the 985 Program. The Cheung Kong Scholar Program has inspired the establishment of similar programs at provincial and municipal levels, such as the Qianjiang Scholar Program in Zhejiang, the Furong Scholar Program in Hunan, and so on. Cities such as Dalian have been working across the municipal government as well as with the central government to attract returnees as well as provide new types of education programs abroad and support local faculty attempts to reach out overseas for collaborative projects.

The CAS program

The One-Hundred Talent Program was set up in 1994 to recruit scientists under the age of 45 years, mainly from abroad but also from other Chinese institutions, with an offer of RMB2 million (US $240 000) for three years, including generous start-up research support, a housing subsidy, and a high salary.[8] This program has become part of the academy's "Knowledge Innovation Initiative" since 1998. Between 1998 and 2004, 899 researchers were recruited into the Program; some 778 of them had worked overseas, including 392 having doctorates from foreign universities.

The NSFC program

Launched in 1994, the National Science Fund for Distinguished Young Scholar Program comes under the jurisdiction of the NSFC, which was established in 1986 on the model of the US National Science Foundation (NSF). It serves as a major agency to fund peer-reviewed basic and mission-oriented (*yingyong jichu yanjiu*) research projects. The fund, again, modeled after the NSF Young Investigator Award, provides support for promising young scientists under the age of 45 from seven scientific fields: mathematics and physics; chemistry; life science; earth science; engineering and materials science; information science; and management science. Award winners are selected based on past performance and allowed to pursue research of their own interests.

Awards were initially made for a three-year period, with award-winners in experimental and technological sciences receiving RMB600 000 (US $72 000), and half that amount being awarded to those engaged in theoretical research. On the occasion of the fund's fifth anniversary in 1999, and in recognition of its achievements, the then Premier Zhu Rongji approved a significant increase in the Fund's budget from RMB70 million (US $8.4 million) in 1998 to RMB180 million (US $21.7 million) in 1999. The grant tenure also has been extended to four years, with funding for experimental and theoretical research increased to RMB800 000 (US $96 000) and RMB550 000 (US $66 000), respectively. In 2002, the funding was further increased to RMB1 million (US $120 000) per award for experimental science and RMB800 000 for theoretical research. Recently, the NSFC has extended the program by providing a select number of the fund's award-winners with continuous support upon successful completion of their grant tenure. The NSFC will give 190 awards to outstanding

---

[8] Funding of RMB2 million (US $240 000) is significant even by international comparison. For example, the Canadian government established research chairs for "rising stars" or young faculty members at universities, which carry a funding of US $70 000 a year (Kondro, 1999).

young scientists every year during the Eleventh Five-Year Plan period (2006–2010). In 2005, the NSFC set up a special program in the National Science Fund for Distinguished Young Scholar Program to support Chinese-origin scientists with foreign nationality, aged under 45, to work full-time in Chinese institutions of learning with similar level of support.

As a whole, the fund has made awards to 1174 young scientists, of whom 32.8 percent have received their doctorates from overseas and another 45 percent have had experience doing research abroad (Cao & Suttmeier, 2001; NSFC, 2004).

The MOP program

The Ministry of Personnel initiated the "One Hundred, One Thousand, and Ten Thousands of Talent Program" in 1995 with the participation of the Ministry of Science and Technology, the Ministry of Education, the Ministry of Finance, the National Development and Planning Commission (it evolved into the National Reform and Development Commission [NDRC] in 2003), the NSFC, the CAS, and the Chinese Association for Science and Technology (CAST). The purpose of the program is to identify outstanding Chinese researchers so that by the year 2010, 100 individuals will be active at the research frontier of international science and technology, 1000 will have the advanced knowledge to lead the development of academic disciplines, and 10 000 disciplinary leaders with high academic attainments will be in reserve. As an academic honor, the program does not carry any monetary award. By 2000, the national component of the program had identified about 10 000 outstanding scholars, while the local component run by provincial governments had also chosen a significant number of scholars. Entering the twenty-first century, the Ministry of Personnel requires that 500 talented individuals are chosen at the national level every two years (MOP, 2002).

Overall, the programs surveyed here are a tangible manifestation of the tremendous efforts of China's political and scientific leadership to address the country's evolving talent problem. They also reveal the current shortages: many of the scholars receiving one award end up being selected for another simply because the number of excellent candidates is limited. For example, the award-winners of the prestigious National Science Fund for Distinguished Young Scholars are most likely to be named as Cheung Kong scholars at universities *and* included in the One-Hundred Talent Program at the CAS. Those selected for these programs are further targeted by the One Hundred, One Thousand, and Ten Thousands of Talent Program at the Ministry of Personnel as the reservoir of China's future academic leaders.

Problems in implementing talent policies

As the leadership of the People's Republic of China has quickly discovered over the last few years, despite its good intentions and substantial increases in funding in pursuit of excellent candidates, it is much easier to identify the existence of a talent problem than it is to actually solve it. Even though the talent problem has been at the top of the agenda of the Chinese political leadership for several years, and the central government has established a leading group to coordinate the tackling of this serious problem, progress thus far has been quite limited. For one thing, after so many years of issuing new pronouncements and starting new initiatives there is a distinct likelihood, based on our field research in China and discussions with various senior- and middle-level officials as well as enterprise leaders, that the leadership actually may not have fully accurate or even up-to-date information on China's talent pool. During our research for this book, early on after discovering some important knowledge and data gaps, we surmised that there might be human resources statistics and information unavailable in the public domain. But, after discussing these issues with China's policy analysts in S&T and human resources management, we realized that this is indeed not the case. This fact is highly disconcerting from a policymaking perspective. It is even more difficult to appreciate when we take into account China's planning legacy and the importance of the "party administers cadre" principle.

Aside from some informal networking and communication, the fact is that there is rather limited coordination or data-sharing among various Chinese governmental ministries, which collect talent data for their own needs.[9] Generally speaking, too many bureaucracies are involved. The Ministry of Personnel, for example, is important for its role in monitoring and managing experts at the high end, such as members

---

[9] The principle exception is probably the defense sector of the People's Republic of China.

(*yuanshi*) of the Chinese Academy of Sciences and the Chinese Academy of Engineering, post-doctoral researchers, and returnees with significant credentials, among others. While people falling into the first two categories are easy to account for in terms of workplace and location, the ministry does not appear to know how large the third group – returnees with significant credentials – is, as many of them have not bothered to register with that agency (but then, what are "significant credentials?"). Similarly, both the Ministry of Science and Technology and the National Development and Reform Commission (NDRC), along with the National Bureau of Statistics (NBS), collect data on S&T and R&D activities, including personnel, but China's formal S&T statistics and indicators on human resources in science and technology (HRST) do not profile the distribution of HRST by gender, age, educational attainment, discipline, geographic location, sector, or professional rank, among others. Surprisingly, we can only conclude that such data are just simply unavailable because they are not being collected and processed in an orderly, systematic fashion. The Ministry of Education is responsible for producing data on university admissions, enrollment, and graduates. Although it knows exactly where Chinese college graduates get their first job, it has probably become too politically sensitive to provide such information, as in recent years too many graduates have not gained employment. On the other hand, the CCP Central Committee's Department of Organization and the Ministry of Personnel, along with the NBS, collect large quantities of data on professionals. Although about one-quarter of all the "professionals" now work for non-government economies, it was not until 1999 that the Ministry of Personnel started to consider including them in national statistics. There also are censuses conducted by the NBS every 10 years, and labor market surveys conducted by the Ministry of Labor and Social Security (now part of the new Ministry of Human Resources and Social Security, as the result of the reorganization of the Chinese government in 2008), whose information is difficult to integrate into the overall plethora of statistics and data on the Chinese talent pool.

One of the consequences of the lack of comprehensive information about the various aspects of the Chinese talent pool is that the leadership apparently does not have a complete picture. Accordingly, it is constrained in its efforts to make informed decisions or to evaluate the effectiveness and efficiency of its policy measures. For example, there is reason to wonder how much the decision to establish many new specialized software colleges at some of the Chinese universities after 2000 was dependent upon accurate information and projections versus how much was driven simply by the hype that China did not have enough software professionals. It also would be interesting to know whether these software schools have produced enough software engineers to meet current demand, whether these software engineers have the right qualifications for their jobs, whether the locations of these schools were correctly decided, and so on. In other words, it is hard to understand how the Chinese government can evaluate whether the country's increasing, though still scarce, talent resources have been deployed and utilized optimally from a sectoral perspective, a geographic perspective, or an innovation perspective.

When reviewing the talent pool situation in China, relying on the existing data sources and limitations, government officials generally agree that the supply of innovative personnel has become a bottleneck in the country's quest to strengthen its technological capabilities. Simply stated, there is a real and apparent need for closer collaboration among government, industry, and academia in the production and harnessing of such personnel. Much of the efforts discussed here have been from a very pro-active government vis-à-vis an academic sector that seems to be growing by leaps and bounds. Interestingly, while complaining, often vociferously, about the lack of competent talent, Chinese industry has not been as engaged in helping to address the talent problem. For one thing, enterprises are reluctant to take students as interns or to create cooperative training opportunities, an important vehicle for cultivating young talent and allowing them an opportunity to translate their academic learning in an applied context.

Conclusion

As noted throughout this chapter, China faces a serious talent challenge, even though it has one of the world's largest S&T workforces and its education system continues to produce large numbers of graduates at the tertiary level. The Cultural Revolution damaged China's education trajectory and retarded the training of the next generation of scientists and engineers and other professionals. The decision to send students overseas for education after China reopened its door to the outside world has brought an undesired consequence – "brain drain" – that is, significant numbers of China's best and brightest S&T talent have overstayed their period of study in the West and Japan. Of course, some of these individuals continue to play an important role in China's S&T system as vehicles for the transformation of new ideas and information about global S&T trends. That important role acknowledged, however, their absence as potential "agents of change" from inside the S&T system remains conspicuous. To add to the challenge, China's population is aging, and this aging is not being offset because of the effect of family planning policies that were instituted in response to concerns about poverty, food, healthcare, and so on. And finally, Chinese scientists and engineers inside both the R&D system and China's university sector, with some notable exceptions, are not working at the same levels of performance, in terms of both quality and sophistication, as many of their Western counterparts. Whether or not this talent pool, as presently constituted, can carry the burden of moving China toward a truly innovative nation remains a major question.

As suggested, China's political as well as scientific leadership appears to realize the seriousness of the country's talent challenge – the continued efficacy of the problem detracts from ongoing efforts to turn the nation into one that can compete effectively in the cutting edge technologies that will define the competitive frontier in the coming years. These concerns have prompted the issuing of various top-down policy measures and the launch of many new programs since the late 1990s. To give even greater emphasis to resolving the talent issue, the CCP has put the nurturing of talent at the top of its agenda to coincide with the arrival of the twenty-first century. These are all very necessary and positive steps. That said and acknowledged, however, it also is clear that the efforts adopted by the leadership to meet the talent challenge continue to encounter an underlying but not dormant range of critical structural, institutional, and societal issues as well as economic problems owing to the incomplete nature of the reform effort, such as the impact of wages on labor supply and demand, and the relative immaturity of the market mechanism in China. Ultimately, when viewed from this perspective, the real challenge facing the leadership is not merely to be found in the realm of science and education or the policies usually associated with them, but in the larger political, societal, institutional, and even cultural milieu that continues to define the context for sorting out the talent dilemmas faced by the regime and the bandwidth that exists (or does not exist) for the expression of creative ideas and innovative thinking.

3 | Human resources in science and technology, and their structure and characteristics in China

One of the essential ingredients for developing and sustaining a high-performance innovation culture is the deployment and effective utilization of scientific and engineering talent. The next five chapters provide a comprehensive and detailed examination of China's scientific and technical talent pool, including a stocktaking of the current science and technology (S&T) workforce, a thorough analysis of higher education in S&T, a discussion about how S&T talent in China is being utilized, an examination of the "brain drain" phenomenon, and a forecast of the demand and supply for scientists and engineers over the next five years. Taken together, these five chapters present a broad, integrated picture of China's S&T talent situation and its international connections. The analysis is built on field interviews as well as in-depth inspection, scrutiny, and analysis as well as the interpretation of a large volume of primary talent-related data from Chinese sources. It is this overall set of data and the accompanying analysis that forms the core of this book.

This chapter starts with a discussion of terminology and focuses on the application of the internationally used definition – human resources in science and technology (HRST) – and its variations in the Chinese context. Particular attention is paid to the latter – the terminological variations that occur in the Chinese situation – to lay a clear foundation for the subsequent discussion about and analysis of the case of the People's Republic of China. This detailed explanation and analysis is necessary in order to go beyond the often simple presentation of data about China's talent pool in the media and secondary literature, and even in China's own formal government statistical publications. From here follows an effort to establish an overall baseline of China's HRST. The chapter examines China's human resources in science and technology measured by occupation (HRSTO), one key component of HRST, by describing and analyzing such variables as HRST stock and other related measures. This discussion complements the analysis contained in Chapter 4, which focusses on an examination of the other component of HRST – human resources in science and technology measured by education (HRSTE). The survey in the present chapter covers an analysis of the characteristics of China's HRSTO in terms of distribution across geography, age, gender, education attainment professional title, discipline, and so on, depending upon operational definitions used in China and data availability. The chapter also offers an assessment of the general quality of Chinese S&T workforce, placing the Chinese case in a comparative perspective in terms of how China has developed its HRST over time along with how China compares with some other countries in terms of its HRST.

Key terms – human resources in science and technology

In Chapter 1 we discussed the concept of human capital and its role in economic development. In reality, however, as mentioned in Chapter 1, from an operational perspective, human capital is difficult to define and measure (see also, for example, Pollak, 1999). Years of schooling, and school enrollment rates at various levels are widely used proxies for human capital stock; human capital may also be raised through experience accumulation, on-the-job training, and continuing professional education. This chapter focuses instead specifically on human resources, a concept that is related to human capital and possesses similar characteristics, but, more importantly, is easier to quantify.

According to the *Canberra Manual* (OECD, 1995: 8), an important document issued by the Organization for Economic Co-operation and Development (OECD), it is the combination of S&T and human resources that is the key ingredient underlying rapid and concerted innovation, national- or firm-level competitiveness, and general economic development, including safeguarding and enhancing the environment. HRST, in this context, refers to those "resources" actually or potentially devoted to the systematic generation, advancement, diffusion, and application of scientific and technological knowledge. Taken from the widest definition, HRST extends to everyone who has successfully completed post-secondary education or is working in an associated S&T occupation; using the narrowest definition, HRST only covers those with at least university-level qualifications in the natural sciences or engineering, or doing an S&T job. The discussion here uses the term "HRST" in the more narrow sense specified above.

Thus, HRST may be defined by, or measured in, terms of two core components – qualifications and occupation – and each corresponds to one critical dimension of HRST: supply or demand. The qualifications component is about the supply of HRST (or the number of people who are currently or potentially available to work at a certain technical or skill level) while the demand for HRST (or the number of people who are actually engaged in S&T activities at a certain level) is reflected in the occupation component. Because demand does not always match supply, and because certain skills may sometimes be obtained outside the formal education system, the *Canberra Manual* proposes a "combined definition" of HRST (OECD, 1995: 16). In this sense, HRST may also be identified by both *occupation* (people employed in S&T professions at the appropriate level) and *qualification* (people with the formal education that enables them to be considered for employment in various specific S&T professions). Therefore, data on S&T occupation tend to relate to demand-side or utilization questions such as "How many people are actually employed as HRST?" whereas data on S&T qualification are most relevant when responding to supply-side questions such as "What is the pool of people potentially available to work in S&T?" Once people have successfully completed their education at the tertiary level in S&T, they become classified as HRST on a permanent basis simply because they have the potential to be employed in S&T-related activities on an ongoing basis, regardless of whether they actually have ever used their education in a job or whether their knowledge is still current for a specific S&T-related job after returning from a non-technical position.

Operationally, HRST are people who have either successfully completed education at the tertiary level in an S&T field of study (HRSTE [education]) or, even if not formally qualified in terms of educational credentials, are employed in an S&T occupation where the above qualifications are normally required (HRSTO [occupation]). Those meeting both criteria at the same time – having successfully completed their education at the tertiary level in an S&T field of study and employed in an S&T occupation – form the HRST core (HRSTC) (Figure 3.1).

The details pertaining to the above-mentioned educational requirements are referred to in a United Nations Educational, Scientific and

HRSTO (Occupation)		HRSTE (Education)			
		Tertiary education			< Tertiary education
		ISCED 6	ISCED 5A	ISCED 5B	ISCED < 5B
HRSTO **(Occupation)**	Professionals	HRSTC (Core)			HRST without tertiary education
	Technicians				
	Managers	HRST non-core			
	All other occupations				
	Unemployed	HRST unemployed			
	Inactive	HRST inactive			

Figure 3.1 Definition of human resources in science and technology.
Source: Organization for Economic Cooperation and Development, 1995.

Cultural Organization (UNESCO) document, the *International Standard Classification of Education (ISCED) 1997*, which was updated recently (UNESCO, 2006). The document classifies educational programs by explicit levels as well as the fields of education. Tertiary education, as mentioned in the *Canberra Manual*, refers to the same Level 5 education and up in the *ISCED 1997*; that is, programs leading to the awarding of an undergraduate and graduate degree. Specifically, Level 5 is the first stage of education at the tertiary level whose programs must have a cumulative duration of at least two years, with 5B being two- to three-year programs that are generally more practical, technical, and occupationally specific than 5A, which is longer, largely theoretically based, and intended to provide sufficient qualifications for gaining entry into advanced research programs and professions with high skill requirements. The second stage of education at the tertiary level are the Level 6 programs, which are devoted to advanced study and original research, leading to the award of an advanced research qualification such as a master's and doctoral degree.[1] Therefore, HRSTE include, but are not limited to, those who

---

[1] It should be pointed out that the *Canberra Manual* (OECD, 1995), published in 1995, uses the *ISCED 1976* where the education levels related to HRST include Category 5 – education at the tertiary level, first stage, of the type that leads to an award not equivalent to a first university degree; Category 6 – education at the third level, first stage, of the type that leads to a first university degree or equivalent; and Category 7 – education at the third level, second stage, of the type that leads to a postgraduate university degree or equivalent. The *ISCED 1997* combines categories 5 and 6 in *ISCED 1976* into *ISCED* Level 5, which in

have received a bachelor's, a master's, and a doctoral degree in the natural sciences, engineering and technology, medical sciences, agricultural sciences, social sciences, humanities, and other fields. This also indicates that HRST is a very broad category that potentially encompasses a large number of people.

HRST may be divided into stocks as well as flows within any national S&T system or within any regional S&T system. HRST stocks are the number of HRST at a particular point in time, available in distributions of age, gender, professional title, discipline, region, and employed sector; HRST flows, on the other hand, measure the mobility of HRST between jobs. HRST flows, in turn, include inflows and outflows – with the former being the number of people who do not fulfill any of the conditions for inclusion in HRST at the beginning of a time period, but fulfill at least one of them during that period; and the latter referring to the number of people who fulfill one or another of the conditions for inclusion in HRST at the beginning of a time period and cease to be qualified during the period. The educational system represents the main source of people moving into the HRST stocks, providing both *real* inflows (graduates) and *potential* inflows (enrolled students) of such stocks. In addition, retirement and death are two major events that lead to HRST outflows. There is another kind of HRST flow that occurs when HRST move or migrate across national boundaries: these are considered to be inflows for the country receiving HRST, but outflows for the country that witnesses the departure of HRST.

The study of HRST also monitors the following variables.

- HRSTU (unemployed) refers to those people who have successfully completed education at the tertiary level in an S&T field of study, but are unemployed; correspondingly, the HRST unemployment rate reflects the number of people who have successfully completed education at the tertiary level in an S&T field of study but lack formal jobs.
- HRST/population ratio, which measures HRST as a proportion of the total population of the age group 15 years old and up (this is

turn is divided into Level 5A and Level 5B, and Category 7 correspondingly becomes Level 6. Here the *ISCED 1997* scheme is used in explaining HRSTE.

because no one below the age of 15 will fulfill either of the requirements for being classified as HRST).

- HRST/workforce ratio measures HRST as a proportion of the total workforce of the age group considered.

In this book, there are various references to these different categories of HRST and the associated ratios. In most cases, even though Chinese data are not always aligned with this classification scheme, an effort has been made to utilize these formal categories to create a close match with international standards and classification systems.

HRST: operational definitions

Under the umbrella of HRST, there are various operational categories or definitions that have been offered by a range of different international organizations. According to UNESCO (1978: 23), S&T activities are systematic activities "closely concerned with the generation, advancement, and application of knowledge in all fields of science and technology." They are composed of three broad types of activities: research and development (R&D); scientific and technical education and training (STET); and scientific and technological services (STS). UNESCO (1978: 25) further defines "scientific and technical personnel" as "people participating *directly* in S&T activities in an institution or unit, and, as a rule paid for their services;" in this category fall scientists and engineers, technicians, and auxiliary personnel. More specifically, scientists and engineers refer to people who, working in those capacities, use or create scientific knowledge along with engineering and technological principles; that is, "persons with S&T training who are engaged in professional work on S&T activities, high-level administrators, and personnel who direct the execution of S&T activities" (UNESCO, 1978: 28). They have either completed education at the tertiary level leading to an academic degree or received tertiary-level non-university education (or training) not leading to an academic degree, but nationally recognized as qualifying for a professional career, or received training, or acquired professional experience that is nationally recognized as being equivalent to one of the two preceding types of training (e.g. membership of a professional association or the holding of a professional certificate or license).

On the other hand, according to the definitions in the widely utilized *Frascati Manual* (OECD, 2002: 92), an OECD document measuring

R&D activities, R&D personnel takes into account all people employed directly in the R&D domain as well as those providing direct services, such as R&D managers, administrators, and clerical staff. Scientists involved in R&D activities are synonymous with researchers and assistant researchers engaged in both the natural sciences and the social sciences and humanities. Researchers are professionals engaged in the conception or creation of new knowledge, products, processes, methods, and systems, and in managing the projects concerned. Researchers sometimes overlap with managers and administrators engaged in the planning and management of the S&T aspects of a researcher's work as well as postgraduate students engaged in R&D, although postgraduate students generally are reported separately in statistics according to the level of their actual involvement (OECD, 1993).

The equivalent to the *ISCED* (UNESCO, 2006) for occupations is the *International Standard Classification of Occupations* (ISCO). The *ISCO 88* distinguishes ten major professional groups, of which two are of specific relevance to the HRST category: the Major Group 2 "Professionals" and the Major Group 3 "Technicians and Associate Professionals."[2] The Professionals group includes those occupations whose main tasks require a high level of professional knowledge and experience in the fields of the physical and life sciences, or the social sciences and humanities. Their main tasks consist of increasing the existing stock of knowledge, applying scientific and artistic concepts and theories to the solution of problems, and teaching about the foregoing in a systematic manner. Most occupations in this major group require education at the Level 5 and Level 6 of *ISCED* (UNESCO, 2006). Other groups such as Major Group 0 "Armed Forces" and Major Group 1 "Legislators, Senior Officials and Managers" also are considered to be of some relevance. Researchers, for example, include all people in Major Group 2 "Professionals" plus "Research and Development Department Managers" (*ISCO 88*).

---

[2] *ISCO 88* is being updated and revised to reflect the occupational realities in the world and provide guidance on its effective use for the production of reliable statistics. The update is expected to be completed by 2008.

Of course, the ISCO definition, when formulated, did not foresee the now widespread trend in which those with higher education in an S&T field perform consulting, technical sales, and service jobs.

And, by convention, any members of the military with similar skills who perform R&D also should be included in this category.

Obviously, the term "R&D personnel" as used under the *Frascati Manual* is both narrower and wider than HRST in scope. The definition of "R&D personnel" excludes from HRST those who are not currently engaged in R&D activities, such as both suitably qualified people working in non-R&D activities and suitably qualified former R&D personnel who are unemployed, retired, or otherwise out of the workforce. However, the "R&D personnel" definition also is wider than HRST as it includes all people involved in R&D activities, regardless of their educational qualifications. That is, although it is rare that R&D personnel have not met the minimum educational qualification and skills requirements for inclusion in HRST, there are people who belong to one of the main components of R&D "Other Supporting Staff," i.e. skilled and unskilled craftsmen and clerical staff who will essentially be found in *ISCO 88* Major Groups 4 ("Clerks"), 6 ("Skilled Agriculture and Fisheries Workers"), and 8 ("Plant Machine Operators and Assemblers"). As R&D activities are part of the S&T activities, as specified by UNESCO, R&D personnel necessarily are included in S&T personnel.

HRST in the Chinese context

The definition and scope of HRST was not introduced into China until 2000 when the *Canberra Manual* was translated into Chinese.[3] In 2003, the data compilation entitled *China Science and Technology Indicators 2002* (MOST, 2003) first used the concept to quantify Chinese HRST. Thereafter, China's S&T statistics have used HRST to refer to the total number of those having at least two to three years of college education in an S&T discipline and those active in the S&T workforce who, despite not possessing formal educational qualifications, engage in S&T activities. This is in essence similar to the notion of HRST defined in the *Canberra Manual*. Interestingly, the *China Science and Technology Indicators 2006* makes a major modification of the HRST statistics (MOST, 2007: 29–30) (to be discussed).

---

[3] Earlier efforts under Asia-Pacific Economic Cooperation (APEC) and the non-governmental Pacific Economic Cooperation Council (PECC) in the mid-1990s to harmonize Chinese data with the statistical approaches used by other Asia-Pacific economies did not obtain much traction.

For quite some time in the People's Republic of China, intellectuals (*zhishi fenzi*) – scientists and engineers belonging in this "class" – were at the core of the country's human resources, although they were more commonly treated as a socio-political stratum.[4] In the meantime, in theory, intellectuals were equivalent in rank, salary, benefits, and sometimes social status to "cadre" (*ganbu*) – who include party and public administration personnel, administrators at public institutions, and top managers at Chinese enterprises. Organizationally, cadres and those intellectuals qualified as "cadres" were under the control of the Chinese Communist Party (CCP) according to the fundamental principle of "party administers cadre" (*dang guan ganbu*) (Zhong, 2003: 99). Nowadays, while this distinction still remains in place, it also appears to be the case that the number of those under the direct administration of the party apparatus is decreasing, albeit gradually. The Department of Organization of the CCP Central Committee continues to play a major role in overseeing the career progression of these cadres. Most recently, however, as the need to fortify the ranks of the CCP with technically competent people has grown, the Department of Organization has become more active in monitoring, managing, cultivating, and developing China's overall talent pool.[5]

During the reform and open-door era, professionals (*zhuanye jishu renyuan*) have largely replaced intellectuals as a category, with the former term emphasizing the aspect of professional knowledge and associated skills, while the latter refers, in particular, to those educated with so-called "independent thinking." More specifically, professionals are those with at least a middle-level vocational education (*zhongchuan*) or working in one of the 17 professions including: engineering; agriculture; scientific research (natural science, social science, and experimental technology); medicine; teaching (from universities to elementary schools); economics; accounting; statistics;

---

[4] Chinese society prior to the reform and open-door era was divided roughly into workers, peasants, soldiers, students and intellectuals, businessmen (*gong, nong, bin, xue, shang*), plus various enemy classes, depending upon the definition of "enemy" at the time. This was mainly a measure of political status and social honor (Kraus, 1981) (see Chapter 5 for a discussion on that).

[5] The clearest expression of this more intense involvement has been the financial support given by the Department of Organization to the "rising stars" among policymakers to attend programs at prestigious overseas universities such as Harvard, the University of Chicago, and so on.

translation; library, archive, culture, and museum; journalism and publishing; lawyers and notary public; broadcasting and television anchors; arts and crafts; sports; artists; and political counselors with professional ranks (*zhicheng*) or titles (*zhiwu*) (NBS & MOST, 2007: 332). In other words, the term "professional" is a very broad category overlapping greatly with HRST but placing more emphasis on occupation than qualifications. Like cadres, this category also was formulated by the party's Department of Organization and the government's Ministry of Personnel, which have authority over the administration of these professionals and collect data on professionals working at state-owned enterprises and institutions (*gongyou qishiye danwei*) and lately non-state-owned enterprises (*fei gongyou qiye*).[6]

Finally, "professionals" constitute only a part of the overall "talent" (*rencai*) pool; the term *rencai* emphasizes the skills and competencies of individual Chinese and especially the great strategic significance of these people to the economy and S&T system. Although the term *rencai* has appeared in Chinese studies of scientists and engineers for many years, the first formal definition of the term was provided only in a 2002 document issued by the CCP and China's State Council. *Rencai* are measured by neither educational qualifications nor job title; in addition to professionals, they are composed of other four categories: party and public administration personnel; managers at enterprises; highly skilled workers; and agricultural personnel (Table 3.1) (General Office of the CCP Central Committee and General Office of the State Council, 2002). Obviously, when the term *rencai* is used in this sense the concept is extremely broad in scope, generally vague in meaning, less strategically oriented, and unfortunately not necessarily comparable with the internationally used concept of HRST. And, when the term is applied simply to those with some formal, albeit perhaps lower, educational achievement, it tends to be less practical and pragmatic than HRST. Therefore, while acknowledging the strategically significant aspects of the term, *rencai* is not used in a formal way in this book, and when used only refers, generally speaking, to educated human resources as a group.

---

[6] In recent years, it has been estimated by Chinese government officials that people falling into this latter group account for approximately half of China's GDP.

Table 3.1 *Category and distribution of Chinese talent* (rencai) *(2000 and 2003) (million persons)*

Category	2000	2003
Party and administrative personnel	5.86	7.72
Professionals	41.00	32.69
Management personnel at enterprises	7.80	2.54**
Others*	8.94	46.20
Total	63.60	89.15

*Includes those with practical skills and those in the rural areas.
** Include those in state-owned enterprises only.
Sources: Chinese Academy of Personnel Science, 2005: 10; General Office of the CCP Central Committee and General Office of the State Council, 2002.

According to data released by China's Ministry of Personnel, of the five types of *rencai* totaling 89.15 million in 2003, professional is the largest single category, with some 32.69 million persons in total (or one-third) (Chinese Academy of Personnel Science, 2005: 10). Moreover, while all the *rencai* are pivotal to China's efforts to become a comprehensive, harmonious, and well-off society, professionals, and especially those in the S&T fields, shoulder one additional key responsibility, that is, turning China into an innovation-oriented nation.

In addition, two other categories are pertinent and highly relevant to the discussion in this book (Du & Song, 2004). The group of HRST who spend at least 10 percent of their time in S&T-related activities – those organized activities closely related with the production, development, dissemination, and application of knowledge in natural sciences, agricultural science, medical science, engineering and technological science, humanities and social sciences – falls into the first category, called S&T personnel (*keji huodong renyuan*). This category counts scientists at independent R&D institutes and universities, engineers at enterprise R&D laboratories, and those working at institutions of S&T information, graduate students at their thesis or final project stages, S&T administrators, and those who provide services to S&T activities, including managerial personnel at the organizations mentioned, and those involved in S&T activities such as planning, administration, human resources, materials supply, facility maintenance, and library staff (NBS & MOST, 2007: 331). Given the variety of S&T activities and the 10 percent time threshold, this definition also is quite broad and encompasses a large number of personnel. Compared with the UNESCO standard, however, the Chinese definition of S&T activities does not include S&T education and training personnel. As a result, the term "S&T personnel" as applied in the Chinese case is not necessarily internationally comparable.

The second additional category is R&D personnel (*yanjiu kaifa renyuan*) who are engaged in conducting, administering, and supporting R&D activities. R&D personnel in the Chinese S&T statistics are counted by their full-time equivalent (FTE), that is, person-years (NBS & MOST, 2007: 331–2), as specified in the *Canberra Manual*. If three people each spend one-third, two-thirds, and one-half of their time on R&D activities, for example, their FTE count is 1.5 person-years, although there are three individuals counted as S&T personnel. The Chinese definition of R&D personnel is the same as that used in the *Frascati Manual*. What should be stressed here is that, according to the Chinese approach, to be classified as either a member of the S&T personnel or R&D personnel category, an individual does not have to meet a tertiary education requirement or standard. There is a range of economic and socio-political as well as historical reasons for this difference; in some cases lacking a tertiary education certificate or degree does not have major quality or performance implications, but in other cases the consequences are quite substantial. But most of the current S&T personnel and R&D personnel do possess appropriate educational credentials as a result of both the retirement of senior persons and, more importantly, the recent addition of graduates from higher education.

One final definition worth mentioning is "S&T workers" (*keji gongzuozhe*), a definition used by the China Association for Science and Technology (CAST). CAST is a professional organization similar to the American Association for the Advancement of Science (AAAS). Their definition is a derivative of the "professional" classification, including only those in such S&T-related professions as engineering, agriculture, scientific research, healthcare, and teaching in the natural sciences at universities and high schools. Therefore, the definition is similar to "S&T personnel" defined by the UNESCO.

The relationship among talent, HRST, professionals, S&T workers, S&T personnel, and R&D personnel is shown in Figure 3.2. In terms

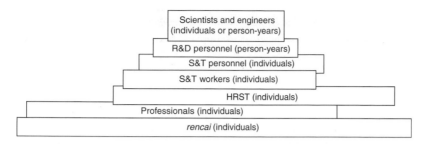

Figure 3.2 Relations between professionals, human resources in science and technology, science and technology personnel, and research and development personnel in China.
Source: Authors' research.

of the operationalization of this array of terms and classifications, it is useful to recognize that the category HRST includes S&T personnel, which in turn includes R&D personnel – both of which overlap with the category defined as "S&T workers," i.e. people working in the fields of engineering, agriculture, scientific research, medicine, and teaching in the natural sciences, which in turn are part of professionals. Talent, however, remains the overarching umbrella category.

Within the categories of S&T and R&D personnel are China's community of active scientists and engineers who either hold professional standing (*zhicheng*) at the middle level and above in an S&T field or have a bachelor's degree and up in an S&T field if they do not have professional credentials yet (NBS & MOST, 2007: 331). Thus, from this distinction, it is clear that there are scientists and engineers engaged in S&T activities in general *and* scientists and engineers engaged in R&D activities in particular, both of whom also are the part of HRST. Our research and the bulk of the discussion in the book is focussed specifically on China's community of scientists and engineers.

In addition to the level of study, there are differences between what constitutes S&T activity in China versus that in the *Canberra Manual* as well as how academic disciplines in higher education are defined in China and in the *Canberra Manual* (Table 3.2). In terms of the disciplines in higher education, the *Canberra Manual* includes not only natural sciences, mathematics and computer science, engineering, medical science and health-related fields, agricultural sciences, forestry and fishery programs, but also social and behavioral sciences, humanities, and education science. However, when Chinese talk about science

Table 3.2 *Tertiary education system: a comparison*

Levels of study	
China's higher education system	*International Standard Classification of Education* (ISCED) definition of tertiary-level education
• Short-cycle (2–3-year) programs at the undergraduate level that lead to a sub-baccalaureate (*zhuanke*) diploma	• Level 5B – education at the tertiary level, first stage, of the type that leads to an award not equivalent to a first university degree, i.e. at undergraduate levels
• Four-year and up programs at the undergraduate level that lead to a bachelor's degree	• Level 5A – education at the tertiary level, first stage, of the type that leads to a first university degree or equivalent
• Programs at the postgraduate level that lead to a master's and a doctoral degree	• Level 6 – education at the tertiary level, second stage, of the type that leads to a postgraduate university degree or equivalent
Fields of study	
China's higher education system	*Canberra Manual* definition
Core fields	
• Science	• Natural science
	• Mathematics and computer science
• Engineering	• Engineering
	• Architecture and urban planning
• Medicine	• Medical science and health-related
• Agriculture	• Agricultural, forestry, and fishery programs
Related fields	
• Economics, part of social science	• Social and behavioral science
• Law, including some fields of social science such as political science and sociology	
• Philosophy, part of humanities	• Humanities, religion, and theology

Table 3.2 (*cont.*)

- Literature, part of
  humanities
- History, part of
  humanities
- Education   • Education science and teacher training
- Military science
- Business administration

Sources: Organization for Economic Co-operation and Development, 1995; United Nations Education, Scientific, and Cultural Organization, 2006.

and technology, in most instances, they means natural science, engineering, medical science, and agricultural science, although social science also is frequently covered in the S&T statistics. This not only causes confusion but also makes international comparisons somewhat difficult.

While most of the statistics associated with China's HRST reported in this book are based upon internationally shared definitions, some clearly derive from the Chinese developed approaches. In what follows, the term "S&T workforce" is used to refer to S&T personnel and scientists and engineers engaged in S&T activities.

Growth of HRST in China

After the Cultural Revolution ended in 1976, and especially since 1990, China has witnessed the steady growth of its HRST stock – the sum of the number of people who have successfully completed higher education in an S&T field plus the number of people who are engaged in S&T activities despite not having received appropriate higher education (Table 3.3). According to China's higher education statistics and population census, the total number of Chinese receiving some higher education between 1949 and 2005 reached 54 million, of whom some 21 million graduated with at least a bachelor's degree. In 2005, the total HRST stock numbered 35 million. As a result, China now ranks first in the world in terms of overall HRST (MOST, 2007: 29).

Table 3.3 *China's human resources in science and technology (HRST)*
(million persons)

	2000	2001	2002	2003	2004	2005
Individuals with higher education	31.5	34.0	38.0	42.0	48.0	54.0
Individuals with bachelor's degrees and up	10.0	10.50	11.0	12.0	13.0	14.5
Stock of HRST	25.0	26.0	28.0	30.0	32.5	35.0

Note: The numbers were estimated from educational statistics and population censuses. The numbers include those who finished higher education through self-study
examinations, but exclude those receiving higher education.
Sources: Ministry of Science and Technology Bureau of Development and
Planning, 2007: 180.

Professionals

As mentioned, "professional" is a special, albeit broad, category used
in China's HRST statistics; it includes people in scientific research,
engineering, agriculture, medicine, teaching, and other professions.
While there were some 27.7 million professionals in China's state-
owned enterprises and institutions (*danwei*) in 2006, those in
engineering, agriculture, scientific research, healthcare, and teaching
numbered 22.3 million (Table 3.4).[7] Among the five categories,
teaching professionals – from university professors to elementary
school teachers – accounted for less than half, while scientific research
professionals accounted for only about 1.2 percent of the five. From
1996 onward, the percentage of engineering professionals has actually
been declining; this also is true with respect to scientific research
professionals, though the latter have recovered recently. Presumably,
large numbers of retirees are leaving the workforce and have contributed to the overall decrease.

---

[7] However, according to the "Outline for Building-Up of China's Talent Pool,"
the total number of talent in 2000 reached 63.6 million, of whom some 41 million
were professional and the number of professionals is expected to increase to
54 million by 2010 (General Office of the CCP Central Committee and
General Office of the State Council, 2002). On the other hand, the numbers of
professionals, according to the National Bureau of Statistics (NBS), in 2002 and
2003, were 30.60 million and 31.13 million, respectively (see Table 3.4).

Table 3.4 *Professionals – total in state-owned enterprises and institutions (1000 persons)*

Year	Total	Scientific research*	Professionals in state-owned enterprises and institutions						
			Total	Engineering	Agriculture	Healthcare	Scientific research	Teaching	Subtotal
1990			22 852	5 101	551	2 720	291	8 243	16 483
1991			23 919	5 024	463	2 758	342	8 581	17 168
1992			24 935	5 205	477	2 828	337	8 750	17 597
1993			25 965	5 364	496	2 916	334	9 014	18 123
1994			26 771	5 535	520	2 996	321	9 287	18 459
1995			27 054	5 626	536	3 035	303	9 634	19 134
1996			28 019	5 745	579	3 131	303	10 162	19 920
1997			28 603	5 720	611	3 214	302	10 648	20 495
1998			28 774	5 657	636	3 255	290	11 075	20 913
1999	30 605	951	29 043	5 655	654	3 330	284	11 508	21 430
2000	30 602	897	28 874	5 551	670	3 372	275	11 783	21 651
2001	30 533	867	28 477	5 316	675	3 390	266	12 051	21 698
2002	30 893	870	28 344	5 289	667	3 402	263	12 239	21 860
2003	31 130	1 128	27 746	4 993	683	3 441	276	12 347	21 740
2004	31 531	1 129	27 504	4 808	705	3 532	282	12 456	21 783
2005	32 010	1 135	27 567	4 791	706	3 581	311	12 589	21 979
2006	32 568	1 184	27 739	4 897	702	3 612	326	12 764	22 298

*Scientific research includes scientific research and technical services for years between 1999 and 2002, and scientific research technical services and geological prospecting for the years between 2003 and 2005.

Sources: National Bureau of Statistics Department of Population and Employment Statistics and Ministry of Labor and Social Security Department of Planning and Finance, various years; National Bureau of Statistics and Ministry of Science and Technology, various years.

However, if professionals in non-state-owned enterprises are included, the total number reached 32.6 million in 2006. In other words, professionals in the non-state sector accounted for some 15 percent of the total, rising from only 5 percent in 1999. The total number of professionals engaged in scientific research, technical services, and geological prospecting reached 1.18 million, or about 3.6 percent of professionals. This translates into only 326 000 professionals in scientific research being in state-owned *danwei*.

S&T workers

As indicated, S&T workers are those professionals in engineering, agriculture, scientific research, healthcare, and teaching in the natural sciences at universities and high schools. According to the estimate by the CAST, using data from the NBS, the Department of Organization of the CCP Central Committee, the Ministry of Personnel, and the Ministry of Science and Technology, the total number of S&T workers in 2002 was 26.39 million. Of these, 22.62 million were at state-owned institutions and enterprises while the rest were with non-state-owned enterprises and private institutions (CAST Research Team on Survey of Chinese S&T Workers, 2004a: 5). Of the remaining 3.77 million S&T workers, 970 000 were with overseas-invested enterprises from Hong Kong, Macau, Taiwan, and foreign countries, 2.33 million were employed by private enterprises, and 460 000 were with other types of non-state-owned enterprises and institutions (CAST Research Team on Survey of Chinese S&T Workers 2004b: 2). Apparently, the number is smaller than the one shown in Table 3.4 because the number in the table covers teachers in all fields and at all levels.

S&T personnel

Overlapping with both HRST and professionals, and covering personnel involved in a broad spectrum of S&T activities, China's S&T personnel surpassed three million for the first time in 2000, after crossing the two million mark a decade early (Table 3.5). In 2006, the latest year in which data are available, China had 4.13 million people engaged in S&T activities, with 2.80 million being qualified as scientists and engineers who either have finished studying toward a bachelor's degree and up in an S&T field or possess a professional rank at or above the

Table 3.5 *Science and technology (S&T) personnel, research and development (R&D) personnel, and scientists and engineers in China*

| | (1000 persons) | | | (1000 persons–year) | |
Year	S&T personnel	Scientists and engineers in S&T activities	Percentage of scientists and engineers among S&T personnel	R&D personnel	Scientists and engineers in R&D activities
1990	2 099	1 190	56.69	617	
1991	2 286	1 321	57.77	671	
1992	2 270	1 372	60.43	674	472
1993	2 452	1 372	55.95	698	489
1994	2 576	1 539	59.74	783	552
1995	2 625	1 554	59.20	752	522
1996	2 903	1 688	58.14	804	548
1997	2 886	1 668	57.80	831	589
1998	2 815	1 490	52.94	755	486
1999	2 906	1 595	54.88	822	531
2000	3 224	2 046	53.47	922	695
2001	3 141	2 072	55.95	957	743
2002	3 222	2 172	57.41	1035	811
2003	3 284	2 255	58.66	1095	862
2004	3 482	2 252	64.68	1153	926
2005	3 815	2 561	67.12	1 365	1 119
2006	4 132	2 798	67.72	1 502	1 224

Source: National Bureau of Statistics and Ministry of Science and Technology, various years.

middle level. If this percentage is used to measure the quality of China's technical community, entering the twenty-first century, China has enjoyed a significant quality improvement among its S&T talent pool – the percentage of scientists and engineers among S&T personnel has gone up to 67%, compared with less than 60% in the 1990s.

R&D personnel

Similarly, China's R&D personnel also have been growing in number over the years (see Table 3.5). In 2006, the nation devoted 1.5 million person-years to R&D, and its R&D scientists and engineers – those with a higher educational requirement – reached 1.22 million person-years. As both figures are calculated on an FTE basis, the exact number of people engaged in R&D activities is unknown, but it is most likely over one million.

It is interesting to recognize that S&T personnel and associated scientists and engineers engaged in S&T activities decreased some-what in the late 1990s, before returning to the growth path begun in the 1980s. At that time, S&T personnel dropped slightly from 2.90 million in 1996 to 2.89 million in 1997 and further to 2.81 million in 1998. The number of scientists and engineers in S&T activities saw an even larger drop in percentage terms. R&D personnel and scientists and engineers in R&D activities also decreased somewhat between these years, although it is difficult to gauge the precise change in terms of "number of people" as the number was measured in FTE terms. Several possible reasons might explain this seeming irregularity, including the retirement of S&T personnel and a change in the def-inition of S&T personnel. The Asian financial crisis, which occurred during 1997–1998 in several Asian economies, also affected China's economic growth; this slowdown, in turn, was likely related to a slight decrease in employment at Chinese enterprises as a whole and to the employment of S&T personnel in particular.

High-end S&T talent

Sitting on top of the human resources hierarchy, there is high-end talent. In the Chinese scientific and technical community, this is the vanguard of the country's talent pool. People in this category include the following.

- Approximately 1400 prestigious members (*yuanshi*) of the CAS and the Chinese Academy of Engineering (CAE) (Cao, 2004a; NBS & MOST, 2007: 23).
- Approximately 1000, most in the scientific and engineering fields, have been recruited to the One Hundred Talent Program at the CAS, appointed to the Cheung Kong Scholar Program by the Ministry of Education, received the National Science Fund for Distinguished Young Scholars from the NSFC.
- Approximately 5200 young and middle-aged (usually under the age of 45) experts with outstanding contributions identified by the State Council.
- Approximately 145 000 outstanding experts who have received special stipends from governments from the central to provincial levels.
- Some 10 000 young scientists identified by the One Hundred, One Thousand, and Ten Thousands of Talent Program of the Ministry of Personnel at national level and an additional 20 000 young scientists at provincial level.
- Approximately 31 000 researchers with post-doctoral experience.
- Some 133 550 with doctoral degrees.

These numbers represent an aggregation of China's top S&T talent. In examining these numbers, however, it needs to be acknowledged that there is frequently some overlap among the various categories of top scientists and engineers. For example, a scientist with post-doctoral experience conceivably could receive a stipend from the State Council as an outstanding expert and also be acknowledged by the Ministry of Personnel's One Hundred, One Thousand, and Ten Thousands of Talent Program. Some middle-aged, or even young, outstanding experts have been elected either CAS or CAE members. A key problem is that some of China's truly leading scientists and engineers have reached, or are approaching, retirement age; the situation is compounded by the "brain drain," thus exacerbating the prevailing shortage of such talent at the high end.

Characteristics of China's S&T workforce

Though quite large in terms of overall size, China's S&T workforce – S&T and R&D personnel and scientists and engineers involved in S&T and R&D activities – is very unevenly distributed across institutions, regions, and sectors. This section addresses the issue of talent deployment and its unique characteristics.

Institutional distribution

Chinese HRST in general and the S&T workforce in particular, as is true of their counterparts in other countries, are deployed across a broad range of institutional settings. In 2006, of China's 4.13 million S&T personnel, 509 000 (12.32%) were employed by universities, 462 000 (11.18%) worked in research institutes, and the rest were engaged in S&T activities within enterprises including FIEs operating in China, of which 1.89 million (45.79%) were employed by large- and medium-sized enterprises (Table 3.6). In terms of FTEs, the distribution of R&D personnel in the same year was 15.45% at universities, 16.18% in research institutes, and 65.78% within enterprises, plus a small percentage working at other types of organizations (Table 3.7).

During the reform era, institutions of higher education have seen their role become increasingly important in terms of China's S&T and R&D activities. They have been transformed from organizations primarily focussed on student training to more active players in scientific research, especially as support from the central government has grown, as manifested in the 211 Program and the 985 Program as well as various initiatives introduced by local governments. While the S&T workforce within universities has become stronger in terms of overall numbers and quality, ironically, its share of the country's total S&T workforce has either remained stable at approximately 12 percent for overall S&T personnel or has declined in terms of total scientists and engineers over the period from 1991 to 2006.

It has been within China's independent R&D institutes that the most significant drop has occurred, not only in absolute terms but also in terms of the relative share, as a result of the restructuring and reform of the organizational and governance mechanisms in place. In 1991, about one-third of Chinese S&T personnel (36.48%) and scientists and engineers (31.35%) were employed by R&D institutes; 15 years later, the respective shares dropped to 11% for both S&T personnel and scientists and engineers. Among independent R&D institutes, the CAS is the most important employer of China's S&T workforce. In 1998, the academy launched the Knowledge Innovation Program, aimed at turning itself into a world-class

Table 3.6 (a) *Institutional distribution of science and technology (S&T) personnel (1000 persons)*

Year	Total	Independent research and development (R&D) institutes	Large- and medium-sized enterprises*	Institutions of higher education
1991	2 286	834	829	292
1992	2 270	751	886	299
1993	2 452	723	918	314
1994	2 576	684	1 179	319
1995	2 625	666	1 234	324
1996	2 903	653	1 455	332
1997	2 886	636	1 474	326
1998	2 815	608	1 410	345
1999	2 906	552	1 454	342
2000	3 224	491	1 387	352
2001	3 141	427	1 368	366
2002	3 222	415	1 367	383
2003	3 284	406	1 411	411
2004	3 482	398	1 449	437
2005	3 815	456	1 679	471
2006	4 132	462	1 892	509

Table 3.6 (b) *Institutional distribution of science and technology (S&T) personnel (%)*

Year	Total	Independent research and development (R&D) institutes	Large- and medium-sized enterprises*	Institutions of higher education
1991	100.00	36.48	36.26	12.76
1992	100.00	33.06	39.02	13.18
1993	100.00	29.50	37.44	12.79
1994	100.00	26.53	45.77	12.39
1995	100.00	25.37	47.01	12.36
1996	100.00	22.49	50.12	11.44
1997	100.00	22.05	51.08	11.31
1998	100.00	21.60	50.10	12.27
1999	100.00	19.00	50.04	11.77
2000	100.00	15.24	43.03	10.93
2001	100.00	13.61	43.55	11.66
2002	100.00	12.88	42.43	11.89
2003	100.00	12.36	42.97	12.52
2004	100.00	11.43	41.61	12.55
2005	100.00	11.95	44.01	12.35
2006	100.00	11.18	45.79	12.32

Table 3.6 (c) *Institutional distribution of scientists and engineers involved in science and technology (S&T) activities (1000 persons)*

Year	Total	Independent research and development (R&D) institutes	Large- and medium-sized enterprises*	Institutions of higher education
1991	1 321	415	503	273
1992	1 372	407	550	281
1993	1 372	402	538	296
1994	1 539	393	690	301
1995	1 554	387	710	308
1996	1 688	391	796	316
1997	1 668	382	802	312
1998	1 490	370	637	311
1999	1 595	343	668	329
2000	2 046	303	769	315
2001	2 072	277	791	359
2002	2 172	271	813	376
2003	2 255	266	873	404
2004	2 252	263	842	364
2005	2 561	319	1 031	395
2006	2 798	329	1 176	429

Table 3.6 (d) *Institutional distribution of scientists and engineers involved in science and technology (S&T) activities (%)*

Year	Total	Independent research and development (R&D) institutes	Large- and medium-sized enterprises*	Institutions of higher education
1991	100.00	31.45	38.08	20.69
1992	100.00	29.66	40.09	20.50
1993	100.00	29.31	39.21	21.54
1994	100.00	25.51	44.84	19.58
1995	100.00	24.90	45.69	19.82
1996	100.00	23.17	47.16	18.75
1997	100.00	22.87	48.09	18.68
1998	100.00	24.80	42.75	20.90
1999	100.00	21.50	41.89	20.63
2000	100.00	14.83	37.59	15.40

Table 3.6 (d) (*cont.*)

Year	Total	Independent research and development (R&D) institutes	Large- and medium-sized enterprises*	Institutions of higher education
2001	100.00	13.36	38.18	17.32
2002	100.00	12.48	37.43	17.32
2003	100.00	11.80	38.72	17.92
2004	100.00	11.68	37.39	16.16
2005	100.00	12.46	40.26	15.43
2006	100.00	11.76	42.03	15.33

* The table lists only S&T personnel and scientists and engineers employed at large- and medium-sized enterprises. But presumably the difference between the total and the numbers at independent R&D institutes and institutions of higher education is the number of enterprises as a whole.
Source: National Bureau of Statistics and Ministry of Science and Technology, various years.

Table 3.7 (a) *Institutional distribution of research and development (R&D) personnel (full-time equivalent [FTE], 1000 persons–year)*

Year	Total	Independent R&D institutes	Enterprises	Institutions of higher education	Others
1991	670.5	274	206	145	45
1992	674.3	283	222	128	41
1993	697.8	259	257	139	43
1994	783.2	257	307	172	47
1995	751.7	245	294	157	56
1996	804.0	230	355	151	68
1997	831.2	254	321	165	91
1998	755.2	228	310	169	49
1999	821.7	233	351	176	61
2000	922.1	227	481	159	53
2001	956.5	205	553	171	27
2002	1035	206	601	181	47
2003	1095	204	656	189	46
2004	1153	203	697	212	40
2005	1365	215	883	227	39
2006	1502	232	988	243	40

Table 3.7 (b) *Institutional distribution of research and development (R&D) personnel (full-time equivalent [FTE], %)*

Year	Total	Independent R&D institutes	Enterprises	Institutions of higher education	Others
1991	100.00	40.87	30.74	21.63	6.77
1992	100.00	41.97	32.94	18.98	6.11
1993	100.00	37.12	36.76	19.92	6.21
1994	100.00	32.81	39.17	21.96	6.05
1995	100.00	32.59	39.10	20.91	7.40
1996	100.00	28.61	44.09	18.81	8.50
1997	100.00	30.59	38.56	19.87	10.97
1998	100.00	30.15	41.04	22.35	6.46
1999	100.00	28.36	42.66	21.42	7.41
2000	100.00	24.62	52.14	17.26	5.78
2001	100.00	21.43	57.84	17.88	2.85
2002	100.00	19.90	58.06	17.49	4.54
2003	100.00	18.62	59.93	17.29	4.17
2004	100.00	17.64	60.45	18.40	3.51
2005	100.00	15.78	64.71	16.65	2.87
2006	100.00	15.45	65.78	16.18	2.66

Source: National Bureau of Statistics and Ministry of Science and Technology, various years.

preeminent center for basic research, a leading institution for cutting-edge high-technology R&D, and a key performer of research in support of "public goods" programs in defense, agriculture, health, energy, and the environment, among others. As a result of hiving off a select number of applied research institutes as well as commercial entities, along with the reorganization of several institutes to reduce duplication, rationalize missions, and bring focus to new intellectual opportunities, the CAS has radically reduced the number of redundant and less productive research and non-research personnel (Suttmeier *et al.*, 2006). This has made the academy into a much leaner, more efficient, and, it is hoped, more effective organization, further reducing the legacy of the "iron rice bowl" mentality that has continued to exist in some domains of the Chinese economy and R&D system. As a whole, in 2006, the academy employed some 60 000 S&T personnel, of whom 55 000 were qualified as scientists and engineers (NBS & MOST, 2007: 28).

In the meantime, China's enterprises have stepped up their S&T and R&D activities, investing more on an overall basis and employing more technical personnel. In 2006, three-quarters of China's S&T personnel worked at such enterprises, representing a sharp rise from just over 50 percent about 15 years ago. It should be pointed out that one of the reasons for the rise is the conversion of some former application-oriented independent R&D institutes into commercial enterprises since 1999, as mentioned above. Similar reasons account for the increase of R&D personnel at enterprises, although measured by FTEs it still is difficult to know the exact number in terms of the total net gain inside the enterprise sector.

Here, it is important to pay particular attention to the S&T workforce employed within FIEs from the perspective of the institutional distribution of China's HRST. After China opened its door in the late 1970s, foreign corporations and especially MNCs, gradually – albeit steadily – have moved more and more of their mission-critical operations to China, as mentioned. Since the late 1990s, MNCs have increased their research presence in China by opening numerous R&D centers – the number reached 1140 as of the end of 2007. Consequently, between 1998 and 2006, FIEs saw their employment of S&T personnel quadruple, and the number of scientists and engineers in their employ increased more than five times (Table 3.8). In 2006, the total number of S&T personnel employed by FIEs operating in China reached almost 350 000, of whom some 219 000 were scientists and engineers, representing 7.84% of China's scientists and engineers – rising from just 2.80% in 1998. Comparing Table 3.8 with Table 3.5, however, we will find that the percentage of scientists and engineers among S&T personnel – a proxy of the quality of S&T workforce – is slightly lower for FIEs than for all enterprises in China as a whole. Although these statistics may not prove at all compelling to indicate that Chinese domestic enterprises have done a better job in employing scientists and engineers, they do provide some evidence that large- and medium-sized FIEs have yet to fully commit themselves to more innovative S&T activities in China. Of course, they are gradually refocussing some of their strategic goals into the knowledge-creation field and are now competing with local firms for more direct access to China's higher-end talent pool.

Table 3.8 *Science and technology (S&T) and personnel scientists and engineers in large- and medium-sized foreign-invested enterprises (FIEs)*

Year	Science and technology personnel (people)	Scientists and engineers in science and technology activities (people)	Percentage of scientists and engineers among science and technology personnel	Percentage of China's science and technology personnel	Percentage of China's scientists and engineers
1998	83 000	41 679	50.22	2.95	2.80
1999	92 000	47 444	51.57	3.17	2.97
2000	107 000	66 243	61.91	3.32	3.24
2001	124 479	79 961	64.24	3.96	3.86
2002	137 453	87 508	63.66	4.27	4.03
2003	172 139	111 280	64.65	5.24	4.93
2004	236 862	141 390	59.69	6.80	6.28
2005	288 718	181 596	62.90	7.57	7.09
2006	350 282	219 454	62.65	8.48	7.84

Source: National Bureau of Statistics and Ministry of Science and Technology, various years.

Geographical distribution

Geographically, the distribution of Chinese HRST is highly uneven – closely corresponding to the different economic development levels across the country's various regions. S&T personnel, and scientists and engineers, are located mainly in Eastern China; respectively, they account for 60.84% of S&T personnel and 61.78% of scientists and engineers engaged in S&T activities in 2006 (Table 3.9). As is generally known, the coastal economy of China, encompassing 14 key cities from Dalian down to Shenzhen, is more advanced technologically and has more money to be spent on S&T and R&D activities. Further, among the top nine provinces and municipalities that each employed more than 4% of the nation's scientists and engineers in 2006, seven are in the East: Beijing (10.95%); Guangdong (9.27%); Jiangsu (8.54%); Zhejiang (6.78%); Shandong (6.71%); Shanghai (5.37%); and Liaoning (4.54%). Otherwise, only Sichuan (4.46%), in

Table 3.9 (a) *Geographical distribution of China's science and technology (S&T) personnel (1000 persons)*

Region	2000	2001	2002	2003	2004	2005	2006	Percentage of total in 2006	Percentage change between 2000 and 2006
Eastern									
Beijing	249.0	241.0	257.3	270.9	302.0	352.6	382.8	9.26	53.72
Tianjin	71.0	70.0	71.2	78.7	83.8	90.7	99.1	2.40	39.51
Hebei	101.0	101.0	109.5	113.5	1?2.6	123.2	130.5	3.16	29.21
Liaoning	165.0	166.0	197.0	159.1	165.9	183.9	186.0	4.50	12.74
Shanghai	183.0	176.0	178.9	175.9	174.0	186.2	200.7	4.86	9.66
Jiangsu	295.0	300.0	328.6	331.8	335.3	375.7	381.1	9.22	29.20
Zhejiang	126.0	136.0	163.9	188.4	209.3	257.7	310.5	7.52	146.45
Fujian	64.0	71.0	67.5	71.5	80.0	85.9	101.1	2.45	57.97
Shandong	231.0	228.0	243.3	260.2	279.2	274.2	285.4	6.91	23.54
Guangdong	222.0	232.0	267.4	277.6	292.9	320.4	368.8	8.93	66.13
Guangxi	49.0	47.0	48.7	46.0	51.4	55.6	58.6	1.42	19.65
Hainan	6.0	4.6	3.6	3.7	5.6	8.7	9.1	0.22	50.88
Subtotal	1762.0	1772.6	1936.9	1977.3	2052.0	2314.8	2513.6	60.84	42.66
Central									
Shanxi	74.0	71.0	75.9	78.6	92.8	108.6	121.8	2.95	64.55
Neimenggu	37.0	33.0	34.3	34.4	35.2	38.0	39.9	0.96	7.72
Jilin	77.0	70.0	64.0	64.8	63.5	77.4	82.0	1.99	6.52
Heilongjiang	92.0	89.0	90.6	92.9	94.5	107.6	109.4	2.65	18.91

Table 3.9 (a) (*cont.*)

Region	2000	2001	2002	2003	2004	2005	2006	Percentage of total in 2006	Percentage change between 2000 and 2006
Anhui	97.0	89.0	88.2	86.0	86.0	90.5	96.7	2.34	−0.30
Jiangxi	59.0	59.0	56.1	64.4	65.0	67.2	71.5	1.73	21.16
Henan	152.0	140.0	143.2	146.4	144.3	157.4	177.3	4.29	16.63
Hubei	168.0	157.0	190.8	192.7	149.7	159.4	170.2	4.12	1.28
Hunan	104.0	99.0	103.8	97.0	104.9	121.4	130.2	3.15	25.23
Subtotal	860.0	807.0	846.9	857.2	835.9	927.5	998.9	24.18	16.15
Western									
Chongqing	62.3	59.7	61.6	65.2	65.9	68.1	75.6	1.83	21.39
Sichuan	177.0	167.0	176.8	172.7	178.6	183.8	194.8	4.72	10.08
Guizhou	34.0	34.0	32.9	31.8	29.9	31.3	36.0	0.87	5.76
Yunan	53.0	60.0	53.6	50.2	48.0	49.7	53.4	1.29	0.70
Tibet	2.8	2.4	2.6	2.9	2.7	3.4	4.1	0.10	47.86
Shaanxi	155.0	141.0	135.3	136.0	133.1	139.8	145.1	3.51	−6.39
Gansu	67.0	71.0	69.5	59.8	51.7	51.1	58.0	1.40	−13.47
Qinghai	10.0	9.9	13.2	9.1	8.8	10.1	10.5	0.25	4.76
Ningxia	11.5	11.2	12.5	10.2	10.2	10.3	13.1	0.32	13.65
Xinjiang	25.1	24.3	24.7	25.2	25.1	27.7	28.5	0.69	13.45
Subtotal	597.7	580.5	582.7	563.1	554.0	575.3	619.0	14.98	3.57
Total	3219.7	3160.1	3366.5	3397.6	3481.9	3817.6	4131.6	100.00	28.32

Table 3.9 (b) *Geographical distribution of China's scientists and engineers engaged in science and technology (S&T) activities (1000 persons)*

Region	2000	2001	2002	2003	2004	2005	2006	Percentage of total in 2006	Percentage change between 2000 and 2006
Eastern									
Beijing	195.0	190.0	208.8	226.3	235.4	283.0	306.4	10.95	57.14
Tianjin	49.0	49.0	50.3	55.6	54.4	61.2	69.0	2.47	40.83
Hebei	71.0	68.0	73.9	78.6	74.8	83.9	89.6	3.20	26.16
Liaoning	114.0	115.0	142.0	117.0	114.9	120.8	127.1	4.54	11.49
Shanghai	120.0	123.0	125.6	123.3	119.8	137.9	150.4	5.37	25.32
Jiangsu	167.0	175.0	201.6	208.9	198.6	228.4	239.0	8.54	43.10
Zhejiang	80.0	88.0	106.9	123.4	125.7	163.6	189.8	6.78	137.26
Fujian	39.0	46.0	48.0	49.2	52.1	56.9	64.8	2.31	66.05
Shandong	139.0	144.0	149.2	162.6	158.5	177.0	187.7	6.71	35.05
Guangdong	148.0	162.0	189.8	198.6	196.5	224.1	259.3	9.27	75.21
Guangxi	32.0	32.0	33.1	32.4	34.1	37.6	40.6	1.45	26.78
Hainan	3.0	2.9	2.1	2.6	3.8	4.5	4.9	0.18	64.80
Subtotal	1157.0	1194.9	1331.3	1378.5	1368.6	1579.0	1728.6	61.78	49.40
Central									
Shanxi	47.0	49.0	51.5	55.1	52.6	62.7	71.2	2.55	51.59
Neimenggu	23.0	22.0	23.0	22.5	22.6	25.9	28.5	1.02	23.98
Jilin	57.0	51.0	48.0	50.0	45.8	57.6	60.7	2.17	6.48
Heilongjiang	66.0	62.0	65.2	66.5	68.3	78.2	78.0	2.79	18.25
Anhui	56.0	55.0	58.0	56.7	52.4	58.6	63.1	2.26	12.70

Table 3.9 (b) (*cont.*)

Region	2000	2001	2002	2003	2004	2005	2006	Percentage of total in 2006	Percentage change between 2000 and 2006
Jiangxi	32.0	32.0	32.2	37.0	35.7	38.8	44.2	1.58	38.12
Henan	91.0	87.0	90.8	93.6	83.0	95.5	108.6	3.88	19.33
Hubei	105.0	103.0	145.1	143.4	103.0	113.7	122.2	4.37	16.42
Hunan	64.0	68.0	68.6	68.0	65.6	80.1	88.0	3.14	37.48
Subtotal	541.0	529.0	582.4	592.8	529.0	611.1	664.6	23.76	22.85
Western									
Chongqing	38.4	41.3	43.7	48.3	46.0	47.7	52.4	1.87	36.39
Sichuan	102.0	100.0	113.2	112.2	113.1	114.2	124.8	4.46	22.33
Guizhou	19.0	19.0	19.0	19.1	18.1	19.0	22.0	0.79	15.83
Yunan	33.0	40.0	34.5	33.0	31.6	33.2	35.1	1.25	6.27
Tibet	1.8	1.6	1.7	2.0	1.7	2.1	2.8	0.10	54.22
Shaanxi	86.0	85.0	82.7	86.7	81.0	88.5	93.2	3.33	8.42
Gansu	41.0	43.0	48.5	42.8	33.8	34.6	39.6	1.42	-3.35
Qinghai	5.9	5.9	9.3	5.9	5.7	6.2	6.8	0.24	14.61
Ningxia	6.7	7.1	8.4	6.7	6.8	6.7	9.0	0.32	34.24
Xinjiang	16.0	16.1	16.8	16.9	16.6	18.4	19.0	0.68	18.69
Subtotal	349.8	359.0	377.8	373.6	354.4	370.6	404.6	14.46	15.67
Total	2 047.8	2 082.9	2 291.5	2 344.9	2 252.0	2 560.7	2 797.8	100	36.63

Source: National Bureau of Statistics and Ministry of Science and Technology, various years.

the West, and Hubei (4.37%), in Central China, possess a significant pool of scientists and engineers.

Moreover, most of the increases in the size of the S&T workforce between 2000 and 2006 occurred in Eastern China. Zhejiang, for example, more than doubled the number of scientists and engineers employed in the province. Other provinces that experienced above-average growth – increase of the total number of scientists and engineers by about 36% during this period – were Guangdong (75.21%), Fujian (66.05%), Hainan (64.80%), Beijing (57.14%), Shanxi (51.59%), Jiangsu (43.10%), Tianjin (40.83%), Jiangxi (38.12%), and Hunan (37.48%).[8] It is surprising to note that Shanghai has been lagging behind many other locations in growing its S&T workforce. Even as the Shanghai economy has been booming, and the Pudong New District has taken off, the municipality has witnessed a mere 10% increase in the number of S&T personnel. Although the number of scientists and engineers increased by 25%, this was less than the national average. Taking into account the sustained pace of economic growth in Shanghai over the last few years, these facts may reflect the possibility that S&T workforce in Shanghai is more efficient and competent than those in some other regions, in terms of performance and output; thus, in comparison with several other regions, its actual contribution to the city's economic growth seemingly has been more robust.

Neither Central nor Western China has grown their S&T workforce as rapidly. In fact, some areas within Western China have experienced a decline, although on an overall basis, Western China has witnessed an increase in the number of scientists and engineers engaged in S&T activities by some 15%. Gansu, for example, has seen an exodus of S&T personnel – declining 23.73% between 2000 and 2006. Even Shaanxi, a stronghold that used to be one of the country's military-related S&T centers in Western China, lost some 6% of its S&T personnel. Presumably, these "mobile" scientific personnel have migrated to Eastern and Central China. To exacerbate the existing shortages, generally speaking not much new blood has been injected into Western China, even taking into consideration Beijing's Western

---

[8] Tibet also experienced rapid growth, but it is a special case because its S&T workforce base is very small.

Development Initiative which was launched around the turn of the century. This initiative contains several specific provisions concerning talent, offering incentives and other preferable treatment to attract and retain talent (Lai, 2002: 456). The continued uneven distribution of the S&T workforce in China could pose a long term problem in terms of closing the regional economic development and associated income gap. The lack of excitement about life, and career opportunities in the West looked at in the context of a growing differential between Eastern and Western China, may be one of the reasons underlying the exodus of some people and thus the current talent shortage. Whether this situation will prevail in the future remains to be seen as more and more FIEs appear prepared to invest in Western China in response to specific government incentives.

Female S&T talent

In post-1949 China, women are supposed to have equal opportunities to participate in all activities. However, there are no concrete gender-related data available showing how many Chinese scientists and engineers are female. Therefore, proxy information must be used to gauge the ratio of females across the HRST category (Table 3.10). The share of women among all professionals and scientific research professionals has remained constant between 1999 and 2005. In 2005, women made up 43 percent of the 32 million professionals and about one-third of the 1.14 million professionals engaged in scientific research, technical services, and geological prospecting.

Of course, the statistics related to "professionals" are not the same as counting the number of women in the Chinese S&T workforce per se. Perhaps a more useful indicator is the size of female representation in China's S&T activities; again, a proxy – the ratio of women among the advisors of graduate students – is used (Table 3.11). Over the years, not only has the number but also the share of female high-ranking scientists and engineers been increasing. In 2006, some 44 000 female professors supervised Chinese graduate students, representing more than quadruple the number just a decade ago and reflecting a much faster increase than the total increase, which was 2.6 times. In the same year, female advisors to Chinese graduate students accounted for some 23 percent of the total, compared with

Table 3.10 *Female professionals (1000 persons)*

	All sectors			Scientific research*		
Year	Total	Female	Percentage female	Total	Female	Percentage female
1999	30 605	12 442	40.65	951	311	32.70
2000	30 602	12 728	41.59	897	310	34.56
2001	30 533	12 838	42.05	867	299	34.49
2002	30 893	13 084	42.35	870	300	34.48
2003	31 130	13 307	42.75	1 128	372	32.98
2004	31 531	13 641	43.26	1 129	380	33.66
2005	32 010	13 791	43.08	1 135	377	33.22

*Same as in Table 3.6.
Source: National Bureau of Statistics Department of Population and Employment Statistics and Ministry of Labor and Social Security Department of Planning and Finance, various years.

Table 3.11 *Females among advisors of graduate students*

Year	Total	Female	Percentage female
1997	71 598	10 749	15.01
1998	74 560	11 300	15.16
1999	80 813	13 026	16.12
2000	88 825	14 782	16.64
2001	101 097	17 440	17.25
2002	115 462	22 473	19.46
2003	128 652	25 651	19.94
2004	150 798	31 472	20.87
2005	162 743	33 321	20.47
2006	188 835	43 769	23.18

Source: Ministry of Education Bureau of Development and Planning, various years.

only 15 percent in 1997. By having one-third of female professionals in scientific research and 23 percent of female graduate student advisors, it may be concluded that at least one-quarter of Chinese scientists and engineers are women.

Age and professional rank

No overall data are available on the age structure of China's S&T workforce. Nonetheless, one thing is certain: the workforce tends to be relatively young compared to its counterparts in the USA and Europe. Over three-quarters of the 27.7 million professionals employed at state-owned *danwei* in 2003 were under 45 years old, with those aged under 35 accounting for 46.8% (Chinese Academy of Personnel Science, 2005: 69). In 2004, 71.6% of those working at civilian R&D institutes and 55% of the senior scientists and engineers were under 45 years old. In the same year, those between 35 and 49 years old composed 51.4% of the total, compared with 44.5% in 1999. The CAS has been successful in adding young scientists to its ranks through the One Hundred Talent Program and other aggressive talent-attraction schemes. As a result of the 14 409 new appointments made by the CAS between 1998 and 2003 through its Knowledge Innovation Program, 67.8% were senior scientists under the age of 45 years (Chen, 2004). This suggests that China's S&T workforce has become more energetic and perhaps more productive as the work years between 35 and 45 are generally viewed as productive for people in the S&T professions.

Even the leadership contingency at Chinese R&D institutes, laboratories, and research groups has been significantly rejuvenated. If, in 1990, senior positions were dominated by those aged between 50 and 59 years, in 2004 those in the 40–49- and 30–39-year-old groups became more important (Table 3.12). Whereas the average age of CAS institute directors and deputy directors in 1991 was 56, by 2003 this had been reduced to 47 (Chen, 2004). On the other hand, the youthfulness of the country's senior professionals does not necessarily imply that they also have the necessary or requisite experience usually associated with those who occupy such positions in the West and Japan and that their experience and capabilities are sufficient to be effective in these senior leadership roles.

The data on the age profiles of advisors for graduate students at Chinese universities also reflect this same rejuvenating trend (Table 3.13). Between 1997 and 2006, the number of graduate student advisors more than doubled, but the average age of these advisors fell from 50.48 to 45.97 years, assuming that the midpoint is the

Table 3.12 *Distribution of professionals, by age and rank, in independent research and development (R&D) institutes (%)*

Age group (years)	<30	30–34	35–39	40–44	45–49	50–54	55–59	>60
1990								
Senior	0.02	0.07	0.13	0.85	17.71	51.57	26.4	3.25
Middle	6.37	10.11	13.94	13.35	25.33	24.33	6.46	0.11
Junior	54.88	16.31	12.98	7.78	4.59	2.61	0.82	0.03
1994								
Senior	0.38	3	4.17	4.02	8.6	31.89	43.09	4.85
Middle	12.55	21.98	15.01	14.36	13.33	14.72	7.79	0.26
Junior	51.9	19.05	12.23	8.26	4.89	2.53	1.09	0.05
1999								
Senior	0.31	8.41	20.32	13.77	13.23	12.81	24.89	6.26
Middle	8.11	25.21	24.48	15.29	13.7	8.46	4.49	0.26
Junior	49.35	12.63	11.74	10.64	8.16	4.52	2.75	0.21
2004								
Senior	0.4	5.1	20.6	29	17.7	14.3	8	4.9
Middle	7.5	24.3	23.1	19.4	13.1	9.6	2.9	0.1
Junior	46.8	21.2	11.4	9.2	6.6	3.7	1	0.1

Sources: Ministry of Science and Technology, 2003: 188; online sources for 2004.

average age of each age cohort (33 for the 30–35-year-old group, 48 for the 46–50-year-old group, and so on). Correspondingly, the average age of the advisors for doctoral students fell from 55.62 to 50.24 years at the same time as the number of such advisors increased by more than 3.6-fold. Again, China is going to benefit from having a large available cadre of young professors in place; but, as these data also show, there currently is a dearth of qualified individuals in the 51–60-year-old age group, suggesting that relying on and securing the benefits derived from the type of career mentoring which frequently occurs in the West may be a bigger, more difficult challenge in China.

Table 3.13 (a) *Age profile of advisors for graduate students (persons)*

Year	Total	Age group (years)										Average age (years)
		<30	31–35	36–40	41–45	46–50	51–55	56–60	>60	61–65	>65	
1997	71 598	283	6 330	7 238	7 614	7 073	12 857	19 319	10 884			50.48
1998	74 560	315	6 966	9 209	9 978	7 507	12 554	17 182	10 849			49.51
1999	80 813	319	6 894	13 090	12 741	8 871	12 151	15 523	11 224			48.58
2000	88 825	322	7 056	17 722	15 057	10 298	12 048	14 670	11 652			47.80
2001	101 097	327	6 772	24 850	17 930	13 258	11 770	14 432	11 758			47.00
2002	115 462	431	6 136	31 260	20 322	18 217	11 635	14 464		8 590	4 407	47.11
2003	128 652	500	7 340	33 232	25 242	22 239	13 119	14 051		8 075	4 854	46.73
2004	150 798	618	8 645	34 045	36 485	27 989	15 868	13 969		7 707	5 472	46.47
2005	162 743	794	9 860	32 114	45 951	29 304	17 545	13 561		7 805	5 809	46.35
2006	188 835	1 118	12 284	34 449	59 708	32 580	21 771	13 232		7 774	5 919	45.97

Table 3.13 (b) *Age profile of advisors for graduate students (%)*

Year	Total	Age group (years)							
		<30	31–35	36–40	41–45	46–50	51–55	56–60	>60
1997	100.00	0.40	8.84	10.11	10.63	9.88	17.96	26.98	15.20
1998	100.00	0.42	9.34	12.35	13.38	10.07	16.84	23.04	14.55
1999	100.00	0.39	8.53	16.20	15.77	10.98	15.04	19.21	13.89
2000	100.00	0.36	7.94	19.95	16.95	11.59	13.56	16.52	13.12
2001	100.00	0.32	6.70	24.58	17.74	13.11	11.64	14.28	11.63
2002	100.00	0.37	5.31	27.07	17.60	15.78	10.08	12.53	11.26
2003	100.00	0.39	5.71	25.83	19.62	17.29	10.20	10.92	10.05
2004	100.00	0.41	5.73	22.58	24.19	18.56	10.52	9.26	8.74
2005	100.00	0.49	6.06	19.73	28.24	18.01	10.78	8.33	3.57
2006	100.00	0.59	6.51	18.24	31.62	17.25	11.53	7.01	3.13

Educational attainment

Not only generally younger, China's S&T workforce also has deepened its level of preparation and training in terms of educational attainment. Of the 27.7 million professionals at state-owned *danwei* in 2003, some 61.4% had received at least a two-year college education. Seen from a broader perspective, of the 32.69 million professionals in the same year, about 58% had a college education, including 432 000 individuals with a graduate education (1.5%) and 5.78 million with bachelor's degrees (20.4%) (Chinese Academy of Personnel Science, 2005: 66–67).

Although no information is available on the overall profile of China's S&T workforce in terms of its educational qualifications, the percentage of those with advanced degrees working at civilian R&D institutes is known (Table 3.14). In 2006, 6.26% and 11.34% of the total had received doctoral and master's degrees, respectively.[9]

---

[9] Other sources indicate different statistics. According to the *2007 China Statistical Yearbook on Science and Technology*, 329 000 scientists and engineers at R&D institutions, 17 777 and 51 981 had doctoral and master's degrees, accounting for 5.4% and 15.8%, respectively (NBS & MOST, 2007: 28). According to a Ministry of Science and Technology (MOST) study, however, the number of those with doctorates at R&D institutes was 18 493 as of the end of 2006 (MOST Development and Planning Bureau, 2007).

Table 3.13 (c) *Age profile of advisors for doctoral students (persons)*

Year	Total	Age group (years)										Average age (years)
		<30	31–35	36–40	41–45	46–50	51–55	56–60	>60	61–65	>65	
1997	12 121	4	323	429	557	616	1 506	3 721	4 965			55.62
1998	13 638	2	330	730	979	713	1 728	3 734	5 422			54.88
1999	15 656	8	376	1 097	1 507	1 046	1 988	3 645	5 989			54.00
2000	22 552	14	630	2 314	2 761	1 849	3 167	4 848	6 969			52.49
2001	21 993	12	406	2 818	3 010	2 336	2 446	4 031	6 934			51.92
2002	25 697	32	313	3 688	3 561	3 420	2 471	4 232		4 503	3 477	52.86
2003	28 925	3	406	4 048	4 584	4 525	2 861	4 436		4 297	3 765	52.20
2004	35 024	38	504	4 332	7 129	6 303	3 756	4 630		4 094	4 238	51.30
2005	38 327	22	507	4 110	9 318	7 142	4 476	4 432		4 079	4 241	50.83
2006	43 844	40	609	4 184	12 186	8 254	5 832	4 401		4 069	4 269	50.24

Table 3.13 (d) *Age profile of advisors for doctoral students (%)*

Year	Total	Age group (years)							
		<30	31–35	36–40	41–45	46–50	51–55	56–60	>60
1997	100.00	0.03	2.66	3.54	4.60	5.08	12.42	30.70	40.96
1998	100.00	0.01	2.42	5.35	7.18	5.23	12.67	27.38	39.76
1999	100.00	0.05	2.40	7.01	9.63	6.68	12.70	23.28	38.25
2000	100.00	0.06	2.79	10.26	12.24	8.20	14.04	21.50	30.90
2001	100.00	0.05	1.85	12.81	13.69	10.62	11.12	18.33	31.53
2002	100.00	0.12	1.22	14.35	13.86	13.31	9.62	16.47	31.05
2003	100.00	0.01	1.40	13.99	15.85	15.64	9.89	15.34	27.87
2004	100.00	0.11	1.44	12.37	20.35	18.00	10.72	13.22	23.79
2005	100.00	0.06	1.06	9.96	24.49	19.18	12.17	11.89	21.19
2006	100.00	0.09	1.39	9.54	27.79	18.83	13.30	10.04	19.02

Source: Ministry of Education Bureau of Development and Planning, various years.

Table 3.14 *Scientists and engineers with advanced degrees in China's civilian research and development (R&D) institutes (%)*

Year	With doctoral degree	With master's degree
1991	0.40	4.17
1996	1.02	5.98
1998	1.49	6.47
2000	2.60	7.48
2001	3.28	7.85
2002	3.83	8.18
2003	4.54	9.11
2004	5.48	10.14
2005	6.28	11.34

Source: Ministry of Science and Technology Bureau of Development and Planning, 2007: 62.

In particular, among the scientists and engineers employed by the CAS, 7124 had doctorates (12.9%) and another 5215 held master's degrees (9.5%) (NBS & MOST, 2007: 28). It is very encouraging that the CAS now has a higher percentage of researchers with doctorates

Table 3.15 *Educational attainment of faculty members at Chinese universities*

Year	Total	Degree (individuals)			Degree (%)	
		Doctorate	Master's	Other	Doctorate	Master's
1990	394 567	3882	60 105	330 580	0.98	15.23
1991	390 771	4591	65 877	320 303	1.17	16.86
1992	387 585	5404	69 433	312 748	1.39	17.91
1993	387 808	6583	73 690	307 535	1.70	19.00
1994	396 389	8691	77 293	310 405	2.19	19.50
1995	400 742	10 443	81 420	308 879	2.61	20.32
1996	402 469	12 532	85 775	304 162	3.11	21.31
1997	404 471	15 500	90 491	298 480	3.83	22.37
1998	407 253	18 921	94 228	294 104	4.65	23.14
1999	425 682	23 136	100 492	302 054	5.44	23.61
2000	462 772	28 228	108 210	326 334	6.10	23.38
2001	531 910	34 853	121 546	375 511	6.55	22.85
2002	731 843	44 466	158 068	529 309	6.08	21.60
2003	724 658	53 612	182 517	488 529	7.40	25.19
2004	858 393	70 487	223 860	564 046	8.21	26.08
2005	965 839	88 450	269 003	608 386	9.16	27.85
2006	1 075 989	108 605	317 823	649 561	10.09	29.54

Source: Ministry of Education Bureau of Development and Planning, various years.

on its staff than do the independent research institutions as a whole, which means that its efforts in recruiting high-quality scientists through the Knowledge Innovation Program appears to have paid off. The CAS intends further to raise the number of doctoral degree holders to 30% of its S&T personnel and to 50% of scientists focussing on basic research. In Chinese institutions of higher education the percentage of professors with doctoral degrees has also increased, reaching more than 10% in 2006, while the same indicator was less than 1% in 1990; of course, not all the professors are engaged in S&T and R&D activities, though the numbers in S&T fields probably reflect the largest percentage given the huge emphasis on science and engineering versus the social sciences and humanities (Table 3.15). However, in 2005, among 643 160 S&T personnel employed at research institutes run by large- and medium-sized enterprises, only 7 168 had doctorates and another 47 811 had received master's degrees, accounting for 1.1% and 7.4%, respectively (NBS & NDRC, 2006: 4), many of whom were probably employed by FIEs. While the 2005 data reflect fivefold and fourfold increases, respectively, compared with the situation in 2000, the statistics also suggest that Chinese enterprises may not be prepared or positioned to create a sustained burst of innovative activities as the current stand on the talent front indicates.

Nevertheless, it is expected that the percentage of Chinese S&T workforce with advanced degrees, especially those with doctorates, will rise in the near future. This will no doubt strengthen China's potential capabilities with regard to the performance and output of R&D activities, and may help to advance the country's goals in the field of innovation. While having an advanced degree is no guarantee of innovative behavior or outcomes, it does enhance the potential for more rapid advances as these more knowledgeable people assume key roles within China's R&D system.

The national R&D resources census conducted in 2000 provides further information on the educational attainment of Chinese R&D personnel at various *danwei* by specialization in that year (Office of the National R&D Resources Census, 2002). Apparently, the number represents only part of the overall pool of Chinese S&T workforce; that said, the R&D personnel surveyed are those who are engaged in serious, sustained innovative activities, and therefore, their educational attainment and field of specialization do reveal some details about the focus and emphasis among China's core S&T workforce (Table 3.16).

Overall, in 2000, only 3.91% of Chinese R&D personnel had doctoral degrees, and another 10.10% had master's degrees. Institutionally, Chinese universities fared best with some 20% of the researchers having doctoral degrees and 32% master's degrees. Enterprises had the weakest research contingent in terms of level of education of their R&D staff, which helps to explain why these were not playing a more central role in China's innovation endeavors. Comparing Table 3.16 with Table 3.15, we also find that, in 2000, Chinese university-based R&D personnel had a higher level of educational attainment than the overall faculty as a whole, as measured by the percentage with graduate education.

From a discipline perspective, among the four science and engineering (*ligongke*) fields – science, engineering, agriculture, and

Table 3.16 *Educational attainment of Chinese research and development (R&D) personnel, by type of* danwei *and disciplines (2000)*

	R&D personnel (individuals)			R&D personnel (%)	
	Total	Doctorates	Masters	Doctorates	Masters
	627 221	24 526	63 352	3.91	10.10
By types of danwei					
Government research institutes	270 682	7 787	24 120	2.88	8.91
Institutions of higher education	68 027	13 811	21 808	20.30	32.06
Enterprises	278 085	2 731	16 777	0.98	6.03
Other research institutes	10 427	197	647	1.89	6.21
By disciplines					
Natural science	60 495	7 197	10 319	11.90	17.06
Engineering	459 038	9 838	36 427	2.14	7.94
Medicine	44 362	2 670	6 233	6.02	14.05
Agriculture	40 846	1 928	4 100	4.72	10.04
Management	1 772	247	594	13.94	33.52
Humanities and social sciences	20 708	2 646	5 679	12.78	27.42

Source: Office of the National R&D Resources Census, 2002: 300–2.

medicine – natural science was the strongest in terms of the quality of its researchers – close to 12 percent of scientists held a doctorate. Management, as a discipline new to China, also attracted a high percentage of scientists with doctoral education. There is no doubt that increasing numbers of Chinese scientists and engineers have continued to receive advanced higher education; however, their overall impact seems to be limited right now. Essentially, anticipated quality improvements have not been that significant, nor have the outcomes to date been that impressive. Although we do not know the percentage of returnees with overseas doctorates among Chinese scientists and engineers, at independent R&D institutes the percentage was less than 10 percent as of the end of 2006 (MOST Development and Planning Bureau, 2007).

Quality assessment

Overall, China has seen gradual but steady quality improvements among its current S&T workforce, as measured by an increasing number of those who have had graduate education. Consequently, there has been a steady increase in the productivity of Chinese scientists and engineers in terms of the number of international papers that have been published. In 2006, Chinese scientists published a total of 172 000 papers in journals catalogued by the *Science Citation Index* (SCI) and the *Engineering Index* (EI) and in international conferences catalogued by the *Index of Science and Technology Proceedings* (ISTP), accounting for 8.40 percent of the world's total S&T publications. This placed China in second place among the world's leaders in scientific publications (Table 3.17). In particular, Chinese scientists published 71 000 papers in the basic research-oriented SCI journals; China's fifth rank placement represented a significant improvement from its twenty-sixth place in 1985. China had held that same ranking three years in a row, behind only the USA, the UK, Germany, and Japan. Of course, Chinese leaders would like to see even greater progress. That said, the fact that Chinese scientists continue to hold their position reflects the increasing integration of scientific knowledge produced in China into the mainstream of global scientific affairs.

According to Wu Yishan, the chief engineer of the Institute of Scientific and Technical Information of China (ISTIC), which has tracked China's international S&T publications for some 20 years, China should not become overexcited about its achievement because Japan, with a much smaller talent base, published a similar number of SCI papers in 1996. That is, there is at least a 10-year *static* gap between China and Japan in terms of the number of publications, even putting the quality dimension aside. At the same time, Chinese scientists should also be proud of themselves. In 1996, Japan already had achieved a GDP of US $50 trillion, a per capita GDP of US $40 000, and was spending about 2.8% of its GDP on R&D; comparatively, China's GDP was only US $27 trillion with 1.42% devoted to R&D and a per capita GDP slightly over US $2000 in 2006 (see Chapter 7: Table 7.1 and Table 7.4). Most importantly, China has grown the number of published papers by 170.6% and the number of citations by 390% between 2003 and 2007, compared with Japan's 6.4% and

Table 3.17 *China's science and technology (S&T) papers, cataloged by the Science Citation Index (SCI), Engineering Index (EI), and Index of Science and Technology Proceedings (ISTP) and their respective shares and ranks in the world*

Year	SCI N	SCI Percentage of total	SCI Rank	EI N	EI Percentage of total	EI Rank	ISTP N	ISTP Percentage of total	ISTP Rank	Total N	Total Percentage of total	Total Rank
1996	14 459	1.62	14	9 147	4.43	6	3 963	1.57	11	27 569	2.04	11
1997	16 883	1.84	12	12 638	4.98	4	5 790	2.28	9	35 311	2.48	9
1998	19 838	2.13	12	9 892	4.31	5	5 273	2.02	10	35 003	2.56	9
1999	24 476	2.51	10	14 807	7.44	3	6 905	2.86	8	46 188	3.27	8
2000	30 499	3.15	8	13 163	5.78	3	6 016	2.94	8	49 678	3.55	8
2001	35 685	3.57	8	18 578	7.66	3	10 263	4.47	6	64 526	4.38	6
2002	40 758	4.18	6	23 224	10.12	2	13 413	5.66	5	77 395	5.37	5
2003	49 788	4.48	6	24 997	8.04	3	18 567	1.50	6	93 352	5.09	5
2004	57 377	5.43	5	33 500	10.49	2	20 479	5.33	5	111 356	6.32	5
2005	68 226	5.30	5	54 362	12.60	2	30 786	6.20	5	153 374	6.87	4
2006	71 000	5.90	5	65 000	14.60	2	36 000	9.00	2	172 000	8.40	2

Sources: National Bureau of Statistics and Ministry of Science and Technology, various years.

32%, respectively, between 1997 and 2001. And, during the respective periods, the number of citations per paper increased 0.83 times for Japan versus 1.17 times for China (*Science and Technology Daily* November 22, 2007).

Nevertheless, measured by total number of citations, China has hovered around thirteenth place in the world for many years. This suggests that the quantitative advances in output have not necessarily been matched by a similar array of qualitative improvements. This situation also has to be examined in the context of China's rapid increase in its investment in S&T and R&D activities, the emergence of an enlarged, more qualified S&T talent pool, and the onset of the 15-year "Medium- to Long-Term Plan for the Development of Science and Technology" (MLP), which specifically calls for Chinese-authored scientific papers to become among the top five in the world in terms of citations by 2020 (Cao *et al.*, 2006).

While a select number of Chinese scientists at leading institutions have done cutting-edge work at the frontiers of international research, much of the work coming out of Chinese laboratories and research institutes still tends to be not yet close to the cutting edge or to be derivative of what has been done elsewhere, with minor new contributions. In terms of visibility and impact, not many of China's overall S&T achievements over the past 25 years have been as significant as those represented by the strategic weapons programs (*liangdan yixing*) during the first 20 years after the founding of the People's Republic of China in 1949. The contribution of science and technology to economic growth also has not been commensurate with the huge investments that have been made. The critical problem lies in the fact that China still lacks a scientific leadership capable of driving a concerted push forward, a kind of leapfrogging, in Chinese science that would yield the types of breakthroughs associated with awards such as the Nobel Prize or major commercial successes. Frustration at the lack of major breakthroughs in scientific research and technological innovation is still ever-present among Chinese leaders, who consistently look to China's S&T system for signs of progress and evidence that the technological gap between China and the West and Japan is decreasing. The anxiety concerning Chinese scientists not having won a Nobel Prize in science, for example, reflects continued domestic concerns about the various quality problems that plague the Chinese science establishment (Cao, 2004b).

As mentioned above, an equally serious problem facing China's innovation system today is the experience gap across the current S&T talent pool. The key reasons for this gap logically may derive from the fact that those fresh out of university do not have the experience to manage various complex tasks which require knowledge and skill sets beyond formal education. For one thing, there is an apparent mismatch between the areas in which students have been trained and the jobs they are asked to perform. In addition, many students were simply not trained with proper skills and knowledge for the new jobs emerging in China. Even those in administrative positions in the 40- or 50-year-old group may not necessarily possess the skills and experience to perform adequately in their leadership assignments. It is therefore no surprise to see the government emphasizing, increasingly, programs to recruit Chinese talent from abroad as well as enhancing the quality of higher education, especially within China's select elite universities (to be discussed further in Chapter 6).

Last, but not least, there is a pronounced concern, as we have learned from our field interviews in China, about the lack of creativity and entrepreneurial behavior among the majority of Chinese scientists and engineers. This lack of creativity also reveals itself in discussions about the limited aptitude of recent graduates for risk-taking and the low level of failure tolerance inside the prevailing operating culture of the innovation system. A Chinese scientist who has not done well in a domestic institution might conceivably produce a 180-degree turnaround in performance and productivity upon moving to a foreign-invested R&D center operating in China (see, for example, Buderi & Huang, 2006, for experience of Chinese scientists who have worked at both Chinese institutions and at Microsoft Research China). The source of this behavioral change, in all likelihood, stems from the important differences in culture and the environment for creative activity inside foreign versus Chinese local R&D organizations. The Chinese scientific community has realized the importance of risk-taking and tolerance in innovation. For the first time, the revised Law of Science and Technology Progress (approved by a session of the National People's Congress Standing Committee in late 2007 and starting to take effect on July 1, 2008) encourages S&T personnel to explore and innovate freely, and shoulder risks bravely: they will not be penalized for failing to achieve their goals in high-risk research if they can prove that they have tried their best (*Science and Technology*

Daily January 4, 2008). While it may seem strange to have to legislate "the right to fail" as part of the S&T process, the implementation of this law could help reduce the inhibitions to taking risks and pushing out the frontier in research endeavors.

China's HRST in comparative perspectives

All indicators seem to point to the dramatic rise of China's HRST. The growth of HRST has been faster than that of overall population and workforce growth, respectively (Table 3.18). Between 1991 and 2006, the population increased by more than 13%, and the workforce grew by more than 18%, but the number of scientists and engineers involved in S&T activities more than doubled and the number of scientists and engineers involved in R&D activities increased three-fold. Consequently, China has witnessed a steady increase in the ratio of HRST among the total active workforce. In 2006, the number of Chinese scientists and engineers per 10 000 workforce reached 36, up from 22 in 1991, and its scientists and engineers per 10 000 population were 21, almost double that in 1991, which was 11.

China's HRST stock reached 35 million in 2005, becoming the world's largest. In the same year, China had 1.37 million person-years devoted to R&D, among the highest in the world. In terms of the number of person-years of R&D scientists and engineers, China's 1.12 million only lagged behind the USA, which already had 1.34 million person-years in 2002. The total number of Chinese who have received higher education at the bachelor's degree level and up reached 14.5 million in 2005, slightly less than that of the USA, which was 15.7 million as of 2003 (MOST, 2007: 30).

Given the country's large population and workforce bases, which were 1.31 billion and 782 million, respectively, in 2006, inevitably China continues to exhibit a very low per capita HRST in international comparisons (Table 3.19). For the period from 1996 to 2004, the number of researchers in R&D per one million head of population, for example, was 663 for China, only about one-fifth of that in Germany, France, and South Korea, and one-seventh of that in the USA. Among the BRIC (Brazil, Russia, India, and China) countries, China is ahead of Brazil and India using this comparative indicator, but lags behind Russia significantly – having only about one-fifth the Russian case. More broadly, among China's 700 million plus in the

Table 3.18 *Scientists and engineers (S&Es) in Chinese population and workforce*

	(1000 persons)				(Persons)			
Year	Population	Workforce	S&Es in S&T activities	S&Es in R&D activities	S&Es per 10000 population	S&Es per 10000 workforce	S&Es in R&D activities per 10000 population	S&Es in R&D activities per 10000 workforce
1991	1158230	660910	1321	471	11	20	4	7
1992	1171710	667820	1372	472	12	21	4	7
1993	1185170	674680	1372	489	12	20	4	7
1994	1198500	681350	1539	552	13	23	5	8
1995	1211210	688550	1554	522	13	23	4	8
1996	1223890	697650	1688	548	14	24	4	8
1997	1236260	708000	1668	589	13	24	5	8
1998	1248100	720870	1490	486	12	21	4	7
1999	1259090	727910	1595	531	13	22	4	7
2000	1267430	739920	2046	695	16	28	5	9
2001	1276270	744320	2072	743	16	28	6	10
2002	1284530	753600	2172	811	17	29	6	11
2003	1292270	760750	2255	862	17	30	7	11
2004	1299880	768230	2252	926	17	29	7	12
2005	1307560	778770	2561	1119	20	33	9	14
2006	1314480	782440	2798	1224	21	36	9	16
Increase of 2006 over 1991 (%)	13.49	18.39	111.81	159.87	86.63	78.91	128.98	119.51

Sources: National Bureau of Statistics, various years; National Bureau of Statistics and Ministry of Science and Technology, various years.

Table 3.19 *International comparison of human resources in science and technology (HRST)*

Country or region	Scientists and engineers in R&D (2005) (1000 individuals)	Researchers in R&D (1996–2004) (per million population)
Brazil	NA	344
China	1119	633
Hong Kong China	NA	1563
France	200 (2004)	3213
Germany	268	3261
India	NA	119
Japan	677 (2004)	5 287
Korean Rep.	180	3 187
Mexico	33	268
Russian Federation	464	3 319
Singapore	24	4 745
UK	158 (1993)	2 706
USA	1335 (2002)	4 484

NA, not available.
Sources: National Bureau of Statistics and Ministry of Science and Technology, 2007: 326–7; Ministry of Science and Technology, 2007: 185; World Bank, 2006.

labor force aged between 25 and 64 years, only about 5.2% have college education, whereas the average in OECD countries reached 24% in 1999 (Research Group on China's Education and Human Resources, 2003: 64).

Conclusion

This chapter has examined China's HRST from various perspectives. China ranks first in the world in terms of its HRST stock and second in terms of the number of scientists and engineers devoted to R&D activities. Chinese scientists and engineers are better educated than in the past, as measured by their higher levels of educational attainment, with more new job entrants having advanced degrees. They also are younger and even the leadership is dominated by those who are less than 50 years old. In a word, possessing an enormous and gradually improving S&T workforce, China is poised to become a significant contender, and an important contributor, to the frontiers of international research activity and high technology development. Indeed, China's progress in the production of international publications has been very impressive, at least in quantitative terms.

Although a larger quantity may eventually lead to higher quality levels among the S&T workforce, and also to enhanced performance and productivity, the reality is that the Chinese situation is still a work in progress in terms of overall output and innovative potential. The current S&T talent pool has to overcome a serious experience gap, which is not an easy task. More problematic is the fact that China's S&T talent pool is unevenly distributed geographically as most of the scientists and engineers are concentrated in the more economically developed coastal regions. Eastern China hosts a significant number of research institutes and universities, a legacy of China's development over the past century. This concentration has been further reinforced by the reform and open-door policies in place over the past 30 years, which have had as their main underpinning a trickle-down-oriented, coastal-focussed development strategy. Consequently, the coastal regions have received a larger amount of foreign direct investment and technology transfer. As the chapter has emphasized, FIEs have, in recent years, shifted from pure manufacturing and cheap labor outsourcing to high value-added R&D activities by employing an increasing number of Chinese scientists and engineers in their R&D centers located in China. The problem is that this presence has attracted a significant number of highly qualified scientists and engineers away from the regions and local job opportunities where there is a substantial need for talent. Without the injection of new, well-trained talent, the prospects for the regions outside the coastal areas to move up economically and technologically are seriously constrained. Consequently, regional economic disparities have grown, exacerbated in some important respects by the differentials in talent as well as knowledge, capital, and technology. These factors, plus the limited size of China's S&T workforce in terms of per capita metrics, mean that China still has a long way to go to further develop its HRST as a whole. This has put tremendous pressure on the development of the country's higher education system to turn out not only more but also more highly qualified personnel. The challenges and related issues associated with upgrading and expanding China's higher education system are examined in Chapter 4.

Finally, it is important to consider whether the larger number of scientists and engineers currently in place will be able to meet the leadership's aspiration of developing China into a more innovation-oriented nation by 2020. As China continues to grow in economic terms, there is an expectation inside the top leadership that the country's technology capabilities will strengthen as well. Whether or not China will become a true "technological superpower" in the years ahead remains to be seen, but it is clear that the strategic focus of the leadership is to derive more of China's growth from the expanded application of technology, with the bulk of that technology increasingly coming from the fruits of indigenously driven and supported innovation. Moreover, the leadership's desire to create a new growth formula – based less on huge inputs of raw materials and natural resources, high reliance on imported petroleum, and an environmentally damaging growth trajectory – demands a significant contribution from the Chinese scientific and engineering talent pool. Movement toward a knowledge economy will necessarily increase the demand for talent as well as the productivity of this talent in terms of new, innovative products and services. The changing dynamics of demand and supply for scientists and engineers in China in the years to come will be discussed more fully in Chapter 7.

4 | *Higher education and scientists and engineers in the pipeline*

The rapid increase of China's human resources in science and technology (HRST), described and analyzed in Chapter 3, is a product of the nation's rapid, continuous, and sustained economic growth during the post-Mao economic reform and open-door era. The country's growth imperative has fuelled the demand for larger and larger numbers of high-quality technical and managerial personnel. This has placed an increasing burden on the higher education system, which has been asked to provide a larger volume of capable graduates to assume crucial positions throughout the economy and society.

In recent years, higher education has become much more desirable and also more affordable to most Chinese, who recognized that investment in higher education can bring long-term benefits in terms of rising levels of compensation and greater social status. As the utility of obtaining a college degree or beyond has become more and more apparent, and taking into account the one-child family planning policies across most of China, there has been a steady acceleration in the number of students seeking higher education in China. Between 1991 and 2006, China's regular institutions of higher education turned out a total of 21 million undergraduates and 1.25 million graduate students, including 193 000 doctorates (see Table 2.1). The total enrollment in higher education, including those in various non-traditional higher education programs – from adult institutions of higher education, radio and TV universities, internet-based education, to self-learning – reached 25 million by the end of 2006. As a result, China's gross enrollment rate in higher education for the group of 18–22-year-olds reached 22% in 2006, up from only 3.5% in 1991 (see Table 2.3). The net addition to China's science and technology (S&T) workforce has been substantial, although not without problems, as discussed. Nonetheless, given the likelihood of continued high rates of enrollment, generally speaking, the development of China's HRST will not be constrained from the supply side in the near future.

This chapter focusses on China's HRST from the perspective of the supply side of the equation. Higher education is a major producer of HRST. In fact, human resources in science and technology (education) (HRSTE), as one of the key components of HRST as noted in Chapter 3, showcases the huge potential in terms of the expansion of China's overall HRST base. In what follows, after a brief review of the development and hierarchy across China's higher education system, we examine and analyze data dealing with new student admissions, total enrollment, and graduates from Chinese universities, especially in the areas of science, technology, and management. The chapter ends with a discussion of the qualitative aspects of the Chinese higher education system largely focused on the capabilities of the graduates trained in that system.

Development of higher education in China

Although some Chinese universities claim to have a longer history, modern higher education was introduced into the country at the turn of the twentieth century (Hayhoe, 1996). Since then, the role of higher education in China has evolved from introducing the modern, and mainly moral and social, order prior to 1949, through serving as a mechanism for Maoist political, social, and economic modernization between 1949 and 1978, to becoming a tool of economic development as well as social, and, to a lesser extent, political reform since 1978 (Turner & Acker, 2002).

The first modern Chinese universities – Tianjin (Beiyang) University, Jiaotong University, and Beijing (Peking) University – were established in the late 1890s. But it was after the 1920s, when Chinese graduates with Western doctorates in mathematics, physics, and other fields of science and engineering returned home, that the Western education and research systems started to form in China. Owing to the commitment and efforts of these scientists and educators, plus support from society, China's undergraduate education quickly approached international standards, and graduate education began to take off (Hayhoe, 1996: 29–71). Even the difficult situation during the Sino-Japanese War in the 1930s and the 1940s did not destroy the foundation of Chinese higher education, as universities such as the Southwest Associated University (*Xinan Lianda*), based on Beijing, Qinghua (Tsinghua), and Nankai universities, which retreated to the hinterland

and continued to turn out excellent students and research (Israel, 1998). Furthermore, in the pre-1949 era, most Chinese university professors viewed themselves as "guardians of that nation's culture in the face of growing nationalistic and secularistic pressures" (Julius, 1997: 143), and universities were positioned largely as the enclave where educated elites tried their best to maintain academic autonomy without being influenced by commercial values and the power of the state (Yeh, 1990).

Since the inception of the People's Republic of China in 1949, however, higher education has been politicized, hyper-politicized, and depoliticized in turn (Sautman, 1991), and has experienced three rather distinct stages. During the first stage, 1949–1978, higher education developed amid various political campaigns from the Three-Anti, the Five-Anti, and the Anti-Rightist campaigns, and, finally, the Cultural Revolution, to which faculty members, along with other Chinese intellectuals, gradually lost freedom and autonomy in research and teaching, if not their overall careers and lives.

Following the establishment of the People's Republic of China, all private and missionary universities were abolished and amalgamated into national ones. In 1952, China's universities started a reform in the name of "adjustment of colleges and departments" (*yuanxi tiaozheng*) (Hayhoe, 1996: 77). The systematic transformation of the university system was carried out under Soviet guidance and supervised by the Chinese Communist Party (CCP). Aimed at charging universities with carrying out party policy and developing techno-centric professional education to support rapid economic growth, *yuanxi tiaozheng* relocated both faculty and students across universities and colleges. The adjustment also arbitrarily merged specialties among universities and colleges. Thus, colleges of arts, law, and natural sciences at Qinghua University, for example, became part of Beijing University, and its college of agriculture was merged into the Beijing Agricultural College. Meanwhile, Qinghua University absorbed all the engineering departments from the Beijing and Yenching universities (Yenching was a missionary institution established by Americans) and became a multidisciplinary polytechnic university – often called "the MIT of China." Later, engineering- and technology-oriented colleges were founded by transferring faculty and students from other existing institutions. As a result of these adjustments and newly formed schools, China's universities began to limit their mission to teaching, while their role in research gradually decreased. This set in place the conditions which permitted the gap between research and education to widen steadily over time. The relocation of specialties broke the internal connection between basic research, applied research, and experimental development, which in turn has had a long-term impact on the training of scientific personnel. It also became a requirement that students take political education courses such as "Marxism, Leninism, and Mao Zedong Thought" and "History of the CCP," among others; this is a convention that still is observed nowadays. During the Cultural Revolution, one of the radical measures introduced was the notion that political correctness, or "redness," rather than academic merit, or "expertise," determined entry into universities, and students were selected largely from the ranks of workers, peasants, and soldiers for higher education by party officials who cared about creating archetypal "red" intellectuals possessing political credentials trusted by the party in conjunction with technical and academic skills (Turner & Acker, 2002).

The second stage, which covers the period from 1978 to the mid-1990s, was characterized by the creation of closer links between education and the economy. Higher education was reinstated after the Cultural Revolution, utilizing various revitalization measures from the restoration of merit-based nationwide examinations for entry into tertiary education, the resumption of graduate education, sending students overseas for undergraduate and graduate studies, and the introduction of the academic degree system that had been denounced as a "bourgeoisie's right." These improvements took place largely in response to the need for initial economic recovery from the Cultural Revolution and later to help support the economic reforms and open-door policy initiated under Deng Xiaoping. One of the most important developments was research becoming steadily, albeit gradually, integrated into the university environment and becoming a valued part of the overall education experience, and especially a vehicle for helping to serve the needs of the national economy.

Since the mid-1990s, the development of China's higher education has entered its third stage. During this period, the university system has taken on an even greater and broader set of academic responsibilities – linked not just to the economy, but also to the country's paramount S&T goals. More specifically, higher education, along with S&T, is viewed as critical to the revitalization of the nation, and to strengthening the talent base of the country through advanced training. Thus, the higher education sector has been booming at an unprecedented rate as expectations of students, faculty, and administrators have risen concerning resource availability and additional investment by the Chinese government at the national and local levels.

In all these stages, the favored subjects offered by the higher education system have varied. In the first stage, S&T, broadly defined to include science, engineering, agriculture, and medicine, was viewed as the most attractive field and offered the brightest career prospects. One commonly used saying exemplifies this perspective: "One would not be afraid of going around the world with a master of mathematics, physics, and chemistry." That same situation continued to prevail during the second stage, not only because many of the social sciences and humanities fields had not yet recovered from the damage done during the Anti-Rightist campaign and the Cultural Revolution, but also because of the tremendous emphasis on the role of S&T in economic modernization by the Dengist political leadership.[1] Nevertheless, the most significant change during this third stage has been the diversification in terms of fields of study. Humanities and social sciences programs have steadily improved, and graduates now can find decent jobs with lucrative pay. In fact, foreign language students with simultaneous interpretation skills are a hot commodity, as are aspiring financial and legal professionals, in terms of earning power. Over the last decade, in particular, the field of management education has emerged as a major attraction, driven by the prospect of high salaries and prosperous careers as well as chances for international travel and work assignments (more of this later on).

Higher education also continues to be seen as a means to secure upward mobility in China. In the past, higher education was largely a privilege for select Chinese, usually the children of affluent and better-educated urban families. More recently, however, through the ladder of higher education, many seemingly disadvantaged Chinese have

---

[1] During the open-door era, China's top political leaders have been predominately technocrats (it was only at the Seventeenth National Congress of the CCP, held in late 2007, that those with training in humanities and social sciences started to move into important leadership roles) (Li, 2001; Suttmeier, 2007). Interestingly, these people technically belong to the HRST group as they were trained and employed in the S&T field before assuming political and government positions.

been able to change their destiny and fortunes. Of course, as well as the "upside," in terms of compensation and career experiences, some new uncertainties and risks have entered the picture. During the first stage and part of the second stage, jobs for college graduates were largely guaranteed. In fact, through the so-called job assignment (*fenpei*) system, aimed at meeting the country's needs for specific types of talent, graduates were "assigned" to various positions by government. This system was maintained for many years even though many graduates did not necessarily like their specific assignments, especially if they had to leave one of China's coastal cities for a job in the interior. The *fenpei* system is no longer in place; higher education, in less than a decade, has become a mass education system, as 15% or more of high school graduates can now receive it. One unintended consequence of more admissions to higher education, to be discussed later, is that about 30% of the 2005–2007 graduates reported that they could not find an acceptable job, let alone a bright career (*Beijing Morning News* October 31, 2007). This phenomenon has started to raise some concerns about whether a college education is still a wise investment for Chinese youngsters from the perspective of career and securing a stable, prosperous life. Although there is no doubt that China will eventually benefit in many respects from increasing the number of its citizens receiving higher education, the present mismatches between supply and demand suggest that officials must take a closer look at curricula and quality issues, and the evolving relationship between the economy and the education system.

Finally, and perhaps most critically, higher education is no longer free. Unfortunately, China's governmental budgetary expenditure on education as a percentage of gross domestic product (GDP) has languished below 3 percent, ironically among the lowest in the world. This level of support, albeit inadequate in many respects, has prevailed despite the fact that government investment was supposed to reach 4 percent by 2000, as stipulated in the 1993 Guidelines of Chinese Education Reform and Development. As higher education is only one part of the government's overall education portfolio (it also includes K-12 education plus vocational education), and there are virtually no other means available to support higher education aside from some very modest examples of private philanthropy and money from the overseas Chinese business community, students and their families now have to pay for both tuition and fees. This could be a significant burden depending upon the economic situation of the families and the quality of the schools – public or private – that students decide to attend. There have been cases reported of students who are unable to enroll in college even though they were granted admission; in such cases, as in the USA and elsewhere, parents have to borrow money, sometimes even from loan-sharks, or, worse yet, have committed suicide as they could not afford their children's college education. In a one-child family type of society, the social pressures remain huge in terms of providing for the one heir in the family.

Major initiatives since the 1990s

In the 1980s, Chinese education in general and higher education in particular began to feel huge pressures in terms of the demands of modernization and internationalization arising from the reform and open-door policy. The CCP and government passed the Resolution on Education Reform in 1985, and the Guidelines of Chinese Education Reform and Development in 1993, which finally led to the formulation of the National Education Act in 1996. These documents, among others, promote the decentralization of institutional administration and management in higher education as well as the diversification of the sources of finance for education, while still stipulating the political leadership's institutional oversight and policy regulation for universities (Wang, 2000). In 1998, the Education Revitalization Action Plan toward the Twenty-First Century was launched, the main components of which included: a compulsory nine-year education requirement; raising the gross enrollment rate for higher education; the 211 Program and the 985 Program; and the Cheung Kong Scholars Program. The Education Revitalization Action Plan was updated in 2004 for the period covering 2003–2007. These new programs and initiatives exemplified the leadership's growing recognition that only with a stellar education system could China build a truly modern, technologically advanced society. And, even taking into account events such as the student-led demonstrations that resulted in the catastrophic incident on June 4, 1989, there is willingness among China's current leaders to accept some of the potential political risks associated with opening up higher education to more and more young people in return for the creation of a cohort of high-end human talent that can ensure China's future economic prosperity and national security.

To proceed with the implementation of the above mentioned policies, the State Education Commission and its successor, the Ministry of Education, have introduced several major initiatives. The first involved the reorganization of China's vast array of colleges and universities, amalgamating many of the small, vocational training-oriented units established in recent years to capture scale benefits and reduce redundancy (Mok, 2005). The rewards for institutions participating in mergers have included increased resources and elevated rankings in the university hierarchy (Wang, 2000). In the meantime, there also has been a trend of promoting "junior colleges" to "colleges," and "colleges" to "universities," although many do not necessarily warrant their new "bigger" names. More notable was the creation of a number of education conglomerates through the government-initiated mergers. For example, by absorbing Zhejiang Agricultural University, Hangzhou University, and Zhejiang Medical University in 1998, the new Zhejiang University became China's mega-university in terms of the number of specialties it offers; the Huazhong University of Science and Technology is the product of the merger of the Huazhong University of Technology, the Tongji Medical University, and two other small and less-known institutions located in Wuhan in 2000; and Shanghai Jiaotong University acquired Shanghai Agricultural College in 1999 and Shanghai Second Medical University in 2005. These mergers have strengthened the comprehensive nature of China's key (*zhongdian*) universities.

More than creating economies of scale, the institutional mergers and amalgamation since the mid-1990s were coincidently related to several other important Ministry of Education initiatives – the 211 Program and the 985 Program – to turn out so-called "world-class universities" in China (see Chapter 2). The central government has allocated special funds to designated universities through these programs, which, in turn, have mobilized support from ministries and provincial and municipal governments to commit funds jointly to build up (*gongjian*) those institutions under their respective jurisdictions. For the 211 Program, and in the Tenth Five Year Plan (2001–2005) period alone, the central government allocated RMB (*reminbi*) 6 billion (US \$725 million) to support the selected universities, which was matched by RMB12.4 billion (US \$1.5 billion) from ministries, local governments, and by the universities themselves. Beijing and Qinghua universities each received RMB1.8 billion from the Ministry of Education over a three-year period initially, plus money from other sources. Beijing University received another RMB1.8 billion between 2004 and 2007 (Geng, 2005). Funds have been used to improve basic facilities, upgrade teaching quality, transform their research results into products, and participate in international collaboration and exchange.

Lastly, China took a very bold step in 1999 to expand its higher education in a radical way. Although the expansion was a response to various government policies, especially the Education Revitalization Action Plan, the main driver was economic. Because of the impact of the 1997 Asian financial crisis, Chinese economic growth had stagnated and even declined after its GDP growth reached 14.2 percent in 1991. Accordingly, it needed new stimulation – domestic consumption and higher education were deemed the most appropriate vehicles according to the economists who promoted the idea (Tschang, 2007). First, an increase in admissions of, say, 300 000 new college students would translate into RMB3 billion of tuition and related spending among the students and their families annually.[2] Second, there was the belief that an admissions expansion would necessitate an upgrade in the infrastructure at universities, thus helping to fuel a significant construction boom. And, third, new construction would generate not only employment but also new consumption by employees. As a whole, it was estimated that there would be at least a two percentage points increase in GDP as a result of the enlargement. In making this threefold argument, the economists emphasized the role of higher education in economic development by using the case of other countries: China had less than 4% of its 18–22-year-old cohort attending college compared with 31% in the Philippines, 37% in Thailand, and 8% in India. In addition, the proposed expansion in higher education admissions was in the interest of the particular generation of Chinese parents who were enthusiastic about sending their children to college, as many of them had lost their opportunity to go there because of the Cultural Revolution. Admitting more high school graduates into colleges also made sense as it would, at least temporarily, relieve the employment pressure for those high school graduates who would otherwise compete for employment with those laid off from state-owned enterprises and migrants from rural to urban areas (Bai, 2006).

---

[2] Assuming that a typical Chinese student spends about RMB10 000 per year on tuition and expenses, an extra-domestic consumption of about RMB3 billion would be generated.

On the other hand, those who were against the expansion in college admissions argued that given the available level of government financial support for higher education, and the existing job prospects for potential graduates, China's higher education policies were already far ahead of its economic development situation and therefore new admissions should be curtailed rather than expanded. However, during the discussion and debate on the growth of higher education no attention was paid to future demographics, including the possible decline of college-bound youth around 2015, although Ministry of Education officials now claim their approach was, in fact, a hedge against this potential problem.[3]

Because more higher education admissions were perceived by the leadership as viable, both politically and economically, the new policies went into effect almost immediately. In 1999, China's regular institutions of higher education admitted 1.60 million new students, 513 000 – not the suggested 300 000 – more than those in 1998, an increase of 47.3 percent. The expansion in admissions was kept at this level between 1999 and 2006: some 28 million new undergraduates were admitted, representing a fivefold increase and an annual growth of 22.8 percent. In addition, some 1.9 million new graduate-level students also were admitted (see Table 2.1). In 2002, China enrolled some 15 percent of its college-age youth, a milestone for higher education in the People's Republic of China; college education, once largely the domain of a small segment of the population, had now turned into a type of "mass education" (see Table 2.3). Moreover, the commitment was strengthened further as manifested in the official goals associated with the Tenth Five-Year Plan for Education Development (2001–2005), which mandated the enrolling of a total of 16 million undergraduate students and 600 000 graduate students.[4] China's achievement in expanding its higher education sector is unprecedented in so far as it took the USA 30 years (from 1911 to 1941), Japan 23 years (from 1947 to 1970), and Brazil 26 years (from 1970 to 1996) to transform higher education from an elite- to a mass-type

---

[3] In fact, Ji Baocheng, President of Renmin University of China, indicated that the shrinkage could occur as early as 2009 (*Nanjing Morning News*, May 18, 2007).

[4] Gross enrollment of higher education in the Chinese statistics includes those receiving higher education through unconventional methods, such as television and broadcasting, online, and adult education.

of education (Research Group on China's Education and Human Resources, 2003: 23). In 2005, China's regular institutions of higher education enrolled a total of 15.6 million students, surpassing the USA, which had a total enrollment of 14.2 million students in that same year. China now unequivocally leads the world in terms of enrolling new college students.

Not surprisingly, however, most Chinese universities were not well prepared for the radical increase in admissions. Many did not have enough classrooms, dormitories, laboratories, or libraries. In many instances, their physical facilities were shabby and, most importantly, there was a serious shortage of qualified faculty members. For one thing, many university campuses having been built decades ago had only limited possibilities for physical expansion; the only available option was the construction of new campuses. This emphasis on new construction became the impetus behind a national mania focussed on the construction of many university towns (*daxue cheng*) – housing clusters of universities – in August 2000. In two years, more than 50 university towns, in 21 provinces and municipalities, had been planned. In 2002 alone, some RMB32.6 billion (US $3.9 billion) was invested. Shanghai alone, for example, built five university towns during this period. In fact, in the name of promoting the Chinese versions of Boston and Oxford, the university-town projects have turned out to be lucrative real-estate development initiatives involving the conversion of farmland into luxurious facilities, including golf courses on some campuses, and the corruption in land acquisition. By following this path many universities borrowed huge sums of money from banks under the assumption that they could repay these loans through government support and increased student tuition fees from the growth in admissions. Unfortunately, quite a number of campuses were unable to muster the funds needed to repay the massive debts incurred to create the new university towns and other related capital projects.

Even more problematic is the fact that some of the universities still remain unable to provide a true, high-quality education to a suddenly increased, more demanding student body. A significant number of graduates have had serious difficulty finding jobs in the fields of their training, or have had to accept jobs with lower pay. In the coming years, higher education admissions will likely, and perhaps necessarily, slow down, which in fact corresponds to the projected decline in the numbers of the college-age youth.

Hierarchy of Chinese higher education

Traditionally, China's institutions of higher education were stratified according to their fields of expertise. The first strata consisted of comprehensive (*zonghe*) institutions in the sense that these universities provide a wide range of programs from natural sciences and engineering to social sciences, humanities, and so on. The second category included polytechnic or S&T (*ligongke*) universities, which specialize in the natural sciences and engineering. Institutions falling into the third category were those that focussed on one specialized field (e.g. medicine, chemical engineering, mining, etc.). Accordingly, Beijing, Fudan, Nanjing, Nankai, Wuhan, and Jilin universities belonged to the first category; Qinghua, Shanghai and Xi'an Jiaotong, and Zhejiang universities used to be in the polytechnic category; and the third category included such institutions as Shanghai Medical University and Beijing Geological College.

Since 1995, and especially since 1999, both polytechnic and specialty institutions of higher education have expanded their turf, becoming more or less "comprehensive," while comprehensive universities have been involved in the merger mania orchestrated by the Ministry of Education to become education conglomerates, as mentioned. Consequently, almost every Chinese university now can claim to be "comprehensive." And some of the institutions, mentioned above, are no longer free-standing as they have been merged into larger universities.

In addition, Chinese institutions of higher education have been stratified into key (*zhongdian*) and non-key (*fei zhongdian*) institutions at national or provincial levels. Their status has been determined mainly by government, rather than earned through organic growth like similar institutions in other countries, although many of them well deserve their higher ranking owing to their record of academic excellence. Once an institution becomes a key unit, it almost always retains the "key" designation for ever. The number of key national universities has changed over time. There were six in 1954, 11 in 1956, and 48 before the Cultural Revolution. The number of key universities rose to 88 in 1978 and to 98 in the 1980s. Some 100 universities were designated as key through the 211 Program, while the 39 institutions supported by the 985 Program are all key universities (see Table 2.5 for a list of these).

Under the direct administration of the Ministry of Education, and in many instances regional governments and government ministries, key universities are more likely to receive continuous support, sometimes unrelated to either academic quality or performance. These campuses have benefited from various prestigious national funding programs, the most high-profile ones being the 211 Program and the 985 Program. Furthermore, not only have key universities been resources-rich, they have also been able to leverage their status to recruit outstanding faculty and excellent students from across the entire nation. For example, more than 80 percent of the Cheung Kong Scholars are concentrated in the flagship 985 institutions (Table 4.1). Of the 560 applicants scoring the highest, so-called *zhuangyuan* by borrowing a title from China's imperial civil service examinations, in college entrance examinations in their respective municipalities and provinces between 1999 and 2006, for example, 315 attended Beijing University and 195 went to Qinghua University (CUAA, 2007). These behaviors tend to reinforce the elitist status of the key universities and make it difficult for second- and third-tier universities to catch up, especially in terms of talent recruitment.

Geographically, many of China's key universities are located in Beijing, Shanghai, and the eastern regions of the country (see, for example, Table 2.5); this pattern is very similar to the geographical distribution of scientists and engineers described in Chapter 3 (see Table 3.9). The planned economy in the 1950s and 1960s left a legacy that key institutions of higher education also were founded in some interior regions, where a concentration of military-related programs initially helped some of these schools become "key" institutions. For example, Xidian University, or the Xi'an University of Electronic Science and Technology, used to be a People's Liberation Army-affiliated institution focused on the training of telecommunications engineers and was moved from Zhangjiakou, Hebei province, to Xi'an in the 1960s. Similarly, the Chengdu Institute of Telecommunications Engineering, Xidian's sister institution, which was established in 1956 in Chengdu, Sichuan province, has now become the University of Electronic Science and Technology.

In general, students who graduate from key universities seem to have an easier time finding jobs and securing higher levels of remuneration. They are more likely to be truly high-achievers in many fields, including science and technology (Cao, 2004a). The relatively

Table 4.1 *Cheung Kong scholars at universities identified by the 985 Program (persons)*

University	Location	1999	2000	2001	2002	2003	2004	2005	2006	Sub-total
Beijing University	Beijing	6	8	9	15	9	10	10	5	72
Qinghua University	Beijing	5	14	6	10	4	7	7	9	62
Fudan University	Shanghai	6	7	3	4	5	7	8	5	45
Nanjing University	Jiangsu	2	6	3	8	5	6	4	5	39
Shanghai Jiaotong University	Shanghai	4	7	7	8	1	4	4	3	38
Zhejiang University	Zhejiang	2	2	3	9	7	4	6	4	37
Southeast University	Jiangsu	2	3	5	5	2	2	1	1	21
Wuhan University	Hubei	3	3	4	3	2	1	3	2	21
Huazhong University of Science and Technology	Hubei	1	4	3	2	1	3	2	4	20
Jilin University	Jilin	3	5	2	3		2	2	2	19
Nankai University	Tianjin	3	1	3	1	2	3	4	2	19
Beijing University of Aeronautics and Astronautics	Beijing		2	5	3	1	3	3	1	18
Sun Yat-sen University (Zhongshan University)	Guangdong	1	2		3	2	4	1	4	17
Tianjin University	Tianjin	1		2	5	5	3		1	17
Tongji University	Shanghai	3	3		2	3	3		2	16
Harbin Institute of Technology	Heilongjiang	1	2	3	2		1	1	5	15
Beijing Normal University	Beijing	1	3	1	3			3	3	14
Central South University	Hunan		2	2	1	1		4	3	13
Shandong University	Shandong	2	1			5	2	1	2	13
Sichuan University	Sichuan		3	2	2	2		3	1	13
University of Science and Technology of China	Anhui	1	1	2	1	5	1	1	1	13
Dalian University of Technology	Liaoning	1	2	2	4	1	2	2		12

Table 4.1 (*cont.*)

University	Location	1999	2000	2001	2002	2003	2004	2005	2006	Subtotal
Northwestern Polytechnic University	Shaanxi	1	3	1	3	1		1	1	11
Beijing Institute of Technology	Beijing	1	1	1	2		1		3	9
China Agricultural University	Beijing	2	1	2	2		2	0	1	9
Northeastern University	Liaoning		2			1	2	2	2	9
Xiamen University	Fujian		1	1	2	1	1	2	1	9
Xi'an Jiaotong University	Shaanxi	1	2		2	1	3			9
Hunan University	Hunan			1	3		1	1	2	8
Lanzhou University	Gansu	1	2				3		2	8
Chongqing University	Chongqing	1	1	1			1	1	2	7
South China University of Technology	Guangdong	1		2		2	1	1		7
Ocean University of China	Shandong		1	1	2		1	1	0	6
University of Electronic Science and Technology of China	Sichuan			1			3	1	1	6
Renmin University of China	Beijing							3	1	4
East China Normal University	Shanghai	1	2					2		5
National University of Defense Technology	Hunan			1	1		1			3
Northwest Science and Technology University of Agriculture and Forestry	Shaanxi				1		1			2
Subtotal from universities identified by the 985 Program		57	94	79	112	69	89	85	81	666
Total		66	112	97	135	84	111	102	106	813
Percentage from universities identified by the 985 Program		86.4	83.9	81.4	83.0	82.1	80.2	83.3	76.4	81.9

Source: www.cksp.edu.cn (accessed on March 9, 2007).

Table 4.2 *Top Chinese baccalaureate-origin institutions of 1999–2003, United States' doctorate recipients (persons)*

Baccalaureate-origin institution	Total	Science and engineering			Life sciences	Social sciences
		Subtotal	Physical sciences*	Engineering		
Beijing University (Peking) (2)**	1 332	1 247	558	189	386	114
Qinghua University (Tsinghua) (3)	1 234	1 203	226	863	92	22
University of Science and Technology of China (5)	988	966	461	291	189	25
Fudan University (7)	626	590	220	80	247	43
Nanjing University (10)	437	422	220	57	118	27
Nankai University (12)	396	371	133	34	177	27
Zhejiang University (16)	357	352	70	212	61	9
Wuhan University (17)	340	324	85	56	167	16
Beijing Medical University (now part of Beijing University) (18)	339	333	57	7	265	4
Shanghai Jiaotong University (19)	334	314	57	224	23	10
Total, China top ten	6 383	6 122	2 087	2 013	1 725	297
Total, all foreign	50 908	40 634	10 928	13 180	11 021	5 505
Percentage total, China top ten of total, all foreign	12.54	15.07	19.10	15.27	15.65	5.40

*Includes mathematics and computer sciences.

**The number after the name of an institution is the rank of the institution in terms of the number of baccalaureates who received United States' doctorates.

Source: Hoffer *et al.* (2005: 79).

better quality of graduates from key Chinese institutions of higher education is internationally acclaimed. Between 1999 and 2003, Beijing University and the University of Science and Technology of China in Hefei, Anhui province, an institution affiliated with the CAS, were the two largest baccalaureate-origin institutions of United States' doctorates in the physical sciences (558 and 461 doctorate recipients, respectively), surpassing both MIT and the University of California, Berkeley, by well over 100 doctorate recipients. In engineering, for the same period, Qinghua University was the largest baccalaureate-origin institution, with more than twice as many graduates earning American doctorates than the largest United States' baccalaureate-origin institution, MIT (863 versus 344) (Hoffer *et al.*, 2005: 79) (Table 4.2). As a whole, the 10 Chinese universities mentioned in Table 4.2 accounted for 15 percent of doctoral degrees in science and engineering that American universities awarded to foreign nationals. In 2006, Qinghua and Beijing universities further advanced to become the top two institutions in terms of their students receiving doctorates – in science and engineering – from American universities (Mervis, 2008).

Admissions in Chinese higher education

China's higher education, as holds true with its counterparts elsewhere, is divided into two main divisions: undergraduate and graduate education. There are two types of undergraduate programs, varying in length and depth. The two- to three-year short-cycle programs (*zhuanke*), similar to community college-level education in the USA, or Level 5B according to *ISCED*, prepare students with practical skills and knowledge, while regular programs, which last for four to five years and lead to a bachelor's degree (*benke*) at the *ISCED* Level 5A, are more theoretically oriented. Most of the graduates from these more traditional-length programs dominate the cohort that pursues advanced studies at home and abroad.

Examinations for entry into undergraduate education are administered nationwide at the same time every year. For many years even the contents of the examinations were uniform across the nation, but in recent years some provinces and municipalities have been permitted to write their own examinations. Nowadays, applicants take examinations according to two broad categories – science and engineering (*ligongke*) and humanities and social sciences (*wenke*). In addition to three mandatory subjects of Chinese, mathematics, and foreign language for all, *ligongke* applicants choose a couple of subjects from physics, chemistry, or biology, and *wenke* applicants select from history, geography, or politics (the "3 + X" scheme).

There are 11 fields of study (*xueke menlei*) at the undergraduate level, including philosophy, economics, law, education, literature, history, science, engineering, agriculture, medicine, and management (one more at the graduate level, military science). The divisions among the fields of study are different for undergraduate and graduate education. For graduate education, underlying each field of study is a specialty (*yiji xueke*); mathematics, physics, chemistry, astronomy, geography, atmospheric science, oceans science, geophysics, geology, biology, systems science, and history of science and technology, for example, are specialties of science. And, generally speaking, a specialty is further subdivided into subspecialties (*erji xueke*); in the case of mathematics, there are several subspecialties: basic mathematics, computational mathematics, applied mathematics, probability and statistics, and operations research and cybernetics. For undergraduate education, there are more than 500 specialties (*zhuanye*). In general, science, engineering, agriculture, and medicine correspond to the *ligongke* fields of study, while the rest belong to *wenke*. The one exception is management, which, as a new specialty added in 2001, may be either a *ligongke* or a *wenke* depending upon the *zhuanye*. Applicants for *ligongke* or *wenke* are admitted into specific fields of study and specialities.

Applicants for undergraduate education may apply for more than one specialty at more than one university, but have to rank their choices. Each applicant is admitted into short-cycle or regular programs based upon both their score on the entrance examinations and their preference of university and specialty. Usually, those who score highest enter key universities and those who perform less well are admitted into *benke* programs at non-key universities, with low-score applicants getting into the short-cycle programs. Those who achieve higher scores can major in the specialties in which they are most interested. Most of the 560 *zhuangyuan* between 1999 and 2006 not only attended Beijing and Qinghua universities but also chose such hot specialties as economics and administration (178), basic sciences (90), life science (50), information (42), and computer science and technology (40) (CUAA, 2007). A limited number of high school graduates with exceptional talents and achievements, such as those winning prizes in national and international science competitions, may be admitted into universities, in most cases, without taking entrance examinations. Finally, unlike the USA, where new college students often change majors and fields of concentration once or twice during their undergraduate training, in China this is generally not the case. Once admitted as a biology major, for example, students will tend to graduate as a biology major. This limits student choices and options, and generally serves as an impediment to self-exploration or creative thinking.

Students with a bachelor's degree can apply for graduate study, usually at the master's level, and in extreme cases, at the doctoral level, either during their senior year or after they finish their under-graduate studies. Someone who does not possess a bachelor's degree but claims to have knowledge equivalent to the degree, is allowed to apply for graduate school as well. The term of study is usually fixed: it takes three years to study for a master's degree and an additional three years for a doctorate, and five years in a joint master–doctorate pro-gram. In addition to universities, some of the Chinese research and development (R&D) institutes, such as those affiliated with the CAS, as well as some ministerial-based R&D institutes, also train graduate students.

Applicants for graduate school have to sit for examinations administered nationwide all together. The subject matter coverage of examinations is determined by the universities or research institutes that admit graduate students, except for political education and foreign languages, and mathematics for science and engineering applicants. The examinations test an applicant's knowledge in the specialized areas in which they apply for study. A graduate applicant may only apply for one specialty at one institution. Those who meet the exam score criteria set by the Ministry of Education for political education, foreign languages, and mathematics, and pass the specialty examinations (*chushi*), are invited to a second examination (*fushi*), which might be a writing test, an interview, or a combination of both. Scores on the *chushi* and *fushi* exams are weighted to produce a candidate list from which new graduate students are admitted. It is possible for some of those who do well in the examinations, but are not admitted to their chosen specialties and institutions, to transfer to other institutions.

A person with a master's degree may apply for study for a doctorate, but also has to go through the above-mentioned admissions process. Recently, this process has started to require letters of recommendation from academic advisors in the student's master's program.

Chinese higher education has had a tradition of "walking on two legs;" that is, catering for a great variety of national needs and student desires. For example, the Chinese government allows and encourages those with skills and knowledge equivalent to advanced degrees (*tongdeng xueli*) to apply for such degrees. People with at least three years of work experience after receiving a bachelor's degree can submit an application for a master's degree to a degree-granting institution, which is responsible for examining their credentials and testing them on relevant courses to determine each individual's qualifications and competencies. Once qualified, students must pass nationwide examinations in a foreign language and a comprehensive examination in the field of their academic specialty, and defend their thesis within four years. A doctoral degree applicant must have five years of experience after receiving a master's degree and demonstrate outstanding achievements in the field of study. When a degree-granting institution determines their candidacy, they have to pass course examinations within a year, and defend their dissertation within another year; during this time, they must work on their dissertation at the degree-granting institution for a period of at least three months under the supervision of a faculty advisor.

Adult higher education is another important component of the Chinese education system; it is carried out at regular institutions of higher education, adult-oriented institutions, and radio and television universities as well as through internet-based education and self-directed studies. It offers both short-cycle and bachelor's degree programs. Although adult higher education produces a significant number of science and engineering majors, and its enrollments are included in the calculation of the gross enrollment rate across higher education, it is excluded in the discussion that follows. This has been done because not only is the reliability of statistics about adult higher education uncertain, but the overall quality of adult higher education is lower than that at regular institutions of higher education. In general, many of the students receiving adult higher education have failed to gain normal admissions through college entrance examinations in the first place, their admissions criteria are much looser, faculty members possess lower qualifications, and research facilities are limited. Also excluded from the following discussion are students in graduate programs that do not exist any more and did not offer or grant a graduate degree (*yanjiusheng ban*), a temporary measure for training advanced students through short-cycle programs, whose number is much smaller than those in regular graduate programs.[5]

Admissions and university enrollments

Undergraduates

The admissions among Chinese higher education institutions have had both highs and lows (see Table 2.1). The good news, generally speaking, is that there have been extraordinary highs since 1999. After the number of undergraduate entrants hit the one million mark in 1997, there has been appreciable growth every year going forward: two million in 2000; three million in 2002; four million in 2004; and five million in 2005. Consequently, while it took 30 years for China to enroll a total of one million new undergraduates (between 1949 and 1979), it took only another nine years and eight years to reach two and three million, respectively. By 2003, the total enrollment increased to 11 million, and the next year the total enrollment of undergraduates-reached 13 million.

In particular, across the science and technology (*ligongke*) fields of study, while all kept pace with the overall upward trend, both engineering and medicine saw admissions in 2006 increase to more than four times those in 1998, the year before the exponential expansion of higher education, reaching 1.99 million and 380 000, respectively. At the same time, new science and agriculture majors have not increased that dramatically (Table 4.3).[6] It is interesting to notice that 87 000 fewer students were admitted into science in 2005 than in 2004, representing a 24 percent drop, although more students were admitted into science in 2006 than 2005. Taking a closer look, we find that science majors at the *zhuanke* level decreased from 109 000, in both 2003 and

---

[5] This is not to say these types of programs are unimportant, but only to stress that the quality of the graduates is uneven and inconsistent.

[6] Before 1994, a different category was used to report undergraduate student enrollment and graduation data.

Table 4.3 Undergraduate admissions (persons)

Total

Year	Total	Philosophy	Economics	Law	Education	Literature	History	Science	Engineering	Agriculture	Medicine	Management
1994	899 846	2 043	143 882	30 526	40 487	125 070	15 513	99 239	344 105	32 876	66 105	
1995	925 940	1 747	152 694	31 939	41 258	131 587	15 672	100 295	352 463	32 590	65 695	
1996	965 812	1 589	153 915	36 687	45 232	138 205	15 866	106 236	366 816	32 690	68 576	
1997	1 000 393	1 636	153 367	41 527	46 681	143 080	16 383	110 443	380 946	35 959	70 425	
1998	1 083 627	1 341	159 207	48 102	50 295	160 862	16 383	120 531	412 393	38 325	75 188	
1999	1 548 554	1 763	237 129	69 048	67 257	230 175	19 070	155 880	607 597	52 251	108 384	
2000	2 206 072	1 847	363 379	114 682	107 259	343 418	22 003	202 466	832 124	68 966	149 928	
2001	2 682 790	1 805	138 746	146 782	158 283	417 604	16 082	258 201	892 356	62 952	174 156	415 823
2002	3 204 976	2 175	182 416	160 618	178 223	509 315	15 351	294 867	1 057 241	69 247	207 909	527 614
2003	3 821 701	1 520	221 410	185 999	218 575	611 021	16 330	329 656	1 242 426	81 619	257 681	654 464
2004	4 473 422	4 067	240 100	195 638	264 251	724 402	17 128	357 070	1 466 459	88 281	299 314	816 712
2005	5 044 581	1 797	264 219	199 521	315 638	760 475	13 379	270 147	1 809 426	97 188	338 563	974 228
2006	5 460 530	2 158	268 773	196 195	334 939	816 922	13 698	281 691	1 992 426	100 020	380 083	1 073 625

Year	Total	Philosophy	Economics	Law	Education	Literature	History	Science	Engineering	Agriculture	Medicine	Administration
Bachelor's degree programs												
1994	409 599	1 039	56 455	14 027	14 049	36 987	5 943	41 285	187 261	17 102	35 451	
1995	447 809	873	66 685	15 681	15 083	42 058	6 258	43 366	203 018	17 903	36 844	
1996	505 323	983	74 458	19 124	18 285	51 262	6 984	49 824	223 058	20 166	41 179	
1997	579 679	1 123	84 062	23 280	21 063	60 460	8 242	59 318	251 608	23 379	47 144	
1998	653 135	1 086	89 481	28 725	24 276	72 676	9 154	67 623	280 301	27 056	52 757	
1999	936 690	1 386	131 459	42 765	35 163	117 599	11 043	99 870	386 458	35 834	75 113	
2000	1 160 191	1 530	165 173	51 467	49 143	151 461	12 803	131 539	465 508	42 099	89 468	
2001	1 381 835	1 600	75 568	68 631	48 944	196 526	10 495	165 609	498 984	37 133	97 512	180 833
2002	1 587 939	1 700	94 337	78 519	59 317	243 324	10 474	191 997	543 447	37 513	105 815	221 496
2003	1 825 262	1 446	114 545	91 920	69 682	297 002	11 496	220 157	535 398	41 637	119 270	262 709
2004	2 099 151	1 695	131 913	102 663	79 374	361 894	12 164	247 995	659 745	44 379	131 218	316 111
2005	2 363 647	1 797	145 512	108 779	86 080	435 484	13 379	268 061	739 668	45 674	147 726	371 487
2006	2 530 854	2 158	152 592	110 019	90 533	470 022	13 698	279 708	798 106	47 312	155 242	411 464

Table 4.3 (*cont.*)

Year	Total	Philosophy	Economics	Law	Education	Literature	History	Science	Engineering	Agriculture	Medicine	Management
Short-cycle programs												
1994	490 247	1 004	87 427	16 499	26 438	88 083	9 570	57 954	156 844	15 774	30 654	
1995	478 131	874	86 009	16 258	26 175	89 529	9 374	56 929	149 445	14 687	28 851	
1996	460 489	606	79 457	17 563	26 947	86 943	8 882	56 412	143 758	12 524	27 397	
1997	420 714	513	69 305	18 247	25 618	82 620	8 087	51 125	129 338	12 580	23 281	
1998	430 492	255	69 726	19 377	26 019	89 186	7 229	52 908	132 092	11 269	22 431	
1999	611 864	377	105 670	26 283	32 094	112 576	8 027	56 010	221 139	16 417	33 271	
2000	1 045 881	317	198 206	63 215	58 116	191 957	9 200	70 927	366 616	26 867	60 460	
2001	1 300 955	205	63 178	78 151	109 339	221 078	5 587	92 592	393 372	25 819	76 644	234 990
2002	1 617 037	475	88 079	82 099	118 906	265 991	4 877	102 870	513 794	31 734	102 094	306 118
2003	1 996 439	74	106 865	94 079	148 893	315 019	4 834	109 499	647 028	39 982	138 411	391 755
2004	2 374 271	2 372	108 187	92 975	184 877	362 508	4 964	109 075	796 714	43 902	168 096	500 601
2005	2 680 934		118 707	90 742	229 558	324 991		2 086	1 069 758	51 514	190 837	602 741
2006	2 929 676		116 181	86 176	244 406	346 900		1 983	1 194 320	52 708	224 841	662 161

Source: Ministry of Education Bureau of Development and Planning, various years.

2004, to merely 2000 in 2005 and 2006. This reduction may reflect a combination of university admissions policies as well as the changing face of student interests and demand.

In reality, *ligongke* are no longer the only hot fields of study. Between 1994 and 2006, the share of *ligongke* students declined from about 60% to 50% of the admitted students as other fields of study also offered good or better career prospects. Literature, for example, is one key field of study that has gained in relative size, especially at the *benke* level, which accounted for 18.57% of new admissions in 2006: more than double those in 1994. In 2004, some 56 specialties each admitted 10 000 or more new *benke* students. English language, a specialty within the literature field, was the favorite, accepting more than 100 000 students. Only a few *ligongke* specialties – computer software, mechanical design, manufacturing and automation, clinical medicine, and civil engineering – were among the top ten *benke* specialties (Table 4.4). Computer software was still the top specialty in terms of total enrollment (close to 450 000 students), most likely as a result of the 2001 software school initiative launched by the central government (to be discussed in Chapter 8).[7]

A comparison of Table 4.4 with Table 4.3 indicates that the top engineering specialties admitted a total of 454 000 new *benke* students, or about 67.85% of the total engineering *benke* students, in 2004. Similarly, "hot" science specialties admitted 64.36% of the total. In terms of enrollment, the significance of the specialties listed in Table 4.4 becomes even more obvious, accounting for about 69% of the *benke* science majors and 72% of the *benke* engineering students. This gives us some idea of the types of evolving skills that are available or demanded in the labor market.

Since 2001, when management was added as a new field of study, the number of new entrants into this field had more than doubled by 2006; however, this phenomenon occurred more at the *zhuanke* level. Since the total pool of economics majors has experienced a relative

---

[7] Of the some 340 specialties taught at the 678 *benke* institutions of higher education in 2007, the top ten specialties offered are English (554 institutions), computing (526), law (407), international economy and trade (384), art and design (382), accounting (382), information and computer science (370), information and information engineering (367), marketing (361), and business administration (356) (*Xinmin Evening News*, April 30, 2007).

Table 4.4 *Admissions enrollment and graduation in favored specialties at the bachelor's degree level (persons)*

Specialty	Field of study	Admissions		Enrollment		Graduation	
		2003	2004	2003	2004	2003	2004
English language	Literature	87 808	102 388	292 957	362 642	40 539	53 466
Computer software	Engineering	98 850	92 422	417 860	442 635	65 004	90 517
Law	Law	59 772	63 005	203 927	237 940	33 881	41 232
International economy and trade	Economics	54 856	60 259	163 384	209 125	19 151	24 760
Chinese language and literature	Literature	47 303	55 326	185 342	215 521	33 876	41 784
Arts and design	Literature	43 840	54 491	127 904	165 609	12 580	20 031
Clinical medicine	Medicine	49 430	49 881	246 532	260 423	31 732	44 516
Mechanical design manufacturing and automation	Engineering	41 913	49 420	156 846	169 827	32 134	34 633
Accounting	Management	38 558	44 940	154 746	180 820	29 294	34 668
Civil engineering	Engineering	37 754	43 756	141 525	156 936	26 468	31 624
Business administration	Management	41 265	43 600	152 630	169 219	26 412	32 677
Electronic and information engineering	Engineering	42 371	41 758	155 430	168 694	23 206	31 149
Mathematics and applied mathematics	Science	33 496	37 944	130 377	143 484	24 351	29 299
Information management and information system	Management	29 807	30 898	105 658	121 259	13 212	19 121
Automation	Engineering	28 563	30 652	112 194	118 873	21 647	25 613
Marketing	Management	23 812	29 491	80 422	100 519	11 873	15 150
Finance	Economics	25 594	27 494	88 958	102 103	13 610	16 441

Communications engineering	Engineering	25 946	26 743	92 250	105 609	11 766	16 215
Physical education	Education	22 976	25 642	78 047	91 856	12 674	15 895
Electric engineering and automation	Engineering	22 146	24 976	82 925	91 468	13 963	16 788
Travel management	Management	18 378	24 217	58 610	76 181	6 618	10 465
Information and computer science	Science	25 570	24 186	78 526	90 000	6 987	11 385
Economics	Economics	18 812	20 771	66 943	72 810	10 169	13 416
Music	Literature	14 988	18 880	48 032	60 548	5 795	8 278
Chemistry	Science	16 905	18 385	64 863	69 438	13 282	15 539
E-commerce	Management	14 557	17 390	27 958	46 101	214	698
Public administration	Management	14 139	17 368	39 392	52 837	3 095	5 631
Environmental engineering	Engineering	16 573	17 061	57 789	63 380	7 677	11 171
Financial management	Management	14 341	16 719	46 863	59 129	4 886	6 858
Electronic information science and technology	Science	13 969	16 549	42 627	55 787	3 217	5 174
Physics	Science	15 922	16 478	63 621	65 772	13 645	15 419
Fine arts	Literature	13 905	15 794	46 592	55 261	6 281	9 021
Chemical engineering and technology	Engineering	14 450	15 668	57 228	58 462	12 669	13 417
Applied chemistry	Science	13 674	15 425	44 916	51 841	6 769	8 681
Software engineering	Engineering	9 476	15 418	21 262	39 130	624	4 125
Biological science	Science	14 770	15 352	52 319	57 448	8 234	10 357
Biotechnology	Science	13 854	15 279	44 386	53 532	4 631	7 248
Engineering management	Management	12 562	14 320	40 081	48 362	5 210	7 466
Measure and control technology and instrument	Engineering	11 648	13 588	41 838	46 725	6 871	8 626
Japanese language	Literature	10 056	13 521	28 778	37 313	3 994	5 063

Table 4.4 (*cont.*)

Specialty	Field of study	Admissions		Enrollment		Graduation	
		2003	2004	2003	2004	2003	2004
Industrial design	Engineering	12 238	13 421	39 185	46 391	3 746	6 464
Biological engineering	Engineering	13 049	13 316	38 829	47 439	3 969	5 827
Nursing	Medicine	10 817	13 097	32 534	43 823	1 649	4 186
Public management	Management	9 703	12 662	30 627	40 116	4 333	5 388
Political education	Law	12 685	12 602	51 144	52 727	11 066	13 155
Human resources management	Management	9 224	12 562	27 936	36 725	2 273	4 593
Sports training	Education	11 322	12 339	31 980	39 698	3 314	4 874
Thermal energy and power engineering	Engineering	10 708	11 998	40 084	42 626	7 838	8 680
Mechanical engineering and automation	Engineering	12 271	11 864	47 462	47 301	10 352	11 402
Food science and engineering	Engineering	10 284	11 752	37 105	40 821	7 485	8 319
Journalism	Literature	9 731	11 526	29 672	37 374	4 431	5 185
Pharmacology	Medicine	8 766	10 742	27 698	34 650	3 466	4 866
Advertising	Literature	8 347	10 587	25 808	32 630	1 944	3 848
History	History	9 920	10 506	37 914	40 017	8 178	9 425
Material formation and control engineering	Engineering	8 063	10 503	28 931	34 584	5 632	6 609
Materials science and engineering	Engineering	8 860	10 139	29 340	33 410	5 260	5 282
Subtotal Economics		99 262	108 524	319 285	384 038	42 930	54 617

Law	72 457	75 607	255 071	290 667	44 947	54 387
Education	34 298	37 981	110 027	131 554	15 988	20 769
Literature	235 978	282 513	785 085	966 898	109 440	146 676
History	9 920	10 506	37 914	40 017	8 178	9 425
Science	148 160	159 598	521 635	587 302	81 116	103 102
Engineering	425 163	454 455	1 598 083	1 754 311	266 311	336 461
Medicine	69 013	73 720	306 764	338 896	36 847	53 568
Management	226 346	264 167	764 923	931 268	107 420	142 715
Total	1 320 597	1 467 071	4 698 787	5 424 951	713 177	921 720

Source: *China Educational News* April 30, 2005.

decrease, this decline presumably reflects the fact that among management majors, those in the business management specialty have been increasing because business was formerly part of the economics field of study.[8]

As a whole, the share of *benke* students in new admissions rose from 45.52% in 1994 to 60.49% in 1999, but has declined ever since, which suggests that China's admissions expansion has occurred mainly at the *zhuanke*-level institutions. This finding may be explained largely by the fact that provincial governments have recently been granted more freedom in approving the establishment of such institutions within their jurisdiction, which in turn admit *zhuanke* students. In 2006, philosophy, economics, law, literature, history, and science admitted more *benke* than *zhuanke* students.

All the fields of study listed in Table 4.3 may be further divided into a wide range of specialties. Engineering, however, is the only one about which there is detailed information on the precise breakdown (Table 4.5). The definition of engineering within China's higher education statistics has evolved over the years, with electrical engineering and informatics, mechanical engineering, and civil engineering being the three dominant specialties admitting the most students. Combined, they accounted for approximately three-quarters of the admissions in engineering in 2006. Other top specialties of engineering, in terms of admissions in 2006, included: transportation; light industry, textile, and food; chemical engineering and pharmaceutics; and materials science. Between 1994 and 2006, transportation and the environment and safety were the two specialties that experienced the largest increases – almost thirteen and twelve times, respectively – indicating the growing importance being given to these two specialties in terms of government policies and priorities. While information on the breakdown by length of programs – *benke* or *zhuanke* – is unavailable (to be discussed further in the Appendix), we do know that roughly half of the engineering majors were enrolled in the *benke* programs (see Table 4.3).

---

[8] There has been discussion as to whether such subspecialties as education administration, public administration, and business administration are suitable for undergraduate students who are too young – 18 or 19 years old when admitted – to have any experience in these subspecialties.

Table 4.5 *Undergraduate engineering admissions by specialties (individuals)*

Year	Total	Applied geology	Materials science	Mechanical engineering	Instruments and meters	Energy and power	Electrical engineering and information	Civil engineering and architecture
1994	344 105	7 758	13 729	65 003	7 852	7 147	111 153	42 904
1995	352 463	6 684	14 394	65 023	8 043	6 941	119 754	45 357
1996	366 816	5 940	14 849	65 409	7 351	7 040	130 186	47 009
1997	380 946	6 140	15 644	67 967	7 324	6 810	135 356	48 863
1998	412 393	6 822	17 101	71 256	7 194	6 750	154 266	51 764
1999	607 597	8 071	22 989	92 223	9 962	9 787	262 431	72 413
2000	832 124	7 924	25 985	107 433	11 337	11 877	411 152	88 616
2001	892 356	8 251	26 503	122 933	12 523	13 805	459 140	93 040
2002	1 057 241	9 411	28 098	150 407	14 059	15 300	554 092	110 977
2003	1 242 426	11 690	34 066	195 293	15 509	18 296	623 361	136 562
2004	1 466 459	16 214	40 920	287 754	19 874	26 511	670 357	157 732
2005	1 796 622	24 692	43 300	314 864	15 596	19 769	850 177	177 881
2006	1 995 634	33 298	43 880	367 912	15 797	22 158	912 063	205 199

Table 4.5 (*cont.*)

Year	Hydraulics	Survey and measure	Environment and safety	Chemical engineering and pharmaceutics	Light industry textile and food	Transportation	Agricultural engineering	Forestry engineering
1994	4396	2097	3148	21213	17829	8246	5057	1921
1995	4321	1975	3381	20454	17468	7930	4716	1649
1996	4384	1753	3660	20569	17538	8607	5204	1675
1997	4794	2013	4319	22326	17212	9225	5623	1699
1998	5195	2107	5638	21990	18470	9383	5780	2013
1999	7661	3857	11119	26197	23972	12373	7515	2802
2000	9785	4667	18220	31701	29404	17411	9164	3577
2001	9896	4549	22478	25301	32698	24789	6441	2370
2002	10809	5044	25945	27175	35742	27847	6367	2144
2003	13603	5928	29755	32946	42641	35946	5795	2304
2004	16388	7823	30513	41800	52607	45575	5659	2912
2005	18482	10742	37093	67184	73127	91134	4758	2133
2006	17984	14033	36908	82654	85690	105173	5178	2552

Table 4.5 (*cont.*)

Year	Public security technology	Aeronautics and astronautics	Weaponry	Engineering mechanics	Management engineering	Biotechnology	Engineering	Ocean engineering
1994	716	1 343	448	831	21 314			
1995	772	1 421	417	698	21 065			
1996	889	1 471	421	888	21 973			
1997	1 074	1 726	298	807	21 726			
1998	1 089	1 882	292	876	22 525			
1999	1 543	2 561	361	1 047	28 713			
2000	1 972	2 844	385	1 356	37 314			
2001	5 811	3 095	1 756	2 151		11 406	1 144	2 276
2002	5 084	3 865	1 800	2 928		15 551	1 969	2 627
2003	4 915	5 046	2 028	3 212		19 862	522	3 146
2004	8 470	6 099	2 716	3 444		18 862	266	3 963
2005	2 394	3 593	2 913	3 284		31 544		1 962
2006	3 048	3 737	2 850	3 225		30 083		2 212

Source: Ministry of Education Bureau of Development Planning, various years.

Postgraduates

Graduate education in China emerged in the 1930s. Between 1949 and 1966, the nation carried out advanced training at the graduate level, but it was heavily influenced by the legacy of close cooperation with the former Soviet Union and no degrees had been awarded. It was only after 1978 that China has seen the growth of Western-style graduate education, with the largest expansion occurring from 1999 onward (Table 4.6; see also Table 2.1). In 1978, new graduate admissions were just over 10 000, but in 2006 new admissions into master's programs grew to close to 400 000, with an additional 56 000 students at the doctoral level, representing a sixfold and 3.74-fold increase over 1998, respectively. The admission of doctoral students has been concentrated at key universities. According to statistics from China's Ministry of Education, 85 percent of doctoral students were admitted into the 211 Program universities (Fang *et al.*, 2006: 208).

Although the absolute number of newly admitted S&T (*ligongke*) graduate students has been rising, the admission of *ligongke* graduate students has not grown as significantly as the number of graduate students as a whole. The one exception has been among the field of medicine, which increased by 6.19-fold at the master's level and 3.81-fold at the doctoral level between 1998 and 2006. Moreover, the relative share of *ligongke* graduate students has been declining, similar to the situation of undergraduate admissions. In 2006, new *ligongke* master's students accounted for less than 61 percent of the new intake, and new *ligongke* doctoral students comprised less than three-quarters of the total. This may seem surprising given the hype that frequently appears in the Western media about the production of engineers in China. Of course, the absolute number continues to increase. Nonetheless, this situation reflects the growing sophistication of the Chinese education market and the growing opportunities for jobs in industry, academia, and government outside of S&T.

In 1980, China enrolled only a total of 22 000 graduate students; in 2006, the total enrollment rose to 1.1 million. With a total enrollment of more than 200 000 in doctoral programs, China is among the top countries in the world in terms of numbers of doctoral students; with new admissions of some 56 000 students into doctoral programs, including 41 000 in S&T in 2006, China is en route to surpass the USA in doctorate production (the USA confers some 45 000 doctoral

Table 4.6 *Admissions of graduate students by fields of study ('persons)*

Year	Total	Philosophy	Economics	Law	Education	Literature	History	Science	Engineering	Agriculture	Medicine	Military Science	Management
1994	50756	636	4977	2559	938	2513	932	8789	22143	1943	5326		
1995	50925	683	4645	2365	927	2858	914	8485	23138	1772	5128		
1996	59194	734	6314	3366	1031	3372	1019	9504	25829	2120	5891		
1997	63232	811	7264	4049	1270	3815	1071	9601	26495	2404	6452		
1998	72262	969	9156	4794	1586	4313	1255	10321	29040	2830	7498		
1999	91762	1301	10770	5583	2455	5429	1553	13182	38718	3450	9321		
2000	123065	1679	14743	8196	3227	7730	2106	17707	55034	4847	12796		
2001	164855	2022	8468	11064	4532	10670	2503	21286	62827	5687	16770	65	18961
2002	202504	2356	11016	13782	5123	13361	2835	26240	79486	6521	19815	118	21851
2003	268747	3103	14411	18472	7671	18892	3634	33969	103171	9693	26501	124	29106
2004	326286	3882	17007	22979	10053	24783	4572	41067	120750	12110	33012	174	35897
2005	364831	4414	18612	24770	12357	28962	5249	45193	131345	13864	38340	219	41506
2006	397925	4742	19635	26868	14340	31351	5481	47749	144841	14841	42200	215	45662

Source: Ministry of Education Bureau of Development, various years; Ministry of Education and Planning and National Bureau of Statistics, various years.

Table 4.7 *Admissions into graduate programs by level of degree (persons, %)*

Year	Applicants	Admissions	Percentage admitted	Applicants	Admissions	Percentage admitted
	Doctoral			*Master's*		
1996	23 811	12 590	52.87	193 291	45 796	23.69
1997	23 437	12 654	53.99	227 581	49 267	21.65
1998	26 989	14 932	55.33	259 090	55 174	21.30
1999	35 387	19 704	55.68	305 174	68 728	22.52
2000	49 291	25 081	50.88	377 182	95 710	25.38
2001	69 568	32 055	46.08	443 962	130 033	29.29
2002	80 895	38 077	47.07	600 612	162 698	27.09
Average			51.70			24.42
	New master's degree holders			*New bachelor's degree holders*		
1996		3 755		81 399	21 546	26.47
1997		3 646		94 855	24 600	25.93
1998		4 095		103 654	25 944	25.03
1999		5 545		126 934	33 413	26.32
2000		6 719		152 968	45 375	29.66
2001		7 849		193 789	63 013	32.52
2002		9 510		266 499	79 828	29.95
Average						27.98

Year	Percentage admitted	Percentage admitted with new master's degrees	Percentage admitted	Percentage admitted with new bachelor's degrees
1996		29.83	42.11	47.05
1997		28.81	41.68	49.93
1998		27.42	40.01	47.02
1999		28.14	41.59	48.62
2000		26.79	40.56	47.41
2001		24.49	43.65	48.46
2002		24.98	44.37	49.07
Average		27.21	42.00	48.22

Source: Ministry of Education Bureau of Students in Higher Education, 2003.

degrees annually), putting aside for the moment the question of quality and standards.[9]

The admissions process for Chinese graduate education is very competitive, especially at the master's level. According to data from the Ministry of Education, between 1996 and 2002, on average, fewer than one-quarter of applicants to master's programs were granted admission, while the admissions ratios for doctoral programs averaged about 52% (Table 4.7). At the master's level, about 28% of undergraduate seniors were admitted. About 27% of the students admitted into Chinese doctoral programs were fresh master's graduates. It may be assumed that admissions rates in recent years have been lower as a result of the overall admissions expansion at the undergraduate level – there may be more total applicants, but according to our field interviews, the qualifications among the total pool have actually been falling.

It should be recognized that there are differences in admissions at master's and doctoral levels, as reflected in Table 4.6 and Table 4.7. Most of the numbers in Table 4.6 are greater than those in Table 4.7; the difference may be attributed to the numbers in Table 4.7 excluding those admitted into military institutions of learning.

Flow of human resources in science and technology

Undergraduates

To fully understand the complexion and capabilities of China's talent pool, it is essential to understand how the "output" of the higher education system translates into graduates with usable skills and knowledge. In 2006, China turned out 3.7 million undergraduates (Table 4.8), with those specializing in science, engineering, agriculture, and medicine – 1.87 million – joining the ranks of China's HRST base. The new injection of HRST into the existing Chinese talent base helps to explain, in part, the capacity of the economy to continue on its remarkable growth path over the last decade. While there remains

---

[9] Commenting on the expansion of graduate education in China, leading labor economist Richard Freeman points out: "The quality of doctorate education surely suffers from such expansion, so the numbers should be discounted to some extent, but as the new doctorate programs develop, the discount factor will decline" (Freeman, 2005: 4–5).

Table 4.8 *Graduates of undergraduate programs at regular institutions of higher education, by field of study (persons, %)*

Year	Total		Philosophy		Economics		Law		Education		Literature	
	Graduates	%	Graduates	%	Graduates	%	Graduates	%	Graduates	%	Graduates	%
Total												
1994	637 417	100	2 117	0.33	80 981	12.70	17 650	2.77	35 234	5.53	92 928	14.58
1995	805 397	100	2 110	0.26	119 042	14.78	23 170	2.88	41 898	5.20	115 969	14.40
1996	838 638	100	1 960	0.23	127 018	15.15	25 852	3.08	40 620	4.84	120 051	14.31
1997	829 070	100	1 183	0.14	132 988	16.04	28 270	3.41	39 595	4.78	116 115	14.01
1998	829 833	100	1 183	0.14	132 900	16.02	29 649	3.57	40 716	4.91	119 583	14.41
1999	847 617	100	1 067	0.13	134 258	15.84	31 500	3.72	40 271	4.75	120 957	14.27
2000	949 767	100	916	0.10	159 299	16.77	44 124	4.65	42 052	4.43	146 997	15.48
2001	1 036 323	100	925	0.09	57 254	5.52	61 474	5.93	52 563	5.07	157 837	15.23
2002	1 337 309	100	1 012	0.08	65 942	4.93	79 966	5.98	79 812	5.97	198 535	14.85
2003	1 877 492	100	1 196	0.06	88 181	4.70	110 416	5.88	117 072	6.24	286 889	15.28
2004	2 391 152	100	1 331	0.06	113 687	4.75	133 364	5.58	146 685	6.13	367 133	15.35
2005	3 067 956	100	1 275	0.04	162 977	5.31	163 529	5.33	280 134	9.13	415 206	13.53
2006	3 774 708	100	1 417	0.04	203 957	5.40	186 164	4.93	322 317	8.54	524 806	13.90

Table 4.8 (*cont.*)

Year	History Graduates	%	Science Graduates	%	Engineering Graduates	%	Agriculture Graduates	%	Medicine Graduates	%	Management Graduates	%
Total												
1994	16 794	2.63	87 845	13.78	228 922	35.91	27 856	4.37	47 090	7.39		
1995	18 117	2.25	100 566	12.49	295 839	36.73	32 975	4.09	55 711	6.92		
1996	16 423	1.96	97 260	11.60	315 005	37.56	33 032	3.94	61 417	7.32		
1997	14 559	1.76	90 513	10.92	314 418	37.92	30 190	3.64	61 239	7.39		
1998	14 179	1.71	92 729	11.17	308 574	37.19	28 941	3.49	61 379	7.40		
1999	13 374	1.58	90 395	10.66	326 180	38.48	28 070	3.31	61 545	7.26		
2000	13 661	1.44	98 200	10.34	354 291	37.30	30 370	3.20	59 857	6.30		
2001	10 220	0.99	115 829	11.18	349 097	33.69	28 543	2.75	62 638	6.04	139 943	13.50
2002	11 683	0.87	131 494	9.83	459 842	34.39	36 284	2.71	79 500	5.94	193 239	14.45
2003	13 905	0.74	173 031	9.22	644 106	34.31	50 057	2.67	111 356	5.93	281 283	14.98
2004	14 502	0.61	207 490	8.68	812 148	33.96	59 564	2.49	154 187	6.45	381 061	15.94
2005	10 694	0.35	164 867	5.37	1 090 986	35.56	69 531	2.27	202 577	6.60	506 180	16.50
2006	10 605	0.28	197 231	5.23	1 341 724	35.55	77 177	2.04	253 252	6.71	656 058	17.38

Table 4.8 (*cont.*)

Year	Total Graduates	%	Philosophy Graduates	%	Economics Graduates	%	Law Graduates	%	Education Graduates	%	Literature Graduates	%
Bachelor's degree programs												
1994	310 291	100	1 394	0.45	29 622	9.55	8 270	2.67	13 084	4.22	28 232	9.10
1995	325 484	100	1 261	0.39	32 075	9.85	9 393	2.89	14 019	4.31	29 835	9.17
1996	347 194	100	1 164	0.34	35 726	10.29	10 501	3.02	14 482	4.17	32 296	9.30
1997	381 647	100	682	0.18	50 134	13.14	12 471	3.27	13 751	3.60	36 216	9.49
1998	404 666	100	780	0.19	58 095	14.36	14 832	3.67	14 611	3.61	38 885	9.61
1999	440 935	100	852	0.19	67 611	15.33	16 363	3.71	15 479	3.51	44 285	10.04
2000	495 624	100	775	0.16	78 205	15.78	19 806	4.00	17 939	3.62	53 826	10.86
2001	567 839	100	873	0.15	35 267	6.21	30 326	5.34	17 965	3.16	62 956	11.09
2002	655 763	100	858	0.13	37 517	5.72	36 332	5.54	22 885	3.49	77 710	11.85
2003	929 598	100	1 127	0.12	48 878	5.26	52 756	5.68	30 977	3.33	126 087	13.56
2004	1 196 290	100	1 239	0.10	61 758	5.16	63 334	5.29	40 164	3.36	168 738	14.11
2005	1 465 786	100	1 275	0.09	80 710	5.51	76 140	5.19	50 342	3.43	226 903	15.48
2006	1 726 674	100	1 417	0.08	104 665	6.06	91 596	5.30	61 740	3.58	283 404	16.41

Table 4.8 (*cont.*)

Year	Total		Philosophy		Economics		Law		Education		Literature	
	Graduates	%	Graduates	%	Graduates	%	Graduates	%	Graduates	%	Graduates	%
Bachelor's degree programs												
1994	6 509	2.10	36 726	11.84	141 654	45.65	15 445	4.98	29 355	9.46		
1995	6 385	1.96	38 029	11.68	148 844	45.73	16 365	5.03	29 278	9.00		
1996	6 241	1.80	39 319	11.32	160 435	46.21	17 443	5.02	29 587	8.52		
1997	5 735	1.50	39 113	10.25	175 439	45.97	16 559	4.34	31 547	8.27		
1998	5 808	1.44	40 213	9.94	181 890	44.95	16 525	4.08	33 027	8.16		
1999	6 097	1.38	42 351	9.60	195 354	44.30	17 453	3.96	35 090	7.96		
2000	6 755	1.36	49 214	9.93	212 905	42.96	19 154	3.86	37 045	7.47		
2001	6 101	1.07	63 517	11.19	219 563	38.67	19 005	3.35	41 468	7.30	70 798	12.47
2002	7 022	1.07	72 526	11.06	252 024	38.43	22 462	3.43	47 320	7.22	79 107	12.06
2003	8 791	0.95	103 409	11.12	351 537	37.82	29 758	3.20	55 927	6.02	120 351	12.95
2004	10 176	0.85	134 164	11.22	442 463	36.99	34 078	2.85	81 098	6.78	159 078	13.30
2005	10 694	0.73	163 076	11.13	517 225	35.29	35 419	2.42	96 011	6.55	207 991	14.19
2006	10 605	0.61	194 807	11.28	575 634	33.34	36 740	2.13	107 210	6.21	258 856	14.99

Table 4.8 (*cont.*)

Year	Total Graduates	%	Philosophy Graduates	%	Economics Graduates	%	Law Graduates	%	Education Graduates	%	Literature Graduates	%
Short-cycle programs												
1994	327 126	100	723	0.22	51 359	15.70	9 380	2.87	22 150	6.77	64 696	19.78
1995	479 913	100	849	0.18	86 967	18.12	13 777	2.87	27 879	5.81	86 134	17.95
1996	491 444	100	796	0.16	91 292	18.58	15 351	3.12	26 138	5.32	87 755	17.86
1997	447 423	100	501	0.11	82 854	18.52	15 799	3.53	25 844	5.78	79 899	17.86
1998	425 167	100	403	0.09	74 805	17.59	14 817	3.48	26 105	6.14	80 698	18.98
1999	406 682	100	215	0.05	66 647	16.39	15 137	3.72	24 792	6.10	76 672	18.85
2000	454 143	100	141	0.03	81 094	17.86	24 318	5.35	24 113	5.31	93 171	20.52
2001	468 484	100	52	0.01	21 987	4.69	31 148	6.65	34 598	7.39	94 881	20.25
2002	681 546	100	154	0.02	28 425	4.17	43 634	6.40	56 927	8.35	120 825	17.73
2003	947 894	100	69	0.01	39 303	4.15	57 660	6.08	86 095	9.08	160 802	16.96
2004	1 194 862	100	92	0.01	51 929	4.35	70 030	5.86	106 521	8.91	198 395	16.60
2005	1 602 170	100			82 267	5.13	87 389	5.45	229 792	14.34	188 303	11.75
2006	2 048 034	100			99 292	4.85	94 568	4.62	260 577	12.72	241 402	11.79

Table 4.8 (*cont.*)

Year	Total Graduates	%	Philosophy Graduates	%	Economics Graduates	%	Law Graduates	%	Education Graduates	%	Literature Graduates	%
Short-cycle programs												
1994	10285	3.14	51119	15.63	87268	26.68	12411	3.79	17735	5.42		
1995	11732	2.44	62537	13.03	146995	30.63	16610	3.46	26433	5.51		
1996	10182	2.07	57941	11.79	154570	31.45	15589	3.17	31830	6.48		
1997	8824	1.97	51400	11.49	138979	31.06	13631	3.05	29692	6.64		
1998	8371	1.97	52516	12.35	126684	29.80	12416	2.92	28352	6.67		
1999	7277	1.79	48044	11.81	130826	32.17	10617	2.61	26455	6.51		
2000	6906	1.52	48986	10.79	141386	31.13	11216	2.47	22812	5.02		
2001	4119	0.88	52312	11.17	129534	27.65	9538	2.04	21170	4.52	69145	14.76
2002	4661	0.68	58968	8.65	207818	30.49	13822	2.03	32180	4.72	114132	16.75
2003	5114	0.54	69622	7.34	292569	30.87	20299	2.14	55429	5.85	160932	16.98
2004	4326	0.36	73326	6.14	369685	30.94	25486	2.13	73089	6.12	221983	18.58
2005			1791	0.11	573761	35.81	34112	2.13	106566	6.65	298189	18.61
2006			2424	0.12	766090	37.41	40437	1.97	146042	7.13	397202	19.39

Source: Ministry of Education Bureau of Development and Planning, various years.

a variety of shortcomings and problems associated with the quality and distribution of this new talent cohort, the availability of more and more well-educated individuals itself, in economic and social terms, has been one very positive factor in helping to sustain China's development burst.

Slightly less than half (45.74%) of the 2006 undergraduates were at the *benke* level. Having fallen since China restored higher education after the Cultural Revolution, the share of *ligongke* bachelor's degree holders among the total number of undergraduates reduced to less than 50% in 2006. Among this group, some 576 000 students were awarded a bachelor's degree in engineering, which accounted for one-third of all the *benke* undergraduates; science majors constituted an additional 11%. Law and literature are fields of study that have seen their share increase among the total number of *benke* graduates. We also have found that three-quarters of the *benke* science and engineering students who finished their education in 2003 and 2004 were included the specialties listed in Table 4.4.

The number of *zhuanke* graduates also has increased drastically. In 2006, China's regular institutions of higher education graduated more than two million *zhuanke* students, including 766 000 in engineering, 40 000 in agriculture, and 146 000 in medicine (science is the only *ligongke* field that has seen *zhuanke* graduates decreasing). The prevailing trend over the last few years has been that there are more *benke* than *zhuanke* among undergraduates as a whole, as well as in science, engineering, agriculture, and medicine – with the exception of 2005 when *zhuanke ligongke* majors outnumbered *benke* ones.

Finally, according to estimates by the then Commission of Science, Technology, and Industry for National Defense (COSTIND), the number of students graduating from its affiliated seven national defense S&T-related universities in 2003 was 34 000, of whom 72% were undergraduates (Cheung, 2007: 40).[10]

---

[10] COSTIND was dissolved in the 2008 government restructuring with its main component being merged into the new Ministry of Industry and Information Technology.

The seven universities are the Harbin University of Technology, the Beijing Institute of Technology, the Beijing University of Aeronautics and Astronautics, the Nanjing University of Aeronautics and Astronautics, Harbin Engineering University, the Nanjing University of Science and Technology, and Northwestern Polytechnical University.

Table 4.9 *Distribution of graduates at postgraduate levels, by field of study (persons, %)*

Year	Total Graduates	%	Philosophy Graduates	%	Economics Graduates	%	Law Graduates	%	Education Graduates	%	Literature Graduates	%	History Graduates	%
Doctorate														
1989	2 046	100	36	1.76	62	3.03	33	1.61	14	0.68	38	1.86	46	2.25
1990	2 457	100	46	1.87	114	4.64	45	1.83	12	0.49	79	3.22	59	2.40
1991	2 610	100	43	1.65	80	3.07	58	2.22	34	1.30	77	2.95	58	2.22
1992	2 528	100	39	1.54	113	4.47	50	1.98	22	0.87	48	1.90	63	2.49
1993	2 940	100	43	1.46	128	4.35	60	2.04	36	1.22	55	1.87	59	2.01
1994	3 723	100	57	1.53	163	4.38	106	2.85	42	1.13	105	2.82	76	2.04
1995	4 641	100	67	1.44	214	4.61	111	2.39	51	1.10	105	2.26	86	1.85
1996	5 430	100	87	1.60	259	4.77	144	2.65	57	1.05	148	2.73	116	2.14
1997	7 319	100	105	1.43	414	5.66	234	3.20	91	1.24	211	2.88	172	2.35
1998	8 957	100	153	1.71	541	6.04	273	3.05	128	1.43	257	2.87	207	2.31
1999	10 320	100	180	1.74	717	6.95	343	3.32	149	1.44	358	3.47	227	2.20
2000	11 004	100	201	1.83	701	6.37	322	2.93	151	1.37	355	3.23	236	2.14
2001	12 867	100	233	1.81	675	5.25	500	3.89	189	1.47	504	3.92	292	2.27
2002	14 638	100	281	1.92	837	5.72	663	4.53	229	1.56	643	4.39	315	2.15
2003	18 806	100	348	1.85	1 204	6.40	770	4.09	307	1.63	837	4.45	454	2.41
2004	23 446	100	392	1.67	1 309	5.58	1 022	4.36	410	1.75	1 033	4.41	473	2.02
2005	27 677	100	436	1.58	1 617	5.84	1 191	4.30	455	1.64	1 216	4.39	547	1.98
2006	36 247	100	524	1.45	2 038	5.62	1 700	4.69	629	1.74	1 660	4.58	603	1.66

Table 4.9 (*cont.*)

Year	Science		Engineering		Agriculture		Medicine		Military Science		Management	
	Graduates	%	Graduates	%	Graduates	%	Graduates	%	Graduates	%	Graduates	%
1989	571	27.91	884	43.21	65	3.18	426	20.82				
1990	652	26.54	974	39.64	109	4.44	367	14.94				
1991	701	26.86	1 026	39.31	109	4.18	424	16.25				
1992	689	27.25	1 080	42.72	90	3.56	334	13.21				
1993	840	28.57	1 214	41.29	101	3.44	404	13.74				
1994	986	26.48	1 495	40.16	134	3.60	559	15.01				
1995	1 307	28.16	1 784	38.44	197	4.24	719	15.49				
1996	1 400	25.78	2 164	39.85	264	4.86	791	14.57				
1997	1 839	25.13	2 964	40.50	346	4.73	943	12.88				
1998	2 284	25.50	3 427	38.26	468	5.22	1 219	13.61				
1999	2 411	23.36	4 039	39.14	460	4.46	1 436	13.91				
2000	2 408	21.88	4 611	41.90	499	4.53	1 520	13.81				
2001	2 638	20.50	5 009	38.93	510	3.96	1 774	13.79	3	0.02	540	4.20
2002	2 808	19.18	5 252	35.88	626	4.28	2 166	14.80	5	0.03	813	5.55
2003	3 705	19.70	6 573	34.95	756	4.02	2 825	15.02	6	0.03	1 021	5.43
2004	4 518	19.27	8 054	34.35	977	4.17	3 700	15.78	13	0.06	1 545	6.59
2005	5 458	19.72	9 427	34.06	1 093	3.95	4 291	15.50	22	0.08	1 924	6.95
2006	7 241	19.98	12 130	33.46	1 544	4.26	5 481	15.12	35	0.10	2 662	7.34

Table 4.9 (*cont.*)

Year	Total Graduates	%	Philosophy Graduates	%	Economics Graduates	%	Law Graduates	%	Education Graduates	%	Literature Graduates	%	History Graduates	%
Master's programs														
1989	32 890	100	578	1.76	1630	4.96	998	3.03	559	1.70	1616	4.91	765	2.33
1990	31 505	100	645	2.05	1615	5.13	1048	3.33	581	1.84	1447	4.59	753	2.39
1991	29 193	100	608	2.08	1605	5.50	1121	3.84	564	1.93	1386	4.75	552	1.89
1992	23 015	100	348	1.51	1341	5.83	864	3.75	522	2.27	1234	5.36	374	1.63
1993	25 167	100	403	1.60	1772	7.04	1147	4.56	503	2.00	1388	5.52	452	1.80
1994	24 181	100	397	1.64	1804	7.46	1189	4.92	478	1.98	1408	5.82	430	1.78
1995	27 123	100	366	1.35	1951	7.19	1258	4.64	517	1.91	1463	5.39	502	1.85
1996	34 026	100	484	1.42	3407	10.01	1710	5.03	663	1.95	2010	5.91	629	1.85
1997	39 114	100	535	1.37	4574	11.69	2024	5.17	808	2.07	2305	5.89	754	1.93
1998	38 051	100	506	1.33	4199	11.04	2112	5.55	765	2.01	2498	6.56	652	1.71
1999	44 189	100	469	1.06	5554	12.57	2914	6.59	859	1.94	2903	6.57	743	1.68
2000	47 565	100	574	1.21	6518	13.70	3498	7.35	1070	2.25	3294	6.93	790	1.66
2001	54 700	100	671	1.23	3306	6.04	4004	7.32	1361	2.49	3666	6.70	887	1.62
2002	66 203	100	942	1.42	3596	5.43	4476	6.76	1717	2.59	4514	6.82	1080	1.63
2003	92 241	100	1214	1.32	5374	5.83	6714	7.28	2457	2.66	6589	7.14	1472	1.60
2004	127 331	100	1462	1.15	6789	5.33	10 075	7.91	3866	3.04	9450	7.42	1934	1.52
2005	162 051	100	1813	1.12	9313	5.75	12 912	7.97	4646	2.87	12 098	7.47	2110	1.30
2006	219 655	100	2593	1.18	12 746	5.80	17 713	8.06	7138	3.25	18 447	8.40	2894	1.32

Table 4.9 (*cont.*)

Year	Science		Engineering		Agriculture		Medicine		Military Science		Management	
	Graduates	%	Graduates	%	Graduates	%	Graduates	%	Graduates	%	Graduates	%
1989	6 099	18.54	15 070	45.82	1 681	5.11	3 894	11.84				
1990	6 006	19.06	14 297	45.38	1 443	4.58	3 670	11.65				
1991	5 635	19.30	13 037	44.66	1 341	4.59	3 344	11.45				
1992	4 554	19.79	10 537	45.78	831	3.61	2 410	10.47				
1993	4 878	19.38	11 385	45.24	837	3.33	2 402	9.54				
1994	4 535	18.75	10 908	45.11	811	3.35	2 221	9.18				
1995	4 718	17.39	12 873	47.46	914	3.37	2 561	9.44				
1996	5 222	15.35	15 391	45.23	1 154	3.39	3 353	9.85				
1997	5 775	14.76	16 954	43.35	1 442	3.69	3 943	10.08				
1998	5 189	13.64	17 254	45.34	1 247	3.28	3 629	9.54				
1999	5 834	13.20	19 285	43.64	1 489	3.37	4 139	9.37				
2000	5 669	11.92	19 752	41.53	1 783	3.75	4 617	9.71				
2001	5 999	10.97	19 716	36.04	1 626	2.97	5 188	9.48	14	0.03	8 262	15.10
2002	7 058	10.66	24 826	37.50	2 164	3.27	6 511	9.83	28	0.04	9 291	14.03
2003	9 515	10.32	34 764	37.69	3 093	3.35	9 382	10.17	26	0.03	11 641	12.62
2004	13 022	10.23	48 020	37.71	4 188	3.29	12 428	9.76	46	0.04	16 051	12.61
2005	16 570	10.23	63 514	39.19	4 945	3.05	15 114	9.33	92	0.06	18 924	11.68
2006	21 896	9.97	82 386	37.51	7 309	3.33	20 934	9.53	82	0.04	25 517	11.62

Source: Ministry of Education Bureau of Development Planning, various years.

Postgraduates

In 2006, China awarded 256 000 graduate degrees to those who pursue advanced education at universities and research institutes, including 36 247 at the doctoral level.[11] These numbers represented historical highs in both cases (Table 4.9). The number of postgraduates with advanced degrees was low in the early 1990s as a result of the reduction in admissions in the aftermath of the 1989 pro-democracy movement and did not pick up again until the early twenty-first century when the 1999 admissions enlargement started to take effect. In 2002, China graduated 66 000 students with master's degrees, almost 12 000 more than in the previous year; in 2003, another 92 000 obtained their master's degrees, representing a 39 percent increase. These increases have been across all fields of study. Again, as suggested earlier, interest in science and engineering was not the only driver.

China started its doctoral programs after the Cultural Revolution, and awarded its first 13 doctorates – in science and technology in 1982. In 1985, only 287 Chinese received their doctorates from within China itself. The rapid development of doctoral education in China has occurred since 1993: although in that year China awarded fewer than 3000 doctorates; in 2006 the number of students emerging from its doctoral programs was over 36 000. This figure represented an increase of more than 12-fold compared with a ninefold increase in the awarding of master's degrees during the same period.

Science, engineering, agriculture, and medicine majors dominate China's postgraduates. Among the doctorates who graduated in 2006, slightly less than three-quarters (26 396) went to students in these *ligongke* fields, while 60% of the master's degrees awarded went to *ligongke* students. Nonetheless, as noted, the share of *ligongke* doctoral and master's degrees has been declining: in 1989 the figures were 95% for doctorates and 81% for masters. Engineering is the largest field in terms of the production of doctorates (33.46%) followed by science (19.98%), and medicine (15.12%). By comparison, in 2006, the USA awarded 45 596 doctorates, with slightly less than half

---

[11] The number of students graduated from master's degree and doctoral programs is slightly different from that of students awarded such doctorates as some of the graduates may not receive their degrees (see Appendix for a discussion). Here, we treat those graduates as degree holders for the convenience of discussion.

(22 316 or 48.55%) going to students in natural sciences and engineering (including 4323 from China), which means that China already produces more doctorates in this category than the USA (NSF, 2007). In fact, while there has been a general increase across all fields, the social sciences and humanities (or *wenke*) have experienced the largest increases in terms of their share of a particular field, with the exception of philosophy and history. Those in the *ligongke* fields as a whole have exhibited a less than average increase. In particular, the number of graduates with master's and doctoral degrees from the seven universities affiliated to the COSTIND reached more than 5100 in 2003 (Cheung, 2007: 40).

The Chinese Academy of Sciences (CAS) is not only China's most important R&D institution, but also the world's largest graduate school. It has expanded its graduate student training in recent years, with total enrollment as of the end of 2006 reaching more than 40 000 at its institutes, its Graduate University, and its University of Science and Technology of China (USTC) campus in Hefei (CAS General Office, 2007: 53). A new CAS university center is now under construction in Beijing. Graduate students usually do their basic coursework at the Graduate University and the USTC, and then move to specific CAS institutes for their research and thesis preparations. In 2006, the academy awarded 7200 degrees, including 4034 doctorates (CAS Graduate University, 2007). The quality of CAS graduates has risen steadily as the quality of the CAS faculty and facilities has improved.

Quality of higher education and graduates

Over the last decade, as a result of the increased attention from government and expanded investments, China's higher education system has shown marked improvements, especially at key institutions. Many of these institutions are now internationally acclaimed and their students are welcome at leading graduate programs in Europe, Japan, and the USA, especially in science and engineering (see Table 4.2). With increased funding from government and other sources, key universities can now afford to attract more highly qualified faculty members (mainly of Chinese origin) from abroad, with higher salaries and significant research support. At Qinghua University, for example, the School of Economics and Management, for example, has recruited a team of overseas Chinese economics professors from such institutions as the

University of California at Berkeley, MIT, Columbia, and the London School of Economics (LSE) to lead teaching and research as endowed professors. Under the leadership of Qian Yingyi, a Chinese-born professor at Berkeley, the school became the first Chinese business school accredited by the Association to Advance Collegiate Schools of Business (AACSB) in 2007. Some Chinese universities have also started to recruit non-ethnic-Chinese scholars. In fact, as early as 2001, Qinghua's Department of Industrial Engineering appointed Professor Gavriel Salvendy from Purdue University as its Chair. Most recently, the Ministry of Education has appointed some non-ethnic-Chinese professors, such as Gary Becker and Joseph Stiglitz, both Nobel laureates in economics, to its Cheung Kong Scholar Program. A broad range of non-Chinese foreign scholars have been appointed as adjunct professors and programs advisors as a means of facilitating the upgrading of Chinese universities.

Having said this, many Chinese universities – and even several of the so-called key ones – still are not on par with (and, in fact, lag far behind) many of their counterparts in developed countries as well as in some Asian countries and regions, including Hong Kong, Taiwan, and Singapore. According to the academic ranking of world universities by China's own Shanghai Jiaotong University, based on four criteria – quality of education, quality of faculty, research output, and size of institution – in 2008, China's most prestigious universities, Qinghua and Beijing, both ranked between 201 and 302 in the world.[12] Consequently, while there are many notable exceptions, students graduating from Chinese institutions of higher education in general are lacking in critical academic areas compared with those from schools in developed countries and regions, especially in terms of overall quality.

Furthermore, there is no doubt that the quantitative increase in enrollments in China's higher education system in recent years has occurred at the expense of necessary quality improvements. China has witnessed an average 25 percent annual growth in new undergraduate enrollments in a matter of seven years (1999–2006); this increase could only be achieved by lowering admissions standards. The same situation applies to graduate education. According to a survey by the School of Education at Beijing University, 57% of advisors of master's

---

[12] Ranking universities, including the efforts by the Shanghai Jiaotong University, is controversial (Enserink, 2007).

students and 48% of advisors of doctoral students have complained about the decline in the quality of students (Min & Wang, 2006: 155). In other words, although China produces many thousands of scientists and engineers and millions of college graduates, it is important not to confuse quantity with quality.

The quality problem is a multifaceted one. First, not all Chinese universities are equal. As already noted, there are so-called "key" versus "non-key" institutions, with the former having greater access to abundant resources, possessing higher-quality faculty, having better physical facilities, and thus graduating better students. This is not very different from the situation in Europe or the USA, but the gap may be widening rather than closing as China's best universities seem to be getting even stronger. Sending more undergraduates to graduate schools around the world, as mentioned above, vindicates the quality of the key institutions. While these key institutions can compare favorably with the best in the West, beyond them the quality of education declines steeply, along with its market value. Also, not all programs are created equal. There are marked differences between the two- to three-year short-cycle (*zhuanke*) programs and the bachelor's degree (*benke*) programs at undergraduate level. As noted, at least half of recent undergraduates have been in the *zhuanke* programs, and the growth of *zhuanke* students has been faster than that of the *benke* students. The program length itself reflects critical quality differences. Although both are at the tertiary level and, in a broader sense, graduates from both programs are considered HRST, only graduates with a bachelor's degree in an S&T field are counted as scientists and engineers when they enter the workforce. Location also makes a big difference – key universities are more likely to be located in China's coastal regions where the economy is much more advanced and the technology infrastructure more sophisticated. Thus, a diploma from Qinghua or Beijing universities is significantly different from one from a three-year program at a little-known college in an interior city or province.

In the meantime, to maintain the pipeline and throughput, graduate schools have an incentive to train ever-increasing numbers of students so that they perform work on research grants that bring money into universities and attract new professors. However, it is quite common that one Chinese professor may advise ten or even more graduate students at one time. Concerns about the quality of graduate education also derive from the trend that has the best students from key universities going abroad for advanced study, leaving those from non-key universities at home to fill the open teaching and research slots at key domestic schools. In other words, in a growing number of instances at graduate level, the higher the level on the educational ladder, the seemingly lower the relative quality of the students.

Second, the quality problems of graduates are closely related to various shortcomings inherent in the nature of the current Chinese higher education system. A student has to overcome many hurdles to be admitted into an undergraduate or graduate program; it is relatively easy, however, for a student to graduate, but rare for one to be ejected for unsatisfactory performance. Without such explicit pressure, some of the students just do not work hard. The rigidity within the higher education system makes it difficult, if not impossible, for a student to transfer from one specialty to another, let alone to another institution. Because students are admitted according to their scores at entrance examinations, those with higher scores get into their preferred specialties; those who achieve lower scores do not necessarily have their interests taken into consideration when school assignments are made. In this fashion, the way that the admissions process operates is random and arbitrary. Moreover, a student's interests can and do change over time. Generally speaking, however, Chinese students rarely have second chances if they seek to move out of a field of study or speciality in which they have little interest and perhaps low performance.

Third, the supply of qualified faculty remains limited. As shown in Table 3.13, on average 10% of Chinese professors hold doctorates, with a higher percentage employed at key institutions of higher education and probably more than half at Beijing and Qinghua universities (an additional 30% have master's degrees). This comparatively low percentage of doctorates among Chinese university faculty on the whole is the reason that the quality of higher education across the country is so uneven. It also helps to explain why China, with such a large contingent of new graduates in science and engineering, is still not able to leverage that seemingly large pool of talent to generate higher levels of innovative output in economic and technological terms. Now, the minimum requirement for a new professorship at key universities is a doctoral degree, and, as in places such as Taiwan, South Korea, and Hong Kong, the competition for an appointment has become fierce. Turning out more and better-quality faculty is not as easy as increasing student admissions as it usually takes eight to ten years to acquire a doctorate and gain needed post-doctoral experience on a full-time basis; it takes much longer to become a first-rate scholar. Until China's educational and scientific enterprises improve so as to reverse the "brain drain," the current problem of low-quality faculty will not readily go away, at least in the short term (see Chapter 6 for an in-depth analysis on this).

Fourth, because specialties are not set to respond directly to the specific market demands of the economy, the curriculum often remains outdated at many schools. Much depends on the quality of faculty members, their knowledge, their pedagogy, and their international networks. As currently constructed, the curriculum inside many fields tends to be narrow, covering only the specific area of study. As a result, Chinese universities have become technique-focussed, neglecting their larger responsibility to society and future. Rote learning, in which students who can answer questions in classrooms may not be able to solve and manage real-life problems, still dominates higher education. With some exceptions, the prevailing approach to teaching does not engage students in active classroom discussion so that students may actively translate theory into actual practice. Creative thinking, entrepreneurship, interpersonal, and intercultural skills, among others, have not been part of the pedagogy or curriculum, even at key institutions. Political or ideological education, which was introduced in 1950 and has evolved over the years, now comprises five required courses: "Introduction to Basic Principles of Marxism;" "Introduction to Mao Zedong Thought, Deng Xiaoping Theory, and Three Represents Important Thought;" "Morality Cultivation and Basics of Law;" "Outline of Modern and Contemporary Chinese History;" and "Current Affairs and Policies" (*China Youth Daily*, April 23, 2007). These courses, which students do not like but have to take, account for about 10 percent of the credits for their entire undergraduate study and occupy a significant amount of time during the freshman and sophomore years.

There are virtually no practitioner or clinical faculty members. Internships and cooperative assignments, which may be critical to undergraduate and graduate training, especially in engineering and technology, are not usually part of the curriculum. To make matters worse, much of Chinese industry does not exhibit great enthusiasm about providing internship opportunities for Chinese students, thus further exacerbating the lack of real-life problem-solving experiences among recent Chinese graduates. In fact, most corporate leaders in

China do not recognize that they may contribute to raising the quality of graduates by building strong university–industry ties on the education front. Student fees allocated for such important practice-oriented experiences have remained unchanged for decades; even if there were ample opportunities, funds are lacking. Consequently, graduates are able to do things by the book, but dare not tear it up. This limits their ability to apply classroom learning to real-world issues.

Last, but not least, the students themselves may also be an integral part of the problem in terms of quality. As mentioned, some students, born during the Deng Xiaoping era of the four modernizations, have not experienced the hardships or poverty of their parents. They also are products of the one-child family policy and thus many are spoiled. Allowing for some exaggeration, they are not willing to work as hard as their parents. Most tend not to use much initiative in their studies and study primarily for the sake of scores. Those who want to further their studies – at graduate schools at home or abroad – often tend to focus only on the subjects to be tested, surrendering breadth of knowledge in exchange for depth and exam performance.[13]

All of these factors have affected the use of students in general, and science and engineering majors in particular, after their graduation. This is the subject of the next chapter. Some of the above discussion may remind us of some of the criticisms that were launched against Chinese academics and intellectuals prior to and during the Cultural Revolution. While it is less the case that the same sort of "ivory tower" mentality still prevails in Chinese education today, it is the case that real-world problem-solving capabilities are lacking among graduates and even among many faculty members. Unless rectified, the absence of these skills and this lack of real-world orientation will continue to limit the immediate impact of new entrants into the economy and R&D system.

Conclusion

This chapter has surveyed China's HRST from the perspective of *flow*; that is, the higher education system through which the country turns

---

[13] These comments are based on inputs from interviews conducted inside and outside China with Chinese professors, academic administrators, and researchers.

out the next generation of scientists and engineers. China is the largest producer of students in science and engineering at both undergraduate and doctoral levels and will soon surpass the USA in terms of the number of doctorates awarded. Such a dramatic increase in admissions to higher education has provided larger numbers of well-educated talent to China's scientific and educational enterprises, and has contributed to Chinese economic development. It is likely that there will continue to be a positive correlation between China's growth and its steadily improved talent resources, especially in science and engineering. In addition, there is no doubt that the benefit of having a large talent pool will be significant for China in its effort to become an innovation-oriented country.

Yet, while it is true that Chinese universities literally graduate millions of students each year, it is an exaggeration to suggest that the growing numbers of science and engineering graduates naturally provide China with unassailable competitive advantages in S&T. There remains a gap between what the numbers suggest and what is actually happening in terms of innovative performance. The gap has emerged from several sources: the quality of faculty members, which clearly needs to be improved; the university curricula that need to be overhauled; the higher education system that needs to be more flexible; and education which has to be oriented more toward problem-solving. In addition, it is no small task to accommodate the broad range of interests among such a large pool of students. In a word, Chinese universities need to do a better job of nurturing their students and society needs to be more integrated into university life so that it, too, shares responsibility for better preparing students for their post-university lives. One reason why China still lacks leadership that might leapfrog to advantage in S&T, as pointed out in Chapter 3, is that China's educational system has been very slow to turn out such creative leaders. In the words of the founder of China's space program, Dr. Qian Xuesen, who told visiting Chinese Premier Wen Jiabao, in the summer of 2005, one of the important reasons why China has not developed as far as desired in S&T is that the nation does not have universities capable of producing innovative S&T personnel. Dr. Qian further emphasized that without unique creativity it is impossible to grow outstanding talent (*People's Daily*, August 1, 2005). Given his status and knowledge, the assessment is not that optimistic.

It also needs to be remembered that as China has emerged from the doldrums of the 1960s and early 1970s other countries have not stood idly by. Many nations, now feeling the pressure of China's rapid rise in both quantitative and qualitative terms, have also been improving their higher education to respond to what they see as "the Chinese challenge." Therefore, if China does not take quality issues in higher education more seriously, and give them immediate attention, its competitive potential may deteriorate. This could have a negative impact on the long-term sustainability of China's high-technology development as well as the overall development and international competitiveness of the Chinese economy. Although such a suboptimal outcome is by no means likely structurally or politically, the problems surrounding the quality of China's talent pool do seem to warrant a thorough review and rethink across the highest echelons of power in the People's Republic.

5 | Utilization of scientists and engineers in China

Although it is clear that the "supply" side of the science and technology (S&T) talent equation is an important component of a nation's innovation capacity and potential, it also is the case that sheer numbers of scientists and engineers is not an adequate proxy for innovative performance and economic contribution. The effective use and deployment of the S&T talent pool is the major factor which truly shapes, as well as yields, meaningful innovative outcomes. Having described the characteristics of China's human resources in science and technology (HRST) and the educational pipeline through which China's S&T workforce has been produced, the purpose of this chapter is to highlight and evaluate how effectively the Chinese S&T workforce has been utilized.

The chapter first lays out how intellectuals, of whom scientists and engineers are an important component, as a social class have evolved in contemporary China. This analysis is followed by a review of the core political and modernization issues involved in the Chinese Communist Party (CCP) policies toward intellectuals in general, and scientists and engineers in particular, since 1949; the attitudes and actions of the CCP have been the major determinant of how Chinese scientists and engineers are treated both politically and economically. The various components of the professional lives and careers of China's high-end talent pool – from job assignments and promotion to career mobility and performance rewards – are discussed. The chapter also looks at the growing impact of entrepreneurship and commerce, especially within China's high-technology sector, and its effect on the utilization of the S&T workforce; in the era of reform and open-door, and the onset of the knowledge-based economy, there are many new imperatives and opportunities driving the individual behavior and attitudes of Chinese scientists and engineers.

When thinking about *utilization* of the S&T workforce, key questions which come to mind are: whether these scientists and engineers are deployed effectively; whether they perform well once at work; and whether they are satisfied with the environment in which they work. The chapter will discuss each of these issues.

Although enhancing income is not the sole driver and motivator of the bulk of the talent pool, it clearly does have a growing influence on career choices, including the critical decision about whether to stay abroad or return to China after foreign education. The last section of the chapter is therefore devoted to an examination of wage trends and compensation issues related to Chinese scientists and engineers. "On the table," from both a policy and management point of view, is a series of emerging questions about the evolving structure of the local labor market, the degree to which there actually *is* a functioning labor market in China, the seemingly growing role of nationalism in post-Deng Xiaoping China versus the 1950s, and the extent to which the Chinese S&T community, taken as a whole, is appropriately utilized and deployed to meet the expectations of the country's leadership in terms of overall performance and substantive contributions to the nation's economic prosperity, national technological strength, and international image and prestige.

Scholar-officials, intellectuals, cadre, and *jibie*

The "science and engineering" professions are relatively new to China. Historically, intellectuals occupied a very high position in the Chinese society: scholars, farmers, artisans, and merchants (*shi, nong, gong, shang*), ranked in that order, were the key four pre-modern Chinese social groups (Bodde, 1991: 203–12; Wortzel, 1987: 15–17). More accurately, "scholars" were scholar-officials, or gentry (*shishen*), who had a good command of the Confucian classics and passed an imperial civil service examination (*keju kaoshi*) at various levels to be appointed as government officials. As a distinct social group in imperial China, scholar-officials dominated the broad array of social and economic affairs, receiving an assortment of political, economic, and social privileges and powers, and basically lead a rather well-off, high status mode of life (Chang, 1955).

That tradition remained in place for several centuries, although *keju kaoshi* was abolished in 1905 and the Qing dynasty was replaced by a republic in 1911. During the nationalist (Kuomintang) government era, intellectuals with advanced education, especially returnees from overseas, were highly respected and promoted to important positions in education, economy, and even politics. One example was that of the National Defense Planning Commission (*guofang sheji weiyuanhui*) and its successor, the National Resources Committee (*ziyuan weiyuanhui*), which recruited the geologist Weng Wenhao, the economist Qian Changzhao, and the mining expert Sun Yueqi, all foreign-trained, to direct the nation's research, planning, and managerial bureaucracy. Weng, not politically ambitious, was even appointed premier (Kirby, 1989).

It was under communist leadership that Chinese intellectuals were considered to pose difficult ideological problems for the regime (to be discussed in the next section). According to Mao Zedong's standard, anyone with a high school education could be called an "intellectual" (*zhishi fenzi*), with those having more education being "big" (*da*) intellectuals and the less educated "small" (*xiao*) intellectuals (Ogden, 1992: 295). In the 1950s, the term "high-ranking intellectuals" (*gaoji zhishi fenzi*) was coined to refer to some 100 000 Chinese professors, senior researchers, senior medical doctors, and so on, with at least a college education. Currently, "intellectuals" are those with education at college-level and above (Li, 1993: 27–30), which is similar to the definition of HRST if the education received is in an S&T-related field. But before 1978, when the reform and open-door policies were initiated, knowledge and education were secondary in China, so that no matter how important they were in the nation's economic, political, and cultural affairs, intellectuals remained only a marginalized social "stratum" (*jieceng*) under the leading class (*jieji*) of workers and peasants, and could not be an independent class on their own (Kelly, 1990). In the words of Mao Zedong, intellectuals were just "hairs attached to the skin" – their social status was attached to the "skin" of the stratified structure of contemporary Chinese society.

With the inception of the communist regime, intellectuals scattered among various professions, including science, engineering, agriculture, medicine, and teaching among others, were classified into the ranks of cadre (*ganbu*), whose salary and benefits, for most of the history of the People's Republic of China, were associated with their work-grade (*jibie*). This elaborate system categorized and encompassed almost every employee at a state-owned work unit (*danwei*), either within an enterprise (*qiye*) or a public institution (*shiye*), denoting with clarity their position in a hierarchy of job-related rewards, income levels, prestige, privileges, and authority. Within it, cadres were assigned to one of 30 grades, with Grade 1 for state president and vice president, and Grade 26 for the lowliest cadre; there were 12 grades for professors, whereas engineers had eight grades, among others, with adjustments for a region's hardship and cost of living (Kraus, 1981: 31–4).

Because cadres were at the center of the *jibie* system, those in other *jibie* had to find an equivalent rank within the cadre *jibie*, which in turn determined their political status and material and non-material benefits.[1] For example, a Grade 8 professor was equivalent to a Grade 17 *ganbu*, which simply but importantly meant that a Grade 8 professor had similar benefits to those enjoyed by a Grade 17 *ganbu* (Chen, 2006: 82–3). Similarly, new graduates from a four-year undergraduate program entered the rank of *ganbu* at Grade 21, and earned a monthly salary of RMB (*reminbi*) 62 if they worked in Beijing, or slightly higher in Shanghai, regardless of whether they were engineers or college lecturers. This linkage between the status of a Chinese professional and the classification within an official *jibie*, which did not necessarily bring with it further privileges, special treatment, economic benefits, or power associated with the *jibie*, is known as "official-centeredness" (*guanbenwei*) (Lü, 2000: 244; Zhong, 2003: 99). Although the *jibie* system no longer operates in its original way, in its current form, the official-centerness correlates a member (*yuanshi*) of the Chinese Academy of Science (CAS) and the Chinese Academy of Engineering (CAE), respectively, to a vice minister in the government hierarchy, an advisor of doctoral students, a bureau chief, a professor, a division director, and so on. Intellectuals remain quite agitated about this system as formal membership of either the CAS or the CAE is viewed as a prestigious academic honor, while a professorship is a professional-educational rank, with both having nothing to do with their "official" title. The appearance of some sort of "relationship" or a correlation between holders of such an academic honor or achievement-oriented rank with holders of office not only strengthens the official-centeredness of the Chinese

---

[1] Benefits were not the right term; "treatment" (*daiyu*) is probably a more accurate description as they include both material and non-material components with the latter sometimes more significant than the former.

personnel system but also seems to depreciate the value and prestige of members of the CAS and the CAE (Cao, 2004a).

CCP policy toward intellectuals

Policies regarding the utilization of intellectuals, including scientists and engineers, and, correspondingly, the social status accorded them have evolved and indeed changed considerably during the history of the People's Republic of China. Relations between the political leadership and the intellectual community have centered on four major issues.

First, since the construction of a modernizing, harmonious, and innovation-oriented society relies on the technical intelligentsia, the CCP has adopted a largely utilitarian policy toward intellectuals in general, and scientists and engineers in particular. Upon taking power in 1949, the CCP faced the immediate challenge of revitalizing the national economy, so the services of Chinese intellectuals at home and abroad were sorely needed. In the mid-1950s, simultaneously complacent about China's completion of the transition to socialism and concerned about the country's continued economic backwardness, the CCP held a conference on intellectuals, during which the then premier, Zhou Enlai, spoke at length about the party's views toward intellectuals and advocated a "blooming and contending" policy, calling on intellectuals to help the party eliminate bureaucratism, factionalism, and subjectivism. In the early 1960s, when an economic crisis emerged after the Anti-Rightist Campaign and the failures of the Great Leap Forward, the party modified its policies toward intellectuals by recalling scientists and engineers and even former "rightists" to key positions in research and education. The CCP convened another conference on intellectuals in Guangzhou in 1962 to reverse the anti-intellectual trend that had prevailed since 1957. As a result, natural scientists enjoyed a measure of prestige and respect between 1962 and the start of the Cultural Revolution, the research environment was far less politicized, and the amount of time scientists spent attending political meetings was limited to one day a working week at most (Nie, 1988: 722–3). In the aftermath of the Cultural Revolution, in order to win back trust from the intellectual community and to mobilize its members to the fullest possible extent, the leadership held a national science conference in 1978, during which the just rehabilitated Deng Xiaoping gave a very upbeat speech celebrating the role of scientists in society. He made it clear that S&T is the principal "productive force" underlying the four modernizations and that scientists form "part of the working class" and are not somehow politically suspect as they had been since the Anti-Rightist Campaign. The party once again withdrew from its overly dominant position, granting scientists greater freedom within their areas of professional competence. In 2000, Jiang Zemin, then CCP General Secretary and Chinese President, put forward the "Three Represents" theory – the CCP represents the development trends of advanced productive forces; the orientations of an advanced culture; and the fundamental interests of the overwhelming majority of the people of China. Various efforts were made to co-opt intellectuals, who, apparently, were viewed as a component within the "advanced productive forces."

At each of the above-mentioned moments, the party typically became more receptive to the ideas and opinions of intellectuals, and natural scientists and technologists in particular; the CCP loosened its control over institutions of learning and allowed scientists to enjoy a certain degree of freedom in their exercise of academic autonomy and maintenance of authority in teaching and research. Renowned intellectuals were appointed to quasi-political positions such as deputies of the People's Congress and members of the People's Political Consultative Conference at national and regional levels. The party even made great efforts to recruit scientists and engineers into its ranks in the mid-1950s and again after the Cultural Revolution, which more or less signified its pragmatic approach to achieving goals during those periods. There is no doubt that intellectuals as a whole have benefited the most from the reform and open-door policies launched under Deng Xiaoping (to be discussed). In fact, the party has offered economic incentives, academic "reputation," political access, and even well-paid government positions, while standing to benefit from their advice and support (Pei, 2006: 89–92).

Second, the utilitarian policy emerged from the party's distrust of Chinese intellectuals. This may seem like an odd perspective, but as the party has reflected on the cost of periodic attacks on intellectuals it has come to recognize the high price that has been paid in terms of the country's economic well-being and technological progress. For a long time intellectuals were not considered part of the working class, China's leading class, but as a part of the despised bourgeois social group. It was not until January 1956 that the CCP began to address this issue in a special conference on intellectuals. In his 1956 keynote speech, Premier Zhou Enlai explained the party view that the overwhelming majority of intellectuals had become government workers in the cause of socialism and that they were already part of the working class. In the early 1960s, while intellectuals as a whole had not recovered from the bitterness of the Anti-Rightist Campaign, Zhou Enlai reiterated at the 1962 Guangzhou conference that the overwhelming majority of intellectuals worked enthusiastically for socialism, accepted party leadership, and were ready to go on remodeling themselves so as to become working class and thus they should not be regarded as bourgeois. Also at the conference Vice Premier Chen Yi declared boldly, "China needs intellectuals, and needs scientists. For all these years, they have been unfairly treated. They should be restored to the position they deserve." He encouraged intellectuals to take off the hat of "bourgeois intellectuals" and put on the crown of "intellectuals of the working class" (*tuomao jiamian*) (Nie, 1988: 722–3).

Nonetheless, during the Cultural Revolution, intellectuals were denounced sharply as the "stinking number nine" (*chou laojiu*) at the bottom of the barrel as social outcasts after landlords, rich peasants, counter-revolutionaries, bad elements, rightists, traitors, spies, and capitalist roaders (leaders who took the capitalist road). In addition, China's political leadership has always perceived any appeal from the Chinese intellectual community, in particular in the form of pleas for greater freedom and autonomy, as threatening to the legitimacy and authority of the regime; as a result, the CCP has felt it necessary to exercise a heavy political hand. This explains why the "blooming and contending" period turned into a retaliatory strike intended to suppress intellectuals; the party could not accept the claims of intellectuals that only experts were capable of properly governing research establishments and only professors were qualified to run the country's colleges (*zhuanjia zhi suo, jiaoshou zhi xiao*). This also helps to explain why even during the reform era of the 1980s, when intellectuals advocated that they should be able to make their own decisions relating to their work and thus required more freedom and autonomy, that such advocacy was regarded as a serious threat to the CCP monopoly on S&T practices.

The party fought back on several occasions, with the Campaign Against Spiritual Pollution in 1983, the Anti-Bourgeois-Liberalization

Campaign in 1987, and the suppression of the pro-democracy movement in 1989 (Goldman, 1994: 256–360; Meisner, 1996: 349–467). Ironically, however, despite the paranoia that seems attached to these actions, the CCP has needed to move in the direction demanded by the intellectual community as well as the imperatives of its modernization goals. Without the contributions of Chinese intellectuals, continued technological progress and economic prosperity could not be ensured, which actually presents a potentially bigger threat to the regime's claims of legitimacy.

Third, the utilitarian value of Chinese intellectuals determined that they should be "united with, educated, and remolded," as the CCP Central Committee defined in the Fourteen Articles on Scientific Work in 1961, so that existing prejudices against intellectuals could be dispelled (Nie, 1988: 719). To "unite" meant that the party was interested in utilizing the expertise of intellectuals, who were, in the meantime, required to be "educated" or to "educate" themselves through engaging in ideological reform and in the study of communist ideology, Marxism–Leninism–Mao Zedong Thought in particular, and to "remold" their bourgeois ideas. Thus, Chinese intellectuals had not only witnessed and participated in, but have also become targets of, political campaigns – from the thought-reform movement in late 1951, the Anti-Rightist Campaign in 1957, and the Cultural Revolution to various campaigns in the 1980s, in which they had been attacked and mobilized to have their bourgeois ideology transformed. For better or worse, most Chinese intellectuals had decided to retreat from taking a pro-active, highly visible stance, by pulling their heads in. Only during the most recent period has the theme of "uniting with, educating, and remolding" undergone a fundamental change.[2] Nevertheless, education focussing on communist ideology still is required for college students. In the aftermath of the 1989 Tiananmen Square crackdown it became mandatory that those newly admitted into colleges should spend their first year in military camps to enhance patriotism and prevent them from following the footprints of their predecessors; this routine still operates, despite a shorter period.

Ultimately, the party's expectation is that intellectuals will become "both red and expert" (*you hong you zhuan,*) and that they will

---

[2] Nie Rongzhen pointed out, "Now that intellectuals are part of the working people, we should no longer use the slogan of 'uniting with, educating and remolding' intellectuals" (Nie, 1988: 719).

maintain their loyalty and support for the CCP. Here, "redness" means possession of political consciousness in adhering to revolutionary lines and implementing party policies, while "whiteness" is used to denote bourgeois, or counter-revolutionary, ideology (Ogden, 1992: 293). The "red versus expert" issue remained a source of great frustration for many Chinese intellectuals from the late 1950s to the 1980s. In order to conquer "whiteness," and eventually become "red experts," intellectuals were subjected to long and difficult processes of "political re-education" and "ideological reform" through attending endless political study sessions, undergoing frequent criticism and self-criticism, and doing manual labor at factories and farms. More often than not the party used the terms "red" and "white" at will, depending on the prevailing emphasis: *virtuocracy* or *meritocracy*. At one time, the party proclaimed that intellectuals were "red" because of their devotion of expertise to China's socialist construction; at another, the CCP articulated a need to take away "white flags" and establish "red flags;" that is, to criticize bourgeois intellectuals and nurture revolutionary intellectuals (Wang, 1994: 237–40).

In the prevailing anti-intellectualism situation found after the 1957 Anti-Rightist Campaign, Nie Rongzhen, who was then Vice Premier and Commissioner of both the State Science and Technology Commission (SSTC) and the National Defense Science and Technology Commission (NDSTC), led an effort, in 1961, to draft "The Fourteen Articles on Scientific Work" (Nie, 1988: 720). The document defined two criteria for being a "red" scientist – supporting the CCP and socialism and using knowledge in the service of socialism. Accordingly, a scientist who had fulfilled these two criteria might be regarded as having become basically "red;" as for those scientists trained prior to 1949 the party only required that they be patriotic and willing to cooperate with the CCP. The document also suggested abolishing the term "white expert," because ambiguous linkage of the concepts of "expertise" and "whiteness" dampened the enthusiasm of those intellectuals who worked diligently in their fields (Yao *et al.*, 1994: 102–3). At the 1978 national conference on science, the first after the Cultural Revolution, Deng Xiaoping, then just rehabilitated, clarified the "red and white" issue by pointing out that working devotedly for socialist scientific enterprises and making contributions to them is a sign of being an expert as well as being "red" (Deng Xiaoping, [1978] 1987: 46). The "Three Represents" theory put forth by former CCP

General Secretary Jiang Zemin also acknowledges the redness of Chinese intellectuals.

Because of the four issues involved in the interaction between the CCP and intellectuals – the utilitarian values of intellectuals; their class characteristics; the "uniting with, educating, and remolding intellectuals" policy; and the "red and expert" requirement, Chinese intellectuals have experienced a sort of "emotional rollercoaster," fluctuating between the highs of high-level recognition and effective utilization and the lows of harsh treatment (Williams, 1999: 83). Now, while giving the highest priority to the development of S&T and initiating the "rejuvenating the nation with science, technology, and education" (*kejiao xingguo*) and the "empowering the nation through talent" (*rencai qiangguo*) strategies, the party has reaffirmed the utilitarian values of intellectuals in general, and technical professionals in particular; increasingly intellectuals are recognized and appreciated for their roles in society and contributions to the economy. The occupational prestige of scientists and engineers has been among the highest, comparable with that in developed countries. For example, the 2003 survey on Chinese public attitudes toward S&T showed that scientists, physicians, and engineers received higher occupational prestige scores, ranking second, third, and seventh out of the 14 occupations identified (the first was teachers) (MOST, 2005: 131). It is against this background that one may examine the utilization of scientists and engineers – a strategically important intellectual stratum that both the party and the state must rely on to achieve the nation's ambitious economic goals and technological objectives.

Job assignment, promotion, mobility, and reward

Under the planned economy, policies concerning the recruitment of science and engineering personnel and their job assignments, as well as promotion and rewards, underwent several changes, though their essence was retained for most of the Maoist period and beyond. During that time, Chinese students not only received free higher education, but also had their jobs secured through a very structured job assignment system (*fenpei*). Indeed, graduates from Chinese tertiary institutions of learning had to fulfill an obligation for the education they received. In this way, they not only worked where they were directed by the state, but also entered a social structure in which a single, bureaucratic framework defined desirable positions in various state-owned institutions and enterprises. They were willing to accept their job assignments because they received stable employment and lifetime job security, the possibility of climbing the cadre ladder, and assorted benefits such as subsidized housing, healthcare, and education for their children, among others. Nevertheless, in many ways, they were often coerced into accepting the options they were given because they were neither allowed nor able to make their own job choices (Davis, 2000). In some cases, husbands and wives were separated because the job system did not pay special deference to the needs of the family. Of course, preferable jobs usually went to the children of politically privileged groups – cadres and party members – because the CCP, through its organizational departments at different levels, maintained firm control of job assignments. As a result, while the Maoist policies on higher education and job assignment were intended to prevent urban bourgeois parents from passing their favored social status on to their children, these policies had the unintended consequence of being utilized by the so-called "new" preferred groups to achieve the same "old" purpose.[3]

Taking into consideration a student's political loyalty, academic credentials, and recommendations from a university (with possible

[3] This is ironic because, in the 1960s and 1970s, Chinese policies regarding so-called "manpower planning" were moving in directions advocated by many key international development agencies. At the time, in many Third World countries, too much money was being spent on educating an elite while the rest of the population was being neglected. Moreover, the education policies in place were indeed focussed on the "ivory tower" of high-end intellectuals and there was too little investment in the basic technical skills and know-how needed to operate the economy at a very basic level. The Chinese-announced emphasis on vocational and mass education was, therefore, not out of step with efforts being made to move many developing nations in the same direction. Unfortunately, as suggested above, over time a serious gap between theory and practice emerged in China, as education for the political elites never really took a back seat to more practical education in trades and basic technologies. Of course, one could cite the *"xiafang"* (sending to the countryside) policies adopted during the Cultural Revolution to bring intellectuals into closer contact with the masses as evidence that the Maoist system was committed to breaking down the ivory tower mentality that prevailed at the time. Although true, and very damaging in terms of its long-term economic consequences, it also is the case that the old system was never dismantled to the point of altering the traditional philosophical foundations of intellectuals as a group.

involvement of professors), unified job assignment to a specific *danwei* – a university, a research institute, an enterprise, or a government agency – as well as the location of the specific *danwei* might or might not be what the individual in question personally desired. Usually, the nation's actual or perceived need rather than a graduate's academic achievement and preference carried more weight in the assignment process. Although there were cases in which job assignments were made outside the specialized skills or training of graduates, in many instances the assignment was "rational" in so far as it did attempt to match a student's field of study, broadly defined, to a specific job. In this way, particular assignments met the interests of both students and *danwei*. For example, a student majoring in chemical engineering might be assigned to a factory to solve its pollution problem, to a research institute to develop new polymers, or to a college to teach introductory chemistry. In other words, at least in theory, the job assignment system represented a bridge between the demands of the economy and the supply side of the education system.

More important, however, a specific job assignment was meant to be permanent, thus determining a student's career prospects. Usually, when an individual started a job they could envision their career path and map all the way until their time of retirement. Given the very low level of job mobility in China at that time, other than the reassignment by the state, if a student did not like the *danwei* or the job, or they did not perform well in the particular job assigned, there really was no institutional mechanism for them to transfer to another *danwei* or job. Until recently, household registration, or residence permit system (*hukou*), further prevented Chinese from migrating not only from rural to urban areas but also from one city to another; the personal dossier (*dang'an*) of an individual, which contained lifelong personal information – from family background, educational attainment, employment history, and political attitude – was controlled by the party branch of an employee's *danwei*, and without formal endorsement there was almost no way to initiate a job change. Meanwhile, the rigidity of the system also meant that *danwei* often had no way of hiring an employee directly, not to mention letting them go. Therefore, many of China's scientists and engineers found themselves underemployed or misemployed; it was often the case that their skills and talents or specialized training could not be leveraged in an optimal fashion.

At present, along with free higher education, the job assignment system has been dismantled except in a few select cases in which students are admitted to a particular *danwei* of importance to the nation, which pays for their study and thus those students are required to work for that particular *danwei*. For example, universities usually enroll some students designated for the military and national defense S&T sector. On one hand, graduates now have an opportunity to choose their job and their own future, and to move to another *danwei* if they do not like the one they have selected. In addition, enterprises and institutions have become more selective in hiring as they seek candidates who not only have excellent potential, but also are willing to grow with them and rise through the ranks. On the other hand, not only does a student have to take on the burden of paying for their education today, but, as Chinese universities have churned out more graduates in recent years, job-hunting has also become more competitive. As graduates are attracted to those jobs with higher pay and brighter career prospects, many positions which do not provide these immediate benefits remain in desperate need of key talent; organizations continue to have increasing difficulty competing for, recruiting, and retaining qualified employees. To some extent, foreign-invested enterprises (FIEs) in China have an advantage over domestic institutions and enterprises, as evidenced by the increasing numbers of scientists and engineers working for them (see Table 3.8), as do some non-state-owned domestic enterprises. Of course, the decision to work for a foreign firm that pays more and offers more job perks does represent a rational response to real market forces. Nonetheless, in many sectors market forces have yet to kick in fully in terms of fostering appropriate wage adjustments and changes in benefits packages to accord with the recruitment challenges that continue to exist throughout the Chinese economy, especially outside the three most-preferred job locations: Beijing, Shanghai, and Guangzhou/ Shenzhen.

With a science and engineering bachelor's degree, a graduate used to start as an assistant engineer at an enterprise, a research assistant at a research institute, or as an assistant lecturer at a university. But nowadays, the minimum requirement for employment at institutions of learning is a master's degree and a doctorate for new faculty at CAS institutes and leading Chinese universities. The inflation of credentials in employment occurs not only because jobs require more advanced knowledge to perform them effectively, but also because more students with higher level education are available for them as a result of the expansion of higher education (see Chapter 4).

Maoist China was characterized by egalitarianism, under which most employees were paid at relatively low wage rates. The salary structure reflected this stress on egalitarianism; since employment was for a life-time, there was a belief that job security offset any unfairness in the system in terms of those who worked harder or contributed more than others. The cradle-to-grave employment guarantee also carried with it benefits ranging from subsidized apartments, healthcare, education for children, and retirement pensions to soap and toilet paper. Promotion was expected every several years and was mainly based on seniority – age and years of experience, but not necessarily on achievement and performance. Promotion was also gradual with differences between grades (*jibie*) in terms of salary being incremental and small. This emphasis on egalitarianism became the underpinning of what eventually came to be called the "iron rice-bowl" (*tie fanwan*) or was vividly described as "every one eating from the same big bowl" (*chi daguofan*); again, the system helped to provide employment stability and security, but it constrained individualism, discouraged competition, limited creativity and initiative-taking, and did not promote entrepreneurship.

Currently, with the "big rice-bowl" having been smashed with the advance of the reform programs under Deng Xiaoping, pay differentials within and across *danwei*, sectors, and ownership structure have become much more significant and promotions more meritocratic. Many foreign and local human resources consultancy firms have been called into enterprises in China, domestic as well as foreign-invested, to restructure the personnel system and create new, performance linked compensation schemes. Entire new job definitions have been developed to ensure that job responsibilities are clearly defined and that performance criteria are unambiguously spelled out. Interestingly, while employment in FIEs may seem attractive in the current economic environment, it also is the case that the competitive pay positions associated with them or non-government entities simply do not provide the same safety net as employment at state-owned *danwei* used to offer. As a result, for many employees, job security has become a real and serious concern. Not only have workers from state-owned enterprises been laid off, professors at universities and senior scientists at research institutes face the possibility of termination for poor performance as tenure is not guaranteed. For example, in implementing the Knowledge Innovation Program, the CAS has streamlined its research institutes according to fields of study to reduce redundancy and raise efficiency; some research personnel have been discharged because of fit and performance issues. The CAS also pioneered the separation of professional rank and appointment, which means that even someone who is qualified to be a senior scientist is not necessarily sure that he or she will receive such an appointment (Suttmeier *et al.*, 2006).

As mentioned, job mobility was almost impossible during the Maoist period and its immediate aftermath. Institutionally, as noted, *hukou* and *dang'an* were barriers that banned scientists and engineers from changing jobs. Worse, the "big rice-bowl" mentality of egalitarianism discouraged them from actively looking for new positions where they could utilize their expertise better and more effectively. Consequently, according to the SSTC, the predecessor of the Ministry of Science and Technology (MOST), only 2% of scientists and engineers changed *danwei* in 1983, and 4% did so in 1985. Likening the immobility of S&T personnel to "a pool of stagnant water," China's scientific leadership vowed to find solutions (Saich, 1989: 126–35). The reform of China's S&T system, which started in the spring of 1985, encouraged and facilitated the mobility of scientific and engineering personnel, especially from institutions of learning to enterprises. Since this represented a major break – not only from the prevailing practices that had become highly institutionalized in China since 1949 but also with the political control of scientific personnel that the CCP had held through the job assignment system – it took many years to overcome a variety of key obstacles and make job mobility for scientists and engineers, and for employees as a whole, possible and easier.[4] Nowadays, more and more Chinese do not believe in working for the same *danwei* for their whole life and they change jobs more frequently, for pay increases as well as career opportunities. Scientists and engineers are no exception.

As described in Chapter 3, since 1999 China has reconstructed its research sector by enterprising a significant number of applied

---

[4] In theory, the CCP, through its organization department at various levels, still controls *dang'an* of all cadres, according to the principle of "the party administers cadres."

Table 5.1 *Mobility structure at China's research and development (R&D) institutes (1998–2005) (%)*

	1998	1999	2000	2001	2002	2003	2004	2005
Moving in from:								
Enterprises	17.2	15.0	13.1	13.2	12.4	11.4	9.3	8.5
Institutions of higher education	47.0	51.4	47.4	41.2	51.7	55.0	59.0	60.5
R&D institutes	7.2	9.0	13.7	15.4	13.5	12.0	9.0	7.9
Overseas	0.5	0.5	0.9	0.9	1.3	1.8	1.7	1.1
Moving to:								
Government	14.8	10.0	12.3	15.8	18.9	19.5	22.2	22.4
Enterprises	51.5	51.6	41.0	34.1	36.7	36.4	36.7	32.5
Overseas	13.8	14.2	16.5	12.0	14.9	11.8	8.2	9.1

Source: **Ministry of Science and Technology**, 2007: 64–5.

research-oriented R&D institutes. In 1998, China had some 590 000 S&T personnel working at 5778 R&D institutes; by 2003, both the numbers of S&T personnel and the number of R&D institutes decreased to some 410 000 and 4169, respectively (MOST, 2005: 45), as a result of the restructuring. R&D institutes have started to see a net increase in employment after several years of decline, mainly from new graduates who are not only younger but also highly educated. In addition to retirements, many S&T personnel have moved from R&D institutes to enterprises, government agencies, and overseas positions, in that order (MOST, 2007: 62–7) (Table 5.1).

Of course, accompanying job mobility is the high turnover rate that exists in all facets of China's labor market. Fears that new, skilled employees will move on within two to three years for better pay, among others, have jettisoned the efforts of the Chinese government to encourage enterprises and R&D institutes to provide more professional training and skills development. Many chief executive officers (CEOs) inside Chinese companies, for example, have refrained from supporting this type of professional cultivation because they feel that such "investments" will be wasted. This is one of the reasons why many enterprise CEOs in China have been criticized for short-term thinking. As the situation suggests, however, when examined in the context of high staff turnover, and from a business and management perspective, this type of thinking may not be totally illogical.

Finally, to encourage sustained high levels of performance, the Chinese government has established a series of science awards to reward scientists and engineers for their achievements and to stimulate their further pursuit of excellence. The nature of these rewards has evolved as well. The 1956 Natural Science Award, China's first, was largely politically motivated. One of the first-class awards went to the aerodynamics scientist Qian Xuesen for his book, *Engineering Cybernetics*, which, according to the initial stipulation, could not be considered as it was published abroad and the award was supposed to target achievements made within China. A special case, however, was made for Qian, who returned from the USA in 1955. Measured by quality, his work no doubt well deserved an award; the decision to reward him, however; was used as a political gesture to lure more returnees (Li, 1995). No more awards were given until 1982 when the reward system was resumed and later was extended from national to provincial and municipal levels. For many years, rewarding scientists by way of such awards was surprisingly linked to increases in their income and improvements in their living conditions; the awards themselves carried token monetary value, but entitled recipients to other material benefits from the *danwei*, such as housing and promotion. They served as a form of bonus to scientists at a time when there were no other ways to do so. As a result, institutions at all levels were empowered to present awards to outstanding technical personnel. Because of these unintended consequences, the reward system was somewhat abused. In 2000, the state decided to abolish all awards at provincial and municipal levels, and consolidated three national science awards – a natural science award, an award for inventions, and an award for the promotion of S&T progress – which are given annually. In the meantime the government established a national superior science and technology prize, which carries a monetary value of RMB 1 million; the prize rewards two Chinese scientists who have made tremendous contributions to national basic and applied scientific research every year.

High-tech entrepreneurship

The reform of China's S&T system in the mid-1980s, mentioned above, also aimed at improving links between research and the economy through technology transfer from institutions of learning to enterprises and more directly through pro-active technical entrepreneurship on the part of the country's S&T talent pool. The earliest expressions of this new emphasis on technical entrepreneurship appeared in Zhongguancun.

Located north-west of Beijing, the capital of China, Zhongguancun is no doubt the nation's most talent-intensive region; it is home to Beijing University, Qinghua University, some 60 institutions of higher education, and more than 200 research institutes affiliated to the CAS, government ministries, and the Beijing municipality. As early as 1980, inspired by the entrepreneurship of the Silicon Valley, Chen Chunxian, a nuclear fusion physicist from the CAS Institute of Physics, founded the first S&T enterprise in Zhongguancun. Back then a significant number of scientists and engineers made great efforts to seek outside support for applied research and development work that could directly benefit the economy and meet market needs. For example, technological findings from the CAS were turned to marketable products by more than one-third of the firms along the so-called "Electronics Street" (*Dianzi Yitiaojie*) in Zhongguancun, including the New Technology Company, a spin-off of the CAS Institute of Computing Technology and the forerunner of Lenovo. Founder, another successful Chinese start-up, was a spin-off from Beijing University, whose Chinese electronic publishing systems have come to dominate the world's Chinese publishing market (Lu, 2000). These companies promoted technology transfer from universities and research institutes and created a series of products with market potential and competitive edge. As a whole, in its initial development Zhongguancun saw a celebration of S&T start-ups not witnessed before in China's history. Those involved in such "risky" business ventures were said to "jump into the sea" (*xiahai*), highlighting the fact that many of these entrepreneurs were willing to give up secure positions within state-owned or state-run organizations for the chance to run their own companies.[5]

The "Electronics Street" evolved into the Beijing Experimental Zone of New Technology and Industrial Development in 1988 and

---

[5] The term, *xiahai*, carried a negative connotation when it was first used, meaning "to give up a respectful profession for a disdained one" such as acting and business. In its current usage, it means to jump on the bandwagon of money-making.

became the Zhongguancun Science Park in 1994. Moreover, the Zhongguancun model has stimulated enthusiasm for the rest of the nation to pursue high-technology entrepreneurship. Thus far, 53 science parks have been established at national level, and more at provincial level, where scientists and engineers have seen their initiatives and talents tapped and used to their full extent (Cao, 2004c).

Of course, the emergence of the Zhongguancun area was not without its challenges. Under former CCP Party Secretary Zhao Ziyang, the Zhongguancun "experiment" was monitored and reviewed carefully by the Chinese leadership, primarily because no one knew how it would evolve over time; nor did the leadership fully grasp the consequences of unleashing this type of entrepreneurial energy. The entire experiment almost met its demise after the June 4 Tiananmen Square event in 1989. Evidence began to appear that several local firms from within the zone had supplied funds and support to the Chinese students who were demonstrating in the square. Foremost among these firms was said to be Stone (*Sitong*), which was headed by successful entrepreneur Wan Runnan. Stone, with the help of some technology imported from a Japanese firm, had developed a Chinese printer that was proving to be popular in the local marketplace. When CCP officials discovered Wan's alleged role in the Tiananmen Square events, the entire Zhongguancun experiment was placed in jeopardy as party officials contemplated what to do about the future of Zhongguancun and whether further entrepreneurship should be encouraged. Many of the entrepreneurs were scientists and engineers who had left the security of state institutions to drive forward China's technological edge. Fortunately, even though many CCP members were skeptical, the decision was made to retain the Zhongguancun experiment, and today it is an area of Beijing that is thriving and represents one of the cutting edge areas of Chinese technological advance (Kennedy, 1997).

Entering the era of a knowledge-based economy, high-technology entrepreneurship has become a new fashion among China's young scientific professionals, many of whom are S&T students, especially computer and information technology, and have overseas study and work and entrepreneurship experience. Such companies as Sina, Sohu, Netease, Alibaba, Shanda, and Baidu, among others, have replaced Lenovo, Stone, and Founder as new symbols in this next wave of entrepreneurship and they are not confined to Zhongguancun any more. Listing some of these high-technology enterprises on the domestic and especially overseas stockmarkets has made their founders and core employees – many educated in the field of science and engineering themselves – into millionaires and even billionaires. These scientist-and-engineer-turned entrepreneurs have started to appear on the Chinese "richest lists," although non-high-technology entrepreneurs, especially real-estate developers, still dominate such lists. These companies may not pay their employees and even executives high salaries compared with their counterparts in the West (Kanellos, 2007), but they promote stock options and other incentives as a means to attract, retain, motivate, and compensate those who have accepted the risks associated with ventures whose longevity and survival are often uncertain even under the best of circumstances.

As mentioned, China has also attracted a significant amount of foreign direct investment, which has moved up the value chain from the labor-intensive manufacturing of toys, clothing, and furniture to more technology-intensive and R&D-intensive high-technology products, from computers and telecommunications equipment to semiconductors. China's coming of age as a new base for R&D endeavors by MNCs has created additional channels of opportunity for the utilization of Chinese technical talent. Some foreign firms, such as Intel, for example, have actually become the source of funds to enable some start-up enterprises to get off the ground. In the late 1990s, Intel created a new-venture fund in China to support the development of Chinese-language content products and software as a means of sparking the growth and expansion of personal computer sales, especially among Chinese consumers. Similarly, IDC, a Massachusetts-based information company that has made major investments in Chinese-language information technology- (IT-) related publications, established a similar fund focused on enabling local high technology start-ups to grow their businesses. Finally, the world of US venture capital has now found its footing in China and is gaining traction in identifying new business venture opportunities among the newest wave of Chinese technology entrepreneurs. Many of these firms have deployed ethnic Chinese staff, many with MBA degrees from some of the best business schools in Europe and the USA, to help build relationships and identify emerging investment opportunities. This all suggests that we have only seen the tip of the iceberg in terms of new career paths for scientists and engineers who are willing to bypass traditional career opportunities and explore the notion of starting and running their own businesses. In addition, this all supports the notion that continues to gain currency in China and is popular among returnees – "it is better to be the head of the chicken than the tail of the ox."

In many ways, the emergence of this new class of "technological entrepreneurs" represents the cutting edge of China's new industrial architecture. The future face of the Chinese economy, and the key source of China's evolving competitive advantage, will increasingly come from this new stratum in the economy. And, moreover, it will likely spearhead the transition to the knowledge economy that Chinese leaders are determined to nuture over the coming years.

Career prospect of young scientists

It is known that many of the most creative advances come from young researchers, and thus having a generation of young scientists and engineers in the pipeline is vital to a country's scientific enterprise. Fortunately, as mentioned in Chapter 3, China's S&T workforce, even at the leadership level, is not only well educated, but is also getting younger with a group of 45-year-olds becoming the core of the talent pool. Given the generation gap wrought by the Cultural Revolution and the "brain drain," young Chinese scientists shoulder more than their counterparts elsewhere, who have a historical responsibility for receiving the baton from the older generation and passing it along to the younger one. Over the years, the Chinese government and various S&T and educational institutions have initiated various programs to nurture leaders of Chinese science, and have made great efforts to lure young and outstanding scientists from overseas. The Cheung Kong Scholar Program under the Ministry of Education, the One Hundred Talent Program at the CAS, and the National Science Fund for Outstanding Young Scientists at the National Natural Science Foundation of China are such programs. As will be discussed in Chapter 6, many returnees have not yet established themselves, therefore, support from these programs has had an effect on them launching a successful career in China and becoming leaders within China's scientific community (Cao & Suttmeier, 2001).

However, given the limited number of scientists included in these programs, their experiences may not be representative. China's doctoral programs produced a record high number of PhDs in science and engineering in 2006, and the pipeline of students studying science and engineering at doctoral level has been filled. To China, the availability of a large number of young scientists willing to work very hard for relatively little financial compensation compared with other professions (to be discussed in the next section) is an asset that could contribute to China's scientific enterprise. Some observers believe that China's major competitive weapon will be its ability to move from an economic model, driven by cheap labor and cheap foreign capital, to a knowledge economy, driven by inexpensively generated intellectual know-how (Stevenson-Yang & DeWoskin, 2005). But, as prospective scientists, newly minted PhDs are certainly concerned about the availability of funding for their careers. Indeed, there is little doubt that the way Chinese young scientists are utilized and the nature of the environment in which they work are critical to maintaining the momentum for China's future development in S&T. In particular, their treatment in obtaining support for their research, promotion, and compensation to some extent will determine whether a scientific career is appealing for future bright students and whether science is a career path for those who are active in the workforce. Data about the number of young scientists receiving grants from the NSFC, China's major funding agency for basic research and applied-oriented basic research, represents a useful proxy of understanding their utilization (Table 5.2).

Among various types of funding at the NSFC, in 2006, general programs (*mianshang xiangmu*) supported projects with an average of RMB260 000 (US$33 000) for three years and projects receiving support under key programs (*zhongdian xiangmu*), involving participants from more than one institution, received average grants of RMB1.5 million (US $188 000) for four years. Apparently, grantees of the general program were, on average, 41.15 years old in 2006 compared with 43.28 years old in 2001, while those supported by the key program have also witnessed a drop in their average age from 52 years old in 2001 to 49 years old in 2006.

In 2001, about a quarter of the general grants went to scientists aged 35 years and younger, at which age they likely had just received their PhDs; by 2006, the grants going to that age group increased to about 30 percent, although the big-money key programs have experienced no percentage change for the same age group of principal investigators in between.

If in 2001 the 31- and 50-year-old age groups accounted for some 70% of general program grants; in 2006 scientists at these ages were

Table 5.2 (a) *Age profile of recipients of general programs at the National Natural Science Foundation of China (persons, %)*

Year		Total	Age group (years)											Average age (years)
			25	26–30	31–35	36–40	41–45	46–50	51–55	56–60	61–65	66–70	71	
2001	N	4435	4	212	858	1331	604	341	238	398	326	95	28	43.28
	%	100.00	0.09	4.78	19.35	30.01	13.62	7.69	5.37	8.97	7.35	2.14	0.63	
2002	N	5808	2	335	1080	1795	843	590	261	419	334	113	36	42.57
	%	100.00	0.03	5.77	18.60	30.91	14.51	10.16	4.49	7.21	5.75	1.95	0.62	
2003	N	6359	2	401	1282	1842	1044	731	303	381	240	103	30	41.83
	%	100.00	0.03	6.31	20.16	28.97	16.42	11.50	4.76	5.99	3.77	1.62	0.47	
2004	N	7711	1	513	1542	1849	1734	939	380	360	247	111	35	41.73
	%	100.00	0.01	6.65	20.00	23.98	22.49	12.18	4.93	4.67	3.20	1.44	0.45	
2005	N	9111	3	582	1906	2010	2368	1047	422	343	275	116	39	41.49
	%	100.00	0.03	6.39	20.92	22.06	25.99	11.49	4.63	3.76	3.02	1.27	0.43	
2006	N	10271	5	725	2312	1939	2906	1106	558	327	239	114	40	41.15
	%	100.00	0.05	7.06	22.51	18.88	28.29	10.77	5.43	3.18	2.33	1.11	0.39	

Table 5.2 (b) *Age profile of recipients of key programs at the National Natural Science Foundation of China*

| Year | | Total | Age group (years) | | | | | | | | | | | Average age (years) |
			≤25	26–30	31–35	36–40	41–45	46–50	51–55	56–60	61–65	66–70	≥71	
2001	N	124	0	0	2	23	26	7	13	13	26	12	2	51.88
	%	100.00	0.00	0.00	1.61	18.55	20.97	5.65	10.48	10.48	20.97	9.68	1.61	
2002	N	208	0	0	8	48	28	28	11	21	35	23	6	51.12
	%	100.00	0.00	0.00	3.85	23.08	13.46	13.46	5.29	10.10	16.83	11.06	2.88	
2003	N	252	0	1	3	52	43	41	15	27	39	22	9	51.08
	%	100.00	0.00	0.40	1.19	20.63	17.06	16.27	5.95	10.71	15.48	8.73	3.57	
2004	N	224	0	0	6	40	52	48	11	22	21	13	11	49.58
	%	100.00	0.00	0.00	2.68	17.86	23.21	21.43	4.91	9.82	9.38	5.80	4.91	
2005	N	303	0	0	5	40	94	61	21	33	18	21	10	49.35
	%	100.00	0.00	0.00	1.65	13.20	31.02	20.13	6.93	10.89	5.94	6.93	3.30	
2006	N	277	0	0	6	26	99	58	22	19	24	15	8	49.08
	%	100.00	0.00	0.00	2.17	9.39	35.74	20.94	7.94	6.86	8.66	5.42	2.89	

Source: www.nsfc.gov.cn (accessed on October 2, 2007).

awarded 80% of such grants. Likewise, in the competition for key program project support, the same age groups of principal investigators had seen the portion receiving grants increase from some 55% in 2001 to almost three-quarters (75%) in 2006. In particular, while the age groups of 41–45 and 61–65 seemed to stand out in 2001 in terms of receiving grants from key programs, five years later, those aged between 41 and 50, the so-called "middle-aged scientists," became important recipients of the key program support – gobbling up more than half of the larger grants. Although we do not know how likely a young scientist compared with an older one is to win an NSFC grant, we may conclude that there has been a trend in so far as younger and younger scientists are receiving larger and larger shares of NSFC grant monies.

Utilization and income of scientists and engineers

In discussing the utilization of scientists and engineers, we cannot ignore the issue of compensation, even though salary rates alone are not an accurate measure of the real value of scientists and engineers as a whole. Compensation trends in China seem to reflect the country's growing integration into the global talent pool, especially among the high-end component of the Chinese talent pool.

In pre-reform China, intellectuals as a whole received a salary higher than that of manual laborers, although it was lower compared with wage levels before 1949 when the People's Republic was established (Chen, 2004). Indeed, high-ranking intellectuals (*gaoji zhishi fenzi*) were in the highest income bracket in China and enjoyed favorable treatment in housing, healthcare, and other benefits (Cheng, 1965: 149–54). Scientists and engineers were especially privileged, enjoying not only higher social and political status but also material benefits associated with that status. Even in the early 1960s, when the country experienced extreme economic difficulties in the aftermath of the Great Leap Forward, and both staples and scarce consumer goods were rationed, those involved in strategic weapons programs, many being very senior in the scientific community and returnees from the West, were given special treatment (Nie, 1988). This is one of the reasons why intellectuals were attacked severely during the Cultural Revolution. Nevertheless, despite being attacked, being sent to factories and the countryside, losing many of their privileges, and having their salaries cut, they still were better off than factory workers economically. College graduates, including those "worker–peasant–soldier students" (*gongnongbing xueyuan*), still earned a salary similar to their predecessors before the Cultural Revolution, which was higher than most others. What frustrated intellectuals the most was that their knowledge was not appreciated and utilized, and that their loyalty was called into question simply because they were honest (and perhaps courageous) enough to state their opinions about what was right or wrong with the regime.

In the aftermath of the Cultural Revolution, the four modernizations drive, launched in 1978, called for the respect of knowledge and talented people. Leaders such as Deng Xiaoping, after traveling abroad to places such as Japan and the USA, recognized just how far behind the rest of the world China had fallen economically and technologically. A major commitment from the highest echelons of the Chinese leadership was made to close the prevailing gap as quickly as possible. Chinese intellectuals saw their "damaged" images cleaned and their political and social status restored. However, higher social prestige was not translated into decent economic benefits during the early reform era; in reality, intellectuals were disappointed by their inability to cash in on the regime's new reforms and open-door policy. Ironically, the early beneficiaries of market-oriented reform, between the late 1970s and the early 1990s, were private entrepreneurs (*getihu*) who became prosperous or rich first by taking advantage of loopholes in the law and engaging in activities, some of which, from the perspective of the twenty-first century, might be considered to be dishonest, unethical, and illicit, if not illegal. This was the new era of Deng Xiaoping and the most popular notion was "to get rich is glorious." This resulted in an "inversion of intellectuals and manual laborers in income" (*nao ti daogua*). There was a frequently quoted saying, "those who made atomic bombs earn less than those peddling tea-leaf-soaked eggs on the street, and those who perform surgery earn less than hair-cutters" (*zao yuanzidan buru mai chayedan, na shoushudao buru na titoudao*),[6] implying that compared with other social groups that benefited more from the reforms initiatives, scientists, surgeons, and intellectuals as a whole earned an income in

---

[6] In Chinese, *dan* in *yuanzidan* and *chayedan* share the same pronunciation, while *dao* is knife of different types in *shoushudao* and *titoudao*.

reverse proportion to their contribution to society. In fact, one of the reasons why intellectuals supported the pro-democracy movement in 1989 was that they felt poorly treated, underpaid, and burdened with difficult living conditions (Miller, 1996).

Intellectuals were also constrained by the cultural tradition (and constraint) of despising money and business. In the mid-1980s, the reform of the S&T management system aimed at not only strengthening the linkage of research and the economy and raising the efficiency of scientific research, but also holding the scientific workforce accountable for results. Consequently, many scientists and engineers had to find funding for their research themselves and to become involved in technology-transfer activities from which they may gain some money to supplement their salary. Quite a number of scientists and engineers from state-owned enterprises and institutions had to "moonlight" at township and village enterprises at weekends, thus receiving the name of "Saturday engineers."[7] In fact, one of the reasons why intellectuals supported the pro-democracy movement in 1989 was that they felt poorly treated, underpaid, and burdened with difficult living conditions (Miller, 1996).

Nevertheless, one of the major sources of difficulty experienced by the more entrepreneurial of these scientists and engineers was the uncertainty surrounding the rules about what they were or were not allowed to do to earn extra income. Several engineers, who ventured out as "consultants" to various localities to assist township and municipal governments address a range of technical problems and issues, soon found themselves in political hot water when they requested payment for their services. Some were reprimanded for violating socialist principles, while others received even harsher treatment when their attempts to secure payment were met with claims of extortion or bribery. There also were several instances where engineers tied their compensation to actual performance and results – a type of "success fee" – only to find that after actually solving one problem or another, their expectations about receiving substantial compensation were deemed unreasonable and underhanded by local officials. In such cases, the engineers were

---

[7] Such moonlighting activities often created problems within the *danwei* as these scientists and engineers could potentially use their facilities and research. Some had their payments confiscated or even were charged with corruption and theft of state property.

threatened with imprisonment or substantial fines if they demanded any more than just a token payment for their services. Many simply walked away highly discouraged as well as extremely frustrated about the lack of legal support for actions that had been encouraged by the central government in Beijing.

A series of salary reforms were carried out in the 1980s and 1990s to correct the shortcomings of the compensation system for China's scientific and technical community (Cooke, 2004). These reforms were also a response to the realization that the country was suffering from a shortage of talented personnel; economic hardship had driven many young qualified academics to leave for better life and career opportunities overseas. This situation gradually led to a "war for talent." The impact of this intensified competition for brainpower may be seen in the changes that were introduced across many Chinese institutions of learning; they included increases in salaries and other benefits. The 1985 salary reform, for example, stipulated that an individual's salary be composed of three parts: a basic component, a seniority component, and a component associated with the position held. One of the considerations in the S&T reforms was to allow scientists and engineers to transfer technology and to set up high- and new-technology companies as a way of supplementing their income. In 1986, the government authorized universities, research institutes, hospitals, and other *danwei* to appoint and promote professionals, with those appointed and promoted receiving a salary increase. By 1992, out of the 23 million professionals, 5.42 million had reached senior ranks (Chen, 2004: 229–45). The government further allowed scientists and engineers to have concurrent positions by legitimating the "Saturday engineer" phenomenon, and to receive part of their income from consulting and technology-transfer. Some provinces started to reward scientists and engineers who had made tremendous contributions to the local economy with passenger cars, houses, and bonuses as high as half a million RMB.

Institutions of learning have also experimented with new incentives to entice and retain excellent scholars. In 1997, for example, Qinghua University started to offer a special stipend to some of its faculty members. In 1999, when the 985 Program was initiated, Beijing and Qinghua universities used part of these government funds to raise the salaries of their faculty members and recruit new professors from overseas. At Fudan University in Shanghai, under a similar scheme, faculty members received an annual stipend ranging from RMB10 000 to RMB200 000 depending upon their appointments. As mentioned in Chapter 2, the Cheung Kong Scholar Program, launched in 1998, mandates that its recipients receive a stipend of RMB100 000 from the Ministry of Education, on top of their regular salary and other benefits, including housing, from the universities where the endowed professors work. The One Hundred Talent Program at the CAS awards a grant of RMB2 million, which includes a housing allowance and a salary component. Universities have also improved living conditions for their faculty members, especially those young and newly recruited, by turning crowded dormitories (*tongzilou*), a kind of building with a long corridor through the middle of each floor lined by small rooms on either side and without private kitchens or lavatories, into truly liveable apartments. In fact, incentives provided at institutional level were sometimes significantly higher than those provided by the programs mentioned above; today, talented professors and scientists can negotiate their salary, housing, research grant, and other fringe benefits directly with their potential employers.

Non-state employers, such as FIEs and especially MNCs, have entered the competition for Chinese talent as well. Those scientists and engineers and other professionals employed by MNCs have seen their salaries and benefits increase several times higher than their counterparts at domestic institutions and enterprises. In fact, according to estimates by the Department of Organization of the CCP Central Committee, employees at China's non-state sector have reached 50 million and growing, including not only workers, peasants, cadres, but also an increasing number of professionals (*People's Daily*, June 11, 2007: 10). Apparently, professionals within the non-state sector have found their knowledge and skills better utilized and better compensated than their counterparts at state-owned enterprises and institutions.

Gradually, scientists and engineers have seen the gap between higher social status and lower material rewards largely disappear. Moreover, since the late 1990s, they have taken important positions and enjoyed not only significant social status but also higher incomes and other privileges, comparable with their predecessors during the pre-Cultural Revolution era and their counterparts in other countries. It appears that today's intellectuals no longer carry the "better performance with cheap compensation" (*jialian wumei*) image of the 1980s. Most intellectuals feel that their overall income level allows them to main-tain a high standard of living and are optimistic about their future status with the nation's active promotion of an innovation strategy. The drive to foster the emergence of an innovation-focussed economy has created the conditions for a more symbiotic relationship between the S&T talent community and the Chinese government. With support for innovation at its apex, there is now a sense that the troubles experienced by intellectuals in the past will not re-appear in the near future, especially as the Chinese leadership is heavily dependent on the S&T talent pool to help facilitate the transition to a new economic and technological foundation for future growth and development.

Income of scientific workforce in the reform era

There is no precise information available on the income of Chinese scientists and engineers, nor is there accurate information on the income of Chinese professionals and those who are counted as HRST. The closest systematic information is annual wage by sectors, which shows how employees in the research sector – scientific research and technical services between 1978 and 2002, and scientific research, technical service, and geological prospecting thereafter (Table 5.3) – have fared relative to those in other sectors. It should be noted that although this is not necessarily the most accurate indicator, it does serve as a useful proxy of the group's income in so far as what is reported here is the average of all the employees in each of the respective sectors of the economy.

In 1978 when the reform and open-door initiative started, employ-ees in the scientific research and technical services sector, on average, earned RMB669 (US $398 at the exchange rate of US $1 = RMB1.68) a year, ranked sixth among all sectors, lagging behind those in pro-duction and the supply of electricity, gas, and water (RMB850), con-struction (RMB714), geological prospecting and water conservancy (RMB708), transportation, storage, post and telecommunications (RMB694), and mining and quarrying (RMB674). In the years to follow, along with all employees, those in the scientific research and technical services sector saw their wages increase. However, their rank remained where it was in 1978.

The year 1992 seems to be a watershed; it was at this time that China's then paramount leader, Deng Xiaoping, toured Southern

Table 5.3 (a) *Average wage of Chinese employees by sector (RMB, 1978–2002)*

Year	National	Farming, forestry, animal husbandry, and fishery	Mining and quarrying	Manufacturing	Production and supply of electricity, gas, and water	Construction	Geological prospecting and water conservancy	Transport, storage, post, and telecommunication	Wholesale and retail trade and catering
1978	615	470	676	597	850	714	708	694	551
1980	762	616	854	752	1 035	855	895	832	692
1985	1 148	878	1 324	1 112	1 239	1 362	1 406	1 275	1 007
1989	1 935	1 389	2 378	1 900	2 241	2 166	2 199	2 197	1 660
1990	2 140	1 541	2 718	2 073	2 656	2 384	2 465	2 426	1 818
1991	2 340	1 652	2 942	2 289	2 922	2 649	2 707	2 686	1 981
1992	2 711	1 828	3 209	2 635	3 392	3 066	3 222	3 114	2 204
1993	3 371	2 042	3 711	3 348	4 319	3 779	3 717	4 273	2 679
1994	4 538	2 819	4 679	4 283	6 155	4 894	5 450	5 690	3 537
1995	5 500	3 522	5 757	5 169	7 843	5 785	5 962	6 948	4 248
1996	6 210	4 050	6 482	5 642	8 816	6 249	6 581	7 870	4 661
1997	6 470	4 311	6 833	5 933	9 649	6 655	7 160	8 600	4 845
1998	7 479	4 528	7 242	7 064	10 478	7 456	7 951	9 808	5 865
1999	8 346	4 832	7 521	7 794	11 513	7 982	8 821	10 991	6 417
2000	9 371	5 184	8 340	8 750	12 830	8 735	9 622	12 319	7 190
2001	10 870	5 741	9 586	9 774	14 590	9 484	10 957	14 167	8 192
2002	12 422	6 398	11 017	11 001	16 440	10 279	12 303	16 044	9 398

Table 5.3 (a) (cont.)

Year	Finance and insurance	Real estate	Social services	Healthcare, sports, and social welfare	Education, culture and arts, radio, film, and television	Scientific research and polytechnic services	Government agencies, party agencies, and social organizations	Others
1978	610	548	392	573	545	669	655	
1980	720	694	475	718	700	851	800	
1985	1 154	1 028	777	1 124	1 166	1 272	1 127	
1989	1 867	1 925	1 926	1 959	1 883	2 118	1 874	
1990	2 097	2 243	2 170	2 209	2 117	2 403	2 113	
1991	2 255	2 507	2 431	2 370	2 243	2 573	2 275	
1992	2 829	3 106	2 844	2 812	2 715	3 115	2 768	
1993	3 740	4 320	3 588	3 413	3 278	3 904	3 505	3 371
1994	6 712	6 288	5 026	5 126	4 923	6 162	4 962	5 213
1995	7 376	7 330	5 982	5 860	5 435	6 846	5 526	6 295
1996	8 406	8 337	6 778	6 790	6 144	8 048	6 340	7 184
1997	9 734	9 190	7 553	7 599	6 759	9 049	6 981	6 838
1998	10 633	10 302	8 333	8 493	7 474	10 241	7 773	8 481
1999	12 046	11 505	9 263	9 664	8 510	11 601	8 978	10 068
2000	13 478	12 616	10 339	10 930	9 482	13 620	10 043	11 098
2001	16 277	14 096	11 869	12 933	11 452	16 437	12 142	12 590
2002	19 135	15 501	13 499	14 795	13 290	19 113	13 975	14 215

Table 5.3 (b) *Average wage of Chinese employees by sector (RMB, 2003–2006)*

Year	National	Agriculture, forestry, animal husbandry, and fishery	Mining	Manufacturing	Production and supply of electricity, gas, and water	Construction	Transport, storage, and post
2003	14 040	6 969	13 682	12 496	18 752	11 478	15 973
2004	16 024	7 611	16 874	14 033	21 805	12 770	18 381
2005	18 364	8 309	20 626	15 757	25 073	14 338	21 352
2006	21 001	9 430	24 335	17 966	28 765	16 406	24 623

Year	Information transmission, computer service, and software	Wholesale and retail	Hotels and catering service	Financial intermediation	Real estate	Leasing and business service	Scientific research, technical service, and geological prospecting
2003	32 244	10 939	11 083	22 457	17 182	16 501	20 636
2004	34 988	12 923	12 535	26 982	18 712	18 131	23 593
2005	40 558	15 241	13 857	32 228	20 581	20 992	27 434
2006	44 763	17 736	15 206	39 280	22 578	23 648	31 909

Table 5.3 (b) (*cont.*)

Year	Management of water conservancy and public facilities	Service to household and other services	Education	Health, social security, and social welfare	Culture, sports, and entertainment	Public management and social organizations
2003	12 095	12 900	14 399	16 352	17 268	15 533
2004	13 336	14 152	16 277	18 617	20 730	17 609
2005	14 753	16 642	18 470	21 048	22 885	20 505
2006	16 140	18 935	21 134	23 898	26 126	22 883

Source: National Bureau of Statistics, various years.

China to revitalize the reform agenda that had been halted after the 1989 Tiananmen Square crackdown. In that year, the annual wage for employees in the scientific research and technical service sector ranked fifth at RMB3115 (US $565 at the exchange rate of US $1 = RMB5.51). Ten years later, in 2002, that sector moved to the second spot, in terms of wages by employment sectors, with an average annual salary of RMB19 113 (US $2308 at the exchange rate of US $1 = RMB8.28), slightly less than finance and insurance's RMB19 135 (in fact, between 1999 and 2002, these two sectors ranked first alternatively on the sector salary list).

In 2003, China changed the way of reporting its national employee wage statistics, not only combining "scientific research and technical service" with "geological prospecting," into "scientific research, technical service, and geological prospecting," but also adding a new sector – "information transmission, computer services, and software" ("information sector" for short). The latter, which presumably employs a significant number of computer scientists and software engineers, was the sector offering the highest salaries – RMB44 763 (US $5616 at the exchange rate of US $1 = RMB7.97), on average, in 2006, followed by finance (RMB39 280 or US $4928) and research (RMB31 909 or US $4004). More noticeably, wages in the sectors of information and research increased along with an increase in employment, and at a pace that has been faster than the national average, especially in the research sector. This is in contrast to the perception that with more graduates entering the job market every year and competition for jobs becoming increasingly intense, salaries for many technical and professional positions would be lower or at least flat.[8] This seems to suggest that scientists and engineers may finally benefit more, if not most, from the reform and open-door policies. Continuous investment in education and scientific research over the past ten years has led to significant changes in the lives of those working in scientific and technical fields.

Within the research sector, which by definition is composed of research and experimental development, professional technical

---

[8] This was what happened in the USA in the 1970s when so many Americans had been getting college degrees that the relative wages of white-collar professionals had started to fall. Consequently, it no longer paid to go to college (Freeman, 1976).

services, services of science and technology exchanges and promotion, and geological prospecting, the S&T workforce includes not only scientists and engineers, but also skilled technicians and other staff. In addition, other sectors also employ scientists and engineers; their wage information is included in these sectors rather than in the research sector. Nevertheless, the research sector, by its nature, appears most likely to employ a higher percentage of scientists and engineers who surely have above-average earning power in the current economic environment. That said, however, because they are deployed across a broad spectrum of the Chinese economy as a whole, the wage rates reported here likely understate the salaries earned specifically by scientists and engineers.

Many of the most competitive pay positions are associated with non-state sectors, most likely FIEs; their employees tend to make more money than their counterparts at state-owned institutions and enterprises in all sectors except higher education and healthcare, where the state still dominates and even monopolizes (Table 5.4). In 2006, state-owned employees earned more than the national average wage and non-state-owned employees, but in the information and research sectors, state-owned employees earned about two-thirds or one-quarter less than non-state employees. In particular, a non-state-owned employee in computer services earned as much as RMB66 749 (US $8375) in 2006. Over the years, the number of non-state-owned employees has closed in on and finally surpassed state-owned employment in the information sector in 2006, although state-owned *danwei* are still the main employers in scientific research with six times more employees than in non-state-owned enterprises.

Again, it is important to recognize that salaries, as reported, represent the average for a sector so that the scientific workforce is quite likely to earn more, sometimes several times more, than has been suggested here. It is reported, for example, that about 40 percent of intellectuals earn an annual salary of more than RMB100 000 (*Nanfang Daily*, January 18, 2003). According to a survey conducted among intellectuals in Shanghai, Guangzhou, and Nanjing, in early 2006, college professors on average earned RMB70 000–100 000 annually (*Outlook Dongfang Weekly*, January 4, 2006).

Over the years, the research sector and the new information sector have been better off when comparing their employees' earnings with the national average. Between the late 1970s and the early 1990s, the

Table 5.4 Average wage in the information and research sectors, by ownership (RMB, 2003–2006)

Sector	2003			2004			2005			2006		
	Average	State-owned	Others	Average	State-owned	Others	Average	State-owned	Others	Average	State-owned	Others
National	14 040	14 577	14 574	16 024	16 729	16 259	18 364	19 313	18 244	21 001	22 112	20 755
Information transfer, computer services, and Software	32 244	26 572	42 867	34 988	29 131	44 683	40 558	31 654	50 509	44 763	34 328	55 135
Telecoms and other information transfer services	30 481	27 096	41 715	32 264	29 458	40 414	36 941	31 590	46 863	40 242	33 947	50 240
Computer services	41 722	14 470	55 406	47 725	22 898	60 701	52 637	32 545	58 470	60 749	41 894	66 327
Software industry	36 873	22 568	38 981	42 835	26 995	44 321	52 784	33 897	54 038	59 385	43 385	60 512
Scientific research, technical service, and geological perambulation	20 636	19 975	26 061	23 593	22 976	29 346	27 434	26 309	35 154	31 909	30 459	41 003
Research and experimental development	22 391	22 307	27 057	25 052	24 851	29 987	29 054	28 597	36 366	33 497	33 065	38 814

Professional technique services	22 046	21 111	26 211	25 349	24 922	28 255	29 460	28 727	33 170	34 723	33 310	41 000
Services of science and technology exchanges and promotion	16 877	15 190	25 981	19 923	18 204	29 852	23 574	19 860	38 608	27 045	23 602	40 372
Geologic prospecting	15 277	15 111	21 427	18 458	17 729	46 494	21 366	20 576	58 293	24 971	24 131	58 046

Source: National Bureau of Statistics, various years.

relative earning power of the research sector was only 1.1, which means that salaries of its employees were 10 percent more than the national average. Later on, the relative earning power of the research sector jumped to around 1.5, while that of the information sector has been over 2.0 since the sector has been treated as a separate item.

Geographically, Beijing, Shanghai, Tianjin, Jiangsu, Zhejiang, and Guangdong are the provinces and municipalities where booming economies have provided employees with a premium salary in almost all sectors (Table 5.5).[9] Employees in the information sector do extremely well in Beijing and Shanghai, and in 2006 saw their salary to be 1.8 times more than the national average in this sector; those in Zhejiang earned 27% more than the national average. For the research sector, Beijing and Shanghai continue to stand out, with employees making 50% more than the national average in 2006, followed by Guangdong and Tianjin. But even in these regions, several non-S&T-related sectors fared better than or as well as the information and research sectors, including finance and public management and social organization. Indeed, civil service, which includes employment in public management and social organization, has become one of the hottest job choices for Chinese graduates, including S&T majors, as such employment not only means a safe job, but also provides good healthcare, a good retirement program and pension, and other such benefits. The earning power of civil service employees in Beijing, Shanghai, and Zhejiang is significantly higher. This explains why, in 2005, about 540 000 people took the civil servant examination, roughly a 16-fold increase over those who took it in 2001 (Fan, 2007).

In addition to the wages paid by employers, Chinese professionals, especially high-ranking ones, also receive various benefits – some intrinsic – from the state and other sources because of official-centeredness, which relates professional title to the *jibie* of a civil servant in terms of benefits. In science and engineering, as mentioned, a member (*yuanshi*) of the CAS or the CAE is entitled to a stipend from the state, though a meager RMB200, life-time employment, and other benefits from regional governments or the institution to which they are affiliated; they also receive de facto privileges equivalent to a

---

[9] The exceptions are Tibet, Qinghai, and Ningxia, three autonomous regions dominated by minorities, which are most likely receiving favorable treatment and subsidies from central government.

Table 5.5 *Average wage of Chinese employees, by region and select sectors (RMB, 2006)*

	Average	Information transmission, computer service and software	Financial intermediation	Real estate	Scientific research, technical service, and geological prospecting	Education	Health, social security, and social welfare	Public management and social organization
National	21 001	44 763	39 280	22 578	31 909	21 134	23 898	22 883
Beijing	40 117	81 851	113 092	32 275	54 231	42 565	48 167	48 714
Tianjin	28 682	43 366	59 796	27 939	44 993	29 512	31 299	32 660
Hebei	16 590	27 394	25 081	15 927	26 102	16 117	16 878	15 973
Shanxi	18 300	22 586	24 628	12 092	19 316	17 726	15 582	16 565
Inner Mongolia	18 469	26 139	24 889	15 197	23 772	21 393	20 510	20 553
Liaoning	19 624	39 741	32 284	16 912	26 823	20 473	20 639	21 708
Jilin	16 583	26 807	22 747	14 762	20 046	17 901	15 483	17 364
Heilongjiang	16 505	32 926	26 793	14 666	22 517	19 545	18 426	19 541
Shanghai	41 188	83 525	69 043	48 420	48 234	40 263	45 267	43 118
Jiangsu	23 782	44 202	43 495	28 444	37 155	25 647	29 394	35 469
Zhejiang	27 820	57 027	59 910	30 069	40 894	39 224	42 016	46 770
Anhui	17 949	25 695	25 532	17 229	21 198	17 599	17 667	18 831
Fujian	19 318	40 817	42 359	21 588	27 701	21 933	24 076	24 645
Jiangxi	15 590	21 810	25 069	13 934	20 592	16 156	18 377	16 195
Shandong	19 228	36 522	33 304	19 241	26 986	21 877	22 950	21 584

Table 5.5 (*cont.*)

	Average	Information transmission, computer service and software	Financial intermediation	Real estate	Scientific research, technical service, and geological prospecting	Education	Health, social security, and social welfare	Public management and social organization
Henan	16 981	24 436	26 988	15 658	22 713	17 213	17 180	16 238
Hubei	16 048	30 328	23 619	16 925	24 693	17 078	17 733	19 436
Hunan	17 850	32 178	25 966	17 831	21 655	18 688	22 124	17 991
Guangdong	26 186	53 121	55 508	26 286	46 587	26 706	33 319	35 142
Guangxi	18 064	30 940	29 576	16 551	22 498	17 039	20 690	20 330
Hainan	15 890	43 621	34 209	16 503	16 651	20 808	20 711	21 161
Chongqing	19 215	34 996	39 755	18 053	27 525	19 133	22 228	22 640
Sichuan	17 852	34 048	31 503	16 993	30 164	16 552	21 436	19 705
Guizhou	16 815	24 067	29 549	12 039	20 411	16 719	18 834	17 750
Yunnan	18 711	27 880	28 797	14 346	21 122	18 666	19 912	18 257
Tibet	31 518	66 882	60 018	34 793	34 625	30 062	32 065	34 234
Shaanxi	16 918	38 484	26 917	17 920	23 705	17 232	16 383	14 446
Gansu	17 246	16 866	19 826	12 239	20 403	18 997	17 491	17 824
Qinghai	22 679	33 080	27 321	12 959	35 352	24 417	24 564	24 163
Ningxia	21 239	35 662	37 628	15 625	22 670	21 026	18 662	20 191
Xinjiang	17 819	28 513	28 647	15 425	21 220	19 663	20 053	20 356

Source: National Bureau of Statistics, 2007: 173–5.

vice minister or vice governor in terms of housing, medical care, and transportation. Professors and other intellectuals at similar ranks enjoy a lesser, but nonetheless still significant, benefits package. Experts designated at national and provincial levels receive special stipends or monthly salary supplements. In 2004, for example, those experts receiving special stipends at the national level reached 145 000 or about 8 percent of senior professionals. In addition, many college professors in Shanghai, Guangzhou, and Nanjing engage in extra teaching outside their home institutions to make extra income (*Outlook Dongfang Weekly*, January 4, 2006). Researchers also earn extra money by publishing in journals catalogued by the *Science Citation Index* (SCI) at a couple of hundreds to hundreds of thousands of RMB depending upon where they publish their work.

Satisfaction of S&T workers

Income aside, self-assessment by scientists and engineers is probably a better way to measure the utilization of their expertise. According to a survey of 7000 S&T workers by the China Association for Science and Technology (CAST), the umbrella organization of Chinese S&T societies, in 2003, less than half of respondents were "very much" and "somewhat satisfied" with their jobs and only 13.8% were "not satisfied" with their job; satisfaction was higher for those in the East and with higher professional ranks. Among them, 6.7% indicated that their ability was fully utilized, another one-third had 80% of their ability utilized, 43.9% saw 50–80% of their expertise utilized, with the rest less than 50% of their ability utilized (CAST Research Team on Survey of Chinese S&T Workers, 2004b: 24–5 and 132). That is, there is still room for improvement to satisfy S&T workers and better utilize their expertise. A similar survey of over 5000 S&T workers at non-state-owned enterprises and institutions by the CAST in 2002 also found that employees wanted their working environment improved and, not surprisingly, their level of satisfaction with the job was correlated to their income (CAST Research Team on Survey of Chinese S&T Workers 2004a: 19–20).

For those working at state-owned institutions, close to 90% of respondents to the CAST survey of S&T workers in 2003 claimed to have smooth relations with members of research teams, which may contribute significantly to their job satisfaction (CAST Research Team on Survey of Chinese S&T Workers, 2004b: 122). Nevertheless, as will be discussed in Chapter 6, the Chinese scientists with domestic doctoral degrees felt that they had been treated unequally compared with those trained overseas.

S&T workers were not so satisfied with the research environment in which they work (CAST Research Team on Survey of Chinese S&T Workers, 2004b: 94). One of their concerns was increasing incidents of misconduct in research. One-third of the S&T workers surveyed had noticed such incidents and an equal percentage of respondents thought the situation "very serious" and "somewhat serious" (CAST Research Team on Survey of Chinese S&T Workers, 2004b: 133). Pressure to perform is surely one of the reasons that have contributed to the rise of misconduct and fraud in science as significant investment in scientific enterprise in recent years has not yielded equally significant achievements. According to surveys, on average, Chinese S&T workers in both state-owned and non-state sectors work 46 hours a week with some individual's working week lasting for more than 60 hours; and usually, the higher the educational attainment, the longer the working week (CAST Research Team on Survey of Chinese S&T Workers, 2004a: 19; CAST Research Team on Survey of Chinese S&T Workers, 2004b: 25–6).

Conclusion

This chapter has discussed various issues involved in the utilization of scientists and engineers in China. Scientists and engineers are part of China's vast community of intellectuals, which, as a social group, has experienced a variety of ups and downs in terms of status, stature, and political standing between 1949 and the present period. Although often mistrusting intellectuals as a group, and periodically uncertain of the loyalties of even top scientists and engineers, the CCP has also been pragmatic toward intellectuals in general, and scientists and engineers in particular, by giving them autonomy in their areas of expertise as long as they do not go beyond certain "politically defined" boundaries. The once very powerful job assignment system has disappeared as market reforms have proceeded, and consequently college graduates have more freedom to choose where they want to work and work satisfactorily. Job mobility has become a reality with more S&T personnel moving from R&D institutes to enterprises, which has made it possible to further strengthen the role of enterprises in China's national innovation system. Young scientists have seen increasing opportunities in terms of receiving grants from the NSFC, China's leading funding agency for scientific research, thus making scientific research as a career option more attractive to young scientists at the onset of their professional lives. The development of China's high-technology industry has also opened more opportunities for S&T personnel, especially those with entrepreneurial aspirations who have the willingness to start their own businesses and assume the risks associated with pursuing that course of careers.

More importantly, Chinese scientists and engineers have seen not only their social status, but also their income raised. As a proxy for the S&T workforce, wages of employees in S&T-related sectors such as scientific research and information technology have outperformed those in other sectors; in fact, R&D and information services have become among the top-paying fields in recent years. On average, in 2006, a software engineer earned twice as much as an average Chinese employee and a researcher one and half times as much. If they happened to be in Beijing and Shanghai and/or employed by an FIE, they would do even better. On one hand, this phenomenon reflects the sustained attractiveness of the S&T professions, which, along with the increasing share of young scientists being supported for their research at the NSFC, sends a clear and strong, positive signal to those who are interested in pursuing a technical career in China. On the other, it may reflect the paucity of talented and qualified scientists and engineers in China, which could be a problem as demand for such individuals is increasing steadily. If the latter is the case, the implications are clear: China's higher educational system needs to do a better job – turning out not only more but also more employable graduates to meet increasing demands across all sectors of the economy. The issues of demand and supply of S&T talent are discussed more fully in Chapter 7.

Finally, to more fully understand the issues surrounding utilization of China's scientific and technical talent, it is necessary to examine the question from within the context of its evolving political, economic, and national security environment. As the regime has become more self-confident, especially in the aftermath of the 2008 Olympics, and as the imperatives of technological advance have grown in importance, the place and position of the S&T community have changed in positive ways from the situation that existed during the Maoist period. These changes, for the most part, reflect the changing agenda of the Chinese leadership – both the party and the state – as well as the different challenges which face the regime today versus those of its predecessors. The Maoist political agenda was of paramount importance during its heyday of the 1950s to the mid-1970s; the regime also felt under siege from within and without. Paranoia and xenophobia were at an all time high during this period, and thus produced policies and actions that clearly saw the S&T community as potentially threatening to regime legitimacy at various points in time. Yet, even during this period, the demands of national security made it necessary to adopt much of an inclusive set of policies toward scientists and engineers to help drive China's advanced weapons programs.

The agenda of the Chinese leadership under President Hu Jintao and Premier Wen Jiabao, although no less challenging in many respects, reflects a rather different set of issues and concerns. No doubt, there remain major apprehensions about maintaining the authority and legitimacy of the CCP. That recognized, it also must be acknowledged that the complexion of the leadership itself has evolved, with more and more scientific and technical personnel in positions of authority, and growing numbers of overseas-trained individuals becoming national- and local-level leaders. Most important, the situation within the Chinese economy commands a new set of skills and talents to move to the next phase of China's modernization drive. As the focus of the 15-year S&T Medium- to Long-Term Plan (MLP) suggests, moving toward a knowledge-centered, innovation-driven economy is no longer simply desirable for China, it has now become a strategic imperative because of the huge environmental damage wreaked upon the country from the growth approach of the last two-plus decades. The Chinese leadership recognizes, as do many foreign observers, that China must wean itself from an economic model that depends so heavily on fossil fuels, heavy inputs of natural resources, and cheap labor to produce adequate levels of economic growth. The new innovation-driven economy that is being touted as the key to China's future requires a highly qualified, highly mobilized, and highly supportive S&T community at the center of the efforts to guide China on its future growth path. This suggests that there will need to be an even closer, more intimate relationship between the political leadership and the S&T talent pool. This all bodes well for the utilization of China's steadily growing S&T community, as this is the time and place in China's modern history for them to showcase their capabilities and resourcefulness. Not only are the Chinese people watching, but so is the rest of the world.

6 | "Brain drain," "brain gain," and "brain circulation"

This chapter examines China's human resources in science and technology (HRST) from the perspective of flow – the outflow of Chinese overseas as students and scholars (*liuxuesheng*).[1] Studying overseas (*liuxue*) is not a new phenomenon in China, but it is the reform and open-door policy initiated in the late 1970s that has offered Chinese more education and training opportunities on a global scale. The expansion of China's science and technology (S&T) and educational exchanges with the outside world has opened up a broad array of new, substantial opportunities for study abroad through both government sponsorship and private channels. The significance of overseas study is reflected not only in the overall number of *liuxuesheng*, but in the critical role of those who have returned to China after finishing their studies. The returnees (*haigui*, literally meaning "sea turtles"), especially those who have returned in recent years to take advantage of a booming economy and the government's favorable policies toward them, are strategically important to China's rise as a global economic and technological power, and even to China's political evolution to some extent as well (Li, 2004, 2005a). China has also experienced a "brain circulation," in which many ethnic Chinese professionals and scientists residing overseas help their native country by acting as information conduits and collaborative partners in new business ventures (Saxenian, 2002, 2006). In fact, according to the Chinese definition of S&T and research and development (R&D) personnel, as discussed in Chapter 3, those directly engaged in China's scientific and technological activities

---

[1] In this chapter, "students" and "scholars" are referred to those who have gone abroad to study and/or conduct research and who may or may not have pursued a degree. However, as we will point out, the Chinese statistics does not specify these.

212

are an integrated component of China's HRST if they work in China and are engaged in S&T and R&D activities.[2]

From multiple perspectives China is in serious need of help from this overseas-trained talent pool. Nonetheless, a significant number of *liuxuesheng* have been reluctant, if not unwilling, to return home and render their services. Not only has China arguably and unequivocally suffered from a "brain drain" in terms of the absolute number of non-returnees, but more problematic is the fact that the bulk of the non-returnees are most likely the best and the brightest. In addition, there are indications that even more students are ready to leave because they perceive they can achieve a better life and a bright career abroad. Therefore, the challenge for China is to attract back a larger percentage of this more highly qualified stratum of talent, especially academics, from abroad so as to realize a substantial "brain gain." Interestingly, to some extent, the Chinese government policies to attract this overseas talent, as well as the behavior of some returnees, have caused domestic resentment toward the *haigui* as a whole. These factors, along with an operating environment that still is not fully conducive to career development and the lack of deep-seated concrete political reform, have further retarded the formation of the benign circle of talent outflow and inflow.

This chapter examines China's outflow of HRST in the context of globalization and international human resource mobilization and migration. In addition to discussing why such a significant number of Chinese have chosen to remain abroad when their studies are over, the chapter offers a series of explanations as to why Chinese government efforts to reverse the "brain drain," especially at the high end, have not been fully successful. The chapter also addresses the implications of "brain circulation" and "brain gain" for China's high-level human resources development.

Overseas study movement in China

Chinese study abroad dates back to 1847 when Rong Hong (known to the West as Yung Wing) became one of the first foreign-bound *liuxuesheng* and *haigui* (Rong returned in 1854 after receiving his

---

[2] But we do not know whether this is the case, and if so how much they account for.

bachelor's degree from Yale University).[3] These early students who returned from Europe, Japan, and the USA, mainly studied literature and humanities subjects to prepare themselves for leadership in the social and political realms. Upon returning to China at the turn of the twentieth century, they became elites in various arenas and exerted a significant impact on the country. Some were pioneers and a powerful force in political activities. For example, Sun Yat-sen, a returnee from Japan, led the 1911 revolution, successfully overthrowing the socio-political system that had hindered China from modernizing. Returnees also participated in the May Fourth Movement of 1919, actively advocating the ideas of "science" and "democracy."

Overseas study reached its first peak during the Republican era, at which time Chinese supported by "the Boxer Indemnity Scholarship Fund"[4] and other sources, including students themselves, were at the forefront of the international research frontier (Wang, 1966; Ye, 2001). Most of these students returned without hesitation upon finishing their studies, bringing back the vision to develop modern science in China and the hope to change their country with scientific knowledge (Wang, 2002). It is because of their efforts that China began to witness the establishment of scientific organizations, independent research institutions, and modern universities on its soil.

After taking control of the China mainland in 1949, the Chinese Communist Party (CCP) also successfully attracted back some of those who left the country when the nationalist (*Kuomintang*) government was in power and initially stayed abroad after the change of leadership. However, several countries such as the USA tried to postpone, if not obstruct, the return of Chinese students. For example, between 1948 and 1955, the US Congress authorized US $10 million

---

[3] It is said that Rong Hong coined the term "*haigui*."

[4] In 1900, the allied army of eight imperialist powers that occupied Beijing after putting down the Boxer Rebellion (*yihetuan qiyi*) demanded the Qing government to pay a huge sum of indemnity. In 1908, the American government considered that the indemnity it received – $24 million – far exceeded its loss during the war so that it decided to use $12 million to train students from China. This included establishing a preparatory school for Chinese studying abroad, the forerunner of Qinghua University, and setting up a Boxer Indemnity Scholarship Fund to support Chinese to study in the USA. Later, Great Britain and other countries adopted similar scholarship programs (Hunt, 1972).

to provide scholarship for 3641 Chinese students, nearly all of the Chinese students then in the USA; the majority remained there afterwards (Bullock, 1987).[5]

In the 1950s and the 1960s, during the height of the Cold War, the key overseas education destinations for most Chinese students were the Soviet Union and Eastern European countries. These government-sponsored students were obligated to serve their country after their studies; indeed, according to the available statistics, more than 95 percent of those Soviet- and Eastern Europe-bound *liuxuesheng* returned. Starting from 1957 onward, China also dispatched a small number of students to select Western countries; most of them also returned. In the meantime, some 2500 Chinese students who were stranded abroad after 1949 for various reasons also returned. Between 1972 and 1976, as the Cultural Revolution started to wind down, China sent students to 49 countries, including the US, mainly for language studies, and these students also came back (Song, 2003). That almost all of these students returned to China probably reflects more the fact that visa policies were sharply enforced during the era of the Cold War as part of national security controls; small groups of select students who went abroad were also highly monitored and watched by Chinese authorities stationed in those countries.

It is probably fair to say, therefore, that during the first 30 years of communist rule China did not experience a serious brain drain problem, nor a serious shortage of high-quality personnel for its economic, educational, and scientific enterprises. For example, 14 of the 23 most important contributors to China's strategic weapons programs – atomic and hydrogen bombs, missiles, and satellites (or the so-called *"liangdan yixing"*) – honored by the state in 1999 had foreign doctorates granted by such institutions as Berlin (2), Cal Tech (2), Edinburgh (2), Michigan (2), Harvard, Yale, and Paris; only two did not have foreign study and research experience! The main talent problem during this period was that the country did not better utilize this rather elite group of individuals. Instead, the group encountered numerous political obstacles and campaigns as well as personal attacks and abuse which in all likelihood left many of them wondering why

---

[5] As a whole, the USA retained some 5000 students, professionals, trainees, visitors, government officials, and others on temporary visas (Pan, 1990: 276–7).

they returned to the "new" China.[6] This is especially true for a large number of computer scientists who left employment with firms such as Burroughs in the early 1950s to help Maoist China build its own modern information technology (IT) and electronics industries, only to find themselves engaged in thought reform to ensure their ideological purity in the aftermath of the Great Leap Forward, or tending pigs in the countryside during the Cultural Revolution if they were lucky not to be persecuted!

In contrast, between 1978 and 2007, 1.21 million Chinese went abroad, attending language preparation courses, pursuing degrees, conducting post-doctoral research, and engaging in studies in fields ranging from natural sciences, engineering, social sciences, and humanities to law and business administration. This wave of overseas study is historically unprecedented in terms of not only the number of students dispatched, but also the number of returnees, which, by 2002, already reached 153 000, exceeding the total number of Chinese who studied abroad between 1847 and 1978 (Sun & Zou, 2003). These *liuxuesheng* who went abroad *after* the late 1970s are the focus of the chapter.

China's post-1978 policy toward overseas study[7]

Immediately after the Cultural Revolution, the Chinese leadership realized the seriousness of the damage to the country's talent pool wrought by the decision to close down universities and numerous research institutes and programs. Simply stated, the country lacked a cohort of young and middle-aged vigorously trained scientists, engineers, and other professionals to fulfill the pressing needs of the four modernizations drive. As a result, in addition to resuming formal undergraduate and graduate education, the Dengist leadership also put high on its agenda the training of high-quality scientists and technical personnel overseas. The imperative was clear – China had to catch up with the West and Japan as rapidly as possible and steadily close the

---

[6] But many of their children have gone abroad after China reopened its doors in the late 1970s.

[7] This section draws much information, unless indicated otherwise, from the website China Scholars Abroad, available at www.chisa.edu.cn/chisa/column/index/index.xml, accessed August 10, 2003.

prevailing technological gap for economic and national security reasons. As early as 1978, Deng Xiaoping, who himself was just rehabilitated, proposed to send students abroad as one of the important ways to quickly raise the level of Chinese science and education regardless of how much scarce foreign exchange would be spent. His remedy for strengthening China's S&T situation was to dispatch students by the thousands, and even tens of thousands, through every possible means. Regarding the possibility of a "brain drain," Deng Xiaoping indicated that even if 100 of the 1000 students sent did not return, there were still 900 left (Jiang, 2003). In the same year, Fang Yi, then Vice Premier, Commissioner of the State Science and Technology Commission (SSTC), and Vice President of the Chinese Academy of Sciences (CAS), discussed the issue of student exchanges with a visiting S&T delegation from the USA. In October, Zhou Peiyuan, in his capacity as Acting President of the China Association for Science and Technology (CAST), Beijing University President, and CAS Vice President, visited the USA and reached an understanding on the exchange of students and scholars with the American side, which was signed into a formal agreement when Deng Xiaoping visited the USA in early 1979 (Bullock, 1996).[8]

Afterwards, the Chinese government decided to send some 3000 students and scholars to foreign countries, including Australia, Austria, Belgium, Canada, Denmark, Finland, France, Germany, Holland, Italy, Japan, New Zealand, Romania, Sweden, Switzerland, Yugoslavia, the UK, and the USA, in 1978–1979. The first 52 visiting scholars bound for the USA departed on December 26, 1978. The dispatch of *liuxuesheng* marked the beginning of the open-door policy (Zweig, 2002: 161–210). In 1981, self-sponsored (*zifei*) overseas study was permitted. Between 1978 and 1987, 64 000 students, mainly government-sponsored (*guojia gongpai*) or institutional-sponsored (*danwei gongpai*), went abroad, of whom 22 000 returned after they finished their studies. In 1987, during a major debate over the lack of returnees, Zhao Ziyang, then General Secretary of the CCP Central Committee, argued that the so-called "brain drain" was in reality a mechanism to "store brainpower abroad," which would be utilized in the future

---

[8] Zhou Peiyuan himself was a returnee. He studied physics at the University of Chicago and Cal Tech where he received his doctorate and conducted research in Germany, Switzerland, and later, the USA.

(Zweig & Chen, 1995). The same argument was supported by then Fudan University President Xie Xide, an MIT PhD and a prominent physicist in her own right, who believed that whether the time was now or in the future these Chinese-trained scientists and engineers would maintain their links to China and become part of the country's overall talent base.

But the 1989 Tiananmen Square crackdown became a watershed event for overseas study as well as the return of Chinese *liuxuesheng*. Because many *liuxuesheng* at least showed sympathy with the pro-democracy students and actually participated in some sort of activities in support of their fellow students in China, they claimed to fear prosecution if they returned and used this as a reason to remain abroad after completion of their studies.[9] More than that, by taking advantage of the images in the minds of many Americans about the violent nature of the crackdown and the severe repercussions handed out to those sympathetic to the so-called pro-democracy movement, Chinese *liuxuesheng* in the USA first persuaded the Bush administration to issue an executive order in 1990 allowing Chinese nationals in the USA to stay and work. They also successfully lobbied the US Congress to pass the Chinese Student Protection Act in 1992; an important piece of legislation that formally granted permanent resident status to Chinese protected by the executive order. The executive order and the Act opened the door for *gongpai* students and scholars on J-1 visas to stay permanently in the USA.[10] Therefore, whether by choice or by design, many Chinese found themselves in the USA again; this time the number topped 50 000 students. Many of the Chinese *liuxuesheng* in other countries also changed their non-immigration status and became permanent residents. This represents the first large exodus of high-quality Chinese students and scholars who were supposed to shoulder an important historical responsibility in China's overall modernization drive.

---

[9] There was doubt whether the motivation of those participants was really to support the pursuit of democracy or to manage to stay in the USA (Orleans, 1992).

[10] United States immigration regulations require that a person on a J-1 (exchange student or scholar) visa resides outside of the USA for two years following the time in which they held the visa in the USA before they are eligible to apply for an immigration visa or certain categories of non-immigration visa, unless the two-year rule is waived by the United States Information Agency with consents from both the American government and the government of another country in which the individual is a citizen.

Immediately afterwards, China put severe restrictions on overseas study. A significant measure was to impose a service period (*fuwuqi*): only those who fulfill a certain number of years of service to the country – five years for undergraduates and two more years for graduate students – would be allowed to go abroad as *zifei liuxue-sheng*. The rationale behind this policy was an apparent belief that after working in China for several years those graduates would lose interest in studying abroad or that foreign universities would be reluctant to admit those who were not fresh out of school. Those with relatives residing abroad were exempt from the service period by paying back their tuition fees. As a result, both the number of *liux-uesheng* who went abroad and the number of returnees dropped.

At this juncture, in early 1992, in the midst of an active political debate over China's future direction, then paramount leader Deng Xiaoping toured southern China, during which he reaffirmed the validity of the reform program and open-door policy. With regard to overseas study, Deng Xiaoping pointed out that China should not stop sending students abroad just because some appreciable number had not returned, and that even if half the overseas students did not return another half remained to help the country in its modernization quest. Deng Xiaoping's remarks reflected a significant lowering of his 1978 expectation, in which he had hoped for a return-rate of 90 percent. In the meantime, he called for the return of all *liuxuesheng* regardless of their previous political attitudes; he tried to convince them through an appeal to their patriotism that they would be better off to come home to make a contribution, hoping to correct the negative impression left across the globe, and especially among the Chinese *liuxuesheng*, by the Tiananmen Square crackdown (Deng Xiaoping, 1993).

Later that year, Li Tieying, then State Councillor and Commissioner of Education, formally proposed the now well-known 12-character policy, "supporting overseas studies, encouraging return, and allowing students to come and go as they will" (*zhichi liuxue, guli huiguo, laiqu ziyou*). The policy was included in the documents passed at the Third Plenum of the 14th CCP National Congress in 1993. Later on, the emphasis shifted from "returning and serving the country" (*huiguo wufu*) to "serving the country" (*weiguo fuwu*). This laid the foundation for a new policy toward overseas study. These changes also are reflected in the decision to loosen the service period requirement in 1993 and, starting from 2003, those who have not finished their service period are not required to repay tuition fees and most students do not even have to obtain approval to study overseas. Consequently, overseas study has reached another peak in a relatively short period of time.[11]

In 2000, when interviewed by *Science*, one of the most prestigious international science journals, then CCP Central Committee General Secretary Jiang Zemin made another significant statement: "for various reasons, quite a number of students have decided not to – at least for the moment – come back, which is understandable" (Rubinstein, 2000). It is clearly impossible, but perhaps also unnecessary, for China to attract all of its overseas students back. Of course, *liuxuesheng* remaining overseas in universities, in research laboratories, and in corporations are not an indication that China has lost them completely and permanently; quite the contrary, they may be among China's greatest assets, from which the nation may benefit in the long run.

It needs to be remembered, however, that in the midst of these changing, more favorable attitudes toward issues such as the "brain drain" in China there were also important public policy issues emerging in the West about national competitiveness as well as national security. Although some countries such as the USA welcomed the net addition of talented Chinese scientists and engineers to the stock of their talent pool, others worried about the growing dependency of the USA on foreign-born talent to staff key positions in universities and laboratories. In addition, as China's defense sector began to reveal signs of rapid progress, concerns emerged about the role of Chinese personnel abroad in serving as a conduit for the transfer of so-called "dual-use" knowledge that potentially could serve Chinese military needs as well as the civilian economy. Combined with the growing number of Chinese technology businesses and so-called technological listening posts in places such as the Silicon Valley and the Research Triangle in North Carolina, the issue of potential Chinese industrial espionage began to surface. Although it is clear that the numbers of Chinese students and scholars engaged in such activities are extremely limited, there continues to be uneasiness about how serious the

---

[11] Even among those who personally and professionally wish to return to China, securing a foreign education and exposure to the outside world is seen as the path to a better career and more prosperous life. It is also the goal of many Chinese parents that their sole child has the opportunity and associated advantages of going overseas for advanced education.

problem might be every time there are press reports of another incident of illegal acquisition of technology. The now famous Cox Report issued by the US Congress in May 1999 (redacted version) further highlighted growing concerns about the activities of Chinese scientists and other technical personnel abroad with regard to the transfer of knowledge that could contribute to the advancement of China's strategic weapons program. These concerns remain today as periodically there are press reports in the USA and elswhere about alleged "illicit" technology acquisition efforts of ethnic Chinese living or studying there.

Is there a "brain drain" in China?

Making sense of the data

Before assessing whether China has indeed suffered a substantial "brain drain" problem, it is necessary to examine the concrete data on students going overseas and on returnees. Unfortunately, Chinese statistics still remain notoriously poor in providing an accurate picture, as was shown in Leo Orleans's seminal study in the late 1980s on Chinese *liuxuesheng* in the USA (Orleans, 1988). Obviously, China has encountered data collection problems similar to those of other countries: the government tends not to keep track of the return of its citizens after studying or working abroad, making return migration extremely difficult to quantify; when reported to authorities, returnees do not necessarily specify where training was received, in which area, at what level, and for how long. In addition, data are not gathered for the purpose of studying "brain drain" or "brain gain," let alone the new phenomenon of "brain circulation." In general, data refer only to "gross" outflows, ignoring the likelihood of returnees moving back and forth in a more-or-less continual pattern (Bhagwati, 1976; Grubel & Scott, 1977).

Moreover, as Orleans (1988: 78) pointed out, "the problems associated with keeping track of the movement of students and scholars in and out of China are magnified by the number of institutions, scattered throughout the country, involved in the process." The size of the country and the diversity of the student body aside, China does not possess a unified agency to collect data on *liuxuesheng*. The primary educational authority – the State Education Commission (SEC) and its successor, the Ministry of Education – was, until 2003, in charge of approving those students who desired to go abroad and collecting statistics on *liuxuesheng*, and the Ministry of Education is still in charge of dispatching *gongpai liuxuesheng*, although many are short-term visiting scholars. The *zifei* group, however, was not included in official statistics before 1990, whereas those who attended overseas high schools and middle schools were included in the statistics in 2001 and 2002. This also raises the question of the definition of *liuxuesheng*, which should take into account at least the level and length of overseas study. The value of the statistics also depends heavily upon the willingness of students to register with overseas Chinese embassies and consulates; clearly, *zifei* students are less likely to do so. Therefore, the Ministry of Education only may have accurate information on *gongpai liuxuesheng*. The Ministry of Personnel (MOP), on the other hand, gathers information on returnees employed by state-owned work units (*danwei*), but many returnees have gone to work for foreign-invested enterprises (FIEs) (*sanzi qiye*) or have become entrepreneurs themselves. And, while the Ministry of Public Security (MOPS) checks the qualifications of applicants for foreign study and issues passports, as well as keeping track of the exit and entry of Chinese citizens, many of the Chinese who first went abroad as students have changed their visa status or even their citizenship (Zhang & Li, 2001). Although the Ministry of Public Security data are not accessible, the Ministry of Education and the Ministry of Personnel have from time to time disclosed statistics on *liuxuesheng* and returnees.[12] Nonetheless, the data are distorted – underreporting in most circumstances and overreporting in the case of inclusion of high school students and short-term visiting scholars, as we will show.

As a result, virtually no one knows the *exact* number of Chinese who have been abroad as students and researchers since 1978. According to the official *China Statistical Yearbook*, presumably using the available flow data from the Ministry of Education, between 1978 and 2006, 917 012 Chinese went abroad, mostly government-sponsored (Table 6.1). The statistics indicate that until 1992, fewer than 50 000 Chinese had gone abroad. The numbers clearly picked up significantly

---

[12] On February 19, 2001, *Beijing Youth Daily* released the numbers of *liuxuesheng* obtained from the Ministry of Public Security for the years between 1997 and 1999 were 35 079, 55 000, and 85 000, respectively, significantly higher than those reported in the *China Statistical Yearbook* (see Table 6.1) (Zhang & Li, 2002).

Table 6.1 *Chinese students leaving for and returning from overseas destinations each year, 1978–2006*

Year	Number of students leaving for overseas destinations	Number of students returning long-term from overseas	Net rate of returnees to departing students (%)
1978	860	248	28.84
1979	1 777	231	18.16
1980	2 124	162	13.46
1981	2 922	1 143	23.22
1982	2 326	2 116	38.96
1983	2 633	2 303	49.07
1984	3 073	2 290	54.04
1985	4 888	1 424	48.13
1986	4 676	1 388	44.72
1987	4 703	1 605	43.06
1988	3 786	3 000	47.12
1989	3 329	1 753	47.61
1990	2 950	1 593	48.08
1991	2 900	2 069	49.65
1992	6 540	3 611	50.39
1993	10 742	5 128	49.92
1994	19 071	4 230	43.25
1995	20 381	5 750	40.17
1996	20 905	6 570	38.66
1997	22 410	7 130	37.58
1998	17 622	7 379	38.05
1999	23 749	7 748	37.36
2000	38 989	9 121	34.92
2001	83 973	12 243	29.36
2002	125 179	17 945	25.01
2003	117 307	20 152	23.34
2004	114 682	24 726	23.03
2005	118 515	34 987	24.02
2006	134 000	42 000	25.09

Note: Numbers for 2001 and 2002 include those who attended overseas high schools and middle schools.
Source: National Bureau of Statistics, 2007: 790.

Table 6.2 *Cumulative totals of Chinese students overseas and back in China each year, 1985–2007*

Up to year	Total number of students dispatched overseas	Total number of students returned	Rate of returnees to total students overseas in year (%)
1985	40 000	16 500	41.25
1986	40 000	17 000	42.50
1987	64 000	22 000	34.38
1988	70 000	NA	NA
1989	80 000	33 000	41.25
1990	NA	NA	NA
1991	170 000	50 000	29.41
1992	190 000	60 000	31.58
1993	210 000	70 000	33.33
1994	230 000	75 000	32.61
1995	250 000	81 000	32.40
1996	270 000	90 000	33.33
1997	300 000	96 000	32.00
1998	300 000	100 000	33.33
1999	320 000	110 000	34.38
2000	340 000	140 000	41.18
2001	420 000	140 000	33.33
2002	583 000	153 000	26.24
2003	700 200	172 800	24.68
2004	815 000	198 000	24.29
2005	933 400	232 900	24.95
2006	1 067 000	275 000	25.77
2007	1 211 700	319 700	26.38

Note: NA, not available.
Numbers for 2001 and 2002 include those who attended overseas high schools and middle schools.
Source: Authors' research.

after Deng Xiaoping reemphasized sending students abroad during his southern tour and the Chinese government loosened restrictions on studying abroad. Still, doubling of numbers of Chinese *liuxuesheng* in 2001 (84 000) compared with 2000 (39 000) may also be attributed to the increase in those who went abroad for high school and middle school education; the same may be said for the numbers in 2002. The smaller numbers of *liuxuesheng* in 2002 (117 000) reflects the change of the statistical scope of *liuxuesheng*, made in 2003, to exclude those students aged under 18 years (MOST, 2005: 26); nevertheless, no adjustment was made to the previous statistics. The most recent Ministry of Education stock statistics, also official but not in any government statistical yearbook, on the other hand, indicate that between 1978 and the end of 2006, the total number of *liuxuesheng* was 1.07 million (by the end of 2007, the number was 1.2 million) (Table 6.2).

While it is genuinely difficult to track down how many Chinese have gone overseas to study, the data from recipient countries seem to confirm that the numbers tend to be very large. For each of the past 18 years, for example, Chinese have accounted for more than 10% of the international student body in the USA with more than 80% in graduate programs, and have constituted another 15–22% of the total number of international scholars (Table 6.3). It was only in the 2001/ 2002 academic year that India replaced China as the leading country of origin for international students in the USA.

Similarly, no one knows how many *liuxuesheng* have returned to China upon finishing their studies abroad. Again, the flow number, according to the *China Statistical Yearbook*, was only 230 045 between 1978 and 2006; but the stock data released by the Ministry of Education indicates that, as of the end of 2006, the number of returnees reached 275 000 (319 700 by the end of 2007). With such variations in the statistics on Chinese *liuxuesheng* and *haigui* from the same source, the Ministry of Education, it is very difficult to reconcile them except to say that both numbers tend to be significant.[13]

Rate of return – a measure of "brain drain"

Originally, China's leadership had hoped for a fairly high rate of student return; as previously noted, in 1978, Deng Xiaoping expected that

---

[13] According to some estimates, the number of *liuxuesheng* was already over one million by 2005. In his presentation to a conference convened by the China Association for Science and Technology (CAST) in September 2005, Bai Chunli, the CAS Executive Vice President, mentioned that close to a million had gone abroad to study, with more than 200 000 returning (*Science Times*, September 27, 2005). Wang Huiyao, who is in charge of the Entrepreneur Alliance of the Western Returned Scholars Association, an organization composed of returnees, also estimated in May 2005 that the number of Chinese *liuxuesheng* should be one million and that of returnees between 300 000 and 400 000 (2005: 68–72).

Table 6.3 *Chinese students and scholars in the USA*

Year	No. of students from China (rank)	Percentage of total international students in the USA	No. of scholars from China	Percentage of total international scholars in the USA
1990/91	39 600 (1)	9.7	NA	NA
1991/92	42 910 (1)	10.2	NA	NA
1992/93	45 130 (1)	10.3	NA	NA
1993/94	44 380 (1)	9.9	11 156	18.6
1994/95	39 403 (2)	8.7	9 866	17.0
1995/96	39 613 (2)	8.7	9 228	15.5
1996/97	42 503 (2)	7.8	9 724	15.6
1997/98	46 958 (2)	9.8	10 709	16.4
1998/99	51 001 (1)	10.4	11 854	16.8
1999/00	54 466 (1)	10.6	13 229	17.7
2000/01	59 939 (1)	10.9	14 772	18.5
2001/02	63 211 (2)	10.8	15 624	18.2
2002/03	64 757 (2)	11.0	15 171	18.0
2003/04	61 765 (2)	10.8	14 871	18.0
2004/05	62 523 (2)	11.1	17 035	19.0
2005/06	62 582 (2)	11.1	19 017	19.6
2006/07	67 723 (2)	11.6	20 149	20.5
2007/08	81 127 (2)	13.0	23 779	22.4

Note: NA, not available.
Source: IIE, various years.

90 percent of the *liuxuesheng* would return. Beijing now recognizes that quite a number of students have decided not to come back to China, at least for the time being. In fact, the reality is that Chinese statistics on the return of *liuxuesheng* point to rather disappointing rates of return (see Table 6.1 and Table 6.2).[14] The flow data, for

---

[14] These numbers are obtained by dividing the total number of returnees by the total number of overseas Chinese students – both flow and stock – up to a particular year.

   The lower rate of return is apparently because some non-returnees are still pursuing their studies. Without such information, however, the chapter has to use rate of return in its current formula to measure "brain drain."

example, gives a net return rate of 25% in the period with available data, and similarly and consistently, the rate of return calculated from the stock data has also been around 25% in recent years.

Between the late 1970s and the early 1980s rates of return were low, which is understandable because it takes time for *liuxuesheng* who have gone abroad to finish their studies or research. Later on, rates of return rose to around 50 percent and, surprisingly, were initially even unaffected by the 1989 Tiananmen Square incident. Two reasons may account for this situation. First, those early overseas students were mainly *guojia gongpai* and *danwei gongpai,* so they had to return, and, second, Chinese student protection laws offered by foreign countries were neither issued nor implemented at this time. The second reason also explains why China saw a drop in the number of returning students after 1992, the year that the US Congress passed the Chinese Students Protection Act and other countries followed suit. The gradual loosening of restrictions on Chinese studying abroad after 1992, and especially after 2003, has caused the departure of more students, especially those in the *zifei* category, which has resulted in a further decrease in rates of return afterwards (Table 6.4). And the actual rates of return, and the five-year and ten-year smoothing rates of return, all show that 1993 seems to be the turning point for the rates of return from increasing to decreasing overall (Figure 6.1).

Rates of return differ for different categories of students: *guojia gongpai, danwei gongpai,* and *zifei.* It is reported that between 1978 and 1996 more than 270 000 Chinese studied abroad and about 90 000 returned, yielding a 33.3% rate of return. Of the 44 000 *guojia gongpai liuxuesheng,* some 37 000 returned (rate of return 84.1%). Around 48 000 of the 86 000 *danwei gongpai* students and scholars returned (rate of return 55.8%), but – pathetically – only 4 000 of the 139 000 *zifei* students returned (rate of return 2.7%) (Chen, 2003). In recent years all three categories of students have experienced an increased inflow, with the rate of return for the *gongpai liuxuesheng* close to 100% as a result of both a financial bond that must be posted (until 1996 there was no legal undertaking of financial bonds for *gongpai* students to return) and the upward mobility opportunities offered to these students in the rapidly growing Chinese economy. It should also be pointed out that many of the *gongpai liuxuesheng* are abroad for less than a year and their return has boosted the number of returnees (Wei, 2006).

Table 6.4 *Chinese students going overseas and returning, by type of support (persons)*

| | Students going overseas | | | | Returnees | | | |
Year	Total	State dispatched	*Danwei* dispatched	Self-supported	Total	State dispatched	*Danwei* dispatched	Self-supported
2000	38 989	2 808	3 888	32 293	9 121	2 456	2 290	4 375
2001	83 973	3 495	4 426	76 052	12 243	2 528	3 016	6 699
2002	125 000	3 500	4 500	117 000	18 000	NA	NA	NA
2003	117 300	3 002	5 144	109 200	20 100	2 638	4 292	13 200
2004	114 700	3 524	6 858	104 300	25 000	2 761	3 965	18 000
2005	118 500	3 979	8 078	106 500	35 000	3 008	4 770	27 200
2006	134 000	5 580	7 542	121 000	42 000	3 716	5 267	33 000

Note: NA, not available.
Numbers for 2001 and 2002 include those who attended overseas high schools and middle schools.
Source: Authors' research.

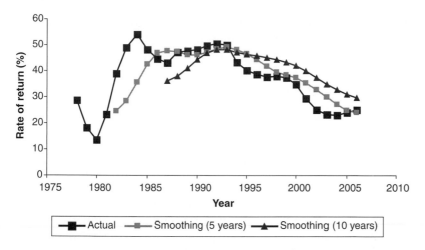

Figure 6.1 Rates of return of overseas Chinese students.
Source: National Bureau of Statistics, 2007: 790.

The return rate for Chinese overseas students also appears to be linked to where they studied. The USA is the country that most Chinese students have targeted for overseas study, and many *liuxue-sheng* in the USA tend not to return. Although the exact number of non-returnees in the USA is unknown, the Chinese Student Protection Act, implemented in 1992, alone allowed at least 50 000 Chinese students to remain as legal immigrants. Such a situation did not change until the USA significantly tightened its admission of immigrants after the terrorist attacks of September 11, 2001. For a while, strong national security concerns prevailed so that those pursuing studies in the high-technology areas from certain countries, including China, had difficulty even getting student visas. The situation has improved recently owing to the extensive lobbying efforts by many university presidents in the USA and a wide array of American companies which depend more and more on foreign talent to staff technical positions. Nonetheless, a variety of obstacles still exists.

In a word, judging by the modest rates of return, we can at least tentatively conclude that China has been experiencing a serious "brain drain." From the perspective of the Chinese government drive to promote more and higher level innovation activities, this problem denies the country some valuable, badly needed talent resources. The key question, therefore, is: What has been the actual impact and long-term consequences of this "brain drain?"

"Brain drain" at the high level

Not only are the highly skilled students disproportionately likely to leave, they are often the "cream of the crop." "Brain drain" is more serious across the highest segments of the talent pool in China. In January 2002, the Ministry of Education issued a circular intended to facilitate the obtaining of entry visas and local residence permits for ethnic Chinese with foreign citizenship, many of whom used to be *liuxuesheng*. Other related government agencies have initiated similar measures and all these ended up with a February 2007 document, jointly released by the Ministry of Personnel, the Ministry of Education, the Ministry of Science and Technology, the Ministry of Finance, the Ministry of Foreign Affairs, the National Development and Reform Commission, the Ministry of Public Security, the Ministry of Commerce, the Bank of China, the State-Owned Assets Supervision and Administration Commission, the Office of Overseas Chinese of the State Council, the CAS, the State Administration of Foreign Experts Affairs, China Customs, the State Administration of Taxation, and the State Administration for Industry and Commerce. In this context, high-level talent refers to the following.

- Those who are appointed department chairs, professors or associate professors, or their equivalents, at institutions of learning.
- Those who have one-year, or longer, teaching, research, or academic collaboration contracts with institutions of learning.
- Those who serve in senior management positions (deputy general managers and above) at domestic enterprises or the enterprises set up by returnees.
- Those who fulfill state, provincial, or ministerial level S&T and key engineering projects signed between central or local governments and foreign countries.
- Those who invest in China with the amount of money exceeding the medium level at a locality.
- Those who fall into the category of Western regional development strategy, engaging in teaching, research, and enterprise ventures.

The issuing of such documents, whose policy measures toward high-level *liuxuesheng* have been reaffirmed in a series of related government documents, indicates that: first, these ethnic Chinese are now foreigners who need visas to enter China, and, second, this group is significant in number and potential impact, thus necessitating central government to issue a document to assist their getting entry visas and other benefits enjoyed by local residents.

Then, how large is this group? According to a CAS official in charge of talent recruitment, *liuxuesheng* may be classified roughly into three categories. The *first*, most outstanding are those who are well-established in their respective fields, possess critical and innovative technology, and lead a team, thus enjoying higher reputation in academia or the business community and having significant social influence. They include tenured professors at universities, principal investigators at research institutions and laboratories, managers at department level or above in corporations. They have made innovative scientific achievements, published significant papers in influential international academic journals, received prestigious awards, or served in foreign government or non-government organizations. The *second* category – outstanding talent – differs from the first in that scientists and professionals in this category are rising toward the first category. Also included in this category are some post-doctoral fellows with excellent and prolific research records. Specialists in particular fields fall into a *third* category. They may be professors, visiting scholars, or even graduate students and their importance is not necessarily measured by their academic reputation and position as long as they possess specialized knowledge or practical technology that China needs or covets.

In terms of numbers, according to the CAS official mentioned above, as of 2003, the first category had fewer than 1000, with two-thirds residing in the USA; the second more than 5000; and the third had a presumably large but unknown number (Wang, 2005: 46–50). The so-called high-level talent category includes all those in the first and second categories, and some from the third category.

Although such a classification is reasonable, the estimation of numbers for each category is outdated. For one thing, according to Yigong Shi, who gave up his chaired professorship at Princeton University and a prestigious fellowship from the Howard Hughes Medical Institute, and now works full-time at Qinghua University in Beijing, in 2007, more than 2500 Chinese-origin life scientists were at the assistant professor level and up in the USA, most likely tenured or on the tenure track, compared with some 100 at the same level in 1997 (*Science Times*, August 6, 2007: A6). In other words, the number of life scientists in academia in the USA alone could exceed the estimate of the first category of the talent made by the CAS official, not to mention scientists in other disciplines and residing in other countries.

Statistics from the US National Science Foundation highlight a similar situation. In the past 25 years, Chinese from the mainland are among the top foreign recipients receiving doctorate degrees in science and engineering (S&E) from American universities, as noted in Chapter 4. Many have also clearly indicated their intention to remain in the USA at the time they receive their degrees; and, in fact, most have managed to stay on. For example, of the 2 779 Chinese who received S&E doctorates from American universities in 1991, 88% were working in the USA in 1995, while in the 1992–1993 academic year, Chinese students who received S&E doctorates from American university increased to 4010, of whom 92% were working in the USA in 1997; in 1996, 1345 Chinese received S&E doctorates in the USA, the stay rate in 2001 was 96% (Finn, 2003; Johnson, 1999, 2001; Johnson & Reget, 1998). As a result, in 2003, 62 500 Chinese S&E doctorates – more than three-quarters receiving their degrees in the USA – were in the American S&E workforce, the largest among for-eign-born United States residents with such degrees (National Science Board (NSB), 2006: Table A3–18).[15]

Not all of those who have studied abroad, including those who have been awarded S&E doctorates in the USA and stayed on, are equally skilled or talented. For example, a significant number of Chinese students more than likely received their doctorates from low-ranking and unranked departments, from 63.2% for biochemistry, 58.6% for chemistry, and 51.3% for physics to 37.8% for economics (Bound *et al.*, 2006: Table 2). However, it is also clear that a significantly higher number of non-returnees are outstanding. In the case of the life

---

[15] Of the 62 500 Chinese-origin science and engineering (S&E) doctorates, some 35 000 were awarded their PhD in the USA between 1983 and 2003; 10 000 earned their degrees before 1983, mostly in the USA but there were also some other foreign doctorates; 1000–2000 were American citizens at the time of receiving their PhDs; and most of the remaining 14 000 received their degrees in China with a fair number (1000–2000 each) earned doctorates in Australia, Canada, Europe, or Japan.

sciences, again, most of the Chinese who have experience running independent laboratories in the USA and other countries have not returned to China. Given that there are some 892 000 Chinese abroad, with 657 000 still students, and that more, especially from Beijing, Qinghua, and other key Chinese universities, are expected to leave, the situation will only get worse in the years to come. This has been a disturbing trend to the Chinese scientific and political leadership. While it reflects China's growing integration into the world of international S&T activities as well as the global talent pool, it also highlights the potential downside of the greater "freedoms" and mobility that have been accorded the future members of China's S&T community.[16]

The seriousness of "brain drain" may also be examined from the perspective of China's scientific manpower. As discussed in Chapter 3, the latest numbers of those entitled to the government's special stipend – some 143 000 individuals – could be used as a rough indicator of the country's senior-ranking scientists. Among these, almost 110 000 had already reached retirement age in 2001, leaving only about 30 000 still active in research and teaching; even with measures that have been taken to delay some of them from retiring the number is probably around 50 000 at best (Zhang *et al.*, 2003). Moreover, according to a bibliographic study of the 1995–2000 publications included in the *Chinese Science Citation* database, Chinese scientists aged 30 years or less and those aged over 60 tend to be the most prolific and publish twice to four times more than those aged between 31 and 60 – with the 40–50-year-old groups being the least productive (Jin *et al.*, 2004).[17] While the younger group is mainly composed of graduate students or new graduates, the older one has reached, or is closer to, retirement age. At the time of continuing to experience the impact of the Cultural Revolution on talent, although to a lesser extent, China is also losing to "brain drain" a contingency of researchers in their most productive ages. It is speculated that most

---

[16] Their actions, while not necessarily political in intent, do have important implications for a regime that is trying hard to maintain its credibility and legitimacy.

[17] However, as discussed in Chapter 5, grant-awarding at the National Natural Science Foundation of China seems to indicate that those aged 50 and younger have come of age.

authors of the papers published by ethnic Chinese in leading inter-national science journals are those in their forties who left China after 1978. In other words, their return could potentially boost China's research and education performance and output.[18]

A number of scientists and engineers with doctorates conferred by Chinese institutions of learning may also have left the country for perceived opportunities elsewhere. As shown in Chapter 3, there was a total of at least 133 550 doctorate holders employed by various Chinese *danwei* – 17 777 at research institutes and 108 605 at universities (in 2006), and 7168 at large- and medium-sized enterprises (in 2005). However, between 1982 and 2006, Chinese institutions of learning produced 154 775 doctorates in science, engineering, medicine, and agriculture (or the so-called *ligongke* fields). Taking into account that some holders of Chinese doctorates may not have been employed when these data were collected and an unknown number (roughly 10–20 percent of the doctorates) were returnees, it appears that at least a couple of dozen thousand of Chinese who earned their doctorates in China were missing from the statistics! In all likelihood, most of them must have migrated to the USA or other countries, as noted above.

Programs attracting Chinese talent abroad

Realizing the seriousness of the "brain drain" and the growing need for more talented scientists and professionals, especially at the higher levels, over the last decade or so the Chinese government has adopted various measures which it hopes will reverse the current trend. Almost all the major national programs in the fields of S&T and education – from the One Hundred Talent Program at the CAS; the Cheung Kong Scholar Program at the Ministry of Education; the National Science Funds for Outstanding Young Scholars Program at the NSFC; to the One Hundred, One Thousand, and Ten Thousands of Talent Program at the Ministry of Personnel – have aimed at aggressively attracting the permanent return of overseas students (see Chapter 2). There have been other programs as well – all have had some success, but not nearly to the degree hoped for by the government (Table 6.5).

---

[18] Of course, simply bringing qualified people back to China does not guarantee innovative results if other factors do not change as well.

Table 6.5 *Programs targeting returnees or attracting the return of overseas Chinese talent*

Program	Year initiated	Agency in charge	Numbers affected
Seed Funds for Returned Overseas Scholars	1990	MOE	11 000
Cross-Century Outstanding Personnel Training Program	1991	MOE	900
One Hundred Talent Program	1994	CAS	1 100
The National Science Fund for Distinguished Young Scholars	1994	NSFC	1 200
One Hundred, One Thousand, and Ten Thousands of Talent Program	1995	MOP	10 000
Chunhui Program	1996	MOE	10 000
Cheung Kong Scholar Program	1998	MOE	800

Source: Authors' research.

Immediately after the 1989 Tiananmen Square incident, the Ministry of Education established a Seed Fund for Returned Overseas Scholars, which thus far has supported some 11 000 returnees with a total amount of RMB350 million. Currently eligible for funding are those who are aged 45 or younger, hold a doctorate, and have been abroad for at least one year.

The Ministry of Education also initiated a Cross-Century Outstanding Personnel Training Program in 1993, which has invested a total of RMB180 million on 922 talented, so-called "cross-century" (crossing the twenty-first century) young scientists, many with foreign study and research experience. The program was renamed New Century Outstanding Personnel Support Program.

The Chinese government has also put aside special funds to accommodate the interests of expatriate Chinese who desire to contribute to their motherland, but chose not to work full-time in Chinese institutions of learning. The Cheung Kong Scholar Program, for example, has a component of special professorships for those able to work for at least four months in China. The Chunhui Program (*chunhui jihua*), launched by the Ministry of Education in 1996, has supported more than 10 000 outstanding overseas students to work short-term, attend conferences, or conduct site visits in China.

In 2000, the Chunhui Program initiated a special component to entice overseas Chinese academics to spend their sabbaticals in China. A similar program at the CAS targets groups of *liuxuesheng* with permanent positions abroad who are able to work alternatively at a CAS institute.

The government has also incorporated the services of overseas Chinese into the nation's important research and economic programs. The Chunhui Program alone has supported more than 90 groups of overseas students and scholars for that purpose. Additionally, 68 special science parks and business incubators targeting returnees have been established; they provide tax breaks, inexpensive real-estate, and other incentives. In Beijing's Zhongguancun Science Park, as of April 2007, about 8 700 returnees, of whom a significant percentage have doctorates and master's degrees and own patents and other intellectual property rights, set up 3 500 firms (*Beijing Business Today*, April 11, 2007). Chinese officials hope that a new class of "technological entrepreneurs" will emerge from these groups, who will help to spearhead China's march toward becoming an innovative nation.

Who are the returnees?[19]

As suggested, the effort to attract Chinese talent from abroad has achieved some degree of success. Accordingly, it is important to understand, more precisely, "Who are the returnees?" There are roughly two different groups: one, high-technology, management, finance, legal, and other professionals; the other, largely academics. Apparently, professionals are finding a myriad of new, exciting high-potential opportunities in China's fast-growing economy where their foreign education, language, skills, cross-cultural experiences and exposure, professional and personal networks, and strong financial support are in great demand. China's entry into the World Trade Organization in late 2001 has further spurred opportunities for professionals who understand business and culture on both sides of the world. Coincidently, the collapse of the NASDAQ, the bursting of the "dotcom bubble," and the deep recession at Silicon Valley and in high-technology industry as a whole after mid-2000 have caused tens of

---

[19] The discussion here excludes those returnees who have become political leaders (Li, 2005a; Wang, 2005).

thousands of employees, including those of Chinese-origin, in the high-technology area to be laid off. Then the tightening of entry visas in the post-September 11 USA, to counter possible security loopholes, has turned away many talented students and researchers, many also being Chinese. The Chinese mentality of being the "head of the chicken rather than the tail of an ox" as well as the "glass ceiling" phenomenon in the USA and other foreign countries have also made Chinese professionals reconsider their career prospects.[20] All this has shifted the balance of comparative advantage, causing increasing numbers of Chinese to consider a career at home and therefore speeding up the return of Chinese professionals to some extent. Those in possession of patents or key technologies are especially highly valued as China has started to pay more attention to intellectual property rights (IPRs) in its bid to become an innovation-oriented nation. And, professionals with financial and banking backgrounds are equally welcome, as former Premier Zhu Rongji promised to offer them salary and benefit packages similar to those they could receive abroad in his speech delivered at the Massachusetts Institute of Technology (MIT) in 1999 and at the Sixth World Chinese Entrepreneurs Convention held in China in 2001.

Although the exact number of returned professionals who definitely possess specialized knowledge, including some who are in the most outstanding category, is unknown, the trend seems to have picked up. According to a fairly recent study, among the Chinese high-technology professionals working in the Silicon Valley, 74% had friends who had returned to work or start businesses, 49% had helped businesses at home, and 43% had considered or are quite likely to consider going home to live (Saxenian *et al.*, 2002). Many more have taken advantage of the numerous incentives offered by China's central and local governments to become "local" entrepreneurs themselves. The companies formed by returnees include US stockmarket-listed Sohu.com, a Chinese language portal; Baidu, "China's Google;" Suntech Power, a solar energy company, among others. At the same time, those who straddle the Pacific Ocean between the USA and China, or the "new Argonauts," also play a very positive role in the movement of ideas, knowledge, and capital (Saxenian, 2006). These persons are sometimes referred to as "amphibians" (*liangqi*) because they spend

---

[20] It remains to be seen how the so-called "global financial crisis" that began in late 2008 will affect behavior of former *liuxuesheng* currently still abroad.

their time on the "sea" – a foreign country, and the land – China. Their role in facilitating the movement of information and knowledge as well as capital and business opportunities to and from China cannot be underemphasized. They represent a sort of vanguard in that they seem to understand the key success factors for building successful business and starting new ventures on both sides of the Pacific.

Also included in this professional group are those who work in FIEs (*sanzi qiye*). They lead or manage the China operations for many multinational corporations (MNCs) and staff the research laboratories of firms such as Microsoft, Intel, and IBM, among others, whose broader global orientation is what has made employment at these enterprises in China so attractive to many returnees who have come back to China from graduate education or even jobs in the USA and elsewhere (see Buderi & Huang (2006) for the case of Microsoft Research Asia).[21] Returnees have campaigned for the introduction of venture capital investment policies to China, and often represent leading foreign venture capital firms seeking a foothold in China (Sheff, 2002). Strictly speaking, while the returnees sit as employees in foreign companies at present, over time they could help to improve China's business environment, corporate governance, and legal infrastructure with the ideas and concepts they bring back to China. Some have used working for *sanzi qiye* as a transition or as a means to accumulate experience and capital for their own entrepreneurial activities. In 2002, a group of researchers who worked at Intel Research China (IRC), led by Yan Yonghong, one-time IRC director and an associate professor of electrical and computer engineering at the Oregon Graduate Institute School of Science and Engineering, Oregon Health and Science University, moved to the CAS to set up a speech laboratory that also is a high-technology company (*Science and Technology Daily*, December 30, 2002).[22]

The second category of returnees are the academics. *Gongpai* students who went abroad in the late 1970s and the early 1980s represent the group of early returnees who now occupy important positions in China's research and education systems, including many members

---

[21] We simply have to examine the changing composition of people living in expatriate housing complexes in Beijing and Shanghai to recognize the large numbers of returnees who are now working for MNCs.
[22] This practice is not yet the norm.

(*yuanshi*) of the CAS and the Chinese Academy of Engineering (CAE), university presidents, chief scientists of many government research programs as well as key professors and senior researchers (Cao, 2004a; Li, 2005b; Wang H, 2005). Recent returnees also have been appointed by the Cheung Kong Scholar Program and One Hundred Talent Program, among others. More significantly, recently returnees with foreign doctorates have been promoted to leadership positions in science and education. The appointment of Wan Gang to Minister of Science and Technology and Chen Zhu to Minister of Health, in 2007, further attests the government's appreciation of returnees and its growing commitment to capture foreign-trained talent and move these individuals up the career ladder very quickly even if they lack some of the political credentials – the CCP membership – that once were deemed so vital.

Unfortunately, the ongoing government and institutional efforts, despite producing some positive outcomes, have not lured back most of the best and the brightest *liuxuesheng*. Data from some of the government programs aimed at attracting high-quality returnees apparently confirm this fact (Table 6.6). Apparently, almost all the Cheung Kong professors, the One Hundred Talent Program appointees, and the Distinguished Young Scholars are *liuxuesheng*, but only between one-third and one-half have received foreign doctorates. According to information obtained from the CAS in October 2006, between 1995 and 2005, the One Hundred Talent Program made 1 067 appointments, of which 849 candidates were recruited from overseas and only 384 possessed foreign doctorates.[23] The National Institute of Biological Sciences (NIBS) is a new, prestigious scientific establishment backed by the Ministry of Science and Technology and the Beijing municipal government. Principal investigators are provided with internationally competitive salaries – around RMB400 000 after tax, which are set halfway between typical levels in the USA and in China – plus benefits that exceed those of China's overall research community.

---

[23] The time frame is different from shown in Table 6.6, but the outcomes are similar: with almost 80 percent of them recruited into the One Hundred Talent Program had foreign experience, only 36.0 percent received foreign doctorates.
  A study of 227 50-year-old and younger outstanding scientists identified by the CAS indicates that only one-third received their doctorates from foreign institutes, although as a whole 74 had foreign post-doctoral experience (Shang, 2007).

Table 6.6 *Effectiveness of the programs attracting the return of high-quality overseas Chinese talent*

Program	Total number	Percentage of foreign experience	Percentage of foreign PhDs
NSFC Distinguished Scholars (1994–2004)	1 176	98.5	32.8
MOE Cheung Kong Scholars (1999–2004)	537	90	37.2
CAS One Hundred Talent (1999–2004)	899	86.5	43.6

Source: Authors' research.

Principal investigators are also promised a significant level of autonomy in research and administration. Thus far, however, a typical principal investigator is an individual who received their doctorate from a Chinese institution of learning and has several years of experience as a post-doctoral researcher overseas, mostly in the USA.

In other words, such high-profile efforts – with enormous resources and incentives attached to them – are only attractive to those who are less likely to find decent, permanent positions abroad and to those who have gone overseas to gain foreign experience after earning their Chinese doctorates. If so, the effort to turn around the "brain drain" in academics has yielded only modest success. Consequently, few of the post-1990s academic returnees are comparable with non-returnees in terms of quality, international reputation, and prestige (Xiao *et al.*, 2005); the best of them, according to a most optimistic estimate, would be in the 50–80th percentile (Zweig, 2006). For example, most of the Chinese-origin life scientists with background and experience running independent laboratories in the USA have not returned;[24] this is the case even though many individuals have hit the proverbial "glass ceiling" abroad and cannot advance beyond this to their desired levels

[24] Prior to Yigong Si, who returned to Qinghua University in September 2007, Yi Rao, Elsa A. Swanson, Research Professor and Director of Research at the Feinberg Clinical Neuroscience Research Institute at Northwestern University Feinberg School of Medicine, was named Dean of Beijing University School of Life Sciences, becoming the first renowned Chinese-origin life scientist to return permanently.

Table 6.7 *Chinese students and scholars who returned from overseas, by level of the education received overseas*

Year	Number of returnees	Bachelor	Master	Doctorate	Post-Doc	Total	Number with doctorates
2001	12 243	6.4	43.2	35.7	14.8	100	4371
2002	17 945	11.4	47.1	28.1	13.4	100	5043
2003	20 152	13.0	57.2	18.6	11.2	100	3748
2004	24 726	11.4	64.2	14.4	10.0	100	3561
2005	34 987	11.6	73.4	9.2	5.8	100	3219

Source: Wei, 2006.

because of bias and even, in some cases, cultural discrimination (Mervis, 2005). Some returnees have returned simply to take advantage of research opportunities unavailable abroad. For example, because stem cell research has not been endorsed in the USA, some Chinese scientists working in this field have returned from prestigious jobs at places such as Stanford University and the National Institutes of Health (Dennis, 2002); sadly for China, they are likely to leave once the restrictions on this type of research are lifted in the USA. Others return on sabbaticals or to take time off from their permanent positions to run laboratories in China. Finally, some of the returnees are working in both industry and academia so as to access the resources and benefits from both sectors.

Interestingly, along with the trend in the twenty-first century of more Chinese returning upon finishing their studies overseas (see Table 6.1 and Table 6.2), is a declining percentage of those with doctoral degrees (Table 6.7). The statistics are misleading as they show that close to 20 000 students had returned with PhDs: most of them were actually visiting scholars, not recipients of foreign doctorates. What the statistics try to indicate is the fact that three-quarters of the 35 000 returnees in 2005 had a master's degree. Considering that it takes only one year for a master's degree in some countries, from which some of the returned degree-holders may not learn much. Therefore it is no wonder that those without the necessary skill sets and experience could become unemployed (known as *haidai*), as the Chinese labor market has become increasingly competitive and employers more demanding (Wei, 2006).

Why have first-rate academics not returned?

There are several reasons why most first-rate academics have not returned to China. Compared with other professionals, salaries for academics have tended to be lower, though in recent years there have emerged many opportunities for outside consulting as a means to earn additional income. There also are problems linked to securing appropriate education for their children and jobs for their spouses. If the family members of returnees still reside abroad, which is often the case, they not only have to travel back and forth, but also put at risk their family situations and even their marriages. Although these factors and issues are acknowledged, in reality, the most important reasons appear to be institutional.

First, China still remains, more or less, a *guanxi*-based society. After these academics have spent between five and ten years, if not more, overseas, it is likely that their connections with their former institutions are no longer as close as before and their advisors are retired or not actively involved in academic activities. That is, they do not have a social network that could help and support them through their initial adjustment period. For returnees, foreign credentials are necessary, but not sufficient, to guarantee professional success; *guanxi* remains, at least equally important. Therefore, only those with close relations with domestic institutions, and, more importantly, with governments, and those having access to the resource allocation process, may achieve their needed support and infrastructure.

Second, because many Chinese scientists are not doing research at international frontiers, returnees may experience another culture shock; that is, they might not be able to easily find an "invisible college" from which to share information, to discuss how to conduct research, or to secure help when needed. As the Chinese research system usually gives preference to quick or instant results and does not readily accept or tolerate failure, vision and thinking are not part of the research agenda. While this situation has improved somewhat with the passage of a special amendment to S&T law in late 2007 that accepts "failure" as part of the creative innovation process, there still is tremendous pressure for results placed on returnees. Moreover, it is very difficult for returnees' research to be judged on an equal footing with those scholars who have not spent their time overseas recently.

Third, academic returnees have to accept the types of political rituals that remain an ever-present part of the Chinese socio-political environment. One biophysicist is an Australian-trained doctorate who also spent seven years at Oxford University before returning to China in 1996. When his group published a paper in *Cell*, the first in the last 25 years by Chinese scientists for work done in mainland China, in July 2005, he indicated that "it is the gift of an ordinary party member to the party on its birthday" (Huo, 2005). Coincidently or not, he was later appointed president of Nankai University.

Fourth, the rampant misconduct in science – some involving returnees – has made *liuxuesheng* really reconsider whether they want to be in a location where there is growing evidence that plagiarism, fraud, and manipulation of data are much more serious problems than has been imagined. Worse, the Chinese scientific community has not taken swift action to address the reality as well as the growing perception of widespread scientific fraud; it is more than just a cloud that hovers over significant segments of the Chinese research world which has led many possible returnees to think twice about coming back to China on a permanent basis.

Fifth, there still are restrictions on the types of social science research that are politically acceptable. It is not a secret that most of the returnees are natural scientists or those with technical and managerial know-how; because the regime needs the skills and services of such people, it has taken a "hand's off" approach in almost all cases. When it was initially launched, the Cheung Kong Scholar Program also indicated its interest in appointing social scientists. However, natural scientists greatly outnumber their social science colleagues. Therefore, expatriate social scientists, except economists, even those who study China, have not returned, although some may have visiting appointments at Chinese institutions of learning.

While a small number of expatriate social scientists are political activists, most are scholars who do not have political agendas in their research. They objectively observe the variety of development problems China has been encountering in its economic and social modernization, and their candid criticisms of the government and its officials are, in many cases, quite constructive. They seem to understand that China cannot afford to grow its economy without the participation of social thinkers and public intellectuals. But, they are cautious about working even part-time in China because of fears about political tightening as well as the harsh treatment that some of their colleagues have received when conducting research in China.

Finally, while the government continues to call for the return of the best and the brightest, institutional leaders may not necessarily welcome those who are more capable and might threaten their positions and leadership. Petty jealousies abound inside Chinese organizations; sometimes called "red-eye disease" (*hongyanbing*), they can lead to obstructionism in the workplace and make it difficult for high performers to do their work in a non-hostile setting. In some extreme cases, the current leaders may even not want to see the return of outstanding scientists to other institutions. Wang Xiaodong, the first among the post-open-door era Chinese *liuxuesheng* to be elected to the US National Academy of Sciences, and the co-director of the National Institute of Biological Sciences, is said to be interested in moving back completely. As a way to stay linked with Wang, the Howard Hughes Medical Institute considered offering to award ten fellowships to those Chinese working with Wang, who is also an investigator at the prestigious Institute. When the Institute solicited opinions about Wang's career in China, however, no one said good words about him or the National Institute of Biological Sciences.

Consequently, while taking several years to set up a laboratory, form a team, recruit students, apply and obtain grants, and start their research, returnees also have to adapt and adjust to a "different" research environment and be involved in an assortment of activities deemed unimaginable when they were abroad. In some cases, they are unable to survive back home because they no longer know the rules of the game or how it is played in China – there may be no rules at all, as in the case of handling misconduct in research – and they have no one to turn to for help as they do not have good *guanxi*.

Serving China in various ways

In addition to some 319 700 individuals who have returned to China permanently, it should be realized that the large Chinese diaspora is a significant asset strategically and practically, especially in terms of transfer of knowledge, the attraction of foreign capital for high-technology endeavors, and local entrepreneurship. In spite of some of the challenges noted above, it is in fact the case that many former *liuxuesheng* who stay abroad still remain connected to China's S&T system by serving as reviewers for China's institutions of learning and various research and education programs. The CAS has set up an expatriate expert database from which the academy selects the best overseas Chinese to evaluate its institutes and researchers. So has the NSFC, which use overseas Chinese in the evaluation of grant proposals. In other cases, many overseas Chinese admit their alumni as graduate students or post-doctorates and collaborate with their former Chinese colleagues.

For those who have formal appointments at foreign universities, research laboratories, or companies, working part-time in China is their best choice to stay connected. Some have become "migratory birds" (*houniao*), flying back at fixed period of time, say, summer. But there are more creative ways – from government, institutions, and themselves – to accommodate the interests of expatriate Chinese academics. The aptly termed "dumbbell" model (*yaling moshi*) is among the most used, where an overseas Chinese academic, who has a full-time appointment at a foreign institution, holds a concurrent appointment in an Chinese institution, like having research bases at both sides of the "dumbbell" – in their formal appointed institution as well as a Chinese unit. And, as noted, they are the "amphibians" (*liangqi*) because they seem to thrive on both the Chinese and foreign environments. They spend a certain amount of time each year at each base, and when they are away from China, the convenience of information and telecommunications technology permits them to "remotely control" their research in China. For example, the National Institute of Biological Sciences is co-directed by biochemist Wang Xiaodong and plant biologist Deng Xingwang, both established Chinese-American life scientists.[25] At times, they shuttle back and forth to China as much as once a month! Liuxuesheng may use this approach as a stepping-stone for their permanent return, as the

---

[25] Wang Xiaodong is the George L. MacGregor Distinguished Chair Professor in biomedical science with the University of Texas Southwestern Medical Center in Dallas and an investigator of the prestigious Howard Hughes Medical Institute. Deng Xingwang, the other director, is the Daniel C. Eaton Professor of plant from the Department of Molecular, Cellular, and Developmental Biology at Yale University. Deng is an expert on the cellular signaling process responsible for the regulation of development by extracellular stimuli. Based on the number of citations, Deng's laboratory at Yale was ranked twelfth in the area of arabidopsis and plant disease resistance in the world.

case of Yi Rao has shown. Rao, the recently appointed Dean of Beijing University School of Life Sciences, had been running laboratories at the CAS Institute of Neuroscience and the National Institute of Biological Sciences, and helping to improve China's research environment before making the formal commitment.

In 2002, a group of expatriate Chinese economics professors from such prestigious universities as Columbia, MIT, the University of California, Berkeley, and Yale set up a special professorship at the School of Economics and Management at Qinghua University. The professors take time off alternately to lecture and advise students at Qinghua for several months a year. Qian Yingyi, one of the special professors and a full professor of economics at the University of California, Berkeley, was appointed first Deputy Dean of the school in October 2005 and Dean a year later.[26] Under his leadership, and because of the contributions of the special professors and other faculty members, the school became the first Chinese business school accredited by the Association to Advance Collegiate Schools of Business (AACSB) in 2007. The CAS is also experimenting with similar approaches for securing help from groups of overseas Chinese academics.

Those who do not have the interest or time to serve their native country may just be "flying kites," contacted by their colleagues or original institutions in China from time to time to keep their interest and any possibilities alive. Some scientists have expressed their wish to return completely to China while they are quite active academically and may conduct first-tier research there. However, whether China can truly provide or develop an attractive academic environment is uncertain, which explains why many scholars end up simply testing the water and working concurrently in China and abroad as a hedge against unanticipated problems or challenges.

Emerging problems

As suggested above, in utilizing the services and knowledge of expatriate Chinese, especially high-level S&T talent, the Chinese government has been quite accommodating. Because the knowledge and skills of this group are crucial to China's development in science, education, and the economy, those who are permanent residents or

---

[26] It seems that Qian did not give up his tenured professorship at Berkeley.

even citizens of foreign countries are warmly welcomed. The government has started to issue permanent resident visas to ethnic Chinese with foreign citizenship if they work and have business operations in China. In essence, they are granted the same privileges as nationals, including approval to apply for entrepreneurial funding, educating school-aged children, purchasing properties, and enjoying social security benefits. Even some political activists are not discriminated against in these circumstances. For example, Fu Xinyuan, a human rights activist who used to sit on the Board of Human Rights in China, and then an associate professor at Yale Medical School (he is now a professor with the National University of Singapore after spending several years at Indiana University School of Medicine), started to run two laboratories in China – one at Nanjing Normal University, his alma mater, and the other at Qinghua University – as early as 2000. His suggestion to combat misconduct in Chinese science was well received by China's scientific leadership – the then Minister of Science and Technology, Xu Guanhua, even met him for his opinions. Shen Tong, one of the key figures in the Tiananmen Square student movement in 1989, is said to be behind the launching of *Focus Interviews* (*Jiaodian Fangtan*), a popular television program shown on Chinese Central Television that reveals cases of corruption in China, while another Tiananmen Square student leader, William Xin (originally Xin Weirong), now Co-chair and Chief Executive Officer of BChinaB, a critical outsourcing solutions provider based in New York, helps foreign companies manage all aspects of production, consolidation, and export from China through local private entrepreneurs (*World Journal Weekly*, [New York], April 13, 2003: 30–1).

Still, although the overall situation remains positive, and continues to improve, several talent-utilization issues have begun to emerge. The first concerns the conflict between those trained abroad (*haigui*, or sea turtles) and those educated at home (referred to as *tubie*, or domestically trained turtles). As discussed above, various programs initiated by the Chinese government are seen as affirmative action-type initiatives designed to give special preferences to *haigui*, who are more likely to become "haves," while those *tubie* remain, "have nots." This conflict was reflected in the failed reform scheme at Beijing University, where *haigui* were favored in faculty recruitment and promotion initiatives. The implication is that the degrees earned by those who have never gone abroad to study are, in effect, worth less. One specific complaint that the *tubie* have is that the *haigui* have made use of their academic capital earned abroad again and again, thus continually putting *tubie* in unfair and disadvantageous positions. More problematic is that some of the *haigui* have been given rewards and resources far greater than their credentials warrant, thus putting key aspects of China's reward and evaluation system in jeopardy. Because of all these benefits, some returnees have been fabricating or exaggerating their credentials, which in turn has discredited not only themselves but returnees as a whole. And, because of the special favor given to *haigui*, of the 93 600 Chinese doctorates granted between 1985 and 2004, only 33 000 did their post-doctoral research in China. Presumably, many more may have gone abroad for such advanced training and are simply waiting for a good opportunity to be attracted back as *haigui*.

Second, while the Chinese leadership has taken a "global" attitude toward overseas study and the brain drain issue, a "nationalist" tendency has been rising from the Chinese scientific and educational community. Some question whether China's long-term development in science and education will benefit from the "dumbbell" and "remote control" models (Cao & Suttmeier, 2001). In the globalized twenty-first century world, on the other hand, this model may actually represent the cutting edge of a new globally deployed talent pool that is highly mobile, highly flexible, and largely borderless in terms of national affiliation. This new talent utilization model has faculty and researchers who are less physically tied to their home campus while they become increasingly embedded in a series of trans-national knowledge networks focussed on different fields and research areas. Nonetheless, in many cases, Chinese attitudes have not caught up with the speed at which an integrated global innovation system has superseded the multiplicity of national innovation systems around the world. As one CAS member, himself a foreign doctorate, indicated in the interview, the development of Chinese science can only depend upon the efforts of those working on Chinese soil. Perhaps his remark is too extreme, but to some extent, it represents the sentiment of many members of the scientific community working within China, regardless of where they have received their training and whether they have worked abroad.

Third, programs to improve the domestic talent pool by recruiting Chinese scientists working abroad also have not avoided the growing problems of fraud and corruption, which have begun to plague Chinese science over the last few years. In some cases, the high salaries and attractive material incentives used in returnees programs have been abused. Researchers have enjoyed the salaries without taking their research responsibilities seriously; that is, without fulfilling the obligations of their appointments. While their new institutions may be satisfied to use the names and publications produced by these "star scientists" to improve their standing and thus qualify for increased funding, the concrete results have been disappointing. As these programs are related to how best to use China's research monies most wisely and efficiently, the scientific community has petitioned for a crackdown on returnees who have received the most sought-after grants, but have failed to devote enough time to research in China (Cyranoski, 2003). Having noticed the problem, the CAS now requires that those recruited into the One Hundred Talent Program work full-time in China during their tenure.

Fourth, some of the overseas Chinese scientists have taken advantage of their foreign positions and research grants to pursue research in China in an unprofessional, if not unethical, way. Quite a number of Chinese scientists who have formal appointments in foreign institutions have a vested interest in "acquiring" the services of bright Chinese graduate students. The most extraordinary and controversial case involves Xu Xiping, then associate professor of occupational epidemiology at the Harvard School of Public Health, who was found to conduct genetic epidemiology studies in China without the approval of the Chinese government nor informed consent from the participants, most being farmers. Although in May 2003 the Office for Human Research Protection of the US Department of Health and Human Services investigating this professor's studies did not find evidence of harm to individual participants, or evidence of fraud in the informed consent procedures, it at least identified a number of procedural lapses in oversight and record-keeping in some of his research projects (Sleeboom, 2005).

Fifth, recent high-profile cases of misconduct in Chinese science involving returnees have not only tarnished the image of returnees as a group, but also generated new doubts within many Chinese institutions about recruiting academics from overseas. For example, Chen Jin of Shanghai Jiaotong University, a returnee from the USA, claimed that he had come up with a new digital signal processing

(DSP) chip – the "China chip" (*Hanxin*), but it turned out that the chip waspurchased from Motorola with Motorola's logo replaced by that of *Hanxin* in an effort to disguise the poor performance of Chen's team.

Finally, China's well-funded institutions of learning are dis-proportionately located in a few coastal cities, as are foreign-educated returnees. Apart from the *haigui–tubie* tension, this increasingly uneven distribution of human capital also presents a major political challenge to the Chinese leadership as it strives to achieve a more balanced regional development scheme (Li, 2004).

Conclusion

This chapter has discussed various issues involved in the overseas study experiences of Chinese in post-1978 China, with especial regard to the return of foreign-trained students and scholars. China has started to see a steady and growing reverse exodus of its overseas professionals and researchers, and a positive momentum in terms of the "brain circulation" phenomenon. However, as noted, "brain drain" has been serious in China in terms of both the low rate of return (about 25 percent) and the non-return of highly qualified Chinese scholars and professionals, especially in the science and engineering fields.

Many observers point out that this situation has been changing for the better as the Chinese economy has begun to occupy a more important position in the world. In making this argument, they tend to use the examples of Taiwan and South Korea to generalize that once a developing economy starts to grow rich, a return flow will build up on its own accord. In the case of Taiwan, initially, few *liuxuesheng* returned (rates of return were 8 percent between 1952 and 1961 and 4 percent between 1962 and 1985). But, the rate of return started to rise from the late 1980s when 34 percent of the island's *liuxuesheng* returned between 1986 and 1989 (Chang, 1992; Council for Economic Planning and Development, 2002: 289–92; Quan & Hoon, 2003).[27] As wages and opportunities at home improved, the government set up high-technology parks and com-panies to offer incentives to returnees. Following this logic, according

---

[27] Students studying abroad without government scholarships have been excluded from the Taiwanese statistics since July 1989.

to the argument, China will be the next to receive considerable return migration of its talent.

Although relevant to the case of the People's Republic of China, it also must be remembered that the return of overseas-trained Chinese back to Taiwan occurred not just in response to the new, emerging economic opportunities in the high-technology area, but also important were the loosening of political controls and the democratization taking place on the island (Choi, 1995). In this regard, political reform has lagged far behind the process of economic liberalization on mainland China. Moreover, potential political instability has remained a concern among overseas-educated Chinese from the People's Republic; in fact, the 1986–1987 anti-bourgeois liberalization movement and the 1989 Tiananmen Square crackdown had a significant negative impact on the return of overseas Chinese students (Orleans, 1988; Zweig & Chen, 1995). Career advancement, to some extent, still depends on political affiliation rather than pure merit, which continues to cause a loss of bright people to societies where talent is highly valued and rewarded. Because of this, many of the returnees retain their foreign passports or permanent resident status, or never give up their positions abroad. There also is the worry about top-down interference in science, education, and business, not to mention rampant corruption. Finally, the protection of property rights, especially intellectual property rights, also constrains some Chinese from returning. In a word, political stability, the rule of law, and a competitive but fair environment are just as critical as pure economic opportunities in encouraging many of those who would otherwise leave to stay in China and lure back some of those who have left. Therefore, many young Chinese scientists who are upwardly mobile simply choose not to return, even on a temporary basis. While becoming fewer in number overall, they still represent an irritant from the perspective of the leadership's S&T goals and objectives. It is hoped that the overall success of the 2008 Olympics in China will ease any outstanding concerns and help energize a "brain gain" movement.

One returnee remarked that "brain drain" will not be reversed unless the USA changes its immigration policy toward international students. This problem became more real than imagined in the aftermath of the September 11 attacks on the World Trade Center in New York. The difficulties Chinese students and scholars experienced in obtaining entry visas, especially for study in sensitive high-technology disciplines, forced many to shift their destinations or postpone their departure for the USA. The problems, however, seem to have proved short-lived. The reality is that American dependence on the influx of talented foreign students and researchers, including many from China, to staff its scientific and technological enterprises, means that closing the door would deny American universities and companies access to a critical knowledge resource. As a result, when problems began to emerge after the September 11 tragedy, American institutions of higher learning lobbied Congress and the Bush administration to lift or at least loosen the restrictions. For example, the National Science Board (2003) recommended that restrictions be lifted in order to "maintain the ability of the United States to attract internationally competitive researchers, faculty, and students" while "enhancing our homeland and national security."

"Brain drain" from China will not diminish in its entirety for the foreseeable future because of the younger age of the current crop of *liuxuesheng*, who are more easily assimilated into foreign culture and society. Also, unlike in the 1950s when thousands of overseas Chinese returned home to help build what they believed would be a new and better country, and in the 1980s when China's *gongpai* students felt an obligation and a responsibility to return to their home country, this time patriotism does not appear to be the primary factor in shaping the decision whether to return or not. On the contrary, such a decision has been mainly driven by personal gain. As members of the "me generation," with some obvious exceptions, many of these students view patriotic dedication and sacrifice as "hollow" notions, and simply appreciate the power of money; or they are following Deng Xiaoping's admonition, "to get rich is glorious." They do not necessarily see themselves as part and beneficiary of the great economic and technological progress that China has made since the reform and open-door policy started. Increasingly, their dreams have much more to do with their own future than with the future of China (Orleans, 1992). From the perspective of career development, therefore, the opportunity costs for the best and the brightest scientists to work in China seem just too high – low efficiency, personal conflict, and possible loss of close contacts with the international scientific community, which helps to explain why overseas Chinese academics, especially the most outstanding ones, are probably less likely to return or to be involved too deeply in China compared with their older counterparts. On the other hand, those younger scientists who are truly upwardly mobile, if they are able to find opportunities abroad, are not very likely to return home, even when a host of benefits is dangled before them. Some do not even bother to return to China on a temporary basis. While these academics may help China through mechanisms and projects that do not damage or inconvenience their career prospects, they may not necessarily focus on China's needs. They would rather delay until their highly productive years are over. Perhaps they should not be faulted as they are a product of the changing society in which they were born and educated. Nonetheless, it does mean that reversing the "brain drain" and achieving "brain gain" will remain an uphill task for the Chinese leadership in raising the overall quality of its human resources in science and technology.

7 | Supply and demand of science and technology talent in China: key drivers

The previous chapters have surveyed the prevailing situation regarding China's scientific and technical workforce and the higher education system that is responsible for producing the next generation of scientists and engineers. In particular, we have argued that the expansion of university enrollments since 1999 has created an increasing supply of graduates, perhaps even oversupply, in science and technology (S&T) and other disciplines. And, we also have shown that, at the same time, despite admissions having increased, both foreign-invested and domestic employers in China continue to face a growing challenge of finding appropriate candidates for employment with not only adequate educational credentials but also the right skills, competencies, and experience for the highly skilled jobs that they increasingly need to fill. In other words, China continues to face a "talent shortage" in terms of the gap between supply and demand. This kind of mismatch derives primarily from the imbalance between quality and quantity, between the specific skills required for jobs available *and* what the job candidates learned in school, and between localities that have open positions *and* the willingness of S&T personnel to relocate, among other issues.

From the perspective of available statistics and data, however, it is one thing to pinpoint the existence of China's talent problem, but quite another to quantify the actual size of the gap between supply and demand. In this chapter, we highlight and analyze the drivers behind both supply and demand for scientists and engineers in China over the next few years. In doing so, we take into consideration China's economic growth trajectory, social developments, and the increasing technological sophistication of the economy and society as well as the "flattening" world in which the mobility of capital, goods, services, and especially talent across national borders has become easier and quicker. In many cases, the effort required to assess the size and dimensions of China's talent gap is more than a statistical exercise as it is necessary to evaluate the reasonableness of our findings, as developed in our statistical model, against the reality that exists in China and to relate the talent issue to developments in the larger national and international context.

In what follows, using the drivers that we have identified as most statistically relevant, we forecast the supply and demand of scientists and engineers in China over the next five years. Scientists and engineers, the core of human resources in science and technology (HRST), as discussed in Chapter 3, refer to those who have formal higher education in an S&T field at the bachelor's degree level or above, and also include those who may not possess a specific formal credential, but who work in an S&T field and hold medium and higher professional rank. Given the growing influx of recent graduates into China's S&T workforce, and the retirement of the older generation, the ratio of those in the latter category has been declining. By using the same definitions identified earlier in this book, and the subsequent results from our statistical analysis, we highlight and amplify what appear to be the core reasons underlying the existence of a shortage of scientists and engineers in China.

Drivers of demand for scientists and engineers

Given the current pace of progress across the spectrum of Chinese science and technology, along with the sustained rate of growth across the Chinese economy, there are few, if any, reasons to challenge the notion that China will not make a radical departure from the very dynamic development trajectory that it has followed over the past couple of decades. An important underlying hypothesis driving the statistical analysis in the present chapter is the belief in the continuous changing complexion of the Chinese economy: the shift from a labor-intensive, low-end manufacturing orientation to a high-end knowledge emphasis is driving the growing overall demand for a technologically more sophisticated human resources base. In particular, the growth of the Chinese demand for not only more but also better scientists and engineers basically is expected to be driven by the following four main factors.

- China's increasing integration into the world economy.
- China's technological development based on the growth of indigenous S&T and research and development (R&D) activities.

- The increasing technological sophistication of the Chinese economy and society and the rising level of Chinese participation in the global value chain, as reflected in the expansion of high-technology exports by Chinese firms and multinational corporations (MNCs).
- The appreciation of the role of scientists and engineers in the Chinese economy and society.

As the Chinese economy "grows" along each of these four dimensions, the demand for scientists and engineers will steadily increase, even allowing for performance improvements, productivity gains, and efficiency enhancements.

During the past two decades, the Chinese economy has been growing at an astounding 9.5 percent annually. As a result of this sustained pace of rapid economic growth, today China is the world's third-largest economy in terms of nominal gross domestic product (GDP), after the USA and Japan. And it's abundant, comparatively low-cost, but highly educated workforce has propelled it to second position after the USA in purchasing power parity terms.[1]

At the same time, China also has been integrated more fully into the world economy, as evidenced by its accession to the World Trade Organization (WTO) in 2001, the growth of its foreign trade, the growing participation of MNCs in the Chinese economy through direct investment, and, more recently, the growing number of Chinese enterprises that are setting up operations abroad – across countries in South-east Asia and Africa as well as North America.[2] More specifically, it is clear that China's overall economic growth has been fueled in many key sectors by large increases in foreign direct investment (FDI) that have occurred since the announcement of the open-door policy in the late 1970s and in particular since the early 1990s. FDI

---

[1] For a discussion of the recent recalibration of China's gross domestic product (GDP), a 40 percent reduction based on purchasing power parity, see Porter (2007).

[2] China's foreign direct investment (FDI) figures are likely to be overstated due to a practice known as "round-tripping," whereby significant sums of money are taken out of China and then brought in again as "foreign investment." Investors therefore benefit from China's preferential policies for FDI. According to some estimates, round-tripping accounts for 20–30 percent of total FDI in China (see, for example, Xiao, 2004). However, even when accounting for this, the FDI flowing into China is still larger than for most other countries.

Table 7.1 *China's gross domestic product (GDP) and its growth*

Year	GDP RMB billion	GDP US $ billion	per capita GDP RMB	per capita GDP US $	Growth (%) GDP	Growth (%) per capita GDP
1978	365		381		11.67	10.19
1979	406		419		7.57	6.15
1980	455		463		7.84	6.50
1981	489		492		5.24	3.90
1982	532		528		9.06	7.46
1983	596		583		10.85	9.26
1984	721		695		15.18	13.67
1985	902	307	858	292	13.47	11.93
1986	1 028	298	963	279	8.85	7.24
1987	1 206	324	1 112	299	11.58	9.81
1988	1 504	404	1 366	367	11.28	9.50
1989	1 699	451	1 519	403	4.06	2.48
1990	1 867	390	1 644	344	3.84	2.33
1991	2 178	409	1 893	356	9.18	7.70
1992	2 692	488	2 311	419	14.24	12.85
1993	3 533	613	2 998	520	13.96	12.66
1994	4 820	559	4 044	469	13.08	11.81
1995	6 079	728	5 046	604	10.92	9.73
1996	7 118	856	5 846	703	10.01	8.86
1997	7 897	953	6 420	774	9.30	8.18
1998	8 440	1 019	6 796	821	7.83	6.80
1999	8 968	1 083	7 159	865	7.62	6.69
2000	9 921	1 198	7 858	949	8.43	7.58
2001	10 966	1 325	8 622	1 042	8.30	7.52
2002	12 033	1 454	9 398	1 135	9.08	8.35
2003	13 582	1 641	10 542	1 274	10.03	9.34
2004	15 988	1 932	12 336	1 490	10.09	9.43
2005	18 387	2 245	14 103	1 722	10.43	9.79
2006	21 087	2 645	16 084	2 018	11.09	10.47
2007	24 662	3 376	18 665	2 555	11.40	NA

Note: NA, not available.
Sources: National Bureau of Statistics, 2007: 57 and 59; NBS, 2008.

Table 7.2 *Foreign direct investment (FDI) (US $ billion)*

Year	FDI utilized	FDI in WOFEs
1979–1983	1.80	
1984	1.26	
1985	1.66	
1986	1.87	
1987	2.31	
1988	3.19	
1989	3.39	
1990	3.49	
1991	4.37	
1992	11.01	
1993	27.52	
1994	33.77	
1995	37.52	
1996	41.73	
1997	45.26	16.19
1998	45.46	16.47
1999	40.32	15.55
2000	40.77	19.26
2001	46.88	23.87
2002	52.74	31.73
2003	53.51	33.38
2004	60.63	40.22
2005	60.33	42.96
2006	63.02	46.28
2007	74.80	NA

Note: WOFEs, wholly foreign-owned enterprises; NA, not available.
Sources: National Bureau of Statistics, various years; National Bureau of Statistics, 2008.

continues to be an important component of China's economic development, although it is probably not going to see the level of significant increases in absolute value as seen in the past – from around US $40 billion in the late 1990s to US $60 billion in 2004 and thereafter (Table 7.2). But there likely will be important quality improvements and structural changes in the content and composition of FDI in the sense that US $60 billion of FDI in 2010 will have a significantly different character than a similar level of FDI in 2004. First, it is evident that the focus of FDI has been shifting from labor-intensive manufacturing in product areas such as toys, textiles, shoes, and furniture, to higher value-added types of investments in computers and office equipment, pharmaceuticals, and micro-electronics. Essentially, FDI has been the principal growth driver of China's information and telecommunications technology (ICT) industries and related high-technology exports and foreign-invested enterprises (FIEs) have dominated China's increasing high-technology exports. Second, operationally, spurred on by new legislation issued by the Ministry of Commerce, plus the increasing attractiveness of China's talent pool, as noted, FDI also has expanded from an almost single-minded focus on manufacturing into the realm of R&D, as exemplified by the increasing number of scientists and engineers employed in FIEs and some 1140 R&D centers established by FIEs, including well-established MNCs, as of mid-2007 (see Table 2.2 and Table 3.8). As a whole, large- and medium-sized FIEs have appreciably increased their R&D spending, which, according to Chinese government statistics, accounted for 14.80 percent of China's total R&D spending in 2006 (NBS & MOST, 2007: 6, 199–200). Third, the ownership structure of FDI projects has also changed, with two-thirds of these projects being wholly foreign-owned enterprises (WFOEs) in 2006, compared with some one-third a decade ago. Within the WFOE structure, foreign firms are more comfortable bringing advanced know-how to China and putting high-technology content into their ventures, apparently leading to critical quality improvements and structural enhancements in the content and composition of FDI over time. Of course, the strategic goals of MNCs are not only to penetrate the huge Chinese market, with its increasing number of affluent consumers, but also to take advantage of China's relatively higher quality but less expensive workforce to climb up the value chain.

More importantly, however, even taking into account the significant impact of FDI on the country's talent situation, demand for S&T manpower in China has been shifting from being highly FDI-driven to other factors, such as the increasing levels of "informatization" and technological sophistication of Chinese society, the increases in domestic spending on S&T, R&D, and education, the introduction of more favorable wages for those in the S&T profession, and growing high-technology exports from both local and foreign investment firms.

There is little doubt that China is on an explosive economic and technological trajectory that will result in its becoming a knowledge-intensive, information society over the next one to two decades. The country already has the world's largest base of mobile subscribers – 600 million as of mid-2008, which will continue to experience rapid growth in coming years (Table 7.3). With 253 million internet users as of mid-2008, China has already replaced the USA as the country with the largest number of internet users (China's internet use among the young population is also the largest in the world); with 84.7 percent, China also overtook the USA in numbers of homes connected to broadband as well. All of this internet activity will further stimulate household personal computer (PC) ownership and the expansion of the indigenous telecommunications infrastructure, thus accelerating even further growth within the ICT industry. In addition, the coming launch of the third-generation (3G) mobile cellphone service will be another stimulant for FDI and China's ICT industry. Fueled by these developments on the civilian side as well as increasing national defense requirements, China's chip-design industry has grown nearly five-fold to 450 companies during the past five years. Informatization is deeply tied to the changing composition of FDI, the growth of China's high-technology industries, and the onset of e-government and e-commerce around the country. The impact of informatization as measured by the percentage of gross value of industrial output (GVIO) from the manufacture of communications equipment, computers, and other electronic equipment (GVIO-IT for short) in total GVIO at all state-owned enterprises and non-state-owned enterprises with an annual revenue of RMB5 million also has picked up (see Table 7.3).

With all these changes taking place, there is likely to be a concomitant rise in the demand for more S&T talent to support the next stage of development. Further demand also is likely to be exacerbated by China's increased emphasis on indigenous efforts concerning its technological development (*zizhu chuangxin*). Top Chinese political and scientific leaders have perceived the very strong positive correlation between the number of scientists and engineers in a country's workforce and that country's level of R&D activity. With a steadily improving talent base, they hope to guide their country toward becoming an innovation-oriented nation by the year 2020, as specified in the comprehensive 15-year Medium to Long-Term Plan for the

Table 7.3 *Level of informatization*

Year	Internet users	Mobile subscribers	Fixed phone subscribers	Mobile per 100 households	PCs per 100 households	GVIO-IT
		(million)		(units)	(units)	(%)
1978			1.93			
1980			2.14			
1985			3.12			
1989		0.01	5.68			3.15
1990		0.02	6.85			3.13
1991		0.05	8.45			3.46
1992		0.18	11.47			3.35
1993		0.64	17.33			3.74
1994		1.57	27.30			3.89
1995		3.63	40.71			4.61
1996		6.85	54.95			4.86
1997	0.6	13.23	70.31	1.7	2.6	5.74
1998	2.1	23.86	87.42	3.0	3.8	7.22
1999	8.9	43.30	108.72	7.1	5.9	8.02
2000	22.5	84.53	144.83	19.5	9.7	8.81
2001	33.7	145.22	180.37	34.0	13.3	9.42
2002	59.1	206.01	214.22	62.9	20.6	10.19
2003	79.5	269.95	262.75	90.1	27.8	11.13
2004	94.0	334.82	311.76	110.4	31.0	NA
2005	111.0	393.41	350.45	137.0	41.5	10.73
2006	132.0	461.10	367.80	152.9	47.2	10.45
2007	210.0	547.29	365.45	NA	NA	NA

NA, not available.

Sources: National Bureau of Statistics, various years.

Development of Science and Technology (2006–2020) (MLP) announced in January 2006 (Cao *et al.*, 2006).

As noted, since 1999, China has increased its spending on S&T, R&D, and education. At 1.49% of GDP in 2007, China's gross expenditure on R&D (GERD) still remains below the level of most developed economies (about 2.7–3.0%) and short of the goal set for 2005 – 1.5% – by top government officials (Table 7.4). Nonetheless, China exhibits the highest S&T spending level among those economies at a similar level of development (GERD as a percentage of

Table 7.4 *China's gross expenditure on research and development (GERD), government expenditure on education, and their percentages of gross domestic product (GDP)*

Year	GERD RMB billion	US $ billion	GERD/ GDP %	Government expenditure on education RMB billion	US $ billion	Government expenditure on education/GDP %
1991	15.08	2.83	0.69	61.78	11.61	3.02
1992	20.98	3.80	0.78	72.87	13.21	2.65
1993	25.62	4.45	0.73	86.78	15.06	2.46
1994	30.98	3.59	0.64	117.47	13.63	2.44
1995	34.91	4.18	0.57	141.15	16.90	2.32
1996	40.48	4.87	0.57	167.17	20.11	2.35
1997	50.92	6.14	0.64	186.25	22.47	2.36
1998	55.11	6.66	0.65	203.24	24.55	2.41
1999	67.89	8.20	0.76	228.72	27.63	2.55
2000	89.57	10.82	0.90	256.26	30.96	2.58
2001	104.25	12.60	0.95	305.70	36.93	2.79
2002	128.76	15.56	1.07	349.14	42.18	2.90
2003	153.96	18.60	1.13	385.06	46.52	2.84
2004	196.63	23.76	1.23	446.59	53.96	2.79
2005	245.00	29.91	1.33	516.11	63.00	2.82
2006	300.31	37.67	1.42	NA	NA	NA
2007	366.40	50.16	1.49	NA	NA	NA

NA, not available.
Sources: National Bureau of Statistics and Ministry of Science and Technology, various years; National Bureau of Statistics, 2008.

GDP was 0.78% for India in 2001 and 1.04% for Brazil in 2000) (MOST, 2007: 194). In fact, China's GERD has been growing at about twice the rate of its rapidly growing economy! At present, there is growing evidence that China is well on its way to making progress toward its goal of spending 2% of its GDP on R&D by 2010 and 2.5% by 2020, as stipulated by the MLP.[3] Most impressive, as

---

[3] As we learned from our June 2008 fieldwork in China on the MLP implementation, this remains a very ambitious goal and it is likely to be difficult to achieve given present trends.

suggested earlier, is the fact that much of the recent growth in GERD has seemingly derived from industrial and high-technology enterprises, including FIEs. As a whole, the contribution from enterprises – some 70 percent in 2006 – has reached the average level of Organization for Economic Co-operation and Development (OECD) countries. As mentioned, there are some unique reasons for the deepening of R&D activities inside Chinese enterprises, such as the transformation of application-oriented R&D institutes into enterprises at the turn of the twenty-first century. Even taking these into account, however, the fact remains that the locus of innovation in China is indeed shifting to corporate actors rather than formal government-direct research institutes, which indicates a further sharp departure from the model adopted from the former Soviet Union in the 1950s.

Similarly, the Chinese leadership also apparently understands the dramatic importance of education to China's potential S&T advance as well as to the country's general economic and social development (see Table 7.4). China has increased educational expenditures over the last decade and will continue to do so in the years to come. In fact, China has much room to grow in this regard. Measured by education spending as a percentage of government expenditure, ironically, China's 2.82% in 2005 remains among the lowest in the world (the same indicator in 2002–2003 was 4.1% for India and 4.3% for Brazil) (World Bank, 2006: 80–1). Again, the nation has not reached the 4% target set for the year 2000. Yet, the investment in the upgrading of Chinese universities has been substantial by domestic standards, with universities now becoming more central players in the R&D system instead of being primarily teaching-only institutions. This is another sharp departure from previous reliance on the former Soviet model. New facilities have been built throughout the country, many with advanced equipment and research laboratories. The principal shortage, as discussed in Chapter 4, has been in the area of qualified faculty to teach the growing number of university students at undergraduate and especially graduate levels. Recruitment of high-quality faculty to staff the growing number of positions at Chinese colleges and universities represents the "Achilles heel" of the higher education sector.

The growing technological sophistication of the Chinese economy and society is reflected not only in the increasing number of Chinese receiving higher education, but also in the increasing share of high-technology exports in the country's overall trade. According to a

Table 7.5 *China's high-technology trade (US $ billion)*

Year	Export	Import	Balance
1985	0.52	4.73	−4.21
1986	0.72	4.99	−4.27
1987	0.92	5.39	−4.47
1988	1.29	8.13	−6.85
1989	1.85	6.85	−5.01
1990	2.69	6.97	−4.28
1991	2.88	9.44	−6.56
1992	4.00	10.71	−6.72
1993	4.68	15.91	−11.23
1994	6.34	20.60	−14.25
1995	10.09	19.19	−9.10
1996	12.66	22.47	−9.80
1997	16.31	23.89	−7.58
1998	20.25	29.20	−8.95
1999	24.70	37.60	−12.89
2000	37.34	52.51	−15.16
2001	46.46	64.12	−17.66
2002	67.87	82.85	−14.98
2003	110.32	119.30	−8.98
2004	165.40	161.30	4.10
2005	218.20	197.70	20.50
2006	281.50	247.30	34.20

Source: National Bureau of Statistics and Ministry of Science and Technology, various years.

United Nations (UN) report, China was already the world's tenth-largest high-technology exporting country in 1998–1999 (UNDP, 2001: 42); in 2006, China's high-technology exports reached US $281.5 billion, representing an almost 100-fold increase over the level of high-technology exports in 1991 (Table 7.5). In recent years, China has seen itself with a high-technology trade surplus – another dramatic departure from its position during 1980s and most of the 1990s.

To a considerable degree, China's high-technology sector has moved up the value chain as a result of both the changing structure of FDI and technology imports *and* China's indigenous efforts. China's movement up the learning curve has been significant; comparing the level of manufacturing know-how that was in place in the early 1980s with the situation in the mid-1990s and since 2001 to the present, there is appreciable evidence of a remarkable transition in overall management and quality, especially as related to the types of tasks and levels of complexity that may be handled by domestic enterprises, large and small, in terms of part and component production, sub-assembly, and final assembly operations. One big question, however, is who controls the intellectual property embodied in most of the products and components being sent abroad; in some sectors, FIEs account for over 80 percent of the export revenues and much of the value added. This fact has not gone unnoticed by the Chinese leadership, especially at a time when countries such as the USA are paying increasing attention to intellectual property rights as a key source of competitive advantage.

Finally, on average, as discussed in Chapter 5, the S&T-related sectors have outperformed other occupations in wage terms, with those working in the ICT sector now being among the best paid in China. Because of the increasing mobility of global talent, and in response to some of the prevailing as well as projected shortages of needed talent, wages in these advanced sectors have been steadily converging with international levels in Europe and the USA. Head-hunters in Beijing and Shanghai report that Chinese firms such as Huawei, TCL, and Datang as well as Lenovo and internet companies find themselves paying rates closer and closer to the relative wages in the USA to attract qualified talent to their R&D laboratories and engineering-design units, and to compete for such talent with MNCs operating in China.

In summary, the demand for scientists and engineers in China in the years to come will largely be driven by China's indigenous efforts, as measured by increasing spending in S&T, R&D, and education, as well as continuous structural changes in the nature of FDI – toward high-end, high-technology, and high-value added. The informatization of Chinese society and the growth of the domestic high-end market mainly serve as key intervening factors, fostered and shaped by the changing face of FDI and *zizhu chuangxin* efforts. In this regard, FDI may have been a stimulus to domestic innovation rather than an inhibitor. What is still somewhat uncertain is the degree to which the Chinese domestic market itself will also become a critically important force underlying the growth of demand for talent, especially if and when the overall supply–demand gap becomes narrower. Nonetheless, there is no reason to believe that technical careers are any less attractive in China; nor does there appear to be any reason to indicate that the emergence of new jobs in finance, business, law, and other professional services will curtail the strong interest in such technical careers to any appreciable degree.

Supply of scientists and engineers

In addition to fortifying the existing S&T talent base in China, the future supply of scientists and engineers, which will be drawn from students graduating in science, engineering, agriculture, and medicine, will be needed to offset the growing ranks of retired S&T workforce members (the older generation); to a lesser extent, returnees with overseas study and work experiences will also be needed to address the retirement problem (to be discussed below). Over the short- to medium-term, however, the increasing supply of college graduates has begun to create a number of unanticipated problems, which began to reveal themselves as early as three to four years in the aftermath of the initial 1999 admissions increase. The main source of these problems is that the growth in overall enrollment occurred with almost no reference or guidance in terms of specialization or niches, no apparent consideration of the skill sets needed to meet the rise in demand, nor any specific preparation for dealing with the qualitative aspects of newly trained, albeit "raw" graduates, as discussed in Chapter 4. The types of job-related, market-derived feedback loops that exist in countries such as the USA do not exist or work very well in China. Therefore, even many of the students enrolled in so-called "hot" specialties have had difficulty finding jobs related to their training.

It must be remembered that the current surplus of college graduates coincides with the growth of the urban working population, the reform at the state-owned enterprises which has led to growing employee layoffs, and the migration of rural youth from the countryside to China's major urban areas. Interestingly, only 22% of the new jobs created in 2006 were for college graduates. Finally, to fully appreciate the extent of the problem, it also must be remembered once again that the number of college entrants has grown from about 3% of high school graduates in the early 1990s to over 22% by 2006, with 23 million Chinese university students in total, counting those in various forms of non-traditional higher education. The government of the People's Republic of China has announced that this percentage is intended to grow to 25% by 2010, which at present rates will surely be exceeded. No wonder that 30% of new graduates between 2005 and 2007 were unable to find jobs, and, of the other 70% who supposedly did, there is no clear explanation to account for the actual match between supply and demand in specific fields.

Consequently, as the economy reaches an even higher level of labor excess among college graduates over the next few years, the supply of scientists and engineers could become even less aligned with China's precise labor market conditions because of the continued expansion of admissions. Under such conditions, wages may not be the most accurate barometer for understanding the supply and demand for S&T human resources in China, as Chinese leaders do not seem prepared to retreat on their "higher education push" and their associated commitment to grow and improve tertiary education. From the perspective of China's top leaders, having an educated society has many virtues and is viewed in very positive terms. Yet, with so many graduates unable to find jobs, let alone ones in their specific fields of training, the situation may also become a source of great frustration and social problems in the future. In a word, if the Chinese economy experiences a state of appreciable labor-excess, there could be political consequences as well as economic ones that could create a new period of brain drain – internal and external – or even socio-political unrest. This also would further complicate efforts to utilize the market mechanism to create a balance between supply and demand as wages would not accurately predict the demand for S&T talent.

The supply of scientists and engineers is also integral to the nation's demographics as well. It is clear that China's college-bound 18–22-year-old cohort will begin to shrink after 2010, apparently because of the one-child policy (Figure 7.1).[4] This further decrease in college graduates will have an impact, likely negative, on the overall number of scientists and engineers seeking entry into the workforce. That is, even if China wants to maintain a large pool of scientists and engineers in reserve, it might be unable to do so because of the country's unfavorable demographics. It is under these circumstances that China probably has a narrow "window of opportunity" from now until 2020 or so to grow its high-quality S&T workforce from the perspective of

[4] The last time in which China saw a dip in the same age group was between 1989 and 2001.

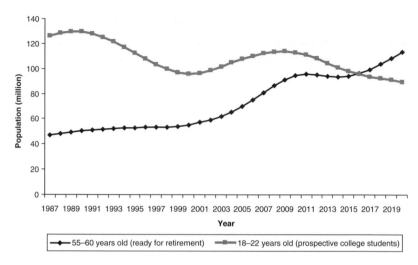

Figure 7.1 China's population change by age groups.
Source: Based on United Nations Population Division, 2005.

ensuring a better match between the demands of the economy and technology system and the types of graduates and professionals being educated within the country's higher education institutions. Granted the increase in admissions of students into China's higher education institutions since 1999 has, to some extent, hedged the coming drain of college-bound youth and provided a "just-in-case" solution to it.[5] Even in a mature market economy such as the USA, such matching of supply and demand is difficult to achieve. In contrast to China, where the market mechanism remains immature and market reforms are still incomplete, however, American labor markets are highly responsive to shifts in supply and demand, and wage rates adjust relatively quickly to changes in the availability of those with skills that are in high demand.

Modeling and forecasting demand and supply of scientists and engineers

The research which provides the principal source of data for this chapter is aimed at analyzing and projecting supply and demand

---

[5] Available online at http://edu.china.com/zh_cn/1055/20051118/12862674.html (accessed on November 30, 2005).

trends regarding China's high-end talent pool to 2010 by use of a linear regression-based methodology.[6] In assessing the dynamics of supply and demand for high-end S&T talent, it looks specifically at scientists and engineers involved in S&T activities in general, and R&D activities in particular, to gauge the technological potential and innovative capacity of China from a human resource perspective.

Dependent variables

- Scientists and engineers (S&Es).
- Scientists and engineers involved in R&D activities (S&Es–R&D).

Independent variables

Statistical modeling is based on discussion in the previous sections; the analysis has yielded the following independent variables:

- Spending: S&T expenditures; GERD; education expenditures.
- Integration of Chinese economy into the world: FDI-utilized.
- Informatization of society: GVIO-IT as percentage of GVIO.[7]
- Technological sophistication: graduating undergraduates and graduate students in science, engineering, agriculture, and medicine; high-technology exports
- Relative wages across the S&T sector versus the national average – a proxy that reflects the role of market forces.

The relationship between the variables is shown in Figure 7.2.

Primary data sources

The analysis is based on national-level data between 1989 and 2006 from the following sources: *China Statistical Yearbook* (NBS); *China Statistical Yearbook on Science and Technology* (NBS & MOST); *China Statistics Yearbook on High-Technology Industry* (NBS, NDRC

---

[6] We have learned how to identify factors correlated with shortages and labor surpluses from Cohen & Zaidi (2002: 59–91).

[7] We have tried other independent variables in this category, such as number of mobile subscribers in population, number of internet users in population, and number of computers in urban households, but they are not significant. Even this variable is embedded in FDI utilized and high-technology exports.

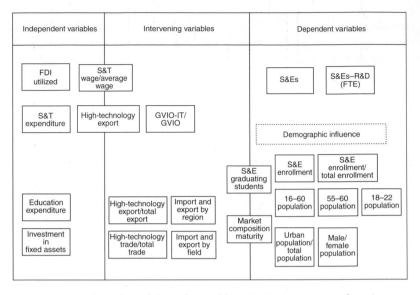

Figure 7.2 Analytical models and variables. S&Es, scientists and engineers; FDI, foreign direct investment; S&T, science and technology; S&E, science and engineering; R&D, research and development; FTE, full-time equivalent; GVIO, gross value of industrial output; GVIO-IT, gross value of industrial output in information technology.

Source: Authors' research.

& MOST); *China Labor Statistical Yearbook* (NBS & MOLSS); *China Educational Statistics Yearbook* (MOEd); and *China Population Statistical Yearbook* (NBS Department of Population and Employment Statistics).

Models

Linear regressions have resulted in two models with significant coefficients:

- Model 1: S&Es (or S&Es–R&D) = f (FDI utilized, S&T expenditure/GERD).
- Model 2: S&Es (or S&Es–R&D) = f (High-technology exports, the S&T wages relative to the national average).

Problems of multi-colinearity were identified owing to the limited number of observations and also the nature of the independent variable; this prevented the inclusion of more independent variables in the regression models. Nonetheless, the models do appear to capture the type of "supply–demand" dynamic previously discussed.

Forecast of demand

In addition to the historical trends noted above, forecasts for supply and demand for China's scientists and engineers utilized a number of recognized sources as references, including forecasts of China's economic growth by Goldman Sachs (known as the BRICs report[8]) (Wilson & Purushothaman, 2003); forecasts of China's population growth by the United Nations Population Division (UNPD); and the Chinese government's policy initiatives in the areas of science and technology as well as higher education, talent growth and development, high-technology development, and several other areas (e.g. ICT). Our goal has been to analyze supply and demand conditions using a linear extrapolation based on recent historical growth trends as well as taking into account discontinuities (non-linear extrapolation) – either acceleration or deceleration – in growth to incorporate possible changes in the drivers of economic development over the next five years. We have come up with six scenarios – two based on historical trends and four assuming discontinuities of both downward and upward possibilities for each of the demand models – between 2007 and 2010 (Table 7.6). From these different extrapolations, we have identified and evaluated a broad range of possibilities representing the lowest, highest, and most likely outcomes on the demand side (Table 7.7).

Our forecast is as follows: in what we assess to be "the most likely scenario," China needed some 3.12 million scientists and engineers in 2007; demand is projected to increase to 3.95 million in 2010. In the meantime, China required 1.40 million and 1.90 million full-time equivalent (FTE) scientists and engineers, respectively, engaged in R&D activities in 2007 and 2010. This forecast is significantly higher than that made by Chinese S&T policy analysts when they prepared for the MLP based on data up to 2001. According to that largely supply-driven forecast, which factored GERD as the only independent variable, China was going to have between 848 000 and 1.75 million FTE scientists and engineers in R&D in 2010 (Li & Yu, 2004).

[8] BRICs refer to such countries as Brazil, Russia, India, and China.

Table 7.6 *Demand forecasting scenarios based on regression (2007–2010)*

Scenario	Model	Change in independent variables	Demand	Note
Trend Historical	1	Using historical trends	f (FDI utilized, S&T expenditure) f (High-technology exports relative wage)	No regression
	2 (Most likely 1)		f (FDI utilized, S&T expenditure)	
Downward	1	FDI 2% annual decreases; S&T expenditure/GERD 5% annual increase		
	2 (low)	High-technology exports 10% increase; relative wage flat after 2006	f (High-technology exports, relative wage)	
Upward	1 (most likely 2)	FDI 8% annual increases; S&T expenditure/GERD 15% annual increase	f (FDI utilized, S&T expenditure)	
	2 (high)	High-technology exports following historical trend; relative wage 10% annual increase	f (High-technology exports, relative wage)	

Source: Authors' research.

Table 7.7 *Forecast of the supply and demand of scientists and engineers in China (1000 persons)*

Year	Supply	Historical trend		Most likely		High		Low		Oversupply or shortage versus the most likely
		S&Es	S&Es – R&D	S&Es	S&Es – R&D	S&Es	S&Es – R&D	S&Es	S&Es – R&D	S&Es
2007	3 011	2 900	1 304	3 062	1 401	3 300	1 468	2 781	1 210	–51
2008	3 253	3 001	1 383	3 298	1 557	3 780	1 694	2 874	1 271	–46
2009	3 523	3 103	1 463	3 534	1 723	4 286	1 927	2 976	1 337	–11
2010	3 825	3 205	1 543	3 771	1 902	4 820	2 170	3 089	1 411	55

Source: Authors' projection.

Forecast of supply

In forecasting the supply of scientists and engineers, we have considered the following factors. On average, 88.7% of males aged between 16 and 60 years and 78.3% of females aged between 16 and 55 years are active in the labor force. In China, the statutory retirement age is 60 years old for males and 55 years old for females; we have assumed that scientists and engineers observe the same retirement age and they have the same rate of retirement as Chinese employees as a whole. Therefore, we have calculated the retirement rate of the existing scientists and engineers as follows.

Retirement rate $(t) = 100$ * (# male at 60 (t) * 0.887 + # female at 55 (t) * 0.785)/(# male at 16–60 * 0.887 + # female at 16–55 * 0.783)

We have assumed that 75% of the graduates with master's degrees or above have become employed as working scientists and engineers upon receiving their degrees. Some of the undergraduates trained in science, engineering, agriculture, and medicine continue on to graduate-level education at home and abroad, while others seek actual full-time employment. Unfortunately, China has had a low and inconsistent record in placing these graduates, but we expect this placement rate to improve gradually as the quality of students also improves and as the labor market matures. Here, the 2007 placement rate for S&T undergraduates into the S&T fields will be the average of the rates between 2001 and 2006, and we have further assumed that thereafter placement will improve incrementally by 5% annually.

The forecast model for the supply of scientists and engineers is as follows.

S&Es (t) = S&Es $(t\text{-}1)$ * (1 – retirement rate) + S&E graduates (t) * 0.75 + S&T undergraduates (1 – advanced studies rate) * job placement rate for S&T undergraduates

Based on these data and above assumptions, we forecast that China was only able to supply 3.01 million scientists and engineers in 2007 and 3.82 million scientists and engineers in 2010 (see Table 7.7). We did not forecast the supply of scientists and engineers involved in R&D activities (S&Es–R&D) as they are counted only as FTE.

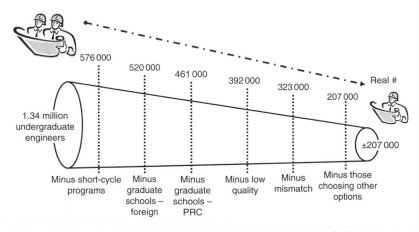

Figure 7.3 From official data to reality: "estimated" size of China's undergraduate engineering graduate pool (2006). PRC, People's Republic of China.
Source: Authors' research.

Here, we would like to illustrate, in a different way, why there has been a relatively smaller number of undergraduates actually entering the S&T occupations than is shown in the data by China's official statistics. This does not mean to say that the data are necessarily inaccurate, but suggest that various attritions may reduce the pool (Figure 7.3). In 2006, for example, China graduated 1.34 million engineering undergraduates. To fully understand the real size of the available talent pool among these graduates, we have to identify the true number actually qualified as well as seeking work in the engineering field. First, it must be recognized that less than half the total number of graduates have the equivalent of a fully fledged four- or five-year undergraduate engineering degree elsewhere, which left with 576 000 at the batchelor's degree level. Second, we have to take into account those who decide to go on to foreign graduate schools (8% of the total) and domestic graduate schools (12%). Third, we also have to account for the percentage of low-quality students (12%) as well as the number of students mismatched, for various reasons, with the nature of available jobs (12%), and finally, those students who have chosen other, non-engineering career opportunities (20%). As a result, in the final analysis only 207 000 (about 20% of the total engineering graduates or about 35% of the engineering majors with a bachelor's degree) remain "available" for employment as scientists and engineers.

Apparently this number is slightly higher than the replacement rate we have used in our forecast of the supply of scientists and engineers, which is around 20%. This discrepancy arises because our estimates are about the number of students actually employed as scientists and engineers while the illustration points to the pool of engineering majors seeking jobs in engineering. This only highlights why there has been unemployment of college graduates as the unintended consequence of the recent admissions expansion.

Possible shortage of scientists and engineers

The above forecasts imply that the economy's demand for scientists and engineers between 2007 and 2009 will not be met by the current supply pool (see Table 7.7). However, quantitatively, the gap between supply and demand is not that significant; in fact, we have noticed a gradual decline in the gap as our previous projections, using data up to 2004, for 2005 and 2010 were in the range of 265 000 and 380 000. According to the current analysis, there even may be an oversupply of scientists and engineers in 2010. There is no doubt that all these developments may be attributed to the post-1999 admissions increase, which has created a significantly large pool of undergraduate and graduate students available for employment in all sectors of the economy, including S&T-related ones. Our research has also assumed that the quality of science and engineering undergraduates will improve gradually, albeit steadily, as shown in the replacement rates. However, the wage factor has not seen sufficient changes to offset the increasing demand for scientists and engineers, although we have also assumed that market and wage adjustments should have some impact. Until then, it is improbable that supply and demand will reach a state of equilibrium. Of course, the severity of the differential will determine how deleterious the impact will be in terms of overall economic growth and innovation outcomes.

Given the projected demographic shift that will occur around 2015 when China will have a larger population in the 55–60-year-old age group than in those aged 18–22 years (see Figure 7.1), it is expected that the supply of S&T graduates could flatten out and perhaps even start decreasing. Although this is not inevitable, also given the fact that a smaller and decreasing percentage of graduates are majoring in science and engineering (still high by the standards of the USA and other developed economies), there could be a serious impact on the supply side. This would be ironic in view of the huge numbers entering S&T fields – past and present.

The unknown: the Chinese diaspora

The one key factor that has not been taken fully into account in our quantitative statistical forecasts is whether the Chinese diaspora will become a significant contributor to the motherland's talent pool and innovation potential, and if so, how significant its impact will be. According to the criteria used in China's S&T statistics, as discussed in Chapter 3 and Chapter 6, those who even work part-time in China are supposed to be counted in the data as long as they spend 10 percent of their work time in S&T-related activities and have "the right credentials," which they surely have. Unfortunately, we have been unable to learn how many have been included in the current statistics because specific detailed data has not been made available.

Theoretically, the Chinese diaspora is a huge potential source of "brain gain," a reverse migration or return of overseas Chinese talent. China's efforts to lure their native sons and daughters back home after being trained overseas, which include various active programs targeting overseas Chinese, mentioned in Chapter 6, have had some success. As a whole, the magnitude of the recent returnees, many in the S&T disciplines, has shown the possibility of making up the prevailing gap, albeit gradually, in supply and demand for talent. Most important, the return of these people may have a catalytic effect on the innovation potential of the R&D system. An increase in the number of returnees would counteract, to some extent, the tendency for Chinese "high-fliers" in research and other professions to go and remain overseas. Moreover, many of these individuals are integrated into trans-national knowledge networks that would help facilitate the flow of new scientific and technical information and data into the Chinese research environment. Still, despite some positive trends over recent years, it remains to be seen whether more high-level, high-quality talent will make a permanent move back to China so as to increase the supply significantly.

Reasons for the shortage

It may seem somewhat incredible to conclude that China lacks an adequate number of scientists and engineers given that the education system has been turning out millions of graduates in recent years, and that at the same time graduates have difficulty finding jobs. The shortage of scientists and engineers appears to be a global phenomenon. As indicated, forecasts of supply and demand of scientists and engineers in most OECD nations reflect questions and debates about "shortages," especially projections about the number of new entrants into S&T fields (see, for example, Kelly *et al.*, 2004).[9] S&T occupations in these countries, and increasingly in China, might not be as attractive as law, business, finance, and other new fields that provide more lucrative incomes, though the decline in China does not seem to be as extensive.[10] Because of supply challenges in their home markets, cost considerations, and growing competitive pressures to innovate continuously, MNCs are engaged in a sustained effort to "capture and harness" talent pools in rapidly developing economies such as China and India.

Putting aside for a moment the forecasts and associated numbers contained in the statistical analysis presented here, our intensive field interviews and continuous conversations in China during 2005–2008 indicate that the seeming shortage of scientists and engineers in China is a reality. Many people, however, continue to wonder why. In general, China, like many other countries, including the most advanced ones, has experienced a slower annual growth of HRST than that of GERD. In addition, according to the McKinsey study on China's looming talent shortage, the bias of higher education toward theory, the limited English-language abilities of young professionals, and the inconvenient location of many universities (which are not close to major international airports) are among factors that constrain the

---

[9] Continuous debates have emerged in the USA in particular about whether there is a real shortage of scientific and engineering talent (Teitebaum, 2003).

[10] In general, returnees with foreign degrees in business administration and law are likely to earn significantly higher salaries than those trained in S&T at both domestic and foreign-invested enterprises in China, although the efforts devoted by those with S&T PhDs are substantially more.

supply of talent (McKinsey Global Institute, 2005).[11] A diagnosis of the quality problems that plague Chinese higher education was presented in Chapter 4. Here, we would like to argue that China's shortages across the S&T workforce are mainly a structural problem of higher education and the labor market.

What causes specific concern is certainly the *quality*, not the size, of the S&T workforce. Many of the new entrants are raw talent: our supply model suggests that close to one million new scientists and engineers – 367 000 with graduate degrees and 612 000 undergraduates in science, engineering, medicine, and agriculture – secured employment between 2000 and 2006, accounting for more than a third of the current total (2.8 million). And, another 1.3 million new students will join the S&T workforce by 2010. Clearly, however, it will take time for these new scientists and engineers to mature and assume responsibility for strategically important S&T-related tasks. In other words, first and foremost, China must overcome the leadership gap that continues to afflict the S&T talent community. Whether this gap is largely attributable to the legacy of the Cultural Revolution or the more recent exodus of the best and the brightest for overseas, the fact is that its continuation will make it difficult to secure the type of performance and outcomes – in terms of both effectiveness and efficiency – that might be expected from such a sizable grouping of human talent.

Apparently, within the ranks of recent graduates, given the rapidity of expansion in the university sector, there have been not enough students trained with relevant skills and knowledge for the current and future job markets. This is one of the paramount problems confronting the Chinese higher education system. As noted, in many Chinese universities, the quality of the faculty is not up to the international standards, facilities are still relatively poor, and curricula are not only out of date, but also sometimes unusable in the real world. For example, although Chinese students devote a huge amount of study time to foreign languages, the bulk of them suffer from deficient communication skills; quite often, there is a conspicuous absence of

---

[11] Although the McKinsey study is not one of the overall S&T workforce per se, many of its findings are applicable to this community of scientists and engineers.

individuals who can provide the right pedagogy for the Chinese learning environment. Employers also bear some of the responsibility for the prevailing skills mismatch. Many students lack adequate work experience because most employers are not willing to provide them with an opportunity to gain the type of on-the-job training necessary for the job situation. In addition, enterprises seem unwilling to hire those fresh out of school and provide them with further training to acquire knowledge and skill-sets because of turnover concerns.

In fact, in certain respects, the shortages may actually be more severe than the numbers reflect as Chinese employers have very specific requirements for experience-based skills that many universities in China simply cannot meet as the curriculum is presently structured and delivered. The problem has caused another dilemma: while employers try to use more aggressive wage measures to reduce shortages, the availability of such a large cohort of "raw" university graduates may actually be creating the conditions for lower starting salaries. Consequently, appreciation of wages among the S&T workforce has not been as significant, especially in recent years, as it should be in terms of prevailing levels of unmet demand.

Even where there are available jobs that match skills, many students are not willing to relocate to work in regions where living standards are lower or the quality of life is not as attractive as in major cities such as Beijing, Shanghai, and Guangzhou Shenzhen. As discussed in Chapter 3 and further examined in Chapter 8, there continues to be a concentration of talent along the east coast and in big cities; these areas have attracted scientists and engineers seeking to move from the West, thus helping to undermine the government's "Western development strategy." Although students with training in science and technology also might contribute to the economy by performing a range of professional and semi-professional roles in manufacturing, services, and non-technical oriented work, what has become worrisome is evidence, albeit anecdotal, that many of them actually leave their fields of training. Some engineers, for example, prefer technical work at financial institutions to design work in construction and civil engineering; medical doctors end up with marketing jobs selling medicines to hospitals and medical practices for local and foreign pharmaceutical companies. People with an agronomy background not only find it difficult to secure jobs, but those with the appropriate training are not willing to work in rural areas.[12] The coal industry, with all its shortcomings in terms of safety and environmental impact, is also finding its development constrained by a talent squeeze (Lague, 2006).

Although the damage of the Cultural Revolution to China's higher education and scientific enterprise has gradually diminished due to the efforts of the past 30 years, the effect of the "brain drain" still is severe and will have significant impact on the further development of China's S&T talent pool, as discussed in Chapter 6. If China were able to attract back more high-quality academics – say 20 percent of those with foreign doctorates who are still overseas – it could significantly boost the quality of higher education and research. Unfortunately, much recent investment in Chinese higher education has been used to construct new buildings rather than to hire outstanding faculty members by offering substantial and attractive packages. Given its ideological importance, higher education is largely a monopoly under the protection of the state, and therefore it faces no real challenges from truly private domestic universities or foreign-based ones. Moreover, most of the reforms and changes introduced into the educational sector have come from government, with very little public input as a force for progressive change.

The statistical model deployed here has focussed on producing a forecast from a quantitative perspective; qualitatively, however, it also is important to highlight the particular areas of deficiency. It is well known that most Chinese education focusses on rote learning. Culturally, Chinese society has tended to have a low tolerance for failure, even though "failure" and the associated learning is part of the process that drives successful technological entrepreneurship and innovation. In addition, the nurturing of creativity has not been integrated into the education process and there have been only limited mechanisms for instilling an aptitude for risk-taking in Chinese students. There also are significant complaints about the lack of "soft skills" among graduates, including everything from leadership ability, communications skills, international exposure, and cross-cultural

---

[12] This situation has improved somewhat with the new emphasis given to the issue of agriculture, rural areas, and farmers (*san nong*).

awareness.[13] In summary, the talent of the twenty-first century, according to Kai-fu Lee (2006), who once directed Microsoft Research China and now leads Google's China R&D operation, should have the following characteristics:

- possess a mastery of the pertinent knowledge in their field and associated problem-solving capabilities
- be able to integrate innovation and practice and approach problems through an interdisciplinary and comprehensive lens
- possess not only a high intelligence quotient (IQ) but also a significant emotional quotient (EQ) and spiritual quotient (SQ)
- be able to communicate well and have strong teaming skills
- be passionate about their work and have a positive and optimistic attitude.

Although finding this package of skills embodied in one person may be a difficult challenge, whether in China or any other country, it is important to recognize that many of these skills and analytic approaches frequently are not a central component of the Chinese university educational experience, which has led to the deficiency in quality of its graduates.

Conclusion

In the chapter, we have identified the four key drivers that will continue to have a significant shaping effect on the demand for scientists and engineers in the years to come. These range from the further integration of China into the global economic system, the increasing technological sophistication of Chinese society and economy, China's indigenous efforts to turn itself into an innovation-oriented nation, and the continuous appreciation of wages across the S&T workforce. At the same time, we also have determined that the supply of S&T talent in China will be constrained by the quality of training received among graduates from the higher education system as well as the demographic trends that will lead China to become an aging society sooner than anticipated. Our forecasts, based on our statistical

---

[13] Of course there is a ubiquitous lack of soft skills as well in developed countries needed for the current job environment, such as people–technology interfaces and cross-cultural management.

analysis, indicate that China is facing a talent shortage, and unless an array of quality improvements are introduced, the severity of the current situation, especially along the quality dimension, could be exacerbated.

In economic terms, the talent shortage could have a negative impact in the near- to medium- term. The ability of employers to attract "the best and the brightest" will be affected by this projected shortage as China could experience the onset of a series of real "talent wars." Using our statistical model, we have determined that FDI will be one of the key drivers influencing the demand for scientists and engineers; if the challenges associated with recruiting high-end talent become too significant, this could alter some of the plans among MNCs to greatly increase the scope of their investments inside the Chinese economy. Consequently, China's pace of economic growth, especially in terms of the development of new, technology-intensive sectors and its ability to attract higher value-added foreign investment, might be put in jeopardy. Although we do not want to overexaggerate the seriousness of this impact, we do wish to sensitize observers of the Chinese situation to the possibility of a type of discontinuity that potentially could moderate the current growth path of the People's Republic of China.

Our analysis indicates that China's limited capacity for overcoming the immediate S&T talent shortage, including its ability to provide training-related quality improvements, will constrain the extent to which the country can advance the development of its indigenous innovative capabilities. This situation will also reduce China's ability to limit its continued dependence on foreign technology and know-how. Reducing this dependency is an integral part of the policy mandates spelled out in the MLP. It is under these circumstances that a rapid policy response is needed by the Chinese government to moderate, if not ameliorate, any possible negative impacts and that, first and foremost, the "fix" must focus on closing experience and competency gaps across the talent pool.

8 | *China's talent in key emerging technologies*

This chapter extends our analysis of China's scientific and technical talent by examining its distribution, deployment, and utilization in key emerging technological fields such as information and tele-communications technology (ICT) as well as biotechnology and nanotechnology – the so-called science-based technologies. The development and advancement of national capabilities in these tech-nological fields has become a high-level priority for the Chinese leadership, as, collectively, they are viewed increasingly as critical engines for the nation's current and future economic growth and national security. Most important, these high-technology fields have witnessed a significant transformation in the structure and size of their workforce and steadily increased the demand for more high-quality talent.

In this chapter we describe and analyze the science and technology (S&T) workforce in high-technology manufacturing, software, life sciences and biotechnology, and nanotechnology. We also discuss the emerging face of talent in the field of management and business administration, an area closely related to technological process since many Chinese managers have technical backgrounds. China's foray into global markets and knowledge networks will stimulate even further the demand for competent, experienced management talent. And, achieving desired improvements inside China's research organizations also will necessitate upgrading the performance of an entire cadre of research and development (R&D) and project managers. The chapter takes stock of the current situation and examines the readiness of talent in these fields. In doing so, we try to provide greater insights into the talent dynamics in priority areas where the Chinese government is making major investments.

High-technology industry: an overview

Before discussing China's talent situation across several high-technology industries, it is important to distinguish and clarify the precise meaning of the term "high-technology." The "high-technology" definition is dynamic owing to the constant and rapid pace of innovation and technological change; it also varies across countries as, for policy reasons, different governments reply on either a narrow- or a broad-based definition in terms of overall scope. Generally speaking, a high-technology industry is one in which competitive success depends largely on the ability to keep up with rapid innovations in products, production processes, and/or services. Microelectronics, biotechnology, new materials, telecommunications, civilian aviation, robotics and machine tools, and computer hardware and software all belong to the high-technology category, and are considered to be key focal points in global competition (Thurow, 1992). Statistical classifications of high-technology industry typically utilize such indicators as the ratio of a firm's R&D expenditure to sales, the share of scientists and engineers on staff, and so on. One of the international benchmarks for being a high-technology firm is that the firm spends at least 5 percent of its sales on R&D. In addition, the US Census Bureau has adopted a separate but important classification code, "advanced technology," in reporting a nation's merchandise trade. Products within this classification must meet the following criteria:

- The underlying know-how is from a recognized high-technology field (e.g. biotechnology, information technology)
- The associated products embody leading-edge technology in that field
- Such products constitute a significant part of all items covered in the "advanced technology" classification (McGuckin *et al.*, 1989; US Census Bureau, 2001; Wilson, 1994).

For a Chinese firm to register and to be certified as a high-technology business, it not only must fall into the above-mentioned technology categories, but also meet the following requirements:

- At least 30% of its employees have college or above education
- More than 5% of its sales are spent on R&D

- More than 60% of its sales are related to technology services and high-technology products.[1]

High-technology industry, as used in this chapter, includes the manufacture of pharmaceuticals, aircraft and spacecraft, electronics and communications equipment, computers and office equipment, and medical equipment and measuring instruments. The scope has been delimited in this way primarily because of data availability issues.[2] This definition has the following specific characteristics. First, apparently, it is oriented toward hardware and manufacturing. Second, certain high-technology sectors, such as computer software[3] and new materials, are not included. Third, exclusive of computer software, the sectors of electronics and communications equipment manufacturing as well as computers and office equipment manufacturing are usually referred to as "ICT," whereas the pharmaceuticals manufacturing sector covers both chemical and biochemical items.

As a whole, over the past decade, China's high-technology industries have experienced a significant expansion of employment of S&T personnel – from about a quarter-million in 1995 to some 400 000 in 2006 (Table 8.1). By sector, as the manufacturing of computers and office equipment grew, the headcount of S&T personnel increased almost five-fold; a similar growth spurt took place in both pharmaceuticals manufacturing and the manufacturing of electronics and communications equipment (both about 2.5-fold).

---

[1] The certification of high-technology enterprises, corresponding to the MLP implementation, not only has been extended to outside the high-technology zones, but also changed the requirement of R&D expenditure, which is no longer 5% of sales revenue across all enterprises. Instead, a new measure has been introduced according to sales of an enterprise: 6% invested on R&D for enterprises with sales under RMB50 million, 4% for those between RMB50 and 200 million, and 3% for those over RMB200 million and over, apparently requiring that start-ups be more innovative.

[2] However, China's trade statistical reporting system has categorized high-technology differently. Until 1998, "high-technology" referred to computers and telecommunications, life sciences, aerospace and aeronautics, electronics, weapons, opto-electronics, computer integrated manufacturing, nuclear technology, biotechnology, and materials. Afterward, China reported high-technology trade statistics under a new scheme, in which external trade in the weapons and nuclear technology are omitted while a new "Other Technology" category was introduced – presumably it includes the combination of military weapons and nuclear technology.

[3] Software will be discussed in a separate section.

Table 8.1 (a) *Science and technology (S&T) personnel in high-technology industry, by sector (persons)*

Sector	1995	2006	Percentage of total in 2006	Change between 2006 and 1995 (times)
Pharmaceuticals	25 059	64 278	16.31	2.57
Aircraft and spacecraft	94 143	55 209	14.01	0.59
Electronic and communications equipment	81 445	202 406	51.37	2.49
Computers and office equipment	8 422	41 442	10.52	4.92
Medical equipment and measuring instruments	36 503	30 652	7.78	0.84
Total	245 572	393 987	100.00	1.60

Source: National Bureau of Statistics, National Development and Reform Commission, and Ministry of Science and Technology, 2007: 79.

Table 8.1 (b) *Scientists and engineers in high-technology industry, by sector (persons)*

Sector	1995	2006	Percentage of total in 2006	Change between 2006 and 1995 (times)
Pharmaceuticals	10 865	42 241	16.01	3.89
Aircraft and spacecraft	26 078	30 669	11.62	1.18
Electronic and communications equipment	33 418	138 837	52.62	4.15
Computers and office equipment	4 745	31 014	11.76	6.54
Medical equipment and measuring instruments	16 205	21 064	7.98	1.30
Total	91 311	263 825	100.00	2.89

Source: National Bureau of Statistics, National Development and Reform Commission, and Ministry of Science and Technology, 2007: 80.

Table 8.1 (c) *Percentage of scientists and engineers among science and technology (S&T) personnel (%)*

Sector	1995	2000	2001	2002	2003	2004	2005	2006
Pharmaceuticals	43.36	59.42	60.75	63.98	66.03	64.98	69.50	65.72
Aircraft and spacecraft	27.70	43.36	46.63	48.46	51.81	43.03	57.37	55.55
Electronic and communications equipment	41.03	66.12	71.52	69.48	69.87	68.09	72.01	68.59
Computers and office equipment	56.34	76.23	78.68	81.10	74.67	69.89	73.46	74.84
Medical equipment and measuring instruments	44.39	58.75	54.68	62.49	64.70	62.37	69.40	68.72
Total	37.18	57.89	61.91	63.32	65.60	62.88	69.26	66.96

Source: National Bureau of Statistics, National Development and Reform Commission, and Ministry of Science and Technology, 2007: 79–80.

Interestingly, the manufacture of medical equipment and measuring instruments, as well as that of aircraft and spacecraft, experienced less than average growth in the ranks of their S&T personnel. This is probably because these sectors already had a sizable S&T workforce.

Many of the new additions to the S&T workforce have been college graduates in science and engineering, but also include those with postgraduate educational and professional credentials. In 2006, approximately 264 000 scientists and engineers, or two-thirds of the total S&T personnel, were employed in China's high-technology industries, almost triple the number in 1995, which totaled only 91 000 at the time. Overall, as a result of new educational opportunities and improvements in skills among all S&T personnel, two-thirds of the S&T workforce employed in China's high-technology industries fell into the formal definition of "scientists and engineers" in 2006, compared with only about one-third in 1995. Of the five sectors identified above, computer and office equipment manufacturing stands out – the number of scientists and engineers increased 6.5-fold over 1995. Both the electronics and communications equipment sector and pharmaceuticals manufacturing employed about four times more scientists and engineers, respectively, in 2006 than they did in 1995. Again, both the manufacturing of medical equipment and measuring instruments, and the manufacturing of aircraft and spacecraft, have lagged behind in terms of growing the number of scientists and engineers in these sectors. In addition, across Chinese high-technology industries as a whole, ICT has led the growth of employment of scientists and engineers – in 2006 close to three-quarters of the S&T personnel employed in the manufacturing of computers and office equipment sector and more than 68 percent in both the electronics and communications equipment sector and the medical equipment and measuring instrument sector were classified as "scientists and engineers."

In Chapter 3, we used the percentage of "scientists and engineers" among S&T personnel to assess the quality of the overall S&T workforce. Although in 2006 there was almost no difference between the ratio of S&T personnel in the high technology industry (66.96%) and the ratio of S&T personnel in the Chinese economy as a whole (67.72%), as shown in Table 8.1 and Table 3.5, the electronics and communications equipment sector – with 75% of S&T personnel qualified as scientists and engineers – is actually one that has outperformed all other sectors. Apparently, this is because the manufacturing of electronics and communications equipment involves high-level chip design and fabrication skills, and advanced telecommunications gear manufacturing requires sophisticated knowledge about specialized software and encryption. Comparing Table 8.1 with Table 3.5 once again shows that there has also been almost no change in terms of the percentage of S&T personnel working in China's high-technology industries as a percentage of the total S&T personnel – 9.54% in 2006 versus 9.36% in 1995. In contrast, the number of actual "scientists and engineers" who were employed in the high-technology sector rose from 5.88% in 1995 to 9.43% in 2006. In other words, China's high-technology industries have increasingly hired better-trained, higher-caliber, and more technologically sophisticated scientists and engineers rather than generalist technicians, which helps to explain the appreciable quality improvements across the high-technology sector. The growth of China's S&T cohort has helped to create a solid foundation for the future development of high-technology industries from both production and R&D perspectives.

In this context, it also is important to examine the S&T workforce in high-technology foreign-invested enterprises (FIEs) operating in China (Table 8.2). In 1995, high-technology FIEs employed fewer than 10 000 S&T personnel, of whom some 52 percent qualified as scientists and engineers; 11 years later, both the number of S&T personnel and scientists and engineers increased to 130 000 and 90 000, respectively, representing 14-fold and 18-fold increases. Again, most of the employment gains occurred in the ICT sector, especially concerning the manufacturing of electronics and communications equipment, which has seen the entry of MNCs such as Intel, Nokia, Cisco, and Qualcomm, as they have moved more higher value-added operations to the China mainland, including R&D and engineering activities.

A comparison of Table 8.2 and Table 3.8 indicates that the employment of S&T personnel and scientists and engineers by high-technology FIEs accounted for 37.09 and 41.05%, respectively, of total FIE employment of such personnel in 2006, rising from 33.51 and 37.03%, respectively. The most significant finding, however, may be seen by comparing Table 8.2 and Table 8.1. In 1995, employment of S&T personnel and scientists and engineers by high-technology FIEs was merely 3.81 and 5.38%, respectively, of the total S&T workforce across high-technology industries, which suggests that much of the FDI coming to China at the time was not very technologically sophisticated; in fact, it supports the notion that the main interest of MNCs doing business in China was largely use of cheap, low-, and semi-skilled labor and entry into the domestic market, not access to high-quality technical talent. This situation stands in sharp contrast to what is happening today in China, where, as presently structured, the general complexion of the high-technology S&T workforce is quite different. In 2006, almost one-third of the S&T personnel *and* scientists and engineers in the high-technology sector were employed by FIEs (in the same year, overall FIEs employed only about 8 percent of China's S&T personnel and scientists and engineers, as shown in Table 3.8). This further indicates that as FDI has become more technologically sophisticated, it is drawing from a very different, more selective but limited talent pool – and, in fact, may be competing with domestic enterprises and research organizations for access to the same talent contingent. The implications are quite critical for China's technological future as this helps to explain at least one of

Table 8.2 (a) *Science and technology (S&T) personnel in high-technology foreign-invested enterprises (FIEs), by sector (persons)*

Sector	1995	2006	Change between 1995 and 2006 (times)
Pharmaceuticals	1 965	11 934	6.07
Aircraft and spacecraft	82	541	6.60
Electronic and communications equipment	5 790	81 579	14.09
Computers and office equipment	930	30 310	32.59
Medical equipment and measuring instruments	592	5 346	9.03
Total	9 359	129 710	13.86

Source: National Bureau of Statistics, National Development and Reform Commission, and Ministry of Science and Technology, 2007: 179.

Table 8.2 (b) *Scientists and engineers in high-technology foreign-invested enterprises (FIEs), by sector (persons)*

Sector	1995	2006	Change between 1995 and 2006 (times)
Pharmaceuticals	1 174	8 550	7.28
Aircraft and spacecraft	24	349	14.54
Electronic and communications equipment	3 031	54 653	18.03
Computers and office equipment	456	22 868	50.15
Medical equipment and measuring instruments	227	3 659	16.12
Total	4 912	90 079	18.34

Source: National Bureau of Statistics, National Development and Reform Commission, and Ministry of Science and Technology, 2007: 180.

Table 8.2 (c) *Percentage of scientists and engineers among science and technology (S&T) personnel in high-technology foreign-invested enterprises (FIEs) (%)*

Sector	1995	2000	2001	2002	2003	2004	2005	2006
Pharmaceuticals	59.75	64.12	68.06	76.03	74.41	72.11	65.13	71.64
Aircraft and spacecraft	29.27	95.81	60.52	68.79	70.86	92.02	84.75	64.51
Electronic and communications equipment	52.35	64.48	72.96	63.66	69.39	65.57	68.15	66.99
Computers and office equipment	49.03	82.85	73.16	82.54	76.58	70.03	73.24	75.45
Medical equipment and measuring instruments	38.34	83.47	67.60	76.11	68.95	49.71	55.42	68.44
Total	52.48	68.53	71.91	68.39	71.17	66.67	68.81	69.45

Source: National Bureau of Statistics, National Development and Reform Commission, and Ministry of Science and Technology, 2007: 179–80.

the sources of the so-called "talent wars" that seem to have emerged in China. It also highlights the underlying reasons behind the growing concerns about the continued impact of FDI among some Chinese policymakers and academics.

Regional distribution of talent in the high-technology industry

China's fast-growing high-technology industries, high-technology exports, and the accompanying demand for S&T talent have been concentrated regionally, which also has become an issue of great concern as income inequality has grown between coastal and interior China. The problems of narrow geographic concentration apply to China's high-technology talent as a whole (Table 8.3). Although there are 53 nationally designated high-technology parks with only three less developed and remote areas – Qinghai, Ningxia, and Tibet – not having one, Chinese S&T personnel, as well as scientists and engineers, in China's high-technology industries are not equally distributed by a significant margin (Cao, 2004b). Eastern China accounted for more than 72% of scientists and engineers across high-technology sectors in 2006. The level of concentration is most intense in Guangdong province (28.89%), which has more scientists and engineers than the combined number in Central and Western China. There also is a high concentration in the Yangtze River Delta region, which includes Shanghai along with the Jiangsu and Zhejiang provinces (22.99%). China's scientists and engineers are more concentrated in the high-technology sector than in overall S&T activities as a whole, which in itself is not an unexpected finding. In comparison, for example, as a whole, about 11% of Chinese scientists and engineers employed in high-technology industries were located in Beijing, while Guangdong employed less than 10% of scientists and engineers. The Yangtze River Delta economies employed 20.69% (see Table 3.9(b)).

Much of Western China has yet to experience the same level of rapid economic growth associated with coastal China; nor has the region received large quantities of foreign direct investment (FDI). In addition, expenditures on R&D are lower when compared with the East. The problems of bifurcated economic growth in regional terms in China date back to the 1850s with the arrival of Western commercial interests in designated "treaty port" cities along the East coast. Thus, it is not surprising that the development of S&T talent even in high-technology sectors has lagged behind outside the Eastern seaboard. Moreover, several provinces, such as Yunnan and Gansu, have witnessed a substantial decrease of scientists and engineers. Some of this may be caused by the closing down of old so-called "third line" defense factories and related facilities. The main exceptions appear to be the Shaanxi and Sichuan provinces, where, as mentioned in Chapter 3, there have been significant levels of government investment in infrastructure and there has been a step up in activity with respect to military-related R&D facilities and projects. These two provinces, supported by the "Western Development Strategy" driven by the central government, have become new hot spots for FDI, as evidenced by the opening of an assembly and testing facility by Intel in Chengdu, Sichuan province, in 2005 as well as decisions by Motorola and Ford, respectively, to locate new facilities in Sichuan.[4]

---

[4] It is still too early, however, to assess how the massive earthquake that occurred in Wenchuan in Sichuan in May 2008 will affect the economic and technological trajectory of the region and its ability to attract new talent.

Table 8.3 *Geographical distribution of China's scientists and engineers in high-technology industry (persons)*

Region	1995	2006	Percentage of total in 2006	Percentage change between 1995 and 2006
Eastern				
Beijing	5 564	11 505	4.36	106.78
Tianjin	2 984	6 228	2.36	108.71
Hebei	1 233	4 954	1.88	301.78
Liaoning	6 506	10 113	3.83	55.44
Shanghai	7 906	14 252	5.40	80.27
Jiangsu	9 048	26 835	10.17	196.58
Zhejiang	1 784	19 556	7.41	996.19
Fujian	564	8 262	3.13	1 364.89
Shandong	3 169	11 471	4.35	261.98
Guangdong	4 526	76 225	28.89	1 584.16
Guangxi	745	1 613	0.61	116.51
Hainan	55	60	0.02	9.09
Subtotal	44 084	191 074	72.42	333.43
Central				
Shanxi	1 259	1 492	0.57	18.51
Neimenggu	253	319	0.12	26.09
Jilin	1 185	2 315	0.88	95.36
Heilongjiang	4 171	6 600	2.50	58.24
Anhui	1 058	2 702	1.02	155.39
Jiangxi	3 151	4 743	1.80	50.52
Henan	2 408	6 089	2.31	152.87
Hubei	2 853	8 771	3.32	207.43
Hunan	3 072	2 900	1.10	−5.60
Subtotal	19 410	35 931	13.62	85.12
*Western**				
Chongqing**	–	3 484	1.32	
Sichuan	10 027	12 020	4.56	19.88
Guizhou	4 168	5 199	1.97	24.74
Yunnan	655	448	0.17	−31.60
Shaanxi	10 915	14 558	5.52	33.38
Gansu	1 837	656	0.25	−64.29
Qinghai	39	39	0.01	0.00
Ningxia	162	355	0.13	119.14

Table 8.3 (*cont.*)

Region	1995	2006	Percentage of total in 2006	Percentage change between 1995 and 2006
Xinjiang	14	61	0.02	335.71
Subtotal	27 817	36 820	13.96	32.37
Total	91 311	263 825	100.00	188.93

* Tibet, part of Western China, does not have scientists and engineers in the high-technology industry so has to be excluded from the statistical yearbook.
** Chongqing became a municipality affiliated to the central government in 1997.
Source: National Bureau of Statistics, National Development and Reform Commission, and Ministry of Science and Technology, 2007: 205.

In many ways, however, the trickle-down approach to economic development that has been in place since the early 1980s – from coast to interior – has not yielded desired economic results. Unlike Eastern China, which has benefited from high levels of foreign investment and closer articulation with the world economy, Western China has been slow to catch up with developments taking place in places such as Dalian, Shanghai, and Shenzhen. The manifestations of this differential may be seen on both the cause and effect sides of the economic development equation – the growth of scientists and engineers in the Guangdong province has been almost 17 times larger over the last 11-year period (1995–2006) than that of scientists and engineers in the next-highest locations of personnel concentration – Jiangsu, Zhejiang, Shanghai, and Shaanxi, put together. During the same period, Fujian and Jiangsu have seen the numbers of scientists and engineers increase by factors of 15 and 11, respectively, in China's high-technology industries, with Hebei, Shandong, and Hubei following closely behind. In absolute terms, Guangdong, Jiangsu, Zhejiang, Shaanxi, and Shanghai are among the top regions in China in terms of the number of scientists and engineers employed in the high-technology industry. Interestingly, Beijing is not as important as it was in 1995 in terms of high-technology manufacturing; nor has it grown its high-technology industry base as rapidly as some other Chinese provinces, such as Guangdong and the Yangtze River Delta.

Shanghai also seems to have experienced a similar relative decline as most of the growth of scientists and engineers in the Yangtze River Delta has been in Jiangsu and Zhejiang. The situation outside these major coastal growth hubs reflects these ongoing talent differences in terms of most key economic and innovation-related metrics.

The regional growth of the S&T workforce by sector reveals the following evolution and development pattern (Table 8.4). Just as the Chinese economy has grown to become one of the most potent economic engines in the world, Guangdong province stands out as the most important driver behind China's rapid development. Using the number of scientists and engineers as the key indicator, in 2006 Guangdong was clearly dominant in the ICT sector and had a substantial contingent in pharmaceuticals and the medical equipment and measuring instruments sector. In the case of the talent situation in pharmaceuticals, Jiangsu, Zhejiang, Hebei, and Shandong showed the highest concentrations. Scientists and engineers employed in the electronics and telecommunications equipment manufacturing sector are clustered in Jiangsu, Zhejiang, Shanghai, and Sichuan. The other wing of the ICT industry – computer and office equipment – exhibits a high concentration of scientists and engineers in Beijing and Jiangsu. Interestingly, Western and Central China account for three-quarters of scientists and engineers in aircraft and spacecraft manufacturing, with Shaanxi, Guizhou, Heilongjiang, Jiangxi, and Sichuan also being quite important, as suggested earlier, a legacy of the military industry building-up during the heyday of the Sino-Soviet dispute in the late 1960s and the early 1970s. Finally, scientists and engineers deployed in the medical equipment and measuring instruments sector also are clustered in Eastern China, especially in Jiangsu, Zhejiang, Beijing, and Shanghai.

With the current human resources pool not sufficient to meet the increasing demand for high-quality technical talent, even in Eastern China where there are a high concentration of institutions of higher education that turn out a significant number of S&T graduates, there has been a significant appreciation of wages. Accordingly, FIEs, which have rising labor needs and tend to exhibit higher levels of demand for scientists and engineers, have started to migrate their operations, even those in high-end activities, to several second-tier Chinese cities that possess a reasonable support infrastructure and operating situation. Intel, for example, has set up an assembly and testing factory in

Table 8.4 *Geographical distribution of scientists and engineers in high-technology industry, by sector (2006) (persons)*

Region	Pharmaceuticals	Aircraft and spacecraft	Electronic and communications equipment	Computers and office equipment	Medical equipment and measuring instruments	Total
Eastern						
Beijing	1 121	1 123	3 911	3 728	1 622	11 505
Tianjin	2 022	123	3 677	300	106	6 228
Hebei	3 740	264	395	36	519	4 954
Liaoning	1 469	3 954	4 108		582	10 113
Shanghai	1 703	962	8 152	1 825	1 610	14 252
Jiangsu	4 568	648	15 149	3 626	2 844	26 835
Zhejiang	4 238		9 834	2 644	2 840	19 556
Fujian	670	125	4 957	2 332	178	8 262
Shandong	3 515	18	4 476	2 451	1 011	11 471
Guangdong	2 309	206	59 878	11 792	2 040	76 225
Guangxi	902		639		72	1 613
Hainan	36		24			60
Subtotal	26 293	7 423	115 200	28 734	13 424	191 074
Central						
Shanxi	519		238	221	514	1 492
Neimenggu	319					319
Jilin	1 994	29	292			2 315

Table 8.4 (*cont.*)

Region	Pharmaceuticals	Aircraft and spacecraft	Electronic and communications equipment	Computers and office equipment	Medical equipment and measuring instruments	Total
Heilongjiang	2 329	3 722	95	97	357	6 600
Anhui	722	511	810	243	416	2 702
Jiangxi	1 062	2 441	910		330	4 743
Henan	1 257	1 396	2 205		1 231	6 089
Hubei	2 178	1 187	4 370	326	710	8 771
Hunan	638	707	249	785	521	2 900
Subtotal	11 018	9 993	9 169	1 672	4 079	35 931
Western						
Chongqing	1 081	107	622	274	1 400	3 484
Sichuan	1 938	2 181	7 610	243	48	12 020
Guizhou	474	3 767	832		126	5 199
Yunan	236		30	91	91	448
Shaanxi	864	7 002	5 032		1 660	14 558
Gansu	163	196	297			656
Qinghai	15				24	39
Ningxia	143				212	355
Xinjiang	16		45			61
Subtotal	4 930	13 253	14 468	608	3 561	36 820
Total	42 241	30 669	138 837	31 014	21 064	263 825

Source: National Bureau of Statistics, National Development and Reform Commission, and Ministry of Science and Technology, 2007: 230, 255, 280, 305, and 330.

Chengdu and a new US $ 2.5 billion semiconductor fabrication facility in Dalian; other MNCs have followed suit in other cities such as Nanjing. Nonetheless, it still remains to be seen how this trend will affect the geographical reconfiguration of China's technical talent over both the short and long term. One thing is clear, however: the strategic role of talent will only increase as time goes on and it will be essential for the Chinese government to devise an effective set of policies to avoid China's talent situation from becoming a deterrent to MNCs that are seeking to locate their advanced facilities overseas – and are considering multiple options along with China.

Software

If it is indeed the case that the combination of the telecommunications revolution in China and the expansion of the internet has stimulated an increased demand for ICT talent in China, then the growth and continued acceleration of India as a global software and outsourcing hub has "provoked" China to address the reasons for the slow pace of its own outsourcing services development (Saxenian & Quan, 2005). In addition, while China has become the second-largest personal computer (PC) market in the world, it continues to underachieve in software development. In 2000, China's software industry had an output value of US $7.17 billion, accounting for only 1.20% of the world, lagging behind India's 1.48% (CSIA, 2004: 50). Of course, initially China seemed to be choosing a different path than India in terms of software development, focussing its efforts on packaged software and porting English language software while India concentrated on services (Arora & Gambardella, 2005; Li & Gao, 2003: 63–8). With the need to move beyond low-wage, labor-intensive manufacturing, China is looking to software services as a vehicle to employ a large number of young people while developing its own software engineering and delivery capabilities. Viewed from this perspective, however, it is reasonably clear that China's chief bottleneck in developing a more vibrant and competitive software industry lies in the shortage of qualified, experienced software engineers and project managers. In 2000, for example, China had only 70 000 software engineers, while actual demand was 180 000, almost three times more than the supply (Table 8.5).

Table 8.5 *Chinese software professionals and supply and demand (1000 persons)*

Year	Software professionals	Software engineers	
		Supply	Demand
1998	132	40	180
1999	150	50	200
2000	210	70	180
2001	290	100	180
2002	590	150	320
2003	620	210	470
2004	720	300	500
2005	940	380	550
2006	1290	NA	NA

Note: NA, not available.
Source: Authors' research.

"Brain drain" is one particular reason causing the talent shortage among China's domestic software companies. Between 2001 and 2005, for example, China turned out 80 000–100 000 software and related professionals annually. Among them, half went abroad or secured work with FIEs. According to a survey of software engineers by Beijing University's Center for Enterprise Research, more than 30% expressed a desire to go to the USA; approximately 40% of the software and computer science majors from Qinghua and Beijing universities intend either to go abroad or work for FIEs. In fact, the China Software Industry Association (CSIA) reveals that almost half of Shanghai's software and computer science graduates have left for the USA or have been hired by FIEs (CSIA, 2005: 124). Moreover, a high rate of attrition from domestic companies to FIEs also has restricted the ability of domestic companies to grow and climb up the value chain.

To catch up and promote a stronger indigenous software capability, Chinese officials have acted in a concerted fashion to address the country's deficiencies in the software sector. On July 14, 2000, the State Council issued a document, "Policies for Encouraging the Development of Software Industry and Integrated Circuit (IC) Industry" (known as "Document 18"), which devoted one entire chapter to a series of policies for fostering and attracting software talent. Two years later, the

State Council General Office issued another key document – "Outline of the Software Industry Rejuvenation" (known as "Document 47"). These policy initiatives, in particular, identified as key priorities the training of new students and the provision of continuing education to existing professionals in computers and software. The stated goal was eventually to churn out some 200 000 software professionals at various levels on an annual basis so that China would have 800 000 software professionals by 2005. This resulted in increased financial support to secure advanced training overseas for a select number of software engineers so that they can learn how to lead and manage a globally oriented software enterprise. Strategic programs were developed by Chinese government organizations such as the China International Talent Exchange Foundation (CITEF) under the State Council's Foreign Experts Bureau with key American academic institutions such as Rensselaer Polytechnic Institute in New York and the Neil D. Levin Graduate Institute of International Relations and Commerce under the State University of New York to provide these technically trained individuals with more of a global perspective and set of critically needed leadership tools to drive future development of the software sector.

Further, in its bid to evolve from a manufacturing powerhouse into a major player in innovation and services, the Chinese government has viewed IT services outsourcing (ITO) and business process outsourcing (BPO) not only in terms of the competition from India, but, more importantly, also in terms of the high-value added dimensions of this business field. Chinese officials support the development of this sector because it will help to create jobs for college graduates, it is environment friendly, and it consumes few natural resources. Specifically, in 2006, the Ministry of Commerce (MOFCOM) issued a special circular to encourage the development of this sector; the Ministry announced its goal to increase software exports to US $10 billion by 2010, doubling that in 2005. An important White Paper, entitled "Building a World-Class IT Services Outsourcing Industry in China," released by Electronic Data Systems (EDS), the world's second-largest IT service-provider, and China's MOFCOM in June 2007, predicts that IT outsourcing service-providers in China could earn as much as US $18 billion by 2010 (*China Daily*, June 22, 2007). In particular, China intends to build ten internationally competitive outsourcing services-base cities, attract 100 MNCs to outsource their services business to China, and nurture 1000 large- and medium-sized enterprises with international reputations (the name given to this initiative is the One Thousand, One Hundred, and Ten Thousands Program). For that purpose, the MOFCOM will set aside a special fund to train college students with special knowledge and skills of service outsourcing, and encourage ITO and BPO firms to create more jobs for new college graduates, especially those still unemployed. Within five years, it is hoped, the ITO and BPO sector will be able to train 300 000–400 000 personnel with practical knowledge and to create jobs for 200 000–300 000 new college graduates (MII Bureau of Electronics and Information Products, MII Bureau of Economic System Reform and Economic Operations, and CSIA 2007: 763–70).

Formation of software engineering schools

At the time Document 18 and Document 47 were issued, along with sending more students overseas for specialized leadership and management training, one of the new measures designed to help achieve the above target was the establishment of pilot software engineering schools at 35 leading Chinese universities in 2001 (two more schools were approved afterwards) (Table 8.6), giving software engineering extra attention amidst the overall admissions surge. This initiative was approved by the Ministry of Education and the then State Planning Commission with the goal of producing graduates who possess not only strong technical capabilities in software development and engineering, but also solid skills in foreign language, management, innovation, and entrepreneurship. These software schools accept transfer students who have completed their sophomore years at the home universities from other disciplines (so-called "2+2" students), admit new students into second bachelor's-degree programs in software engineering, and admit new students into master's degree programs in software engineering directly from graduating seniors from either the same or other institutions. To lend its support, in 2002, Microsoft signed an agreement with the Chinese Ministry of Education to initiate a so-called Great Wall Program, committing RMB200 million (US $25 million) over three years. Through Microsoft Research Asia, the money was designated for curriculum development, faculty and managerial training, academic exchange, international collaboration, equipment, and textbooks for the software

Table 8.6 *Pilot software engineering schools and affiliated universities*

Location	Affiliated university	Assessment in 2006	
Beijing (7)	Beijing University	Q	
	Qinghua University		Q-
	Beijing University of Engineering		Q-
	Beijing University of Aeronautics and Astronautics	Q	
	Beijing Institute of Technology		Q-
	Beijing University of Post and Telecommunications			Q–
	Beijing Jiaotong University (designated in 2006)		
Tianjin (2)	Nankai University			Q–
	Tianjin University		Q-
Liaoning (2)	Dalian University of Technology		Q-
	Northeastern University			Q–
Jilin (1)	Jilin University		Q-
Heilongjiang (1)	Harbin Institute of Technology	Q	
Shanghai (4)	Fudan University	Q	
	Tongji University	Q	
	Shanghai Jiaotong University	Q	
	Eastern China Normal University		Q-
Jiangsu (2)	Nanjing University	Q	
	Southeastern University		Q-
Zhejiang (1)	Zhejiang University	Q	
Anhui (1)	University of Science and Technology of China		Q-
Shandong (1)	Shandong University		Q-
Hubei (2)	Wuhan University		Q-
	Huazhong University of Science and Technology		Q-
Hunan (2)	Hunan University			Q–
	National University of Defense Technology			Q–
	Central South University (designated in 2007)		
Guangdong (2)	Sun Yat-sen University (Zhongshan University)			Q–
	South China University of Technology			Q–

Table 8.6 (*cont.*)

Location	Affiliated university	Assessment in 2006	
Sichuan (2)	Sichuan University		Q–
	University of Electronic Science and Technology of China	Q-	
Chongqing (1)	Chongqing University	Q-	
Yunnan (1)	Yunnan University		Q–
Shaanxi (3)	Xi'an Jiaotong University	Q-	
	Northwestern Polytechnic University	Q	
	Xi'an University of Electronic Science and Technology	Q-	
Fujian (1)	Xiamen University	Q-	

Note: Q, qualified; Q-, basically qualified; Q–, having problems or not qualified in certain areas and will be re-evaluated in a year.
Source: Ministry of Information Industry Bureau of Electronics and Information Products, and Bureau of Economic System Reform and Economic Operations, and China Software Industry Association, 2007: 121.

schools as well as post-doctoral fellowships and student internships (Buderi & Huang, 2006: 130–46).[5]

About 15 000 students were enrolled in 2002 under this scheme, including 7000 advanced students on graduate programs. In 2003, software schools graduated their first 1892 "2+2" students; in 2004, the pilot schools graduated another 3685 with bachelor's degrees as well as 2516 with master's degrees in software engineering. By June 2006, these schools had turned out a total of 10 092 students with 3498 holding postgraduate degrees, and total enrollments reached 64 039 – with 26 174 at the postgraduate level. These schools are predicted to dispatch 18 000 graduates annually over the next several years (Wu, 2006).[6]

---

[5] The support from Microsoft reflects part of the company's "new" strategy to harness high-quality Chinese talent to support its growth in the Chinese market as well as the overall Asia-Pacific region.

[6] Please note the numbers given here by the Vice Minister of Education Wu Qidi are different from those in Table 8.7.

Unfortunately, when these pilot software engineering schools underwent a formal evaluation in 2006, only nine received a "qualified" rating and another 17 were assessed to be only "basically qualified" (see Table 8.6). Three problems stand out as plaguing the various schools, even those at some of China's most prestigious universities. First, the schools lack adequate numbers of competent faculty who are familiar with and fully understand the dynamics of the global software industry and the rapidly evolving technical requirements that need to be conveyed to students if they are to be attractive in the job market and have industrial experience. Because of the dearth of available faculty, some schools, such as Beijing University, have taken to relying on "foreign experts" or retired executives from MNCs operating in China to teach classes and develop the curriculum. The second problem, closely related to the first, is continued reliance on an increasingly outdated curriculum. Although the industry needs personnel with knowledge in embedded software, Java, Linux platform, and database, many of the standard courses taught at these schools are still built around the "C" language. Therefore, the graduates turned out by these schools are actually not quite employable without some substantial retraining (MII Bureau of Electronics and Information Products, MII Bureau of Economic System Reform and Economic Operations, and CSIA 2007: 124). Thirdly, the linkages between Chinese and foreign software firms and these various schools are limited and immature; there are very few internships and cooperative programs offered to students as a way to enhance their training and "test" them in a real working situation. The ratio between theory and practice at software engineering schools is three to one at best (Chen, 2007). Because most of these students lack work experience their training is seen as largely academic by many potential employers in China. And, given the huge turnover rate in the job market, many employers – foreign and domestic – are not willing to invest in upgrading the training for these new hires.[7] Obviously, there are some exceptions such as the links that have been forged between Motorola

---

[7] The irony is that the employment rate for the graduates from the software schools has been close to 100% – 98% for undergraduates and 99% for graduates, which testifies to the shortage of software engineers (MII Bureau of Electronics and Information Products, MII Bureau of Economic System Reform and Economic Operations, and CSIA, 2007: 71).

and the Software School at Beijing University; as a whole there is a long way to go before many of these schools will produce the type of qualified graduates in high demand. Nevertheless, the graduates, especially those with master's degrees, from these schools seem to be well-received by employers. According to a survey of more than 100 software firms, graduates not only work hard, and work with teams, but have self-study ability, innovative capability, suitable knowledge structure, project development experience, and foreign language proficiency (Chen, 2006).

More broadly, in 2006, 750 000 students graduated with degrees in software and related disciplines, with 29 000 having graduate degrees. As of 2006, it was estimated by the CSIA that there were about 3.77 million Chinese studying computer software and related specialties at college level (Table 8.7).[8] Indeed, computer and IT-related majors have been "hot" in China according to statistics from the Ministry of Education (see Table 4.4). It seems that these fields have not hit the peak of demand yet.

As a result of the increasing supply of graduates majoring in software and related disciplines over the past few years, there was a slight respite regarding the shortage of software professionals (see Table 8.5). Nonetheless, in 2005, there was still a country-wide shortage of some 200 000 individuals.[9] In fact, the demand for software professionals forms a moving target.[10] In the north-east coastal city of Dalian, China's only "Software Industry Internationalization Exemplary City," designated by the Ministry of Science and Technology, there are approximately 30 000 software professionals, but estimated demand is thought to be 80 000–100 000. More specifically, the demand ratio for software developers at senior, middle, and junior

---

[8] Software-related disciplines include information and computer science, geographic information system, electronics and information science and technology, electronics and information science and technology (new specialty), automation, electronics and information engineering, network engineering, information confrontation technology, and information security.

[9] Others claim that there did not appear to be major shortages of most types of personnel (Tschang and Xue, 2005).

[10] According to some predictions, in the next five years, the sector will have a workforce of approximately 2.5 million, up from 1.29 million in 2006. In Shanghai alone, the gap was estimated to be about 60 000 (*Morning News*, April 5, 2004).

Table 8.7 Graduates and enrollment in software and software-related specialties (2002–2006) (persons)

	2002		2003		2004		2005		2006	
	Graduates	Enrollment	Graduates	Enrollment	Graduates	Enrollment	Graduates	Enrollment	Graduates	Enrollment
Software										
Doctoral	336		418	3 593	515	5 354	11 249	51 437	14 001	6 708
Master	3 491		4 694	23 885	7 281	38 520	11 249	51 437	14 001	49 858
Undergraduate	37 918		66 548	437 161	5 542	51 327	6 831	75 931	40 371	214 992
Undergraduate-short course	47 693		77 105	376 905	4 162	55 732	6 702	82 249	26 338	109 342
Total	89 438	718 500	148 765	846 544	17 500	150 933	24 782	209 617	80 710	380 900
In which 35 software schools										
Graduate		6 828		13 403	2 516	14 943	2 400	26 599	n.a.	22 000
Undergraduate		8 073	1 892	15 659	3 685	16 740	3 067	27 886	n.a.	40 000
Total		14 901	1 892	30 062	6 201	31 683	5 467	54 485	n.a.	62 000
Software-related										
Doctoral			639	6 204	458	3 839	15 783	34 652	15 307	11 446
Master			5 334	29 609	3 682	19 741	54 062	15 783	34 652	15 307
Undergraduate	33 048		77 178	553 069	183 709	1 042 912	262 537	1 166 185	240 938	1 039 275

Table 8.7 (*cont.*)

	2002		2003		2004		2005		2006	
	Graduates	Enrollment	Graduates	Enrollment	Graduates	Enrollment	Graduates	Enrollment	Graduates	Enrollment
Undergraduate short course	15 117		33 221	218 442	141 337	642 692	127 562	791 660	412 260	2 281 326
Total		482 600	116 372	807 324	329 186	1 709 184	405 882	1 992 497	668 505	3 386 109
Computer software and related										
Doctoral			1 057	9 797	973	9 193	27 032	86 089	29 308	18 154
Master			10 028	58 494	10 963	58 261	103 920	27 032	86 089	29 308
Undergraduate			143 726	990 230	189 251	1 094 239	269 368	1 242 116	281 309	1 254 267
Undergraduate short course			110 326	595 347	145 499	698 424	134 264	873 909	438 598	2 390 668
Total	89 438	1 201 100	265 137	1 653 868	346 686	1 860 117	430 664	2 202 114	749 215	3 767 009

NA, not available.

Sources: China Software Industry Association, 2004: 62–70; Ministry of Information Industry Bureau of Electronics and Information Products and CSIA, 2005: 50–6; Ministry of Information Industry Bureau of Electronics and Information Products, and Bureau of Economic System and China Software Industry Association, 2006: 51–7; Ministry of Information Industry Bureau of Electronics and Information Products and Bureau of Economic System and China Software Industry Association, 2007: 67–71.

levels was 1:2:7, or, in Dalian, the demand for middle- and senior-level personnel accounts for about 30 percent (Li, 2005).

On top of the skills hierarchy are software architects, working in the field for at least eight years and having good command of Japanese, English, or both. Middle-level project managers and system engineers require three or more years of experience, a command of Japanese, English, or both, and one year's experience in project management; programmers are required to have one year's work experience and to achieve Level 3 in the official Japanese language proficiency test and Level 4 or above in the English language proficiency test (Li, 2005). It is obvious by looking at the prevailing needs in the industry that the principal problem facing China's software industry lies in the "olive-shaped" structure of the talent pool. That is, China lacks those with ample technological expertise as well as extensive project management skills at the high end *and* lacks junior programmers who are able to do basic coding at the low end; few software engineers have much international experience that would allow them to handle the types of large-scale outsourcing work from MNCs. In this regard, the graduates from the software schools are not ready for high-end positions, but actually overqualified for low-end jobs. In fact, they have reinforced the structure of Chinese software professional pool by stacking it with too many middle-level, albeit less experienced engineers.

International certification to boost outsourcing

Generally speaking, Chinese software companies have been less focussed on outsourcing services and more oriented toward developing application software packages that meet the needs of domestic clients. Without a larger cadre of software professionals with higher-level skills and experience, it is hard to demonstrate the credentials and create the confidence that is needed to attract a large volume of ITO and BPO assignments from overseas. Therefore, since 1999, existing software companies have put great efforts into getting international certifications, such as the Capability Maturity Model (CMM) for software and the upgraded Capability Maturity Model Integration (CMMI), both developed by the Software Engineering Institute of Carnegie Mellon University (SEI/CMU), to enhance software development capability, improve software process, and internationalize the

Table 8.8 *Chinese software companies with CMM/CMMI certification (2000–2006)*

	CMM2	CMM3	CMM4	CMM5	CMMI2	CMMI3	CMMI4	CMMI5	Total
2000	0	0	0	2	0	0	0	0	2
2001	4	1	0	0	0	0	0	0	5
2002	27	4	0	1	0	0	0	0	32
2003	28	22	1	1	1	0	0	1	54
2004	30	61	8	7	4	3	0	3	116
2005	6	32	1	3	18	28	5	7	100
2006	1	4	0	0	34	103	4	13	159
Total	96	124	10	14	57	134	9	24	468

Source: Ministry of Information Industry Bureau of Electronics and Information Products and Bureau of Economic System and China Software Industry Association, 2007: 245–7.

Chinese software industry (Table 8.8) (Wu *et al.*, 2006). These certifications have become a domestic (as well as international) standardized qualification measure of a software company but also of the company's talent pool.

According to statistics from SEI/CMU, in 2002, only 18 Chinese software companies passed the CMM certification, compared with India's 153. By 2006, the Chinese number increased to 354, still slightly lagging behind India, which had 422 companies. China is expected soon to surpass India in the number of its software companies appraised by CMM. Cumulatively, a total of 468 companies passed CMM/CMMI appraisal by 2006 with 24 at CMM4 and CMM5 levels and 33 at CMMI4 and CMMI5 levels. Beijing (127, 14 at levels 4 and 5), Shanghai (120, 14), Hangzhou (49, 2), Dalian (24, 7), and Shenzhen (24, 4) are the top cities in terms of the number of CMM/CMMI-certified software companies (MII Bureau of Electronics and Information Products, and Bureau of Economic System Reform and Economic Operations, and CSIA, 2007: 244–54). Nonetheless, overall the number of CMM/CMMI certification is still quite low compared with the entire Chinese software industry, which had a total of more than 13 000 software companies in 2006. In addition, of the 38 companies with the CMM/CMMI Level 5 qualification, about half have been set up by MNCs, such as GE, HP, NEC, Accenture, BearingPoint, IBM, Motorola, and Tata (MII Bureau of Electronics and Information Products, MII Bureau of Economic System Reform and Economic Operations, and CSIA, 2007: 110–11), indicating that many high-quality Chinese software engineers are employed by MNCs, which compete fiercely for local talent in China. This fact also may reflect the limited recognition of Chinese brands in the IT outsourcing space in so far as there is no Chinese company that can come close to rivaling Indian powerhouses such as Wipro, Infosys, and Tata. In general, Chinese software companies still are too small to be competitive and to achieve the economies of scale of their India counterparts – of the 13 000 software companies in 2006, only 35 had annual sales of more than RMB1 billion (Hu, 2007).[11]

Indeed, while the improvement of software process capabilities has made possible some companies' forays into the ITO and BPO space, many challenges still remain. In 2006, close to 1000 software exports and outsourcing services companies were active in six software exports bases – Beijing, Shanghai, Tianjin, Shenzhen, Xi'an, and Chengdu, and additional services outsourcing bases – Dalian, Nanjing, Wuhan, Jinan, and Hangzhou (there are a total of 11 services outsourcing bases). Nevertheless, China only exported RMB46.8 billion (US $6.06 billion) worth of software and related services in 2006,[12] accounting for less than 10% of the software industry – with 60% going to Japan and only about 20% to Europe and the USA (MII Bureau of Electronics and Information Products, MII Bureau of Economic System Reform and Economic Operations, and CSIA, 2007: 59–60). While statistics indicate that China's share in the world software industry grew to 7.1% in the same year, larger than India's 4.5%, the latter exported five times more software and IT services, and the gap between these two countries in this area has been expanding (MII Bureau of Electronics and Information Products, MII Bureau of Economic System Reform and Economic Operations, and CSIA, 2007: 57, 94, and 102). This indicates that despite

---

[11] According to the statistics from the *Annual Report of China Software Industry 2007* indicate the number of software companies certified by 2006 was 15 723 (Bureau of Electronics and Information Products, MII, Bureau of Economic System Reform and Economic Operations, MII, and CSIA, 2007: 55).

[12] According to the EDS–MOFCOM white paper on IT outsourcing in China, China's software outsourcing companies brought in US $1.4 billion in revenue in 2006 (*China Daily* June 22, 2007).

government pronouncements and the activities promoted by various programs, the Chinese software industry still is focused on domestic market because of its continued domestic growth opportunities; most Chinese local software companies have a long way to go in ITO and BPO capability development to challenge India's domination on the services side (David, 2007).

Characteristics of software professionals

Of the estimated 590 000 Chinese software professionals in 2002, those with postgraduate degrees, bachelor's degrees, and those who had finished a two- to three-year college education accounted for 7, 33, and 17%, respectively (Table 8.9). In other words, more than 40% of Chinese software professionals did not have a formal college education – it is not surprising, therefore, that those engaged in software development represented only one-quarter of the total number of software professionals. Of course, the recent injection of graduates from the high-end specialized software schools, noted above, and more generally, from computer-related disciplines has changed the complexion of the ranks of software professionals in terms of their educational attainment, though the experience gap has been not as easy to narrow.

Again, most of the country's software professionals are located in China's eastern region, with Jiangsu, Beijing, Guangdong, Shandong, and Zhejiang leading the nation; these data dovetail nicely with data regarding software industry output in these provinces and municipalities (Baark, 2003: 21–3; Saxenian & Quan, 2005: 121–4). Unbalanced geographical development remains one of the key obstacles that the Chinese software industry has to overcome.

Shortages in specific areas

While problems remain with creating a large-scale take-off in the field of outsourcing services, there are some important emerging demands for software professionals in several other fields, such as online gaming. As the world's largest and fast-growing online gaming market, China has only some 3000 developers; estimates are that real demand is for at least 15 000. Network security, testing, and technical

Table 8.9 *Geographical distribution and educational background of China's software professionals (2002) (persons)*

Region	Total	R&D personnel	Percentage of R&D personnel	Education background		
				Graduate degree	Bachelor's degree	Associate degree
Eastern						
Beijing	91 882	43 667	47.53	12 552	49 079	17 705
Tianjin	6 438	2 146	33.33	369	3 179	1 579
Hebei	9 406	1 190	12.65	115	1 783	2 028
Liaoning	27 241	11 242	41.27	574	5 048	2 021
Shanghai	32 591	10 730	32.92	3 505	14 154	5 177
Jiangsu	110 558	7 335	6.63	99	1 340	13 577
Zhejiang	41 603	5 706	13.72	1851	13 662	8 797
Fujian	4 484	2 031	45.29	343	2 587	651
Shandong	46 659	6 161	13.20	1 606	12 904	6 284
Guangdong	90 125	26 237	29.11	13 328	41 887	12 309
Guangxi	2 606	640	24.56	65	709	679
Hainan	974	341	35.01	67	539	231
Subtotal	464 567	117 426	25.28	34 474	146 871	71 038
Central						
Shanxi	713	256	35.90	45	332	270
Neimenggu	2 388	387	16.21	65	1430	634
Jilin	11 864	3 521	29.68	722	4808	3251
Heilongjiang	5 680	2 496	43.94	418	2 587	1 208
Anhui	3 612	1 552	42.97	301	1 745	958

Table 8.9 (*cont.*)

Region	Total	R&D personnel	Percentage of R&D personnel	Education background			
				Graduate degree	Bachelor's degree	Associate degree
Jiangxi	7 731	798	10.32	170	1 426	1 183
Henan	4 993	891	17.84	219	1 433	1 718
Hubei	719	130	18.08	376	223	22
Hunan	13 461	4 748	35.27	769	4 406	2 860
Subtotal	51 161	14 779	28.89	3 085	18 390	12 104
Western						
Chongqing	7 684	1 355	17.63	292	2 227	1 906
Sichuan	14 518	4 316	29.73	1 349	5 330	3 512
Guizhou	6 715	560	8.34	89	1 024	982
Yunnan	3 980	1 031	25.90	121	1 636	971
Shaanxi	36 661	15 036	41.01	3 522	18 663	6 991
Gansu	5 698	1 651	28.98	227	1 589	1 325
Ningxia	851	318	37.37	41	334	319
Xinjiang	535	133	24.86	8	87	282
Subtotal	76 642	24 400	31.84	5 649	30 890	16 288
Total	592 370	156 605	26.44	43 208	196 151	99 431
Percentage with related education				7.3	33.1	16.8

Source: Hu, 2003.

services represent other areas where software professionals are in high demand in China.

Software engineers are among those professionals who change jobs most frequently. They tend to seek work with FIEs with an expectation of higher salaries, better benefits, and more attractive, long-term career opportunities (see Table 5.2). Companies such as Accenture, which offer opportunities for advanced training as well as overseas assignments, for example, hold much greater attraction than their domestic competitors. Those in the high demand areas, such as online gaming, mobile phone software development, and e-commerce, easily command high salaries.

Life sciences and biotechnology

China is gearing up to make serious inroads into the life sciences and biotechnology sectors (Chen *et al.*, 2007). As is well known, China successfully synthesized bovine insulin in the 1960s. This "world first" won international recognition, and was considered to be a Nobel Prize-level achievement (Cao, 2004b). At the turn of the twenty-first century, China joined France, Germany, Japan, the UK, and the USA in an international effort to sequence the human genome and effectively finished its assignment ahead of schedule. Although this only encompassed a very small portion of the entire human genome, this stellar performance earned China a place as one of the major players in the international genomics arena. Chinese genomic scientists also have been involved in the production of other genome sequences, including the superhybrid rice (*indica*), which was completed well in advance of the dawdling international rice genome consortium led by Japan, a country with many more resources (Yu, 2007). In early 2004, Chinese life scientists were among the worldwide groups that identified that a coronavirus was causing severe acute respiratory syndrome (SARS) and their subsequent publication on the molecular epidemiology of the SARS coronavirus in China was widely acknowledged around the world.

China has committed itself to develop advanced agricultural biotechnologies. As one of the first countries in the world to engage in research on and commercialization of agricultural genetically modified (GM) organisms, over the past two decades, China has mobilized its agricultural scientists to achieve substantial results that have generated indigenous intellectual property rights (IPRs); Chinese farmers have devoted some of their lands for cultivating GM crops, especially Bt-cotton. The seeds from Bt-cotton are genetically modified to contain a common bacterium, *Bacillus thuringiensis*, which protects the cotton from bollworm – the most common pest that attacks cotton crops. Given initial progress in this field, China's aspiration is nothing less than becoming a global leader in the field of GM technology. The scientists hope not only to meet their country's increasing demand for food with higher yields, but also to improve nutrition, enhance resistance to pests and diseases, alleviate the huge pollution problems that come from extensive pesticide use, and ensure food security (Williams, 2001). Similarly, the health biotechnology sector has experienced the most rapid development with R&D and manufacturing on a wide range of products from testing and diagnostics, generic medicines, and vaccines to innovative research and applications such as gene therapy and stem cells, to provision of contract research services (Dennis, 2002; Frew *et al.*, 2008).

Some technology professionals and experts have suggested that if the twentieth century was the informatics century, the twenty-first century will be the biotechnology century. Given forecasts about the central place of biotechnology in the next round of the global technology revolution and associated knowledge economy, China started investing in biotechnology in the mid-1980s. The depth of the Chinese commitment is best reflected in the very high priority accorded to biotechnology among other high-technology fields in the "National High-Tech Research and Development Program," known as the 863 Program. In addition, in the "National Basic Research and Development Program," also known as the 973 Program, which was launched in the late-1990s, life sciences underpin many fields that have been supported, such as agriculture, population and health, and resources and environment (Chen *et al.*, 2007: 952–3). China invested over RMB1.5 billion (US $180 million) in biotechnology between 1996 and 2000; this level of support was increased to RMB12 billion (US $1.5 billion) between 2001 and 2005. An investment of RMB100 billion (US $12.3 billion) has been announced for R&D activities in this field over the next five to ten years. Only with such a sustained level of financial support will China have the ability to maintain the current level of momentum and also to achieve its goal of becoming the world leader in biotechnological applications in agriculture and pharmaceuticals (Jia, 2004; Wu, 2005). Because of this ambitious goal, the MLP (2006–2020) contains multiple provisions for continued support for advancing Chinese biotechnology. In fact, two life sciences-related programs – developmental biology and protein science – are among the four mega basic science programs and another one – agricultural GM products – is among one of the 16 mega engineering programs, expected to receive funding on the scale of "billions of RMB." It is estimated that as a result the output of China's biotechnology industry will hit RMB2–3 trillion, or 7–8 percent of GDP, in 2020 (MOST CNCBD, 2005: 14).

This stated commitment to make huge investments in biotechnology over the coming years has generated a great deal of enthusiasm among China's life scientists. It is interesting to note that when China reopened its universities after the Cultural Revolution, biology was one of the top disciplines in so far as it attracted the best and brightest applicants. Now, more than 60 000 scientists are active in life sciences research at 300 institutions of learning. There are approximately 389 biology programs inside China's university system and the Chinese Academy of Sciences (CAS), with 89 conferring doctoral degrees, graduating more than 2000 PhDs in biology and related fields each year. Between 1996 and 2002, China enrolled 15 000 doctoral students into biology and related disciplines. Overall employment in some 6000 pharmaceutical companies and 300 R&D institutes – large and small – reached 20 000–30 000 scientists; about 100 produce medical products based on gene technologies (Qi & Wang, 2006; Zhu, 2005).

Yet, while there is a great deal of optimism about China's potential role in the global biotechnology space, broadly speaking, the paucity of their numbers among the ranks of leading scientists is a serious problem that constrains the building up of the country's capabilities in the life sciences and biotechnology. This stands in sharp contrast to the USA, whose scientific progress continues to benefit from a geographically rich and quantitatively deep pool of high-quality scientific talent. In this regard, the biotechnology field in China suffers from the same sort of talent issues that exist in many other scientific fields. Many Chinese graduates with training in the life sciences have gone abroad to study and have stayed there to work in foreign laboratories and universities. In the 1980s, the China–US Biochemistry Examination and Admission Program (CUSBEA) placed more than 425 top Chinese doctoral students in 80 universities throughout the USA, including many of the leading Chinese-origin life scientists who are currently active in China, the USA, and elsewhere (Chen & Zhang, 2006). In the USA alone, as discussed in Chapter 6, more than 2500 Chinese-origin life scientists are employed at the assistant professor level and up. Unfortunately, from the perspective of China itself, those who have been willing to return lack the experience and credentials, in most cases, of those who remain abroad. Consequently, among those life scientists working within China as of 2005, only 147, including those who have concurrent overseas appointments, had been correspondent authors of at least one paper published in one of the top 50 life science journals *or* correspondent authors on more than five papers published in journals listed in the *Science Citation Index* (SCI) *or* correspondent authors of papers published in journals with a cumulative impact factor of more than five (General Biologic, 2005). In addition, according to a somewhat broader productivity measure – publication of eight papers in a journal with an impact factor of at least two – including at least one in a journal whose impact factor is five or above, only about 500 biologists within China can be classified as "productive," while over 3000 of Chinese descent in the USA, many originally from mainland China, fall into this category (Wu, 2004).

Of course, it must be acknowledged that biotechnology as an emerging sector worldwide has not yet been really successful financially or operationally (Pisano, 2006). One thing clear, however, is that the transformation of new ideas and discoveries in life sciences into commercially viable products and services requires specialized skills beyond general scientific knowledge. To build an internationally competitive biotechnology industry, China is expected to need an additional 30 000–40 000 research scientists, 40 000–50 000 engineers capable of engaging in new product development, and 10 000–20 000 management personnel with ample knowledge of the science behind the biotechnology, new development trends in biotechnology, adequate market knowledge, and so on (Zhu, 2005). Legal professionals, especially those with knowledge of IPRs, international regulations, and standards for IPR protection, manufacturing, and product registration, are in high demand (Frew *et al.*, 2008: 52). This is in addition to having adequate funding, equipment, and related personnel who can help bring new products to market on a national and global basis. Simply stated, overcoming these hurdles remains a challenging task for China's biotechnology talent at all levels.

Nanotechnology

Nanotechnology, another leading-edge science-based technology, is emerging as an important component of the knowledge economy, and one of the most intensively competitive areas in the twenty-first century. As a highly interdisciplinary technology, nanotechnology's talent requirements are multidimensional. It needs to attract scientists from a wide spectrum of disciplines – from physics, chemistry, biology, and information technology to materials science. Because it relies on specialized equipment and instrument manufacturing, nanotechnology requires engineers who are able to execute the ideas of scientists as well. The development of nanotechnology also requires business managers who have both a grasp of the nanotechnology field and relevant high-technology management expertise; there also is a need for legal experts and social scientists because of the societal implications and impact of nanotechnology.

For developing countries such as China, nanotechnology offers both exciting possibilities and significant challenges; only those countries with a strong and sustainable innovative capability and high-quality human resources are able to meet the technological challenges and take advantage of the emerging economic opportunities. Nanotechnology, while positioned at the global scientific and technological frontier, may actually be a field in which China does not lag that much behind the West. Like several other countries, Chinese scientists have been paying special attention to developments in nanotechnology since the 1980s, hoping to achieve some type of leap-frog position (Appelbaum *et al.*, 2006; Bai & Wang, 2007). China is estimated to have more than 5000 scientists at some 50 universities, some 20 CAS institutes, and more than 300 enterprises engaged in nanotechnology R&D, thus, according to Sishen Xie, China's leading nanotechnology scientist, forming a critical mass for engaging in a credible basic research effort (Wang, 2007). These resources are concentrated in Beijing, where a National Center for Nano Science and Technology, several CAS institutes, and Beijing and Qinghua universities are home to some of the leading Chinese scientists active in the frontiers of nanotechnology research. In Tianjin, with the recent approval of the Binhai New Development Zone by central government, a new National Academy of Nanotechnology and Engineering will play an important role in facilitating technology transfer and promoting technological entrepreneurship by harnessing the expertise of scientists in Tianjin and nearby Beijing. The CAS Suzhou Institute of Nano-Tech and Nano-Bionics is a newly established "green field" operation. With direct support from the Ministry of Science and Technology in addition to that from the CAS, this institute is focused on tackling practical problems in nano-electronics and nanobiology. In fact, from a scientific vantage point, China's nanotechnology research output is among the most prolific in the world measured by the number of scientific publications (Zhou & Leydesdorff, 2006).

Even though nanotechnology has become a national S&T priority, and is one of the central targets stipulated in the MLP, the supply of well-trained specialists in nanotechnology-related fields is woefully inadequate. On one hand, China needs more experienced, senior scientific leaders. Some of the Chinese scientists who have studied overseas have returned, but, as in many other fields, the most outstanding have stayed overseas. This does not necessarily mean they are divorced from communication or direct interaction with their counterparts in China; many continue to engage in fruitful types of collaboration and some even "direct" secondary laboratories on Chinese soil. In this way, they have helped China's scientific enterprise to make progress and keep abreast of trends abroad. Based on interviews with several of these experts, the creation of an environment more conducive to cutting-edge research and commercialization, and the improvement of IPR protection, might provide incentives to warrant their return. On the other, much of the really critical demand lies in recruiting individuals capable of the development and application of nanotechnologies; according to one prediction, the near-term need for such personnel is projected to be at least 10 000; this need is projected to expand several-fold by 2010.

Accordingly, on-the-job training for existing scientists working in disciplines related to nanotechnology has become critical. As of the end of 2007, however, there were no Chinese universities that offered a specialty in nanotechnology at the undergraduate level and only a few have such programs in place at the graduate level. Most Chinese universities do not have enough qualified nanotechnology specialists who are strong in both research and training. In Shanghai, therefore, the

"Training Program of Scarce S&T Talent for Nanotechnology" was initiated in 2003 to tackle the nanotechnology talent problem. By 2006, the program had turned out more than 1100 nanotechnology personnel with much-needed creative and explorative capabilities. Concurrent with giving increasing attention to the task of attracting high-end talent from overseas, Shanghai also has focused on nurturing talent by rotating scientists from laboratory to laboratory, providing post-doctoral fellowships to PhD holders, and enhancing international exchange programs. At present, these training programs have been extended to the higher education sector and to the entire Yangtze River Delta to form a large-scale nanotechnology talent training network (Wang, 2007).

Management

Along with having to address the dearth of qualified S&T talent, China also faces a critical shortage of highly skilled, highly experi enced managers. The nation has an astounding number of companies in operation – some 25 000 state-owned enterprises, more than 4.3 million private firms, and tens of thousands of FIEs, many set up by major MNCs. However, even the relatively small number of Chinese companies trying to expand overseas will need up to 75 000 inter- nationally experienced leaders over the next 10–15 years; currently, there are only 3 000–5 000 such men and women in China (McKinsey Global Institute, 2005). The problem is becoming further aggravated as Chinese companies have started to speed up their overseas expan- sion activities (Dyer, 2007).

It also is anticipated that demand for those with skills in the fields of financial management and investment banking will increase appre- ciably over the next few years as China opens up its capital markets as well as its financial sector. In particular, there should be a wealth of lucrative banking positions opening in 2008 and beyond as free- market competition takes hold in many areas of the financial services sector (*Forbes*, September 5, 2005: 154). Although large salaries have been offered to those Chinese who have obtained MBA degrees at leading Western business schools, many individuals have chosen to remain abroad or secure their overseas residence permits while engaged in China business-related work assignments. That situation may now change with the promise of dramatic changes in China's financial services sector, the arrival of venture capital, and China's growing integration into the global financial markets.[13]

Putting the numbers aside, based on the aggregate views of those interviewed for this book, as well as the views of many other foreign experts and observers of the Chinese situation, the stark reality is that most Chinese managers are ill-equipped to handle the multiple challenges of leading and managing a modern enterprise and competing effectively in the highly competitive, rapidly changing global economy of the twenty-first century. Most managers in China tend to "think large-scale, have tremendous drive, and are quick at execution, but lack experience dealing with global stock markets, marketing, profit-making, and communicating a vision," according to Nandan Nilekani, the Chief Executive Officer (CEO) and Managing Director of India's Infosys (*Economist*, April 16, 2005: 53–4). And, often, they also are very cautious about strategic initiative- and risk-taking, being a first mover, and engaging in real collaboration. In many ways, from a Western perspective, China does not yet have a professional managerial class, one that has a mindset of common understanding about the requisites for enterprise success and high-level performance, in the current economic environment.

Many of these prevailing deficiencies may be attributed to the legacy of the planned economy, during which managers did not have to take individual initiatives, exert leadership, or articulate a grand business vision. They also are tied to the effect of the Cultural Revolution, during which many of the current managers missed out on a formal education. Other deficiencies derive from the lack of appropriate incentives and rewards. Many Chinese managers also lack familiarity with conditions abroad and the global aspects of business. In part, these assorted shortcomings also might be attributable to a lack of foreign education or language skills, overemphasis on theory at the expense of practical knowledge, and a lack of cultural fit, including interpersonal skills as well as attitudes toward teamwork and flexible work (McKinsey Global Institute, 2005).[14] An array of these problems has come to the surface as Chinese companies have

---

[13] The international financial crisis in late 2008 may accelerate the return of some who used to work in American financial institutions on the one hand, and slow down the demand for these types of individuals in the short-term on the other. But over the long term, the demand promises to grow significantly.

[14] This was amply highlighted at the "Summer World Economic Forum," held in Dalian in summer of 2007, when many Chinese CEOs discussed their

tried to engage in international or cross-border mergers and acquisitions such as the failed attempt by China National Offshore Oil Corporation (CNOOC) to acquire UNOCAL, the California-based United States oil company, as well as in the aftermath of the acquisition of IBM's personal computer (PC) business by Lenovo, China's top computer company, in one of the more well-known cases of Chinese overseas merger and acquisition activity.

There are some specific "indirect" reasons why top-level leadership is scarce. China's one-child policy, for example, is said to have made it harder for Chinese to find natural team players. For Jeff Barnes, Chief Learning Officer at General Electric (GE) in China, Chinese managerial talent is first-generation and thus does not have role models (*Economist*, April 16, 2005: 53–4). High-technology start-ups usually are headed by scientists who are not good at such tasks as marketing and sales and do not understand the role of venture capital in the expansion of their activities. Culturally, the mentality of preferring to be "the head of a chicken rather than the tail of an ox" creates more "leaders" than are really required. There also are trust problems which derive from the nature of the *guanxi*, or a relationship-driven culture, which survives even in the midst of economic reform and related structural changes. And other cultural factors such as respect for age and hierarchy, orientation toward groups, and the preservation of "face" may also have impeded Chinese managers' learning of management theories and techniques which were originally developed in the Western cultural context (Lau and Roffey, 2002).

Education

To find and prepare well-trained managers to run its booming economy, China has embraced Western-style business education (Goodall *et al.*, 2004; He *et al.*, 2007). In 1991, China's State Education Commission, the predecessor of the Ministry of Education, authorized nine Chinese universities to set up programs that would lead to the award of a master's degree in business administration (MBA); the current number of MBA programs approved by the Ministry of Education has been expanded to 120, with numbers of students admitted annually rising from 86 in 1991

limitations about globalizing their businesses due to lack of familiarity with overseas business environment.

to more than 20 000 in 2006, and more than 80 000 MBA degrees granted. Nevertheless, the number of graduates still does not meet the evolving level of demand, and many of these programs suffer from the same problem challenging China's higher education system in general – quality – with few exceptions (Bradshaw, 2005a; Delaney, 2004).

The China Europe International Business School (CEIBS) in Shanghai, a joint venture between the Chinese government and the European Union, has demonstrated major gains from both a quality and prestige perspective by hiring professors from internationally acclaimed schools, the use of Harvard Business School case studies, and seeking international accreditation (Goodall *et al.*, 2004: 319–21; Southworth, 1999). Most of its graduates, with 20 percent of its 180 full-time students per class from outside China, have taken high-demand supply-chain and logistics jobs at domestic manufacturers and within FIEs. In 2005, the CEIBS executive MBA program claimed to be one of the world's largest, turning out 550 EMBA graduates a year, and was ranked as the world's top-thirteenth in the *Financial Times* EMBA rankings (Bradshaw, 2005b). In 2007, the Qinghua University School of Economics and Management became the first business school in the Chinese mainland to earn accreditation from the Association to Advance Collegiate Schools of Business (AACSB).

Just as there are still relatively few Chinese managers with MBA degrees, there is an even greater shortage of vigorously trained academics who can teach the academic content of advanced economics, business strategy, or executive leadership skills, and can teach using a Western-style case method (Berrell *et al.*, 2001). Every Chinese business school with an international outlook is aware of the problem and most have formed a four-pronged approach to improve their programs. The first is to attract back Chinese professors who are teaching overseas or to recruit new academics who recently received their doctoral degrees in Europe or the USA. In addition to CEIBS and the Cheung Kong Graduate School of Business, a private institution backed by Hong Kong businessman Li Kai-shing, the Beijing University Guanghua School of Management and the Qinghua University School of Economics and Management are the leaders in this regard. Qinghua University, in fact, has an internal policy on recruitment: for every PhD hired locally it has to have two with American PhDs. As a result, one-third of its more than 100 member faculty have degrees from foreign universities. Recently, the Shanghai University of Finance and Economics has been aggressively recruiting those with doctorates from leading American business schools. Major business schools also dispatch teams to the annual meeting of the American Economic Association and others to recruit new faculty members. However, new hires are mainly those with doctorates in economics, just as those with American business school PhDs and doctorates in business administration (DBA) allegedly have higher salary offers and better academic opportunities in the USA (*Twenty-First Century Economic Herald*, September 14 and 19, 2007). The second is to send existing faculty members to train at some of the top foreign business schools, especially those in the USA. But, with more fresh doctorates returning, this approach is only applicable for the top schools. Third, Chinese business schools attract top American and European professors to teach on their campuses as visiting faculty and learn from them.[15] And, finally, Chinese business schools cooperate with their foreign partners to run joint programs. As early as 1984, the School of Management of the State University of New York at Buffalo, established the first American MBA program in China, which was supported by the then Chinese State Economic Commission and the US Department of Commerce. Similarly, the China MBA Program, headquartered at the Dalian University of Technology, graduated more than 200 students before it ended in 1988 (the agreement was not renewed because of the Tiananmen Square incident in 1989) (Goodall *et al.*, 2004: 316). Now, well-known China–foreign cooperative MBA programs include those between Qinghua University and MIT, and Fudan University and Washington University in St Louis, among others.

In the meantime, an increasing number of Chinese managers are opting for an overseas MBA education. In China, where science, engineering, and medicine have long attracted the best and the brightest, only recently has business become an attractive career. Growing prosperity also has meant that young Chinese students now can afford the cost of a foreign MBA. And, ambitious young Chinese have one more very good reason to pursue a foreign MBA: high salaries. That is, an overseas degree is a critical stepping-stone for securing a better career opportunity in China. In the mid- to late-1990s, given the limited availability of managers with such credentials, when Chinese students with a foreign MBA returned to China, they likely had many attractive job offers. Working

---

[15] For example, one of this book's authors holds visiting management professorships at the Dalian University of Technology and Dalian Maritime University.

for an MNC in China was especially appealing because it offered not only a high salary, but also the chance to make better use of the skills acquired abroad and many more chances for career advancement. More recently, however, this situation has changed somewhat owing to the fact that many Chinese enterprise leaders realize that a large percentage of the knowledge acquired abroad about markets, marketing, industrial structure, and human resources management is simply not applicable in China. Foreign-trained MBA holders have found themselves frustrated by the retention of traditional practices in many enterprises or the fact that the onset of a true market economy in China remains impeded by a plethora of socio-political factors. Many have found that the role of *guanxi* has not receded as they attempt to build their careers on the basis of achievement rather than ascriptive criteria. In addition, many fresh foreign-trained MBA graduates have faced petty jealousies and criticism in the workplace because they have commanded high salaries, but have not lived up to expectations.

Many of the issues facing foreign-trained MBA graduates derive from the gap between the teaching materials deployed in the West and the day-to-day realities of managing in China. These issues have confronted many leading foreign management consulting firms such as McKinsey, Accenture, and the Monitor Group, all of which have sought to leverage their global knowledge capital in China only to find that they cannot utilize a great many of their "off-the-shelf" solutions in the highly fluid Chinese political-economic context and cultural environment. The learning curve for these firms has been very steep at times even after hiring freshly minted Chinese MBA graduates from leading management schools in Europe and the USA. In this regard, the apparent value of a foreign MBA degree in China has been diluted to some extent because of these difficulties. It is clear from this situation that there is a huge need for a truly Chinese-style MBA curriculum, with a set of locally derived cases, that matches up better with the shifting demands of the enterprise operating environment and strategic context found in China. Fortunately, some domestic MBA programs have identified these continuing issues and problems, and have taken initial steps toward altering their teaching materials to accord better with the requisites for success in the steadily evolving Chinese economic context.

According to "the Third Annual Survey of Chinese Business Schools" conducted by the US-based *Business Week* magazine in late 2007, in a poll of 253 recruiters from such leading-edge companies as Huawei,

Nokia, and General Electric, 34% of the respondents called the supply of high-quality talent from China's MBA programs "excellent" or "good" compared with 19% the previous year (*Business Week*, December 4, 2007). These results may be attributed to the curriculum becoming more relevant through use of business case studies which document the successes and failings of key Chinese firms. As the reputation of these domestic programs has improved, there now seems to be a growing tendency for interested Chinese students to explore local MBA options rather than immediately opting for overseas education. The fact that the salaries being offered to MBA graduates from prominent domestic institutions also have improved has not hurt either. In addition, many of the top Chinese MBA programs have linkages with high-quality foreign institutions, such as the Qinghua University ties with the Sloan School at MIT, mentioned above. This allows for a more blended approach to MBA training in China which qualitatively and quantitatively better reflects the challenges local managers will face, irrespective of whether they work for a state-owned enterprise, a local high-technology start-up, or an FIE.

Undergraduate education in economics and business administration has been improving, and has been strengthened, by the enhancement of teaching materials as well (Zimmerman, 2001). The total number of students enrolled in four-year programs already reached one million in 2004, although its share of China's total four-year program enrollments remains almost unchanged (Table 8.10; see also Table 4.4). The highest demand areas for economics and business administration include marketing, human resources, accountancy, international economics and trade, business administration, and finance, among others (MOEd Bureau of Higher Education, 2005) (Figure 8.1). The career climb for many of these newly trained undergraduates is a steep one as they often lack the ability to translate the theoretical knowledge they acquired in the classroom into usable tools and skills in the Chinese enterprise or FIE work environment, as their counterparts in science and technology.

From the perspective of management skills, different regions in China obviously have different sets of talent needs. Marketing is in high demand in all regions, as is human resources expertise. Establishing a true performance-oriented culture inside many Chinese enterprises is a real challenge because of the lack of managerial expertise in the human resources field. In Northern and Central China, more than one-fifth of the units surveyed by the Ministry of Education want more

Table 8.10 *Enrollment in economics and business administration programs and total enrollment at bachelor's degree level (1999–2003) (persons)*

Enrollment	1999	2000	2001	2002	2003	2004
Economics and business administration programs	385 525	484 579	560 785	728 596	916 208	1 065 736
Total	2 724 421	3 400 181	4 243 744	5 270 845	6 292 089	7 378 436
Percentage of students enrolled in economics and business administration programs	14.15	14.25	13.21	13.82	14.56	14.44

Source: Ministry of Education Bureau of Higher Education, 2005: 246.

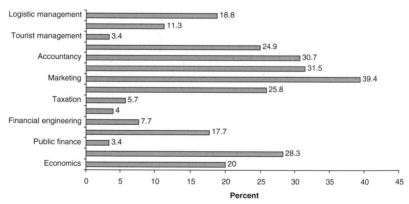

Figure 8.1 Demand for undergraduates in economics and business administration (2004) (%)
Source: Ministry of Education Bureau of Higher Education, 2005: 35.

undergraduates with solid training in economics; 43.3% and 25% of units in the South need majors in international economics and trade, respectively, as well as in finance. Financial engineering is in high demand in the South-west; insurance skills are a high priority in central China, and accountancy knowledge and competency are highly valued in the East (MOEd Bureau of Higher Education, 2005).

Ironically, close to 65% of potential employers believe that undergraduate majors of economics and business administration are in oversupply, especially in the East and among state-owned enterprises; only 12.4% think otherwise. FIEs seem to believe that supply and demand for economics or business graduates is in equilibrium. Again, this likely reflects the gap between education and experience. Domestic firms are finding it a real challenge to identify appropriate talent among fresh undergraduates that can add value quickly to the firm once they begin employment.

Utilization

Since the majority of domestic graduates lack adequate work experience and have not been tested in the trenches of domestic and overseas competition, as noted, Chinese returnees and seasoned entrepreneurs have been plugging some of holes at the most senior levels. MNCs have mainly depended upon expatriates, and Chinese from Taiwan, Hong Kong, and Singapore, for senior candidates to run their China operations. Nevertheless, simply speaking the language does not necessarily guarantee that these expatriate executives understand the current Chinese operating environment and business culture as they have been changing so rapidly. We heard many stories during our fieldwork, but probably none is more remarkable than the saga that occurred at EMC China in 2006. Back then, the "private" email exchanges between the venture's president, who was Singaporean, and his local Chinese secretary, over a misplaced key were leaked to the internet, eventually leading to the resignation of the president. The incident is a typical example of the lack of awareness of many foreign managers, even those of Chinese descent, of local culture and politics (Burns, 2006). As one observer commented to us, "They don't know what they don't know, nor how much they don't yet know!" Further, these executives have their own status and vested interests to protect so they do not always take on risky initiatives or engage in innovative behavior as they have been expected to do by their bosses overseas. Therefore, we have been told that the practice of bringing on highly paid Chinese ethnic talent from abroad has generated resentment among local managers in some cases. The managers do not see themselves being fully appreciated and trusted, nor are they pleased as their chance to run an operation has been preempted by the arrival of colleagues from overseas locations, especially if they, too, are of Chinese ethnic descent (Gamble, 2000).

Still, because of the pressing need for advanced managerial skills and knowledge, China has not retreated in its efforts to attract more foreign talent. For example, Lenovo, which bought IBM's personal computer (PC) business, mentioned above, has remarked quite candidly that much of the attraction of the offer was related to access to IBM managerial know-how rather than the PC business itself. This explains why the company moved its headquarters to the USA, initially retained an American CEO, then hired another American CEO when the first CEO decided to step down, and continues to have a major presence in the USA. Lenovo may have decided to create more distance between itself and IBM in terms of business culture and operations, but it is not any less committed to or dependent upon inputs of Western managerial know-how to transform itself into a truly global business firm.

In the meantime, fierce competition over a limited supply of high-end management talent has resulted in high turnover for managers. Western search firms that specialize in talent recruitment are finding China to be a very lucrative market as there continues to be growing demand for competent managers and great difficulty in filling evolving needs. Cultivation of the next leadership cohort, which for political and operational reasons should increasingly be drawn from mainland-born candidates, also is proving to be a serious challenge, especially in view of the ambitious growth plans that many MNCs apparently have in place in China (and India as well) to grow their businesses – both to serve China's thriving domestic market and to meet the needs of global clients and customers.[16] Accordingly, the recruitment, retention, and localization of staff are at the top of the agenda for firms – both state-owned and foreign-invested – in China (*Economist*, April 16, 2005: 53–4).

---

[16] Firms such as IBM have launched special customized "accelerated leadership" training programs to ensure that there is an ample supply of well-prepared managers in the pipeline to assume key leadership roles over the next 3–5 years and beyond.

Conclusion

While previous chapters have focused on providing an overall picture of China's S&T talent, this chapter has examined the talent situation in some of the key science-based technology sectors and with regard to management resources as well. In a word, China still suffers from a dearth of qualified "specialist" scientists and engineers as well as other key professionals to meet the immediate demands of its rapidly changing technological and economic development.

The nation also is facing a geographical dislocation problem with its S&T workforce as rising wages may impact further development of coastal regions. This may be good news for many of China's second-tier cities as they now have some substantial opportunities for harnessing foreign investment and building up their infrastructure to achieve higher growth rates during the next phase of economic development. Encouraging a certain amount of internal talent migration would not only solve the oversupply problem that exists in certain regions, but also bring an assortment of long-term economic and societal benefits, thus contributing to the onset of a more harmonious society. At the same time, however, it is clear that there needs to be a critical mass of talent and infrastructure resources to achieve the level and type of progress that Chinese leaders have indicated. Without this type of "agglomeration" of talent in selected areas, the deployment of the talent pool will be too diffuse to engage in the kinds of collaborative activities needed to drive the S&T advance. Certainly, in this era of internet, advanced telecommunications, and rapid modern transportation, everyone does not need to be co-located in a physical sense; the virtual workplace can become a reality in China as well. Nonetheless, in the context of current deployment and utilization of talent, and associated constraints and limitations, some degree of concentration does not appear to have many negative ramifications. In many cases, it is the absence of a "critical mass" that is hindering China's potential for progress along the innovation curve.

In the meantime, meeting the growing demand for scientific leaders and experienced managerial talent who are capable of driving sustained innovation, and even leap-frogging, in selected critical S&T fields remains one of China's most urgent challenges. As noted, it appears that the more advanced a scientific field, and the closer it is to the frontiers of international research, the more serious the talent gap, especially in the area of senior leadership. To a large extent, the lingering effects of the "brain drain" continue to undermine efforts to address the problem. As is the case in other areas, China's political and scientific leaders seem fully aware of the severity of the challenge, even if they do not have the full array of data needed to solve the problems systematically as presently defined. Having a contingent of overseas Chinese scientists and engineers and managers with affective as well as scholarly and commercial ties back to the Chinese mainland will temporarily help to alleviate some of these problems, though the availability of these individuals is not a long-term solution. Nurturing of an environment more suitable for the development of a creative, innovative, and more entrepreneurial talent pool is the key to resolving many of the dilemmas confronting the Chinese leadership in these critical domains. Only by further support for increased normalization of the research environment, the adoption of more standardized performance criteria in personnel affairs, better enforcement of IPR laws, and provision of more capital to support start-up ventures will China's leaders be able to establish and have full confidence in the capacity of the country's indigenous innovation system to yield desired results and outcomes.

9 | *Whither China's talent pool?*

This book has focused on providing a detailed stocktaking of the science and technology (S&T) talent contingent in China, accompanied by an in-depth analysis of the potential role of this evolving talent pool in Chinese current and future economic growth and technological development. As discussed in earlier chapters, during the reform and open-door era, China has gradually changed its development strategy from one heavily dependent on natural resources and capital investment to one more focussed on knowledge and talent as the key drivers of enhanced economic performance. The Chinese leadership has exhibited a pervasive sense of urgency about the need to catch up with the developed economies and has recognized that solving the country's talent issue is a crucial ingredient in terms of China's ability to cope with an increasingly competitive international environment, build a comprehensive well-off and harmonious society, and, more importantly, consolidate and fortify the ruling base of the Chinese Communist Party (CCP). It further understands that the successful creation and growth of a knowledge-driven economy requires a greatly enhanced talent pool composed of high-quality scientists, engineers, and other professionals.

In fulfilling the policies of "rejuvenating the nation with science, technology, and education" (*kejiao xingguo*) and "empowering the nation through talent" (*rencai qiangguo*), China literally has turned out millions of college students, especially in S&T, and more recently in management, to meet the new innovation challenges. It has tried to upgrade the existing Chinese S&T workforce by dispatching many talented individuals overseas for advanced training and research experience to expose them to international standards of world-class science. Today, it almost has become common practice, even for larger numbers of Chinese undergraduates, along with their counterparts at the graduate level, to obtain foreign study experience. Exposure to Western education and market economies appears to have

stimulated entrepreneurial activities among many returning Chinese
S&T personnel as they seek to harness their know-how and convert
it into new, commercially viable products and services. China also
has encouraged multinational corporations (MNCs) to move up the
value chain in their China operations, upgrading their manufacturing
activities and adding a research and development (R&D) capability to
their local presence in China. MNCs also are actively seeking to access
the best and brightest Chinese talent, thus creating the context for the
possible emergence of a series of so-called "talent wars" in China.

The new, very positive orientation toward talent and knowledge
seems to have begun to pay off, as China in the early twenty-first
century is significantly different from the China that existed when the
reform and open-door policy started, or even in the early 1990s when
China tried to step out of the shadows of the Tiananmen Square
crackdown. In fact, it is increasingly clear that China is now in a better
position to become a true economic and technological power on both
regional and global levels. Moreover, it is also obvious to Chinese
political and scientific leaders that much of this progress explicitly
may be attributed to the nation's emerging talent assets. The rise of
China as a global technological power, even taking into account many
of the shortcomings mentioned in this book, will have important
consequences for the country, internally as well as externally. Then
what are the specific economic and socio-political implications of
China having a dynamic, pro-active S&T talent pool? And, what
broad potential impact will China's talent pool have on global technological competition and international scientific advance during the
first part of the twenty-first century? In this concluding chapter, we
intend to address these and several other related issues.

China as a global technological power

Various indicators, mentioned throughout the book, suggest that
China is well on its way to becoming a recognized global technological power. What is most relevant in this regard, however, is not
simply that China has increased its gross expenditure on R&D
(GERD), that its GERD as a percentage of gross domestic product
(GDP) is expected to reach the level of developed economies within
a decade or so, or that China's share of publications in the international S&T literature has been increasing. These indicators are

important, but they will become almost operationally as well as economically irrelevant unless Chinese leaders can spur on the sustained development, deployment, and mobilization of a high-quality, high-performance cohort of scientists, engineers, and R&D professionals who can position China at the cutting edge of global innovation and scientific advance. As highlighted in this book, China today possesses the second-largest "army" in the world in terms of scientists and engineers who are devoted to R&D activities, and the country remains the largest producer of S&T students at the undergraduate level and soon at the doctoral level.

To say that China will soon emerge as one of the most innovative and technologically formidable players in global science and technology affairs, however, does not necessarily indicate that a growing confrontation between China and the incumbents is on the horizon. Instead, when viewed from the perspective of talent, the most likely scenarios for the future are characterized by a much more positive-sum set of possibilities and outcomes (Hollingsworth *et al.*, 2008). First, while China has yet to become a full-fledged so-called "epicenter of *technological* development," its domestic scientists have become actively involved in the production of new *scientific* knowledge. One of the key indicators that underlie this orientation is the rather impressive Chinese S&T publication record. In 2006, Chinese papers accounted for 5.90% of the total in journals cataloged by the *Science Citation Index* (SCI) and, as a whole, Chinese scientists and engineers contributed more than 8% of the world's S&T literature (see Table 3.17). In addition, with Chinese science steadily moving toward the international frontiers of scientific research, more and more foreign scientists have sought collaborative opportunities with their Chinese colleagues. Between 1996 and 2005, for example, the number of China's international collaborative papers doubled every 3.81 years, slightly faster than the total number of Chinese papers cataloged by the SCI, which doubled every 3.97 years. Between 2001 and 2005 China's leading S&T collaborators, measured by the number of co-authored papers cataloged by the *SCI*, include, the USA, Japan, Germany, the UK, Australia, Canada, France, and South Korea, all technologically advanced nations. In other words, China's scientific community has become steadily enmeshed and increasingly ever-present in the transnational and cross-border networks of new knowledge creation that now dominate international S&T affairs (Bai & Cao, 2008).

Despite the problems it will face as it implements the "Medium- to Long-Term Plan for the Development of Science and Technology" (MLP), there is little doubt that China is becoming an important player in the world's scientific research and technological innovation. Foreign governments and corporations will be affected by China's development trajectory, and face the challenge of devising strategies to prepare for, and take advantage of, the changes in China. Not surprisingly, governments throughout the world are entering, or expanding, S&T relations with China, and, as noted, a growing number of MNCs that are increasingly concerned about tapping into the global talent pool are establishing R&D centers in China (to be discussed further). In addition, there is a rush among universities and research centers in Asia, Europe, and North America, to build relationships with Chinese educational and research institutions to facilitate cooperative research and the exchange of students and research personnel. The changing complexion of China's S&T relations and cooperative linkages reflects the deepening of the country's talent pool and strengthening S&T capabilities.

Second, as mentioned in Chapter 7, foreign direct investment (FDI) in China has been moving steadily up the value chain over the past three decades. Since China joined the World Trade Organization in late 2001, many MNCs have decided, for strategic business reasons, to relocate more and more of their high-end business operations to China, including the establishment of R&D laboratories. The purpose of these R&D laboratories is not simply localizing technologies generated in their home-base headquarters, which, no doubt, is still a major task, but, rather, is to take advantage of the Chinese local talent pool to carry on genuine R&D activities that could benefit the MNC's global as well as regional operations. Microsoft Research Asia (set up as Microsoft Research China in 1998) illustrates the strategy of MNCs tapping into the Chinese talent pool to support the firm's overall global growth (Buderi & Huang, 2006). Microsoft Research Asia has expanded into an organization that employs over 300 researchers and engineers, most hired locally; has published 1500 papers in top international journals and conferences; and has achieved many important, albeit incremental in most cases, technological breakthroughs. Technologies from Microsoft Research Asia have not only made it into Microsoft products, but also have had an influence on the broader information technology (IT) community. MNCs now see enhanced prospects for migrating more of their outsourcing operations to China.

Foreign firms also have expanded their collaboration with Chinese institutions of learning on various research fronts. Obviously, tapping into China's talent pool requires a local presence and what better place to find talent than in conjunction with a close university affiliation?

Third, China's S&T talent has the ability to help support scientific enterprises in other countries. The quality of Chinese graduates, especially those at the top universities, is well known internationally. Chinese graduates are working all over the world, and it is no secret that many of the outbound students with fully paid offers from some of the world's leading universities indeed are China's best and brightest, who are less likely to return home immediately after finishing their foreign stint. In the USA, some 62 500 Chinese-origin PhD holders were in the S&T workforce in 2003, and it is certain that other highly-qualified Chinese-origin scientists and engineers are now staffing universities, research laboratories, and enterprises in many technologically advanced countries (see, for example, Zhang, 2003). Singapore, for example, has actively competed with other countries for talent, including Chinese talent, especially life scientists, as the city-state strives to build itself into a biotechnology powerhouse (Heenan, 2005; Lee, 2001).

Fourth, as Chinese companies become more internationally active and expand their operations beyond the physical borders of the People's Republic of China, they will extend their overseas technological reach – not only deploying their skilled research personnel, but also looking for new opportunities to hire "local" scientists and engineers. The acquisition of IBM's personal computer (PC) business by Lenovo represents the type of effort by which a Chinese-based firm, albeit one globally oriented, secures access to critical knowledge, high-end talent, and advanced management know-how. Cross-border merger and acquisition activities involving Chinese MNCs will occur with increasing frequency in the future, thus significantly changing the pattern of international competition for goods and services, and, more importantly, leading first to the reconfiguration of the landscape of international S&T affairs and, second, further alteration of the already fluid complexion of the so-called "global talent pool."

China's talent challenge

In Chapter 2, we put forth the argument that China has been facing a serious talent challenge owing to a combination of four factors. First, the pain and aftereffect of the Cultural Revolution, especially in terms of the dislocations that happened in the realm of higher education, continue to be felt more than three decades later; that is, a talent gap. Second, the overseas study initiatives that have occurred in conjunction with China's open-door policy have created an unintended and highly undesirable consequence – "brain drain" – the flight of talent has constrained domestic access to the best and the brightest human resources within China. While it is true that there continue to be positive links between those who have remained abroad and China's domestic S&T community, the forward momentum of China S&T enterprise, no doubt, has been affected negatively from the departure of some of the people with the greatest potential. Third, as Chinese society has begun to age as well, the changing demographic composition of the scientific community in terms of age and work experience has also started to have an impact on the potential for progress in the future. And, finally, the majority of Chinese S&T graduates still are not up to the international quality standards required to meet the steadily increasing skill demands of the overall economy. If, as Orleans argued in the early 1980s (1983: 63), "the shortages, the poor quality, and the inefficiencies associated with scientific and technical personnel have been the primary impediment to China's economic growth and modernization," in early twenty-first century China, the evolving talent challenge may not be as problematic in this regard, but it is no less significant in terms of hurdles affecting China's innovative potential.

Throughout this book, the discussion about China's S&T workforce and higher education has focussed on the key issues of quantity and quality. Assorted cautions have been introduced about taking the publicly available statistics at face value. With higher education being expanded since 1999, and student enrollments continuing to increase steadily, the overemphasis on quantity has led to a series of corresponding problems on the quality side. In fact, the quality issues among many Chinese college graduates contribute, at least in part, to significant numbers of graduates having difficulty in finding jobs related to their academic training, raising many questions about the value of their education and training. Unmet expectations increasingly fill the air among the ranks of recent graduates. Interestingly, there seems to have been an idealistic expectation among some Chinese officials, who also seemed to have been lulled into a state of unreality: a quantitative leap in enrollments would be likely to yield to substantial qualitative improvements across the ranks of the available talent pool. Unfortunately, China has yet to experience the type of scientific or technological leap forward that is so seriously and explicitly sought at the highest levels of its government and the party. It will obviously take more time than desired by the current leadership for the type of sustained concerted advance in S&T and innovative outcomes to occur.

Further, having an overall large S&T workforce in place does not necessarily confer a significant quality improvement in terms of other various other metrics associated with S&T progress. We have pointed out that given the size of its population, China still lags behind most developed countries in terms of the number of researchers engaged in R&D activities on a per capita basis (see Table 3.19). Indeed, using this metric, China still has a long way to go before even catching up with the talent situation in South Korea, Russia, and Singapore. Of China's 758 million individuals in the labor force aged between 25 and 64 years in 2005, only 6.8% had attained a tertiary level of education (NBS Department of Population and Employment Statistics and MOLSS Department of Planning and Finance, 2006: 8 and 62), while across the Organization for Economic Cooperation and Development (OECD) countries, the average percentage is 26% – almost four times greater (OECD, 2007b: 36). The fact remains that the dramatic increase in student admissions in China in recent years has not been matched by a corresponding increase in government investment in higher education. As a result, China's overall investment in education still ranks among the lowest in the world, thus further complicating and confounding the task of growing its S&T workforce and improving its quality.

At this point, it also is important to consider the evolving demographic shifts that in years to come will influence both China's high-end talent pool in S&T and its counterparts around the world. As noted, China has started on the path toward becoming an aging society with a larger percentage of its workforce reaching retirement age and surpassing the percentage of those in their college-bound years around 2015–2017 (see Figure 7.1); some expect that Chinese universities will face an admissions challenge as early as 2009. As an aging society, China will move into a comparatively disadvantageous position vis-à-vis its chief competitor India, which has a younger population. This is likely to translate into an edge for India in terms of potential advantages regarding technology progress and economic growth. Accordingly, China must take full advantage of the narrow "window of opportunity" that exists between now and the onset of an aging society to expand and improve the ranks of the educated to create a more qualified, highly competent talent pool capable of meeting the country's goals in S&T. Otherwise, the goal of becoming "an innovative nation" by 2020 will not be realized.

With these challenges in mind, China could do several things to better ensure that its talent pool evolves and grows in the right directions. First, China has to overcome the structural obstacles that exist concerning the training and utilization of the S&T workforce, such as filling in the gap between classroom education and quickly evolving job requirements, attracting qualified high-end talent to assume leadership positions, providing continuous on-the-job training to upgrade the knowledge of the existing workforce, and so on. One of China's distinctive attributes is its second-tier provinces and cities that are not necessarily inferior to coastal regions in S&T development and education. Therefore, more attention should be given to Anhui, Hebei, and Shandong provinces, along with Liaoning, Shaanxi, and Sichuan, in terms of development of local talent as well as the local S&T infrastructure. Shandong is geographically close to the Yangtze River Delta and Hebei is near Beijing and Tianjin, the latter being China's newest development hot spot. Hefei city in Anhui province is home to the famous University of Science and Technology of China, under the Chinese Academy of Sciences (CAS), one of the strongest S&T talent training centers in the country. Another city that is on the rise is Dalian, located in North-east China: Dalian aspires to become the "Bangalore of China" as it seeks to establish itself as China's key software and outsourcing base.[1] Ultimately, these provinces and cities will become an important driving force behind the demand for talented personnel owing to the underlying trade and investment factors which have helped to propel forward the overall Chinese economy. The key question is whether these regions can make themselves more attractive to high-end talent by creating more highly paid jobs and fostering an environment that offers a good quality lifestyle as well as

---

[1] Noticeable development includes, in 2007, Intel – the world's largest semiconductor manufacturer – broke ground in Dalian for its new 300 mm wafer fabrication facility (Fab 68). This first such advanced plant that Intel has built in a developing country is expected to realize annual sales of RMB20 billion by 2020. Intel's investment is said to be in the range of US $2.5 billion.

facilitating career growth and providing unique professional development experiences. In this regard, for example, Dalian is moving to diminish its dependence on Japan and South Korea in these areas by expanding English language training and better preparing graduates for working inside and with MNCs.

Second, China ought to further increase its investment in R&D not only to absorb more scientists and engineers, but also to raise the sophistication level and efficacy of their activities. In view of the inefficiencies and frustrations associated with the utilization of talent by domestic institutions and enterprises, an increasing number of skilled young scientists and engineers and other professionals choose to work for foreign-owned businesses and joint ventures in China as they seek out their best career opportunities. Although unintentional, the internal "brain drain" to FIEs, at least in the short term, has begun to affect the build-up of an indigenous innovation capability. Meanwhile, the underutilization of the Chinese S&T workforce, generally speaking, has also opened the door for MNCs to outsource more of their operations to China as those in the domestic talent pool are looking for better, more prestigious career opportunities and work experiences. Retention and effective utilization of the current talent pool are both extremely important tasks, as the talent currently in place represents the reservoir of needed scientific, engineering, and managerial human capital that is indispensable for China's future S&T development.

Third, China needs to instill, more deeply and more broadly, a culture of creativity into its students and S&T workforce. Rote learning has been attributed to the lack of creativity among many Chinese. Students are seldom encouraged or even taught to think "out of the box," take risks, or tolerate failure as a means to progress. Following the tradition of respecting the elderly and experienced, Chinese are sincere in their deference for their seniors; consequently, students feel uneasy about daring to challenge their teachers and other forms of authority. Therefore, Chinese education needs to not only reconfigure new curriculum to embrace the rapidly changing reality inside the country to accommodate the new evolving social, economic, legal, and political environment, but also introduce a new pedagogical approach to stimulate more inventive and innovative thinking. This task must involve not only the formal education system, but also the entire social system in China – a rather daunting task in view of the cultural and socio-political complexities that must be addressed in the process.

In a word, China's top priority regarding the growth of its talent pool will be to lift the professional standards of its S&T workforce so as to change the nation from simply being the world's largest manufacturer to a leading nation in innovation. While this is, of course, a high-level strategic goal requiring long-term commitment and investment, Chinese leaders have to take concrete steps now to enhance the chances of substantially realizing China's innovation goals in the future.

Talent and China's political development

Thus far, the analysis provided in this book rarely has touched upon the relationship between talent and politics in China; a discussion of the nexus between these two issues is both necessary and highly relevant to the subject matter at hand. It is necessary because Chinese politics are deeply rooted in the interconnectivity between knowledge and talent. The plight of intellectuals throughout the history of the communist regime has been inextricably linked with the ebb and flow of Chinese politics, most noticeably and decisively during the heyday of the decade known as the Cultural Revolution. The links run historically deep as well. For example, it was the intellectuals in China who advocated the enlightenment value of science and democracy during the May Fourth Movement of 1919. This same type of advocacy became embedded in the pro-democracy movement and demonstrations that occurred in Tiananmen Square 70 years later (Calhoun, 1992). It was also the intellectuals who introduced Marxism into China and eventually helped establish it as the guiding ideology of the Chinese Communist Party (CCP). The ranks of the leadership of the People's Republic of China over the past 20 years have been dominated by technocrats, most having been educated in science and engineering; this trend had been maintained until late 2007 when China started to see those trained in economics and law appearing in the top ranks of the leadership (Suttmeier, 2007). As members of the talented stratum, they are supposed to understand and be sensitive to the ways of and thinking within the intellectual world, even though it is quite often the case that the most intense debates occur and tensions emerge within and across the ranks of the intellectuals as a distinct definable group.

It is also relevant in that as various key political events have unfolded, they have had a huge impact on the talent situation in China, often a rather deleterious one. The tremendous damage wrought by the

Cultural Revolution on higher education aside, the Tiananmen Square incident of June 1989 curtailed the return of a significant number of overseas Chinese students under Chinese government sponsorship, thus exacerbating the current dearth of Chinese talent at the high-end. Within the current institutional climate that has been established under President Hu Jintao and Premier Wen Jiabao, there is every reason to believe that Chinese leaders in power today recognize the huge costs and damage to the country from the unbridled intervention of politics into the realm of science, technology, and education affairs. Accordingly, barring any sudden reversals in the prevailing political climate in China, it is expected that knowledge, expertise, and talent will be valued in their own right as well as in the context of the imperatives of improving the innovation system and sustaining the economic growth trajectory of the country.

In reality, Chinese S&T talent has both benefited from and been disadvantaged by the extraordinary changes that have swept through China since the onset of the reform programs launched by Deng Xiaoping. And, if the reforms and open-door policy since 1978 have produced discrete categories of "winners" and "losers" in the midst of these changes, it is relatively clear that scientists, engineers, and related professionals definitely have been among the former, especially since the 1990s. The regime has become a less intrusive force in terms of operation of the S&T domain; Chinese scientists and engineers have been granted more authority in areas related to their profession as they are not viewed as posing a direct challenge to state power. Rather, they are viewed as instruments that actually enhance the power of the state by helping to boost economic performance, raise Chinese prestige abroad, and ensure greater national security through the technological modernization of Chinese national defense capabilities. Furthermore, because intellectuals were one of the primary socio-political forces that intensively pushed the CCP to undertake more progressive and substantive political reforms to make China more democratic during much of the 1980s, the post-1989 leadership has changed its tactics and strategy toward managing intellectuals (they are now classified as members of the professional ranks) and private entrepreneurs by co-opting them and giving them new elite status (Pei, 2006: 88–95). Professionals have been recruited into the CCP and appointed to powerful administrative positions in universities and research institutions. In the spirit of support and encouragement, the government also parcels out professional recognition, along with material perks, to a select group of intellectuals and scientists as rewards for their achievements and contributions. In some cases, even non-CCP members such as Wan Gang and Chen Zhu, respectively, have even been appointed full ministers, the former in S&T and the latter in public health. These appointments demonstrate the willingness of the leadership to somewhat further depoliticize the realm of S&T to remove any fears and apprehensions that may linger from earlier periods.

Within today's China, a middle class has been newly created with professionals as the core. According to the estimates of the Department of Organization of the CCP Central Committee, the number of employees working in China's non-state sector have surpassed 50 million and continue to grow; this group includes not only workers, peasants, cadres, but also an increasing number of professionals (*People's Daily* June 11, 2007: 10). Apparently, despite the premium that the Chinese government has placed on the role of S&T talent, professionals in the non-state sector have found that their knowledge and skills are better utilized and they are better compensated than their counterparts employed at state-owned *danwei*. Although talented Chinese professionals as a "group" are neither organized nor primed to be mobilized as a democratizing force, they have political interests, even in the midst of their often rather fluid identities. One day, however, they may feel a need to assert themselves politically, if not for larger democratic values than for their own self-interest. Along with other members of the middle class, in all likelihood they will demand an increase in political choices commensurate with their increased economic ones, and perhaps agitate for greater political openness and participation. Therefore, it remains to be seen how long Chinese professionals will maintain their "cozy" relationship with the China's political leadership, which soon may need to develop some new tactics to manage the potential political rise of China's new and perhaps increasingly cohesive "talent pool."

What does the future hold?

It would be unfortunate if we ended this book without addressing what stands out as the most critical question in the minds of those interested in issues such as global talent, global competition, and global cooperation and conflict: Will China's emerging S&T talent pool enable the People's Republic of China to become a true global techno-power or will the problems within and across that talent pool prove to be a major limitation on future Chinese economic growth and technological advance? Even taking into account the multiple challenges and issues that the Chinese leaders must address in cultivating and nurturing an effective human resources pool in the S&T realm, it should be clear from this study that China's science, technology, and managerial base does constitute a critical source of competitive advantage in economic and technological terms. However "raw" or immature the Chinese talent pool may be at this time, there are good reasons to believe that the present set of shortcomings, which frequently have made talent issues into a serious liability, are now being addressed in a concerted, coherent fashion. From our perspective, the issue is not *if* talent will become a source of competitive advantage, but, rather, only *when* and under *what* conditions it will reach this stage. While there clearly are no guarantees, there is a confluence of forces at work that indicates that the global S&T community should not discount China in terms of its future potential as an important source of both invention and innovation.

At various points in this book we have identified critical bottlenecks and constraints that have prevented the country from fully benefiting from the large growth in the numbers of scientists and engineers entering the workforce from Chinese and foreign universities. Our goal was to suggest, as was explained, that we cannot simply extrapolate from this new large volume of talent that China is headed for a major technological leap forward. Quality is just as, if not more, important as quantity in terms of talent when assessing China's real innovative potential. There are ample indicators that Chinese officials have reached the same conclusion in their deliberations about why their national system of innovation has not produced both the type and level of output anticipated. Simply stated, the overall rate of progress in the S&T system has not been satisfactory from the standpoint of the top leadership in Beijing. Based on the findings in this book, the critical missing piece of China's innovation puzzle seems to lie in better deployment and utilization of the evolving contingent of S&T talent. The associated hurdles that must be overcome are as much about the workplace environment and performance expectations as they are about macro-strategic issues revolving around the setting of the right S&T priorities and providing sufficient funds to ensure a high probability of success.

Some observers have suggested that there are deep cultural inhibitors standing in the way of the establishment of a more creative, innovative atmosphere in China. Clearly, culture plays a role to the extent that it is part of the DNA that shapes the operating milieu representing the face as well as the internal workings of Chinese society – even in its most modern aspects. The persistence of the *guanxi* or relationship culture, for example, is one of the most important elements that continue to influence the nature of cooperation and economic exchange in China. That said, however, it is our contention that the more significant underlying shortcomings derive from the still "transitional" nature of the reforms and incomplete structural changes taking place in the S&T as well as the political system. In essence, China has yet to fully realize the onset of an achievement-oriented set of norms and values that fully define the framework of performance, compensation, rewards, and incentives. Another way of saying this is that there still is too much "socialism" left in the Chinese research system. Nor have many Chinese organizations been able to assimilate completely into their own operating environment critically needed notions of personal responsibility and accountability that sociologists such as Talcott Parsons and others long have associated with socio-political and economic advance in the West (Parsons, 1951). Thus, there will continue to exist real limitations on the pace of technological progress in China in so far as it is highly dependent upon getting the bulk of the talent pool in place to perform at new and ever higher performance and skill levels, and with the added intensity that is called for by the growing exigencies of international competition. While these limitations are not sufficient to any degree to derail China in terms of its scientific and technological ambitions, they remain ever-present and continue to create enough friction to diminish the efficacy of many of the new policy initiatives and financial investments coming out of Beijing.

Appendix: Understanding Chinese science and technology human resources statistics

Throughout this book, we have relied upon a vast array of statistics and related data concerning China's human resources in science and technology (HRST), as well as Chinese science and technology (S&T) and education activities. The bulk of our research has focused on the use of primary statistical data from Chinese government sources, mainly because there are not many, if any, alternative reliable sources of such data in this field and also because we wanted to develop a picture of the S&T human resources situation in China that is similar to the one used by Chinese policymakers and scholars. In relying heavily on these Chinese sources, we recognized from the start that there remains a huge gap between China and developed countries, especially Europe and the USA, in collecting and reporting statistics. A host of cautions was certainly warranted as we used these data, even after scrubbing for inconsistencies and associated problems. Indeed, as we have pointed out in various sections of the book, problems with these data raise some serious questions about the ability of Chinese policymakers to develop appropriate policies and incentives given their dependence on data that sometimes pose more questions than answers.

These issues and minefields acknowledged, however, we also believe it is just as important to recognize the tremendous progress that the People's Republic of China has made in developing a more uniform, coherent, and systematic series of statistics concerning domestic S&T activities and outcomes (Gao *et al.*, 2007; Schaaper, 2004). For example, in 1990, China first started formal publication of an S&T statistical yearbook and a bi-annual S&T indicators report. The publication of an educational statistical yearbook dates back to 1984. Without all three of these critical reports, scholars would find it almost impossible to study China's S&T and education system;

nor would it have been possible for us to write the current book with any degree of confidence in the value of the data – raw and in processed form.

This appendix is devoted to an in-depth examination of China's S&T and education statistics and especially their relevance to our study of HRST. It begins with a discussion about the reliability of official Chinese government statistics in general. Then, it provides an overview of the evolution of China's S&T statistics system while highlighting the main sources of such statistics. At the same time that we point out some of the particular problems related to China's talent statistics, the appendix also provides our assessment about how to best use and interpret these numbers.

Official Chinese statistics and their reliability

Quality aside, the reliability of Chinese official statistics has long been a topic of discussion and debate in the academic community, mainly by economists. The lack of complexity regarding many facets of the Chinese economy during the 1950s and 1960s made for relatively clear assessments about the reliability and completeness of Chinese data. Like many other developing countries, while China suffered from an underdeveloped statistical system, its economy had not reached the level of sophistication of its counterparts in the West. Other than availability issues, statistical measures of economic activity, especially under the planned economy, presented few unique or special challenges. At the same time, it also was the case, as occurred during the Great Leap Forward, that there were numerous incidences of falsification of statistical data. This type of purposeful misreporting often was done to obscure problems that might result in job dismissal or political attack. It also contributed to misman-agement of the economy as decision-makers did not have accurate information from which to formulate and implement a variety of critical policies. Then, the Cultural Revolution destroyed China's statistical system completely.

The post-Cultural Revolution period was characterized by a strong effort for the state to regain control over the operation of the economy and reinstitute a more reliable system for reporting data from the localities to the center. Many foreign scholars were mystified by the lack of reliable data; some even went so far as to believe that

China actually did have a great deal of data and information about the economy in its possession, but was outwardly reluctant to release accurate data about the economic and related situation because of concerns about national security or even embarrassment. Problems related to the underdevelopment of the statistical system began to magnify as the economy started to grow and it was realized that the quality of the prevailing data was quite poor in many cases.

In the late 1990s, upward falsification of output statistics caught the attention of several Chinese and foreign scholars and Chinese leaders. For example, by analyzing the anomaly between increasing gross domestic product (GDP) and decreasing energy consumption between 1997 and 2000, economist Thomas Rawski (2001) concluded that real GDP growth in 1998 was not the official 7.8% but 5.7% or even less due to the "wind of falsification and embellishment." More recent glitches in China's statistics went to the other extreme – instead of overstating output to meet "official" growth targets, there has been underreporting of economic growth. The first national economic census conducted in 2004 discovered that in such service sectors as transportation, storage, post and telecommunications; wholesale, retail, and restaurant; and real-estate, where the emerging private economy had a larger share than thought, underreporting was significant, which resulted in a 16.8% upward revision of China's GDP for 2004 and corresponding revision of statistics for the years between 1993 and 2004. Nevertheless, most recently, Chinese-origin, Princeton University-based economist Gregory Chow, who had access to top Chinese leaders from Zhao Ziyang and Zhu Rongji to Jiang Zemin, optimistically comments that "Chinese official statistics are by and large reliable because of the assigned responsibility of the officials preparing them, of their being used in government decision-making that is open to public scrutiny, and in many published articles in referred journals" (Chow, 2006: 396). But he also proposes that "some data are not reliable" so that in using official data, one should "exercise caution to make sure that the data are reliable for the purpose at hand" (Chow 2006: 398).

In order to achieve a better understanding of Chinese S&T statistics, it is necessary to have an appreciation for the structure and operation of China's official statistical system. Upon the founding of the People's Republic, China set up a statistics division within the State Council, which evolved into the National Bureau of Statistics

(NBS) in 1952.[1] Statistics apparatuses also were established in various government ministries and at the regional level; they were responsible for collecting data in sectors and regions under their jurisdictions and reporting the information back to the NBS in Beijing. Through conducting nationwide and sector-wide surveys, statistical work became an integrated and important component of China's planned economy. On the occasion of the tenth anniversary of the founding of the People's Republic of China, in 1959, the NBS published *Ten Great Years*, a compendium of statistics covering achievements in infrastructure; industry; agriculture; transportation, post, and communications; trade; employment; culture and education; people's living, and so on. As noted, even though there clearly had been serious exaggerations under the Great Leap Forward, which led to a host of propaganda-driven, unrealistic economic growth targets, the first statistics compilation in Chinese history provided observers of the country's economy with a useful baseline and a rare opportunity to understand China from a quantitative perspective. Both Orleans (1961) and Cheng (1965), the respective pioneers of the Western studies of China's post-1949 HRST, for example, used this book extensively. Their work both benefited and suffered from the strengths and weaknesses of this statistical compilation.

Generally speaking, China's statistics system was decimated during the Cultural Revolution, which lasted approximately ten years between 1966 and 1976. Statistics bureaux at central and local governments were repealed between 1967 and 1969, and in 1969 the NBS was merged into the then State Planning Commission (SPC). Statistical data collected prior to the Cultural Revolution were destroyed and employees skilled in statistical analysis as well as mathematics and economics were dispatched to engage in irrelevant work, including working on pig farms in the Chinese countryside. Eventually, in 1970, some formal statistical work was restored, albeit on a limited and gradual basis. And, in 1974, the NBS was separated from the SPC.

Recognizing the need for more accurate statistical data to better manage the economy in the aftermath of the Cultural Revolution, and especially after the initiation of the reform and open-door policy in the

---

[1] The English name, the National Bureau of Statistics (NBS), is used here to refer to China's national statistical apparatus, which was the State Statistical Bureau (SSB) before 1998.

late 1970s, statistical work in China began to receive almost unprecedented attention from the central government. By 1978, the NBS was fully restored, which, gradually, but steadily, began to rebuild the integrity of the Chinese statistical system. In 1982, the NBS began publication of the *China Statistical Yearbook*. It also was during this time that China conducted its third population census (the previous two were carried out in 1953 and 1964, respectively). In December 1983, the third session of the Standing Committee of the Sixth National People's Congress (NPC) passed a National Statistics Law, which was enacted on January 1, 1984, replacing the 1963 State Council Temporary Regulations on Statistical Work. Later on, the National Statistics Law was revised in accordance with a resolution passed by the nineteenth session of the Standing Committee of the Eighth NPC. The law required that organizations and individuals under statistical investigation "provide truthful statistical data." In particular, the law stipulates that altering statistical data without authorization, fabricating statistical data, or compelling or prompting statistics institutions or statisticians to tamper with or fabricate statistical data are violations subject to criticism and administrative sanctions or even crimes whose committers shall bear legal consequences accordingly. This makes it more unlikely that those who collect and compile data actually falsify statistics under the pressure from the central, local, or ministerial governments for political purpose – one of the common Western criticisms of China's official statistics. Changing statistical reports requires not only direction from the Chinese leadership and cooperation from statistical bureaus or other agencies responsible for data collection and reporting, but also sophistication to survive the scrutiny of the international community (Chow, 2006).

Nevertheless, it should be recognized that a two-track statistical work system caused considerable problems in data collection and reporting. On one hand, local statistics bureaus receive professional guidance from the NBS and are responsible for collecting data and reporting them to the NBS and fulfilling the tasks as stipulated by the Statistics Law. On the other, their budgets mainly come from local governments, which also tend to carry more weight in appointing and promoting staff members. When a conflict between these two roles arises and creates a very awkward situation, local statistics personnel may feel pressures to subordinate their professional ethics to satisfy and even pander to local leadership. This explains why there have been numerous instances of exaggeration or underreporting regarding key statistical data. Interestingly, if statistical data distortions during the Great Leap Forward period served a distinctly political purpose, the distortions of recent years more or less reflect the specific interests of both local leaders and local statistics personnel (Zhao, 2006). The NBS has been working hard to ensure that these types of local distortions do not occur with any frequency; and indeed, over the last decade in particular, the NBS has become a much more professionally sophisticated organization. The quality of its work continues to improve.

Bearing these factors in mind, let us now move to a discussion on China's S&T and education statistics.

China's S&T statistics

Evolution[2]

The development of China's S&T statistics dates back to 1954 when the NBS surveyed the quantity, quality, and distribution of engineering personnel. The survey targeted not only engineers at universities, research institutes, and other organizations offering a college education, but also technicians and even workers who had been promoted to technical positions. In 1958, the then State Science Planning Commission, the precursor of the State Science and Technology Commission (SSTC), which became the Ministry of Science and Technology in the 1990s, and the NBS conducted a survey of research institutes affiliated with the Chinese Academy of Sciences (CAS), government ministries, institutions of higher education, and enterprises. In 1960, in order to put together a national S&T cadre development plan, another important survey was conducted, covering technical personnel across scientific research, engineering, agriculture, healthcare, and teaching at non-military and non-national defense-related institutions and enterprises. This survey aimed at obtaining the numbers of technical cohorts by institution, professional title, fields of study, industrial sector, and ownership. In 1966, on the eve of the Cultural Revolution, the SSTC and the NBS initiated an investigation of organizations in the natural sciences to obtain the names, locations, numbers of employees (including research and technical personnel,

---

[2] This section is based on Liu (2006).

supporting staff, professional management personnel, and testing staff), areas of research, and tasks.[3]

In 1978, at the onset of China's reform and door-opening, with the role of S&T and talent being given special emphasis, the NBS, the then SPC, the then SSTC, and the Ministry of Civil Affairs jointly carried out a census of Chinese personnel in the natural sciences and technology fields at non-military and non-national defense state-owned enterprises and institutions. The scope of the census included personnel in production, scientific research, and teaching in science, engineering, agriculture, and medicine, with particular focus on anyone who qualified as S&T cadre, that is, having an S&T professional title, being a graduate from a college or specialized vocational school (*zhongzhuan*) in an above-mentioned field, or being promoted from workers or peasants. Information on political background and age of these S&T cohorts also was collected.

In 1985, the SSTC led and organized, along with the NBS and the State Education Commission, the predecessor of the Ministry of Education, a census of China's S&T system, thereby laying a preliminary foundation for the birth of China's formal S&T statistics system. In designing and developing a system of S&T statistical indicators for the census, these agencies consulted the definitions and classification standards used in the *Manual for Statistics on Scientific and Technological Activities*, a United Nations Educational, Scientific, and Cultural Organization (UNESCO) publication, and then took the special circumstances of the Chinese situation into consideration. The introduction of the manual represented a first step toward making China's S&T statistics internationally comparable. The census also started an annual reporting system composed of three separate subsystems – government research institutes, institutions of higher education, and large- and medium-sized industrial enterprises, from which to generate the nation's aggregated S&T statistics. The results of the census were published in the *Statistical Materials on Science and Technology*, the precursor of the *China Statistical Yearbook on Science and Technology*, which started publication in 1990. Because the three subsystems did not follow the exact same definitions, the

---

[3] However, in view of the Cold War and China's sense of external threat – first from the USA and later from the former Soviet Union – a great deal of the statistical information collected during the above-mentioned surveys was never made public for national security reasons.

aggregation did not necessarily reflect China's S&T activities as a whole statistically speaking.

In 1988, the then SSTC studied and evaluated the international standards of S&T statistics and the Chinese situation again, on which China's S&T statistical indicators were revised. A sampling survey on R&D inputs was conducted, through which China obtained for the first time information on R&D expenditures by large- and medium-sized industrial enterprises, research institutes, and universities. In 1990, the SSTC conducted a survey of societal S&T inputs in 20 provinces and municipalities. By formulating clearer and more precise definitions of China's R&D activities, the survey data were not only internationally comparable, but also laid a solid foundation for a uniform national annual S&T statistical reporting system, which started to operate in the following year. The further normalization of statistical indicators has led to more comprehensive information about S&T activities in the People's Republic of China; the new data highlighted the rather complex situation across China's S&T activities and became an important tool in S&T management and macro decision-making. Also in 1990, China released its R&D statistics, which analyzed the scale and distribution of gross expenditure on R&D, known as GERD, as well as the R&D intensity, or GERD as a percentage of GDP. Between 1985 and 1995, the scope of S&T statistics remained focused on three main players: research institutes; large- and medium-sized industrial enterprises; and institutions of higher education.

In recent years, and especially since the onset of the twenty-first century, S&T activities in all facets of society have been expanded and strengthened. For example, high-technology enterprises and non-government enterprises that used to be excluded in the statistical data collection process started to be included; in particular, enterprises in agriculture, medicine, and post and telecommunications have been actively carrying out S&T activities since the early 1950s. Therefore, in 1995, the NBS expanded the scope of S&T statistics collection from large- and medium-sized industrial enterprises to state-owned small-sized industrial enterprises and enterprises in construction; transportation, storage, post and telecommunications; agriculture, forestry, husbandry, and fishery; geological survey and hydraulics; medicine; and state-designated high-technology parks, and it has adjusted the historical data accordingly. This enlarged component is surveyed systematically every five years using increasingly sophisticated sampling techniques.

In 2000, approved by the State Council, the Ministry of Science and Technology, the successor of the SSTC, the NBS, the Ministry of Finance, the then SPC, the then State Economic and Trade Commission (SETC) (the SPC and SETC were merged into the National Development and Reform Commission [NDRC] in 2002), the Ministry of Education, and the Commission of Science, Technology, and Industry for National Defense (COSTIND)[4] jointly organized China's first comprehensive societal R&D resources census. The census included all enterprises and institutions within national economic sectors having R&D activities; the census had the same coverage as the GDP statistics collection and calculation efforts. The organizers issued a "Regulation on S&T Input Statistics" to unify the statistical definitions, scopes, and technical standards used in the three major parts of the S&T activities. The indicators that the census used also became ever closer to existing accepted international standards, thus having better cross-national compatibility. The census is believed to provide highly accurate and rich information about China's R&D resources and their structures, including human resources devoted to R&D activities. Finally, in the national economic census conducted in 2004, mentioned above, information was collected not only on scientific research as a service sector, but also on S&T and R&D activities at enterprises, including foreign-invested enterprises (FIEs).[5]

The past two decades have seen not only various expanded and improved S&T related statistical activities, but also a broadening of content among S&T statistics. In terms of inputs, for example, in 1990, the then SSTC and the Ministry of Finance set up a system of surveying regional government's S&T funding to monitor the share of regional government's S&T expenditure in the nation's investment and the category of such investment. In 1996, surveys started to include national programs for S&T development, such as the State High-Technology Research and Development Program (863 Program), the State Key Basic Research and Development Program (973 Program), the State S&T Tackling Program (*gongguan*), projects under the Torch

---

[4] The COSTIND became a bureau within the newly founded Ministry of Information and Industry in mid-2008. But the discussion here still treats it as a separate government agency. So are the cases of the Ministry of Personnel and the Ministry of Labor and Social Security, which merged to form a new Ministry of Human Resources and Social Security.

[5] In fact, the 2000 R&D resources census also covered FIEs.

Program and the Spark Program, the S&T Achievement Spreading Program, among others. The culmination of these efforts was the internal publication of the *Annual Report of the State Programs of Science and Technology Development*. This publication provides a thorough overview of the state of various Chinese S&T initiatives and contains a useful collection of current data.

In addition to comprehensive surveys and censuses, there have been specialized surveys on different topics, such as national high-technology zones, national S&T achievements, non-government S&T enterprises, technological markets, S&T international collaborations and exchanges, soft science research institutes, productivity promotion centers, S&T popularization, and so on. One key player in these efforts has been the National Research Center for Science and Technology for Development (NRCSTD), recently reorganized to become the China Academy of Science and Technology for Development (CASTED), an important think-tank under the Ministry of Science and Technology (to be discussed).

S&T statistics system[6]

China's S&T statistical work is carried out by four major performers of S&T activities along four central line ministries (*tiao*, or *xitong*) to cover institutions and enterprises under their respective jurisdictions through a combination of censuses and rolling surveys (Figure A.1). In particular, the Ministry of Science and Technology and the S&T bureaus at the provincial and lower levels are responsible for collecting and reporting data on the S&T activities of independent R&D institutes; the NBS and lower-level statistics bureaus gather data on enterprises; the Ministry of Education, through its Department of Science and Technology, and its provincial and regional bureaus of education, gathers data on regular institutions of higher education as their roles in S&T and R&D activities have been grown within and across them; and the COSTIND collects and processes data on its affiliated national defense industry groups, which in turn consist of research institutes and enterprises. The data collected range from personnel, expenditures raised and used, achievements, programs, and organizations related to S&T and R&D activities. Within each *xitong*,

---

[6] This section is based on Gao *et al.* (2006), Liu (2003), and Liu (2006).

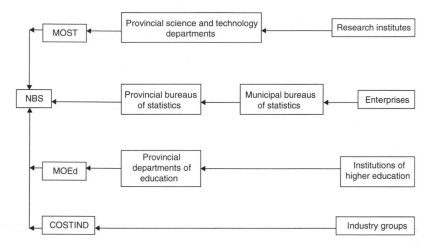

Figure A.1 China's science and technology (S&T) statistics system.
Note: NBS, National Bureau of Statistics; MOST, Ministry of Science and Technology; MOEd, Ministry of Education; COSTIND, Commission of Science, Technology, and Industry for National Defense.
Source: Liu, 2003.

a lower-level agency is in charge of statistical work assignments, personnel training, data collection, and is responsible for reporting statistics to a higher-level agency for review and appraisal until the statistics reach the top of the *xitong*. Also involved in the collection of S&T statistics are such government agencies and organizations as the Ministry of Finance (S&T-related government budget appropriations of the central government), the State Intellectual Property Office (SIPO, patent statistics), and the Institute of Scientific and Technical Information of China (ISTIC, S&T publication and citation statistics). The joint efforts of China's government ministries and regions are designed to safeguard the overall quality of S&T statistics and avoid the type of distortions and problems from occuring.

While various ministries collect S&T statistics within their respective jurisdictions, the NBS, entrusted by the National Statistics Law and through its Department of Population, Social, and Science and Technology Statistics, organizes the nation's S&T statistical work, guides and coordinates concerned parties, and cooperates closely with them to complete the work. It also serves as a gate-keeper and clearing house to assemble S&T indicators of all key performers and conduct the final examination, scrubbing, and approval. In addition, the Department of Industry and Transport Statistics of the NBS has specific responsibility for collecting S&T data for the business sector and other structural and industrial statistics. Regarding patent statistics, the NBS mainly collects the total number of patent applications and patents granted to industrial enterprises from the SIPO, which registers and collects detailed patent information.

The collection of education-related statistics also is a multi-ministry, nationwide effort. The Ministry of Education, through its Department of Development and Planning, collects statistics on the basic situation, expenditures, enrollments, and teaching, among others, at different levels of the education system, and so on from provincial and municipal education bureaus, and compiles and publishes an official statistical yearbook on education. The Ministry of Education provides a set of aggregate data and related information to the NBS, which also produces data on the educational status of the population from censuses, which are conducted every 10 years, and sampling surveys, which are carried out in between censuses, such as literacy rates, average years of education, enrollments, and so on. One more education-related data source comes from vocational training under the Ministry of Labor and Social Security (MOLSS). The data from these sources constructs a complementary and comparable picture of China's education and population quality.

Finally, after the December 2003 talent conference, the Department of Organization of the CCP Central Committee, the MOP, the MOLSS, the Ministry of Agriculture, and the NBS established China's talent resource statistical indicator system, which covers talent in five categories – professionals, party and administrative personnel, managers at state-owned enterprises, skilled personnel, and agricultural personnel. A survey was conducted in late 2004 to come up with the total numbers of talent, but the results have not been released yet except for the mentioning of numbers in each of the five types of *rencai* in a book published by the Chinese Academy of Personnel Science (2005).[7]

---

[7] The launch of this survey, however, does highlight the increasingly activist role of the CCP Central Committee, through its Department of Organization, in addressing China's evolving talent needs and requirements, especially at the highest levels.

Major centers on S&T statistics

With all the S&T statistics collected, it is centers for S&T statistics that are responsible for analyzing such data and reporting findings. Approved by the Ministry of Science and Technology, the former NRCSTD set up a Center for S&T Statistics and Analysis devoted to the study of S&T statistics and indicators in 2003. The center, now placed under the new CASTED, is mandated to establish and maintain an S&T indicators database to support S&T policy decision-making, train S&T statistical workers, carry out theoretical and methodological research on S&T statistics, and participate in international exchange related to S&T statistics. The center also is involved in the publication of *China Statistical Yearbook on Science and Technology*, *China Science and Technology Indicators*, and other key publications containing S&T statistics.

The Center for S&T Statistics and Information at the Huazhong University of Science and Technology, located in Wuhan, Hubei province, also is important in the study of China's S&T statistics. Established in 1986, the center used to be part of the management school of the Ministry of Science and Technology. In 2000, it was merged into Huazhong along with the management school. Now, being part of the Huazhong's management school, the center collects S&T statistics from public research institutes and maintains a website on China's S&T statistics (www.sts.org.cn), which not only updates S&T statistics in a timely fashion, but provides analysis on various topics related to S&T either at the center or elsewhere.[8]

Major publications

Based on the above-mentioned data collection and statistical reporting activities, various related government ministries, independently or along with the NBS, publish annual statistical yearbooks (Table A.1). For example, the Ministry of Science and Technology and the NBS

---

[8] There are also a growing number of quasi-government and non-government entities that have appeared on the scene in terms of offering statistical data related to S&T and talent. Several of these organizations aim to take advantage of the commercial opportunities to "sell" data on the market, especially to foreign companies anxious to better understand quantitative trends in the economy and S&T system.

Table A.1 *Major publications on China's science and technology (S&T) and related statistics*

Title	Authors	Coverage in the latest book	First publication	Publication cycle	Publisher
China Science and Technology Indicators (or *"Yellow Book on Science and Technology"*)	MOST	Human resources in science and technology R&D expenditure S&T activities in government research institutes, higher education, and large- and medium-sized industrial enterprises Outputs of S&T activities Development of high-technology industry Public scientific literacy and attitudes toward S&T	1990	Biannual – Chinese in even year, English in odd year	Scientific and Technical Documents Publishing House
China Statistical Yearbook on Science and Technology (successors to *China Statistical Materials on Science and Technology* between 1986 and 1990)	NBS and MOST	Overview Independent research institutes Large- and medium-sized industrial enterprises and high-technology industry Institutions of higher education National programs for S&T development Results of S&T activities, S&T services International comparison	1986	Annual	China Statistics Press

Title	Compiler	Contents	Year	Frequency	Publisher
Compilation of China Statistical Materials on Science and Technology	MOST	Newest S&T statistics; International comparison of major S&T and economic indicators; Annual report on China's S&T statistics; Results of monitoring S&T progress of the nation and regions; Indicators and rankings of regional monitoring		Annual	MOST
China Statistical Yearbook on High-Technology Industry	NBS, NDRC, and MOST	Production and finance; S&T activities; Employment and technical personnel; Investment in fixed assets; Exports; International comparison	2003	Annual	China Statistics Press
China Statistical Yearbook on Education (renamed *China Statistical Yearbook on Education Enterprise* between 1992 and 1997)	Department of Development and Planning, MOE	Development of educational enterprise: overview; education at various levels; geographical distributions of education; Physical facilities: public expenditure; capital construction investment; S&T activities: natural sciences and technology; social sciences	1984	Annual	People's Education Press

Table A.1 (*cont.*)

Title	Authors	Coverage in the latest book	First publication	Publication cycle	Publisher
China Statistical Yearbook	NBS	Distributions of administrative areas and natural resources General survey National accounts Population Employment and wages Investment in fixed assets Energy Government finance Price indices People's livelihood General survey of cities Environment protection Agriculture Industry Construction Transport, post, and telecommunications services Domestic trade Foreign trade and economic cooperation Tourism Financial intermediation Education, science, and technology Cultural, sports, and public health Other social activities Main social and economic indicators of Hong Kong and Macao International comparison	1982	Annual	China Statistics Press

Publication	Compiled by	Contents	Year	Frequency	Publisher
China Labor Statistical Yearbook (successors to China Labor and Wage Statistical Yearbook between 1989 and 1990)	Department of Population and Employment Statistics, NBS, and Department of Planning and Finance, MOLSS	General survey Employment and unemployment Employment and earnings in urban units, state-owned units, urban collective-owned units, and other ownership units Employment in township and village enterprises Vocational training and skill appraisal Labor relations Labor and social security inspection Social security Trade union works Employment indicators of Hong Kong and Macao International comparison	1989	Annual	China Statistics Press
China Population Statistical Yearbook	Department of Population and Employment Statistics, NBS	National 1% population sample survey in 2005 Historical population statistics Household registration Family planning International comparison	1988	Annual	China Statistics Press

Note: NBS, National Bureau of Statistics; MOST, Ministry of Science and Technology; MOEd, Ministry of Education; COSTIND, Commission of Science, Technology, and Industry for National Defense.
Source: Authors' research.

publish the *China Statistical Yearbook on Science and Technology*, *China Statistical Yearbook on High-Technology Industry* (along with the NDRC); the Ministry of Education publishes the *China Statistical Yearbook on Education* and the *China Statistical Yearbook on Education Expenditure*; S&T and related statistics may also be found in the *China Statistical Yearbook*, *China Labor Statistical Yearbook*, and the *China Population Statistical Yearbook*. The statistical yearbooks usually contain information for the previous year or more. Although the statistics in the *China Statistical Yearbook on Science and Technology* are obtained through surveys involving the NBS, the Ministry of Science and Technology, the Ministry of Education, and the COST-IND, other government agencies, such as the Ministry of Finance, the Ministry of Personnel, the Ministry of Land and Resources, the Ministry of Commerce, the General Administration of Quality Supervision, Inspection and Quarantine, the State Intellectual Property Office, the CAS, the Chinese Academy of Engineering (CAE), the State Seismological Bureau, the State Metrological Bureau, the State Oceanic Administration, the State Bureau of Surveying and Mapping, and the China Association for Science and Technology also contribute their data.

The Ministry of Science and Technology also publishes the *China Science and Technology Indicators* biannually, and two annual pocket data books – *China Science and Technology Statistical Data* (from 1992) and *China High Technology Industry Data* (from 2002), which contain condensed information released prior to the publication of the full-blown *China Statistical Yearbook on Science and Technology* and the *China Statistical Yearbook on High-Technology Industry*. In the meantime, the Ministry of Science and Technology publishes an annual *Compilation of China Statistical Materials on Science and Technology*, which is something between statistical yearbooks and pocket data books and contains a special section devoted to the results derived from monitoring S&T progress at national and regional levels. In the *China Educational Yearbook*, published by the Ministry of Education, there also is a series of aggregate educational statistics, such as the number of college graduates and the number of advanced degrees awarded. The Ministry of Science and Technology also publishes an *Annual Overview of National S&T programs*, which contains very useful data and updates regarding the latest developments in the 863 Program, the 973 Program, and so on. It also contains an update about China's international S&T activities.

Starting from 1998, the NBS, the Ministry of Science and Technology, and the Ministry of Finance jointly put out an annual statistical bulletin on national S&T expenditures, which summarizes information on R&D expenditures, sources of funds and expenditure for S&T activities, and government appropriations for S&T. The bulletin usually is released in March on the occasion of the annual session of the NPC. Similarly, the Ministry of Education publishes an annual statistical bulletin regarding the implementation of education expenditures and a statistical bulletin of education enterprise development.

In addition, the Ministry of Science and Technology and various Chinese government ministries publish and update statistics under their jurisdiction through their official websites. Some of these sites contain English-language as well as Chinese versions.

The key sources for HRST-related information include the *China Science and Technology Indicators*, *China Statistical Yearbook on Science and Technology*, *China Statistical Yearbook on High-Technology Industry*, and the *China Statistical Yearbook on Education*.

Problems of China's S&T human resources statistics

China's HRST statistics, as part of the overall set of S&T statistics, are collected by the Ministry of Science and Technology, the Ministry of Education, the COSTIND, along with the NBS, and are disclosed in various statistical yearbooks, mentioned above. In addition, as noted in Chapter 2, the Ministry of Personnel, which is important for its role in monitoring and managing experts at the high end of the talent pool, and the Department of Organization of the CCP Central Committee, also along with the NBS, collect data on cadres and professionals based on the "party administers cadres" principle. However, the statistics collected by the Ministry of Personnel and the Department of Organization are not available to the public. The NBS conducts population censuses and sampling surveys, and the MOLSS conducts labor market surveys, all collecting talent data. With the involvement of various government agencies, then, the major challenge is how to reconcile data from different sources so as to get an overall picture of China's talent situation. This is the first major hurdle that an observer of the Chinese talent situation encounters and has to overcome.

Second, it is necessary to understand the differences between HRST and "talent" (*rencai*) in China to have a better sense of what each definition includes (see Chapter 3). As mentioned, talent is an evolving concept – from cadre to intellectual to professional, a broad concept with "Chinese characteristics" and not internationally comparable; of course, the breadth of the definition has important policy implications. One of the problems with this concept is that its definition is fluid and open to change over time. In its most recent context, talent is defined as anyone with knowledge and certain ability, able to engage in creative work and contribute to the construction of China's political, spiritual, and material civilization (General Office of the CCP Central Committee and General Office of the State Council, 2002). Technically speaking, this means that education is not a prerequisite for being classified as "talent." Indeed, Chinese talent is not confined to scientists and engineers and other professionals, it also includes party and public administration personnel; managers at enterprises; highly skilled workers; and agricultural personnel; therefore, its number is huge (see Chapter 3). Even within each of the categories, the statistics collected also have evolved. For example, although about one-quarter of the professionals now work for non-government economies, it was not until 1999 that the Ministry of Personnel started to consider collecting data on them.

Third, ironically, China's statistics on HRST do not profile the distribution of HRST in gender, age, educational attainment, discipline, geography, professional rank, and employment, among others, which concerns students of China's S&T development. One possibility is that such data are just simply unavailable, but that is doubtful. For one thing, the population censuses and labor market surveys cover most, if not all, information, as we have found in the *China Population Statistical Yearbook* and the *China Labor and Social Security Yearbook*. The problem is that data in these statistical yearbooks are aggregate and not organized in such a way that allows researchers to easily draw useful information about Chinese S&T talent for further analysis. If it is understandable that such information is not accessible to scholars from outside China for various reasons, at least China-based scholars should have better access to it. As noted, talent, for example, was one of the research topics of strategic importance to the formulation of China's "Medium- and Long-Term Plan for the Development of Science and Technology (2006–2020)" (MLP). Although the outcome of the research has not been made public, we have not found information beyond what was disclosed in various

S&T and education statistical yearbooks in the publications of the researchers involved. Nor does the report on HRST done by OECD of China's innovation policy, with inputs of China-based scholars, contains such information (OECD, 2007a). Because of this, in the present book, we had to piece together a wide range of disparate information from different sources, a task akin to putting together a complicated jigsaw puzzle! Although in several cases our efforts did not yield the full picture in its entirety, the analysis appears to be far more comprehensive and of greater sophistication than what apparently has been done by our China-based colleagues.[9]

Fourth, to the extent that the lack of information as described above is real and somewhat understandable because of the complexities involved in collecting and compiling such information, there also are cases where some key information appears to be intentionally concealed. For our purposes, it would have been nice to have a breakdown for the educational fields and subfields in the tables in Chapter 4. The reason that we were unable to do so, and had to use the lumped-together information, is not the unavailability of data. The *China Statistical Yearbook on Education*, for example, publishes annual data on admissions, enrollment, and graduation at the undergraduate and graduate levels from the Ministry of Education. It is interesting to note that the data are available concerning the number of students newly admitted, total enrolled, and graduated by fields of study (*xueke meilei*) such as science, engineering, agriculture, medicine, and so on, but there are no further breakdowns of specialties (*zhuanye*) except in engineering. Given the specialty breakdown in engineering, one might assume or take for granted that a similar breakdown must have been available in other fields of study. Also, when the *Yearbook* releases undergraduate enrollment data, this is broken down by length of study – two- to three-year short-cycle programs versus regular bachelor's degree programs – and by fields of study, which is wonderful. What is puzzling, however, is that in presenting the undergraduate breakdown by specialties of engineering, the *Yearbook* only indicates the total in the specialties without a similar breakdown by length of

---

[9] Nevertheless, it also is clear that China's specialists on S&T talent have done a remarkable job while working within the limits of the data and the policy constraints that they face on a regular basis.

programs. That is to say, there is aggregated information on the levels of programs and specialties but no information on their interaction. Further evidence that the Ministry of Education possesses detailed information on Chinese university students is that the ministry, in May 2005, made public a list of the "hot" specialties which admitted more than 10 000 undergraduates at the bachelor's degree level in 2004, along with numbers of enrollment and graduation (admissions, enrollment, and graduation information for the year 2003 also was made available for comparison) (see Table 4.4). This gives us reason to suspect that other government ministries also limit public release of similar information. Although the planning economy mentality has been fading, the point holds that "the Chinese simply have not had the figures that Western analysts and visitors regard as indispensable for governing a planned economy" (Orleans, 1980: 17).[10] The question is how to reconcile the incomplete and problematic statistics on HRST, on one hand, and some superficially "accurate statistics," on the other.[11]

Indeed, the problems discussed here have created unique challenges in our study of China's talent. Ultimately, they probably make it difficult, if not impossible, for the Chinese government to make informed decisions and to evaluate the effectiveness and efficacy of its various policy measures. In Chapter 2, we have raised a series of questions, asking whether the establishment of software colleges at some Chinese universities in 2001 was a market information-driven decision and whether these schools have helped alleviate the shortage of China's software professionals. Similar general questions are: What is the rationale behind the government's allocation of resources – financial, physical, and human? How does the leadership know whether the country has too many mathematicians, but may lack chemists or vice versa? What is the mechanism through which education effectively reacts to actual job market signals about the lack of talent in particular

[10] "The Regulations of the People's Republic of China on Open Government Information" started to be in effect on May 1, 2008, which at least provides possibilities for China-based scholars to ask for detailed statistics concerning S&T and education.

[11] For example, in 2006, China employed 4 131 542 S&T personnel, including 2 797 839 qualified as scientists and engineers, and graduated 255 902 with advanced degrees (NBS and MOST, 2007: 4 and 22).

areas? What is the structure of the Chinese scientific workforce in terms of age, disciplines, qualifications, and compositions, and is this structure appropriate for China's innovation push? What is the impact of the demographic change on Chinese talent, S&T capability, and international competitiveness? Without an effectively functioning labor market and wage system, answers to many of these questions will remain more the purview of China's government than is the case in the countries such as the USA.

Realizing the various problems involved in sorting through China's talent statistics and the importance of having a clear picture of the Chinese talent situation (our sense is that the leadership does not have such information), in late 2004, China's government introduced new talent and human resources statistical indicators system to replace the cadre statistical system that had been used since the 1950s. According to the Department of Organization of the CCP Central Committee, the new system covers the entire society, reflecting the quantity, quality, distribution, structure, training, recruitment, and utilization. The target of the system includes five types of *rencai* – party and administrative personnel, enterprise management personnel, professionals and institutional management personnel, skilled personnel, and agricultural personnel – as specified by the 2002 "Outline for Building-up of China's Talent Pool Between 2002 and 2005," with the latter two types being the new additions (General Office of the CCP Central Committee and General Office of the State Council, 2002). The new system is supposed to help the formulation of a new talent-building strategy and provide data support to policy research and macro-guidance. Based on that, a macro-human resources database is to be built. The new system, first implemented by the Department of Organization and the Ministry of Personnel, started to trial in late 2004 and was completed by May 2005. Unfortunately, we have not seen significant output from this survey.

How to use China's human resources statistics

In this final section, we provide our perspectives on the right strategy for using China's human resources statistics. This is based on not only our recent research on China's HRST but also our many years of experience working with China's S&T statistics as a whole.

Understanding Chinese definitions

While China has made tremendous progress in improving its HRST statistics and making them internationally comparable, some of its HRST statistics simply are a Chinese creation. As we have pointed out throughout this book, including in this Appendix, "professional" is one such broad definition having so-called "Chinese characteristics;" so are *rencai* and "S&T personnel." Taking into consideration the evolution and reality of China's HRST statistics, these Chinese "innovations" should be treated seriously; that is, it is vital to understand what is being said and defined in these categories, whether there have been changes over time, and whether there are corresponding categories used internationally. Otherwise, it is difficult, if not impossible, to study China's HRST and to exchange views with Chinese colleagues who use such definitions and statistics.

For example, "S&T personnel" are defined so that anyone who spends 10 percent of their time engaged in S&T activities in China is counted. This implies that overseas-based scientists, Chinese- or non-Chinese-origin, are S&T personnel in China's S&T statistics if they are working for a Chinese *danwei* for more than a month, either within or outside China. Of course, their R&D activities also should be counted in the full-time equivalent (FTE) measure. However, it is questionable as to whether all S&T statisticians treat them in this way. Also, ideally, it would be helpful to know how large this group really is. Related to this is the issue of how students studying overseas (*liuxuesheng*) and returnees are defined. Originally, *liuxuesheng* were referred to only those with an undergraduate education who have spent at least a year overseas pursuing an advanced degree or conducting research. But at one time the threshold was reduced to include those going overseas for undergraduate education or even language studies. Then, how about those who, with an advanced degree, just go abroad for less than a year?

Exhausting all the sources

As statistics on China's HRST are collected and published by various government agencies, it is necessary to exhaust many sources to find relevant data. The usual starting point is the *China Statistical Yearbook on Science and Technology*, which is most systematic and comprehensive, has been improved over the years, and has added new sections almost every year. For example, the 2005 *Yearbook* started to provide information on educational attainment of researchers at research institutes. While the *China Statistical Yearbook on Science and Technology* has information on the numbers of professionals employed in state-owned institutions and enterprises, it also is useful to consult or cross-check with the *China Population Statistical Yearbook* or the *China Labor Statistical Yearbook* for data on professionals.

It is well-known that the statistics collected in the 2000 census on societal R&D resources and the 2004 economic census are more accurate and reliable than most other similar data. Although some of these data have been included in various statistical yearbooks, including those in S&T, the compiled data from both censuses have detailed information on human resources and may be considered a valuable benchmark for previous and latter years.

In addition, we also have paid special attention to research done by China-based scholars which may provide new insights and data. For example, *China Science and Technology Indicators*, known as the "Yellow Book" because of the color of its cover, always devotes an entire chapter to HRST; in fact, the *Indicators* is the only Chinese publication that reveals the complete number of HRST. The Chinese Academy of Personnel Science, a think-tank affiliated to the Ministry of Personnel, discloses the total numbers of *rencai* in its *China Talent Report* (2005), which presumably will become a fully fledged series. The report released the results of China's first talent survey, held after the 2003 talent conference: the total numbers of talent in five categories – professionals, party and administrative personnel, managers at state-owned enterprises, skilled personnel, and agricultural personnel. The Chinese Academy of Social Sciences, one of the most influential social science think-tanks in China, started to publish a *Report on the Development of Chinese Talent* as one of the so-called "Blue Book" series, also because of the colour of its cover in 2004, which has now become an annual publication. Each year, the blue book on talent has a central analytic theme in addition to a general description of China's talent as a whole. Of course, we should not overestimate the value of such publications, and exercise caution in using them as many of the data cited are not always current, are frequently inconsistent within the same book or between different books in the same series, are sometimes careless in presentation and interpretation, and are secondary sources without mentioning who collected the data from where, how, and in which year.[12]

One final source in dealing with China's HRST statistics is Chinese scholars at key research centers such as the CASTED and the Huazhong University of Science and Technology, mentioned above. Our study of China's talent has benefited greatly from interviewing and discussing with this small but very capable cadre of experts on China's S&T statistics. One of the highlights of our fieldwork in China was a unique meeting organized for us that brought together representatives from six or seven of the above-noted organizations. It was apparent that these groups, despite working on similar problems and issues, do not often get together to share data and experiences or collaborate across bureaucracies. The simple exercise of having these persons in the same room together for 2–3 hours opened up new insights about differences in definition, terminology, and so on.[13]

Finding and recognizing discrepancies

Because China's S&T statistics have been collected by different government ministries that, respectively, may have a different understanding of the appropriate definitions and scope of terms, discrepancies often exist. That said, it also is clear that the *China Statistical Yearbook on Science and Technology* has made great efforts to normalize and minimize these differences, and the Ministry of Science and Technology deserves kudos for its work in this area. Sometimes, however, publications, even those from the same government ministry, may convey the data in different ways and imply different meanings. Therefore, it is important to identify and recognize these discrepancies very early on in data collection and assessment efforts. Here, one specific example helps to illustrate the different ways to report numbers of graduates, in the *China Statistical Yearbook on Education* and the *China Educational Yearbook*, both published by the Ministry of Education (Table A.2).

---

[12] For example, one of the articles in the talent Blue Books cites a secondary-source information: since 1985, 76% and 82% of high-technology specialties at Beijing and Qinghua universities had gone to the USA (Pan & Lou, 2004: 21). A fair guess is that happened in 1985; but the authors just make an exaggerating claim without even having a second thought on the possibility and reliability of such statistics.

[13] The limited communication among them is less a reflection of specialization and more a consequence of bureaucratic compartmentation.

Table A.2 Postgraduates in academic and calendar years (persons)

Year	Calendar				Academic			
	2002	2003	2004	2005	2001–2002	2002–2003	2003–2004	2004–2005
Master's degree								
Philosophy	942	1214	1462	1813	979	1379	1536	1840
Economics	3596	5374	6789	9313	6067	6976	9171	10735
Law	4476	6714	10075	12912	5065	7170	10216	11782
Education	1717	2457	3866	4646	1851	2845	3698	5104
Literature	4514	6589	9450	12098	5636	7715	11087	12733
History	1080	1472	1934	2110	1097	1467	1819	2035
Science	7058	9515	13022	16570	7037	9782	12627	15938
Engineering	24826	34764	48020	63514	27845	39813	51950	63086
Agriculture	2164	3093	4188	4945	2289	3137	4096	5049
Medicine	6511	9382	12428	15114	9571	12347	15653	18432
Military science	28	26	46	92	1151	1553	2624	3089
Administration	9291	11641	16051	18924	6473	8435	12287	13941
Professional					13738	17567	31694	44243
Total	66203	92241	127331	162051	88799	120186	168458	208007

Table A.2 (*cont.*)

Year	Calendar				Academic			
	2002	2003	2004	2005	2001–2002	2002–2003	2003–2004	2004–2005
Doctorate								
Philosophy	281	348	392	436	263	323	366	396
Economics	837	1204	1309	1617	855	1040	1254	1379
Law	663	770	1022	1191	615	683	906	1038
Education	229	307	410	455	197	276	274	319
Literature	643	837	1033	1216	648	829	955	976
History	315	454	473	547	311	428	449	473
Science	2808	3705	4518	5458	2813	3580	4213	5083
Engineering	5252	6573	8054	9427	4968	6242	7797	9126
Agriculture	626	756	977	1093	648	742	899	1102
Medicine	2166	2825	3700	4291	2444	3073	3714	4401
Military science	5	6	13	22	91	98	161	228
Administration	813	1021	1545	1924	765	1095	1431	1660
Professional					88	216	174	211
Total	14638	18806	23446	27677	14706	18625	22593	26392

Source: Ministry of Education Bureau of Development and Planning, various years; Editorial Board of *China Educational Yearbook*, various years.

At first glance, there are two sets of numbers of graduates with significant differences at the master's degree level and up. It is only after a careful reading of the numbers and with help from experts on China's HRST in China that we figured out what has caused the differences. First, the numbers represent two different reporting periods – calendar year versus academic year. Obviously, different time periods produce different numbers of graduates.

Second, in fact, the numbers report graduates differently: the numbers for the calendar year include only the graduates from regular institutions of learning who may or may not receive their degrees, whereas the numbers for the academic year are the exact numbers of advanced degrees awarded to graduates. Further, the numbers for the academic year also include those who have become qualified for advanced degrees through on-the-job (*zaizhi*) study, mentioned briefly in Chapter 4. That is, the difference in the numbers reflects a distinction between postgraduates and actual advanced degree holders. Because of the overlap between academic and calendar years, one cannot assume that the numbers of postgraduates always are greater than those of advanced degree holders, or vice versa, as some of the graduates will not be awarded advanced degrees, but *zaizhi* students included in the table have surely received their degrees.

Third, presumably and overall, it is easier to get a master's degree than a doctoral degree through *zaizhi* study, thus explaining the larger discrepancy between the two reporting methods at the master's degree level. However, students from military science are more likely to obtain their degrees – both master's and doctoral – through *zaizhi* study.

Fourth, one also should recognize the definitional differences between two reporting methods. For example, "professional" is a type of degree, but is not available in regular institutions of learning approved and certified by the Ministry of Education.

In the final analysis, wading through the melange of statistical yearbooks and annual reports can be as rewarding as it is often frustrating. It proved to be extremely exhilarating at times simply correlating one data set with another. Quite clearly, more work remains to be done. Our hope is that this Appendix will help open the door for other scholars interested in learning more about China's growing contingent of scientists and engineers – their numbers, their deployment and utilization, and most important, their achievements.

References

Appelbaum, R. P., Gereffi, G., Parker, R., and Ong, R. From Cheap Labor to High-Tech Leadership: Will China's Investment in Nanotechnology Pay Off? Trier, Germany: SASE Conference on "Constituting Globalization: Actors, Arenas, and Outcomes," 2006. Available online at www.cggc.duke.edu/pdfs/workshop/Appelbaum%20et%20al_SASE%202006_China%20nanotech_27%20June%2006.pdf (accessed on April 30, 2007).

Arora, A. and Gambardella, A. The Globalization of the Software Industry: Perspectives and Opportunities for Developed and Developing Countries. In A.B. Jeffe, J. Lerner, and S. Stern, eds. *Innovation Policy and the Economy 5.* Cambridge, MA: MIT Press, 2005; pp. 1–32.

Baark, E. The Evolution of China's Software Industry. Troy, NY: Conference on "China's Emerging Technological Trajectory in the Twenty-First Century," 2003. Available online at www.law.gmu.edu/nctl/stpp/us_china_pubs/6.3_Evolution_of_China_software_industry.pdf (accessed on July 20, 2006).

Bai, C. and Cao, J. Crossing borders, challenging boundaries: reflections on a decade of exchange at the Chinese-American Kavli Frontiers of Science Symposium. *Proceedings of the National Academy of Sciences* 2008; **105**(4): 1101–2.

Bai, C. and Wang, C. Nanotechnology Research in China. In L. Jakobson, ed., *Innovation with Chinese Characteristics: High-Tech Research in China.* Hampshire, UK: Palgrave Macmillan, 2007; pp. 71–98.

Bai, L. Graduate unemployment: dilemmas and challenges in China's move to mass higher education. *China Quarterly* 2006; **185**: 128–44.

Barro, R. J. Economic growth in a cross section of countries. *Quarterly Journal of Economics* 1991; **106**: 407–43.

Becker, G. S. *Human Capital: A Theoretical and Empirical Analysis, with Special Reference to Education.* 1964. Chicago, IL: University of Chicago Press, 1994.

Human Capital. In D.R. Henderson, ed., *The Concise Encyclopedia of Economics.* Indianapolis, IN: Liberty Fund Inc., 1993. Available online at www.econlib.org/library/Enc/HumanCapital.html (accessed on March 10, 2007).

Behrman, J. R. *Human Resource Led Development: Review of Issues and Evidence*. New Delhi, India: International Labor Organization Asian Regional Team for Employment Promotion, 1990.

Benhabib, J. and Spiegel, M. M. The roles of human capital in economic development: evidence from aggregate cross-country data. *Journal of Monetary Economics* 1994; **34**(2): 143–73.

Bergheim, S. 2005. Human capital is the key to growth: success stories and policies for 2020. *Current Issues: Global Growth Centres*. Frankfurt, Germany: Deutsche Bank Research, 2006. Available online at www.dbresearch.com/PROD/DBR_INTERNET_EN-PROD/PROD0000000 000190080.pdf (accessed on August 10, 2006).

Berrell, M., Wrathall, J., and Wright, P. A model for Chinese management education: adapting the case study approach to transfer management knowledge. *Cross Cultural Management* 2001; **13**(1): 28–44.

Bhagwati, J. The brain drain. *International Social Science Journal* 1976; **28**(4): 691–729.

Bodde, D. *Chinese Thought, Society, and Science: The Intellectual and Social Background of Science and Technology in Pre-Modern China*, Honolulu, HI: University of Hawaii Press, 1991.

Bound, J., Turner, S., and Walsh, P. Internationalization of US doctoral education, 2006. Available online at www.nber.org/~sewp/Bound Turner_022006jbset.pdf (accessed on October 4, 2007).

Bradshaw, D. China's lust for business learning. *Financial Times* 2005a; August 1: 9.

Profile CEIBS: bullish on opening up shop in China. *Financial Times* 2005b; October 24: 6.

Brown, P. Skill formation in the twenty-first century. In P. Brown, A. Green and H. Lauder, eds. *High Skills: Globalization, Competitiveness, and Skill Formation*. Oxford and New York, NY: Oxford University Press, 2001, pp. 1–51.

Brown, P., Green, A. and Lauder, H., eds. *High Skills: Globalization, Competitiveness, and Skill Formation*. Oxford and New York, NY: Oxford University Press, 2001.

Buderi, R. and Huang, G. T. *Guanxi (The Art of Relationships): Microsoft, China, and Bill Gates's Plan to Win the Road Ahead*. New York, NY: Simon & Schuster, 2006.

Bullock, M. B. American Exchange with China, Revisited. In J. K. Kallgren and D. F. Simon, eds. *Educational Exchanges: Essays on the Sino-American Experience*. Berkeley, CA: Institute of East Asian Studies, University of California, 1987; pp. 23–42.

American Science and Chinese Nationalism: Reflections on the Career of Zhou Peiyuan. In G. Hershatter, E. Honig, J. N. Lipman, and

R. Stross, eds. *Remapping China: Fissures in Historical Terrain.* Stanford, CA: Stanford University Press, 1996; pp. 210–23.

Burns, S. EMC China chief "to quit" in email fiasco, 2006. Available online at www.vnunet.com/vnunet/news/2155655/china-email-embarasses-emc (accessed on December 20, 1997).

Calhoun, C.C. Science, Democracy, and the Politics of Identity. In J.N. Wasserstrom and E.J. Perry, eds. *Popular Protest and Political Culture in Modern China: Learning from 1989.* Boulder, CO: Westview Press, 1992; pp. 93–124.

Cao, C. *China's Scientific Elite.* London and New York, NY: Routledge-Curzon, 2004a.

Chinese science and the "Nobel Prize Complex." *Minerva* 2004b; **42**: 151–72.

Zhongguancun and China's high-tech parks in transition: "growing pains" or "premature senility"? *Asian Survey* 2004c; **44**: 647–88.

Cao, C. and Suttmeier, R.P. China's "brain bank": leadership and elitism in Chinese science and engineering. *Asian Survey* 1999; **39**: 525–59.

China's new scientific elite: professional orientations among distinguished young scientists. *China Quarterly* 2001; **168**: 959–83.

Cao, C., Suttmeier, R.P. and Simon, D.F. China's 15-year science and technology plan. *Physics Today* 2006; **December**: 38–43.

Chang, C-L. *The Chinese Gentry: Studies on Their Role in Nineteenth-Century Chinese Society.* Seattle, WA: University of Seattle Press, 1955.

Chang, I. *Thread of the Silkworm.* New York, NY: Basic Books, 1996.

Chang, S.L. Causes of brain drain and solutions: the Taiwan experience. *Studies in Comparative International Development* 1992; **27**(1): 27–43.

Chen, C. Survey of quality of graduates from pilot software schools (in Chinese), 2006. Available online at http://unesco.bjtu.edu.cn/view_-report.jsp?reportid=5 (accessed on March 5, 2008).

Chen, M. *Intellectuals and the RMB Era* (in Chinese). Shanghai: Wenhui Press, 2006.

Chen, S. An investigation into the emergency of the IT talent (in Chinese). *China Computer World* 2007; **22**: A26–8.

Chen, X. Talent mobility and the effects of overseas study (in Chinese), 2003. Available online at www.chisa.edu.cn/newchisa/web/0/2003–07-09/news_4873.asp (accessed on July 24, 2003).

Chen, X. and Zhang, D. CUSBEA Program and its influence on the development of life science in China (in Chinese). *Journal of Dialectics of Nature* 2006; **28**(1): 53–61.

Chen, Z. Historical missions of young science administrators: rational thinking on the younger leadership of China's research institutions (in Chinese). *Nature* 2004; **432**: A24–9.

Chen, Z., Wang, H-G., Wen, Z-J., and Wang, Y. Life sciences and biotechnology in China. *Philosophical Transactions of the Royal Society B: Biological Sciences* 2007; **362**: 947–57.

Cheng, C-Y. *Scientific and Engineering Manpower in Communist China, 1949–1963*. Washington, DC: National Science Foundation, 1965.

Cheung, T. M. Innovation within China's Defense Technological and Industrial Base. In S.E. Johnson and D. Long, eds. *Coping with the Dragon: Essays on PLA Transformation and the US Military*. Washington, DC: National Defense University Center for Technology and National Security Policy, 2007; pp. 27–46.

China Association for Science and Technology (CAST) Research Team on Survey of Chinese S&T Workers. *Survey of Working Condition of Chinese S&T Workers (2003)* (in Chinese). Beijing: China Science and Technology Press, 2004a.

Research Team on Survey of Chinese S&T Workers. *Survey of Career Development Needs of Chinese S&T Workers at Non-State-Owned Enterprises and Institutions* (in Chinese). Beijing: China Science and Technology Press, 2004b.

Department of Study and Development Research Center. *Research Report on the Development of China's Human Resources in Science and Technology* (in Chinese). Beijing: China Science and Technology Press, 2008.

China Software Industry Association (CSIA). *Annual Report of China Software Industry 2004* (in Chinese). Beijing: CSIA, 2004.

Chinese Academy of Personnel Science. *Report on China's Talent 2005* (in Chinese). Beijing: People's Press, 2005.

Chinese Academy of Sciences (CAS). General Office, comp. *Yearbook of the Chinese Academy of Sciences 2007* (in Chinese). Beijing: CAS, 2007.

Graduate University. The Graduate University awarded 4034 doctorates and 3186 master's degrees (in Chinese), 2007. Available online at www.cas.cn/html/Dir/2007/09/28/15/25/80.htm (accessed on October 1, 2007).

Chinese University Alumni Association (CUAA). *An Investigation into the Career of the High Score Achievers in the College Entrance Examinations* (in Chinese), 2007. Available online at www.cuaa.net/cur/gkzyzydc/10.shtml (accessed on August 10, 2007).

Choi, H. *An International Scientific Community: Asian Scholars in the United States*. Westport, CT: Praeger, 1995.

Chow, G. C. Are Chinese official statistics reliable?' *CESifo Economic Studies* 2006; **52**(2): 396–414.

Cohen, M. S. and Zaidi, M. A. 2002. *Global Skill Shortage*. Cheltenham: Edward Elgar, 2002.

Cooke, F. L. Public-sector pay in China: 1949–2001. *International Journal of Resource Management* 2004; **15**(4): 895–916.

Council for Economic Planning and Development. *Taiwan Economic Statistics*. Taiwan: Council for Economic Planning and Development, 2002.

Cyranoski, D. Petition calls for clampdown on absentee Chinese researchers. *Nature* 2003; **421**: 3.

David, R. Could China supplant India in outsourcing? *Forbes* 2007; July 7.

Davis, D. S. Social class transformation in urban China: training, hiring, and promoting urban professionals and managers after 1949. *Modern China* 2000; **26**(3): 251–75.

Delaney, M. China MBAs fail on quality. *Times Education Supplement* 2004; October 15: 12.

Deng Xiaoping. Speech at the Opening Ceremony of the National Conference on Science, 1978. In R. Maxwell, ed. *Deng Xiaoping Speeches and Writings*, 2nd expanded edition. Oxford: Pergamon Press, 1987; pp. 40–53.

Excerpts from Talks Given in Wuchang, Shenzhen, Zhuhai and Shanghai (18 January – 21 February 1992) (in Chinese). In *Selected Works of Deng Xiaoping, Vol. III (1982–1992)*. Beijing: People's Press, 1993; pp. 378–83.

Dennis, C. China: stem cell rises from the East. *Nature* 2002; **419**: 334–46.

Drucker, P. F. *Landmarks of Tomorrow*. New York, NY: Harper, 1959.

Du, Q. and Song, W. The definition of S&T talent and the related statistical issues (in Chinese). *China's Forum on Science and Technology* 2005; **5**: 136–40.

Dyer, G. Lack of executives thwarts growth. *Financial Times* 2007; December 18.

Editorial Board of *China Education Yearbook*. *China Education Yearbook*. Beijing: People's Education Press, various years.

Enserink, M. Who ranks the university rankers? *Science* 2007; **317**: 1026–8.

Ernst, D. Innovation offshoring: Asia's emerging role in global innovation networks. *East-West Special Reports*, No. 10. Honolulu, HI: East-West Center, 2006.

Ertl, H. European Union policies in education and training: the Lisbon Agenda as a turning point? *Comparative Education* 2006; **42**(1): 5–27.

Falkenheim, J.C. *US Doctoral Awards in Science and Engineering Continue Upward Trend in 2006*. NSF 08-301. Arlington, VA: National Science Foundation Division of Science Resource Statistics, 2008.

Fan, M. In China, a state job still brings benefits and bragging rights. *Washington Post* 2007; May 29: A7.

Fang, H., Liu, C., and Pan, C. Current Situation, Problems, and Solutions to the Development of Chinese Talent at the Doctoral Level (in Chinese). In Pan C, ed., *Report on the Development of Chinese Talent*. Bejing: Social Sciences Academic Press, 2006; pp. 205–27.

Finn, M. G. *Stay Rates of Foreign Doctorate Recipients from US Universities, 2001*. Oak Ridge, TN: Science and Engineering Education Program Oak Ridge Institute for Science and Education, 2005. Available online at http://orise.orau.gov/sep/files/stayrate03.pdf (accessed on December 10, 2005).

Florida, R. *The Rise of the Creative Class: And How It's Transforming Work, Leisure, Community, and Everyday Life*. New York, NY: Basic Books, 2002.

Freeman, R. B. *The Overeducated American*. New York, NY: Academic Press, 1976.

   Does globalization of the scientific/engineering workforce threaten US economic leadership? *NBER Work Paper Series*, No. 11457. Cambridge, MA: National Bureau of Economic Research, 2005.

Frew, S. E., Sammut, S. M., Shore, A. F., Ramjist, J. K., Al-Bader, S., Rahim, R., Daar, A. S., and Singer, P. A. Chinese health biotech and the billion-patient market. *Nature Biotechnology* 2008; **26** (1): 37–53.

Friedman, T. L. *The World Is Flat: A Brief History of the Twenty-First Century*. New York, NY: Farrar, Straus & Giroux, 2005.

Gamble, J. Localizing management in foreign-invested enterprises in China: practical, cultural, and strategic perspectives. *International Journal of Human Resource Management* 2000; **11**(5): 883–903.

Gao, C., Lundin, N., and Schaaper, M. S&T indicators in China: an evolving national innovation system in a globalizing economy. *Chongqing: OECD–Chinese MOST Workshop on "Indicators for Assessing National Innovation Systems,"* 2006.

General Biologic. *IMPACT! Selected Life Scientists in China*. Beijing: General Biologic, 2005.

General Office of the CCP Central Committee and General Office of the State Council 2002. An outline for building-up of China's talent pool between 2002 and 2005 (in Chinese), 2002. Available online at www.people.com.cn/GB/shizheng/3586/20020611/750475.html (accessed on July 1, 2002).

Geng, J. Beijing University president led a delegation to visit National Taiwan University and was invited to lecture (in Chinese), 2005. Available online at *http://tw.people.com.cn/GB/14813/3955042.html* (accessed December 19, 2005).

Gereffi, G. *The New Offshoring of Jobs and Global Development.* Geneva: International Institute for Labour Studies, 2006.

Godo, Y. and Hayami, Y. Catching up in education in the economic catch-up of Japan with the United States, 1890–1990. *Economic Development and Cultural Change* 2002; 50: 961–78.

Goldman, M. *Sowing the Seeds of Democracy in China: Political Reform in the Deng Xiaoping Era.* Cambridge, MA: Harvard University Press, 1994.

Goldman, M., Cheek, T. and Hamrin, C. L. eds. *China's Intellectuals and the State: In Search of a New Relationship.* Cambridge, MA: Council of East Asian Studies, Harvard University, 1987.

Goldman, M. and Gu, E. eds. *Chinese Intellectuals between State and Market.* London and New York, NY: RoutledgeCurzon, 2004.

Goodall, K., Warner, M., and Lang, V. HRD in the People's Republic: the MBA "with Chinese characteristics"? *Journal of World Business* 2004; 39: 311–23.

Grubel, H. C. and Scott, A. *The Brain Drain: Determinants, Measurements, and Welfare Effects.* Waterloo, Canada: Sir Wilfred Laurier University Press. Oxford and New York, NY: Oxford University Press, 1977.

Hagel, J., III and Brown, J. S. *The Only Sustainable Edge: Why Business Strategy Depends on Productive Friction and Dynamic Specialization.* Boston, MA: Harvard Business School Press, 2005.

Hamrin, C. L. and Cheek, T. eds. *China's Establishment Intellectuals.* Armonk, NY: ME Sharpe, 1986.

Haq, M. ul and Haq, K. *Human Development in South Asia 1998.* Oxford and New York, NY: Oxford University Press, 1998.

Hauser, S. M. and Xie, Y. Temporal and regional variation in earnings inequality: urban China in transition between 1988 and 1995. *Social Science Research* 2005; 34(1): 44–79.

Hayhoe, R. *China's Universities 1895–1995: A Century of Cultural Conflict.* London and New York, NY: Routledge, 1996.

He, W., Wang, X., and Yu, K. A visible hand: government as the change agent in the transformation of management education in China. *International Journal of Management in Education* 2007; 1 (1–2): 5–20.

Heckman, J. J. China's human capital investment..*China Economic Review* 2005; 16: 50–70.

Heenan, D. *Flight Capital. The Alarming Exodus of America's Best and Brightest.* Mountain View, CA: Davies–Black Publishing, 2005.

Hinton, W. *Hundred Day War: The Cultural Revolution at Tsinghua University.* New York, NY: Monthly Review Press, 1972.

Hoffer, T. B., Selfa, L., Welch, V., Jr. *et al. Doctorate Recipients from United States Universities: Summary Report 2003.* Chicago, IL: National Opinion Research Center at the University of Chicago, 2005.

Hollingsworth, J. R., Müller, K. H., and Hollingsworth, E. J. The end of the science superpowers. *Nature* 2008; **454**: 412–13.

Hu, H. Independent innovation boosts China's software industry, 2007. Available online at http://fec2.mofcom.gov.cn/aarticle/theoryresearch/200707/20070704852183.html (accessed on November 30, 2007).

Hu, K. The development of China's software industry and the demand for talent (in Chinese), 2003. Available online at http://tech.ccidnet.com/pub/article/c322_a62698_pl.html (accessed on October 6, 2005).

Hunt, M. H. The American remission of the Boxer indemnity: a reappraisal. *Journal of Asian Studies* 1972; **31**(3): 539–59.

Huo, Y. First *Cell* paper by mainland Chinese scientists in twenty-five years (in Chinese), 2005. Available online at www.ibp.ac.cn/c/msg/info/archive/2005/07/20050701_01.html (accessed on July 5, 2005).

Institute of International Education (IIE). *Open Doors: Report on International Education Exchange.* New York, NY: IIE, various years.

International Labor Organization. *World Employment Report, 1998–99.* Geneva: ILO, 1998.

Israel, J. *Lianda: A Chinese University in War and Revolution.* Stanford, CA: Stanford University Press, 1998.

Jia, H. Biotech research: bumpy road to a promising future. *China Business Weekly* 2004; February 2–8: 25–6.

Jiang, B. Deng Xiaoping's thinking on dispatching students overseas (in Chinese), 2003. Available online at www.chisa.edu.cn/newchisa/web/8/2003–05-27/news_481.asp (accessed on July 5, 2003).

Jin, B., Li, L., and Rousseau, R. Long-term influence of interventions in the normal development of science: China and the Cultural Revolution. *Journal of the American Society for Information Science and Technology* 2004; **55**(6): 544–50.

Johnson, J. M. *Statistical Profiles of Foreign Doctoral Recipients in Science and Engineering: Plans to Stay in the United States.* NSF 99–304. Arlington, VA: National Science Foundation, Division of Science Resources Studies, 1999.

  Human Resource Contributions to US Science and Engineering from China. NSF 01–311. Arlington, VA: National Science Foundation Division of Science Resources Studies, 2001.

Johnson, J. M. & Reget, M. C. *International Mobility of Scientists and Engineers to the United States – Brain Drain or Brain Circulation?* NSF 98–316. Arlington, VA: National Science Foundation Division of Science Resources Studies, 1998.

Jones, C. I. Time series tests of endogenous growth models. *Quarterly Journal of Economics* 1995a; **110**(2): 495–525.

R&D based models of economic growth. *Journal of Political Economy* 1995b; **103**: 759–84.

Julius, D. J. Will Chinese universities survive an emerging market economy? *Higher Education Management* 1997; **9**(1): 143–50.

Kanellos, M. China's new weapon: low executive pay. *New York Times* 2007; June 4.

Keely, J. and Wilsdon, J. *China: The Next Science Superpower?* London: Demos, 2007.

Kelly, D. Chinese intellectuals in the 1989 democracy movement. In G. Hicks, ed. *The Broken Mirror: China after Tiananmen*, Chicago, IL: St. James Press, 1990; pp. 24–51.

Kelly, T. K., Butz, W. P., Carroll, S., Adamson, D. M., and Bloom, G. eds. *The US Scientific and Technical Workforce: Improving Data for Decisionmaking*. Santa Monica, CA: Rand Corporation, 2004.

Kennedy, S. The Stone Group: state client or market pathbreaker? *China Quarterly* 1997; **152**: 746–77.

Kirby, W. C. Technocratic Organization and Technological Development in China, 1928–1953. In D. F. Simon and M. Goldman, eds. *Science and Technology in Post-Mao China*. Cambridge, MA: Council of East Asian Studies, Harvard University, 1989; pp. 23–44.

Kondro, W. Canadian universities: massive hiring plan aimed at "brain gain." *Science* 1999; **286**: 651–3.

Kraus, R. C. *Class Conflict in Chinese Socialism*. New York, NY: Columbia University Press, 1981.

Lague, D. Chinese paradox: a shallow pool of talent. *International Herald Tribune* 2006; April 25: 1.

Lai, H. H. China's Western development program: its rationale, implementation, and prospects. *Modern China* 2002; **28** (4): 432–66.

Lall, S. *Competitiveness, Technology and Skills*. Cheltenham: Edward Elgar, 2001.

Lau, A. and Roffey, B. Management education and development in China: a research note. *Labor and Management in Development Journal* 2002; **2**(10): 3–18.

Lee, K. Singapore focuses its life science strategy on humans. *Current Biology* 2001; **11**(1): R3.

Lee, K-F. A Letter to Chinese institutions of higher education: please training talent the twenty-first century's enterprises need (in Chinese), 2006. Available online at www.5xue.com/modules/wordpress/?p=17 (accessed on June 17, 2007).

Li, C. *China's Leaders: The New Generation.* Lanham, MD: Rowman & Littlefield, 2001.

Bringing China's best and brightest back home: regional disparities and political tensions. *China Leadership Monitor*, No. 11. Stanford, CA: Hoover Institute, 2004.

Political Aspects of the Returnees: Their Rise to Power and Growing Political Influence. Hong Kong: Conference on "People on the Move: The Transnational Flow of Chinese Human Capital," 2005a.

Coming Home to Teach: Status and Mobility of Returnees in China's Higher Education. In C. Li, ed. *Bridging Minds across the Pacific: US–China Educational Exchange, 1978–2003.* Lanham, MD: Lexington Books, 2005b; pp. 69–110.

ed. *Bridging Minds across the Pacific: US–China Educational Exchange, 1978–2003.* Lanham, MD: Lexington Books, 2005c.

Li, M. and Gao, M. Strategies for developing China's software industry. *Information Technologies and International Development*, 2003, **1**(1): 61–73.

Li, Q. *Social Stratification and Mobility in Contemporary China* (in Chinese). Beijing: China Economics Press, 1993.

Li, X. and Yu, J. A forecast on the number of R&D scientists and engineers in China (in Chinese). *Science Research Management* 2004; **25**(3): 124–30.

Li, Y. Will Dalian become 'Bangalore'? (in Chinese). *China Computer World* 2005; August 15: A14–15.

Li, Z. 1956: Positioning China's science system under the planning economic system (in Chinese), *Journal of Dialectics of Nature* 1995; **17**(6): 35–45

Liu, S. The Situation of Development of S&T Statistics in China (in Chinese), 2006. Available online at www.sts.org.cn/fxyj/other/documents/fzgk20060510.htm (accessed on January 10, 2007).

Liu, W. Statistical Coordination among Various Producers of Social Statistics in China. New York, NY: United Nations Statistics Division Expert Group Meetings on "Setting the Scope of Social Statistics," 2003. Available online at http://unstats.un.org/UNSD/demographic/meetings/egm/Socialstat_0503/docs/no_17.pdf (accessed on June 4, 2007).

Lu, Q. *China's Leap into the Information Age: Innovation and Organization in the Computer Industry.* Oxford and New York, NY: Oxford University Press, 2000.

Lü, X. *Cadres and Corruption: The Organizational Involution of the Chinese Communist Party.* Stanford, CA: Stanford University Press, 2000.

Lucas, R. E., Jr. On the mechanics of economic development. *Journal of Monetary Economics* 1988; **22**(1): 3–42.

The industrial revolution: past and future. Minneapolis, MN: Federal Reserve Bank of Minnesota, 2003. Available online at www.minneapolisfed.org/pubs/region/04–05/essay.cfm (accessed on December 7, 2006).

Lueck, J. A. *Chinese Intellectuals on the World Frontier: Blazing the Black Path*. New York, NY: Bergin & Garvey, 1997.

Maurer-Fazio, M. In books one finds a house of gold: education and labor market outcomes in urban China. *Journal of Contemporary China* 2006; **15**: 215–31.

McGuckin, R. H., Abbott, T. A., III, Herrick, P. E., and Norfolk, L. Measuring the trade balance in advanced technology. *Center for Economic Studies Report*, 89–11. Washington, DC: US Bureau of Census, 1989.

McKinsey Global Institute. *The Emerging Global Labor Market*. San Francisco, CA: McKinsey & Company, 2005.

Meisner, M. *The Deng Xiaoping Era: An Inquiry into the Fate of Chinese Socialism, 1978–1994*. New York, NY: Hill & Wang, 1996.

Mervis, J. US workforce: a glass ceiling for Asian scientists? *Science* 2005; **310**: 606–7.

Top PhD feeder schools are now Chinese. *Science* 2008; **321**: 185.

Miller, H. L. *Science and Dissent in Post-Mao China: The Politics of Knowledge*. Seattle, WA: University of Seattle Press, 1996.

Min, W. and Wang, R., eds. *China Education and Human Resources Development Report 2005–2006* (in Chinese). Beijing: Beijing University Press, 2006.

Mincer, J. Investment in human capital and personal income distribution. *Journal of Political Economy* 1958; **66**(4): 281–302.

Ministry of Education (MOEd). Statistics on overseas study in 2007 (in Chinese), 2008. Available online at http://www.js-edu.cn/Html/200804/07/20080407102041.htm (accessed on May 10, 2008).

Bureau of Development and Planning, comp. *China Statistical Yearbook on Education* (in Chinese). Beijing: China Education Press, various years.

Bureau of Higher Education, comp. *A Survey of Demand and Training of Economics and Business Administration Majors at Institutions of Higher Education* (in Chinese). Beijing: Renmin University of China Press, 2005.

Bureau of Students in Higher Education, comp. *1996–2002 Statistical Yearbook of National Graduate Student Admissions* (in Chinese). Beijing: Beijing University of Aeronautics and Astronautics Press, 2003.

National Bureau of Statistics (NBS), and Ministry of Finance (MOF) Annual report of the implementation of national educational expenditure (in Chinese). Beijing, China: MOEd, NBS, and MOF, various years.

Ministry of Information Industry (MII) Bureau of Electronics and Information Products, and China Software Industry Association (CSIA), comp. *Annual Report of China Software Industry 2005* (in Chinese), 2005.

Bureau of Electronics and Information Products, and Bureau of Economic System Reform and Economic Operations, and China Software Industry Association (CSIA), comp. *Annual Report of China Software Industry* (in Chinese), various years.

Ministry of Personnel (MOP) Implementation of the One Hundred, One Thousand, and Ten Thousands of Talent Program (in Chinese), 2002. Available at www.mop.gov.cn/Desktop.aspx?PATH=rsbww/sy/xxll&Gid=65f5e54a-10e8-4b0c-b70c-b97b85ff492f&Tid=cms_info (accessed on December 30, 2003).

Ministry of Science and Technology (MOST), comp. *China Science and Technology Indicators* (in Chinese). Beijing: Scientific and Technical Literature Press, various years.

Bureau of Development and Planning. An analysis of doctoral degree holders at government affiliated R&D institutes (in Chinese). 2007. Available at www.most.gov.cn/kjtj/tjbg/200710/t20071026_56714.htm (accessed on October 1, 2007).

China National Center for Biotechnology Development (CNCBD). Biotechnology and bio-economy in China (in Chinese), 2005. Available online at www.intec-online.net/uploads/media/Biotechnology_and_Bio-economy_in_China_Government_Document_.pdf (accessed on December 10, 2007).

Mok, K-H. Globalization and educational restructuring: university merging and changing governance in China. *Higher Education* 2005; **50**(1): 75–88.

National Bureau of Statistics (NBS), comp. *China Statistical Yearbook*. Beijing: China Statistics Press, various years.

Statistical bulletin of 2007 national economy and social development (in Chinese), 2008. Available at www.stats.gov.cn/tjgb/ndtjgb/qgndtjgb/t20080228_402464933.htm (accessed on March 6, 2008).

National Bureau of Statistics (NBS) Bureau of Comprehensive Statistics on National Economy, comp. *China Compendium of Statistics, 1949–2004*. Beijing: China Statistics Press, 2005.

Department of Population and Employment Statistics and Ministry of Labor and Social Security (MOLSS) Department of Planning and

Finance, comp. *China Labor Statistical Yearbook*. Beijing, China: China Labor and Social Security Press, various years.

National Bureau of Statistics (NBS) and Ministry of Science and Technology (MOST), comp. *China Statistical Yearbook on Science and Technology*. Beijing: China Statistics Press, various years.

National Bureau of Statistics (NBS) and National Development and Reform Commission (NDRC), comp. *Statistics on Science and Technology Activities of Industrial Enterprises* (in Chinese). Beijing: China Statistics Press, 2006.

National Bureau of Statistics (NBS), National Development and Reform Commission (NDRC), and Ministry of Science and Technology (MOST) comp. *2007 China Statistical Yearbook on High-Technology Industry*. Beijing: China Statistics Press, 2007.

National Natural Science Foundation of China (NSFC). Celebration of the tenth anniversary of the National Science Fund for Distinguished Young Scholar Program (in Chinese), 2004. Available at www.nsfc.gov.cn/nsfc/desktop/jjyw.aspx@infoid=6105&moduleid=399.htm (accessed on September 12, 2005).

National Science Board (NSB). *The Science and Engineering Workforce: Realizing America's Potential*. NSB 03–06. Arlington, VA: National Science Foundation, 2003.

　　Science and Engineering Indicators. Arlington, VA: National Science Foundation, various years.

Nelson, R. R. and Phelps, E. S. Investment in humans, technological diffusion, and economic growth. *American Economic Review* 1966; **56**(2): 69–75.

Nie Rongzhen. *Inside the Red Star: The Memoirs of Marshal Nie Rongzhen*. Beijing: New World Press, 1988.

Office of the National R&D Resources Census, comp. *Comprehensive Statistics on the 2000 National R&D Resources Census* (in Chinese). Beijing: China Statistics Press, 2002.

Ogden, S. *China's Unresolved Issues: Politics, Development, and Culture*, 2nd edition. Englewood Cliffs, NJ: Prentice Hall, 1992.

Organization for Economic Cooperation and Development (OECD). *The Measurement of Scientific and Technical Activities: Standard Practice for Surveys of Research and Experimental Development (Frascati Manual)*. Paris: OECD, 1993.

　　The Measurement of Scientific and Technological Activities: Manual on the Measurement of Human Resources Devoted to S&T (Canberra Manual). Paris: OECD, 1995.

　　OECD Science, Technology and Industry Outlook 2006. Paris: OECD, 2006.

OECD Reviews of Innovation Policy: China. Paris: OECD in Collaboration with the Ministry of Science and Technology, China, 2007a.

Education at a Glance 2007: OECD Indicators. Paris: OECD, 2007b.

Orleans, L. *Professional Manpower and Education in Communist China.* Washington, DC: National Science Foundation, 1961.

Manpower for science and engineering in China. *Science and Technology in the People's Republic of China Background Study,* No. 4. Washington, DC: US Government Printing Office, 1980.

The training and utilization of scientific and engineering manpower in the People's Republic of China. *Science and Technology in the People's Republic of China Background Study,* No. 5. Washington, DC: US Government Printing Office, 1983.

Chinese Students in America: Policies, Issues, and Numbers. Washington, DC: National Academy Press, 1988.

Perspectives on China's Brain Drain. In Joint Economic Committee, Congress of the United States, ed. *China's Economic Dilemmas in the 1990s: Problems of Reforms, Modernization, and Interdependence.* Armonk, NY: ME Sharpe, 1992; pp. 629–43.

Pan, C. ed. *Report on the Development of Chinese Talent* (in Chinese). Beijing: Social Sciences Academic Press, various years.

Pan, C. and Lou, W. An Analysis on the Current Situation of Talent and the Environment for Talent Development. In C. Pan, ed. *Report on the Development of Chinese Talent,* No. 1 (in Chinese). Beijing: Social Sciences Academic Press, pp. 1–46.

Pan, L. *Sons of the Yellow Emperor: The Story of the Overseas Chinese.* London: Secker & Warburg, 1990.

Pan, Y. *Tempered in the Revolutionary Furnace: China's Youth in the Rustication Movement.* Lanham, MD: Lexington Books, 2003.

Parsons, T. *The Social System.* Glencoe, IL: Free Press, 1951.

Pei, M. *China's Trapped Transition: The Limits of Developmental Autocracy.* Cambridge, MA: Harvard University Press, 2006.

Pisano, G. P. *Science Business: The Promise, the Reality, and the Future of Biotech.* Boston, MA: Harvard Business School Press, 2006.

Pollak, M. Counting the S&E workforce – it's not that easy. NSF 99–344. Arlington, VA: National Science Foundation Division of Science Resource Studies, 1999.

Porter, A. L., Newman, N. C., Jin, X-Y., Johnson, D. M., and Roessner, D. J. *High Tech Indicators: Technology-Based Competitiveness of 33 Nations, 2007 Report.* Atlanta, GA: Technology Policy and Assessment Center, Georgia Institute of Technology, 2008.

Porter, E. China shrinks. *New York Times,* 2007; December 9.

Qi, C. and Wang, C. An Overview of Development of Biotech Industry during the Eleventh Five-Year Plan Period (in Chinese). In Bureau of High-Tech Industry of the National Development and Reform Commission and Chinese Society of Biotechnology, comp. *Annual Report on Biotech Industry in China: 2005*. Beijing: Chemical Engineering Publication House, 2006; pp. 3–15.

Qu, S. *A Developmental History of University Education in China* (in Chinese). Shanxi: Shanxi Education Press, 1993.

Quan, Y. and Hoon, H. T. Catch-up growth based on international talent mobility in an idea-based world. *SMU Economics & Statistics Working Paper Series*, No. 11–2003. Singapore: Singapore Management University, 2003.

Rawski, T. G. What is happening to China's GDP statistics? *China Economic Review* 2001; **12**(4): 347–54.

Research Group on China's Education and Human Resources. *Stride from a Country of Tremendous Population to a Country of Profound Human Resources* (in Chinese). Beijing: Higher Education Press, 2003.

Romer, P. M. Increasing returns and long-run growth. *Journal of Political Economy* 1986; **94**(5): 1002–37.

  Endogenous technological change. *Journal of Political Economy* 1990; **98**(5): S71–102.

Rubinstein, E. China's leader commits to basic research, global science. *Science* 2000; **288**: 1950.

Saich, T. *China's Science Policy in the 80s*, Atlantic Highlands, NJ: Humanities Press International, 1989.

Sautman, B. Politicization, hyperpoliticization and depoliticization of Chinese education. *Comparative Education Review* 1991; **35**(4): 669–89.

Saxenian, A. L., with Montoya, Y. and Quan, X. *Local and Global Networks of Immigrant Professionals in Silicon Valley*. San Francisco, CA: Public Policy Institute of California, 2002.

  The New Argonauts: Regional Advantage in a Global Economy. Cambridge, MA: Harvard University Press, 2006.

Saxenian, A. L. and Quan, X. China. In S. Commander, ed. *The Software Industry in Emerging Markets: Origins and Dynamics*. Cheltenham: Edward Elgar, 2005; pp. 73–132.

Schaaper, M. An emerging knowledge-based economy in China? Indicators from OECD databases. *STI Working Paper*, No. 4. Paris: Statistical Analysis of Science, Technology and Industry, OECD, 2004.

Schultz, T. W. Investment in human capital. *American Economic Review* 1961; **51**(1): 1–17.

Nobel lecture: the economics of being poor. *Journal of Political Economy* 1980; **88**(4): 639–51.

Science for the People. *China: Science on Two Legs*. New York, NY: Avon Books, 1974.

Serger, S. S. China: from shop floor to knowledge factory? In M. Karlsson, ed. *The Internationalization of Corporate R&D: Leveraging the Changing Geography of Innovation*. Sweden: IPTS, 2006; pp. 227–66.

Shang, Z. The effective way for the current Chinese scientific talent to enter into the international scientific community: a study of the scientific talent younger than fifty-years-old in the Chinese Academy of Sciences (in Chinese). *Science and Technology Management Research* 2007; **8**: 225–7.

Sheff, D. *China Dawn: The Story of a Technology and Business Revolution*. New York, NY: HarperBusiness, 2002.

Sigurdson, J., with Jiang, J., Kong, X., Yongzhong Wang, Y. and Tang, Y. *Technological Superpower China*. Cheltenham: Edward Elgar, 2006.

Simon, D. F. ed. *The Emerging Technological Trajectory of the Pacific Rim*. Armonk, NY: ME Sharpe, 1997.

Sleeboom, M. The Harvard case of Xu Xiping: exploitation of the people, scientific advance, or genetic theft?' *New Genetics and Society* 2005; **24**(1): 57–78.

Solow, R. M. A contribution to the theory of economic growth. *Quarterly Journal of Economics* 1956; **70**(1): 65–94.

Song , J. One hundred years of overseas study movement' (in Chinese). *Guangming Daily* 2003, April 15.

Southworth, D. B. Building a business school in China: the case of the China Europe International Business School (CEIBS). *Education & Training* 1999; **41**(6/7): 325–31.

Stevenson-Yang, A. and DeWoskin, K. China destroys the IP paradigm. *Far Eastern Economic Review* 2005; **168**(3): 9–18.

Stringer, H. and Rueff, R. *Talent Force: A New Manifesto for the Human Side of Business*. Upper Saddle River, NJ: Prentice Hall, 2006.

Sun, C. and Zou, S. Chinese overseas students are in more than 100 countries and regions (in Chinese), 2003. Available online at http://news.xinhuanet.com/weekend/2003–10/05/content_1110988.htm (accessed on October 6, 2003).

Sun, Y., von Zedtwitz, M. and Simon, D. F. eds. *Global R&D in China*. London and New York, NY: Routledge, 2007.

Suttmeier, R. P. Engineers rule, OK? *New Scientist* 2007; November 10: 71–3.

Suttmeier, R. P., Cao, C. and Simon, D. F. "Knowledge innovation" and the Chinese Academy of Sciences. *Science* 2006; **312**: 58–9.

Teitebaum, M. S. Do we need more scientists? *Public Interest* 2003; **153**: 40–53.

Thurow, L. C. *Head to Head: The Coming Economic Battle among Japan, Europe, and America.* New York, NY: William Morrow, 1992.

Tschang, C-C. China's college graduate glut. *Business Week* 2007; June 7.

Tschang, T. and Xue, L. The Chinese Software Industry: The Implications of a changing Domestic Market for Software Enterprises. In A. Arora and A. Gambardella, eds. *From Underdogs to Tigers: The Rise and Growth of the Software Industry in Brazil, China, India, Ireland, and Israel.* Oxford and New York, NY: Oxford University Press, 2005; pp. 131–70.

Turner, Y. and Acker, A. *Education in the New China: Shaping Ideas at Work.* Basingstoke: Ashgate, 2002.

United Nations Development Programme (UNDP). *Human Development Reports 2001: Making New Technologies Work for Human Development.* Oxford and New York, NY: Oxford University Press, 2001.

United Nations Educational, Scientific and Cultural Organization (UNESCO). Recommendation Concerning the International Standardization of Statistics on Science and Technology. In *Resolutions: Volume One of the Records of the Twentieth Session of the General Conference, Annex 23–35.* Paris: UNESCO, 1978.

International Standard Classification of Education ISCED 1997, new edition. Montreal, Canada: UNESCO Institute for Statistics, 2006.

United Nations Population Division (UNPD). *China's Population Growth Projection.* New York, NY: UNPD, 2005.

US Census Bureau. *US International Trade in Goods and Services: Information on Goods and Services.* Washington, DC: US Census Bureau, 2001. Available online at www.census.gov/foreign-trade/Press-elease/current_press_release/explain.txt (accessed on November 15, 2001).

News release: Census Bureau Data Underscore Value of College Degree (CB06–159). Washington, DC: US Census Bureau, 2006. Available online at www.census.gov/Press-Release/www/releases/archives/education/007660.html (accessed on December 1, 2006).

Wadhwa, V. and Gereffi, G. *Framing the Engineering Outsourcing Debate: Placing the United States on a Level Playing Field with China and India.* Durham, NC: Master of Engineering Management Program, Pratt School of Engineering, Duke University, 2005. Available online at http://memp.pratt.duke.edu/outsourcing/ (accessed on December 31, 2005).

Wadhwa, V., Rissing, B., Saxenian, A.L. and Gereffi, G. *Education, Entrepreneurship, and Immigration: America's New Immigrant Entrepreneurs, Part II.* Durham, NC, Berkeley, CA, and Kansas City, MO: Pratt School of Engineering, Duke University, School of Information, University of California, Berkeley, and Ewing Marion Kauffman Foundation, 2007. Available online at http://papers.ssrn.com/sol3/papers.cfm?abstract_id=991327#PaperDownload (accessed on December 31, 2007).

Wang, C. From manpower supply to economic revival: governance and financing of Chinese higher education. *Education Policy Analysis Archive* 2000; 6(26). Available online at http://epaa.asu.edu/epaa/v8n26.html (accessed April 19, 2007).

Wang, H. *Returning Times* (in Chinese). Beijing: Central Compilation & Translation Press, 2005.

Wang, W. China has more than 5000 scientists engaged in nanotechnology research (in Chinese), 2007. Available online at http://news.xinhuanet.com/newscenter/2007–11/21/content_7122966.htm (accessed on November 25, 2007).

Wang, Y. *Hua Luogeng* (in Chinese). Beijing: Kaiming Press, 1994.

Wang, Y. C. *Chinese Intellectuals and the West, 1872–1949*. Chapel Hill, NC: University of North Carolina Press, 1966.

Wang, Z-L. ed. *2005 Report of Multinational Corporations in China* (in Chinese). Beijing: China Economics Press, 2005.

Wang, Z-Y. Saving China through science: the science society of China, scientific nationalism, and civil society in republican China. *Osiris*, 2nd Series 2002; 17: 291–322.

Wei, Z. Some thoughts on overseas students returning to serve the country and serving the country in the new era' (in Chinese), 2006. Available online at www.chisa.edu.cn/news/article/20060922/20060922019073_1.xml (accessed on March 5, 2008).

Williams, J. H. Fang Lizhi's big bang: a physicist and the state in China. *Historical Studies in the Physical and Biological Sciences* 1999; 30(1): 49–87.

Williams, T. GM crops – savior or saboteur? Agricultural biotechnology in China today. *Colorado Journal of International Environmental Law & Policy Yearbook* 2001; 203–24.

Wilson, D. and Purushothaman, P. Dreaming with BRICs: the path to 2050. *Global Economics Paper*, No: 99. New York, NY: Goldman Sachs, 2003.

Wilson, J. S. The US 1982–1993 performance in advanced technology trade. *Challenge* 1994; 1: 11–16.

Wood, A. and Berge, K. Exporting manufacturers: human resources, natural resources, and trade policy. *Journal of Development Studies* 1997; 34(1): 35–59.

World Bank. *2006 World Development Indicators*. Washington, DC: World Bank, 2006.

Wortzel, L. M. *Class in China: Stratification in a Classless Society*, Westport, CT: Greenwood Press, 1987.

Wu, C. Biotech research investment advocated. *China Daily* 2005; September 5: 2.

Wu, Q. A speech at the conference of pilot software engineering schools (in Chinese), 2006. Available online at http://rjb.bjtu.edu.cn/view_law.jsp?lawid=24 (accessed on December 10, 2007).

Wu, R. Making an impact. *Nature* 2004; **428**: 206–7.

Wu, Z., Christensen, D., Li, M., and Wang, Q. A survey of CMM/CMMI implementation in China. *Lecture Notes in Computer Science* 2006; **3840**: 507–20.

Xiao, G. People's Republic of China's round tripping FDI: scale, causes and implications. *ADB Institute Discussion Paper*, No. 7. Tokyo, Japan: Asian Development Bank Institute, 2004.

Xiao, L., Wang, B., Zhang, Y., and Zhu, B. A second thought on China's policies of attracting personnel studying abroad (in Chinese). *Science of Science and S&T Management* 2005; **October**: 90–4.

Yao, S., Luo, W., Li, P. and Zhang, W. A Developmental History of the Chinese Academy of Sciences (in Chinese). In Q. Linzhao and G. Yu, eds. *The Chinese Academy of Sciences*, Vol. 1. Beijing: Contemporary China Press, 1994; pp. 1–230.

Ye, W. *Seeking Modernity in China's Name: Chinese Students in the United States, 1900–1927*. Stanford, CA: Stanford University Press, 2001.

Yeh, W-H. *The Alienated Academy, Culture and Politics in Republic China, 1919–1937*, Cambridge, MA: Council on East Asian Studies, Harvard University, 1990.

Yu, J. Biotechnology Research in China. In L. Jakobson, ed. *Innovation with Chinese Characteristics: High-Tech Research in China*. Hampshire: Palgrave Macmillan, 2007; pp. 134–65.

Yue, C. J. The impact of education on income difference in urban China (in Chinese). *China Economic Quarterly* 2004; **13** (Suppl. 3): 135–50.

Zhang, G. Migration of highly skilled Chinese to Europe: trends and prospectives. *International Migration* 2003; **41**(3): 73–95.

Zhang, G. and Li, W. International Mobility of China's Resources in Science and Technology and Its Impact. In *OECD*, ed. *International Mobility of the Highly Skilled*. Paris: OECD, 2001; pp. 189–200.

   The scale of "brain drain" of China's S&T talent and its impact (in Chinese). *Research on Quantitative Economics and Technological Economics* 2002; **1**: 5–9.

Zhang, J., Zou, S., and Liu, Z. Only 30 000 high-level talent for a country of 1.3 billion (in Chinese), 2003. Available online at http://news.xinhuanet.com/newscenter/2003–12/18/content_1236736.htm (accessed on December 25, 2003).

Zhao, S. Typological analysis of statistics distortion in contemporary China (in Chinese), *Modern China Studies* 2006; **4**. Available online at www. chinayj.net/StubArticle.asp?issue=060410&total=95.

Zhao, W. and Zhou, X. Institutional transformation and returns to education in urban China: an empirical assessment. *Research in Social Stratification and Mobility* 2002; **19**: 339–75.

Zhong, Y. *Local Government and Politics in China: Challenges from Below*. Armonk, NY: ME Sharpe, 2003.

Zhou Enlai. On the Question of Intellectuals, 1956. In R.R. Bowie and J.K. Fairbank, eds. *Communist China 1955–1959: Policy Documents and Analysis*. Cambridge, MA: Harvard University Press, 1962; pp. 128–44.

Zhou, P. and Leydesdorff, L. The emergence of China as a leading nation in science. *Research Policy* 2006; **35**: 83–104.

Zhu, Y. China's Biotechnology Talent Strategy (in Chinese). In Bureau of High-Tech Industry of the National Development and Reform Commission and Chinese Society of Biotechnology, comp. *Annual Report on Biotech Industry in China: 2004*. Beijing: Chemical Engineering Publication House, 2005; pp. 50–7.

Zimmerman, A. Undergraduate business education in the People's Republic of China: adaptation to the market economy. *Journal of Teaching in International Business* 2001; **12**(4): 15–28.

Zweig, D. *Internationalizing China: Domestic Interests and Global Linkages*. Ithaca, NY: Cornell University Press, 2002.

Competing for talent: China's strategies to reverse the brain drain. *International Labor Review* 2006; **45**(1–2): 65–89.

Zweig, D. and Chen, C. *China's Brain Drain to the United States: Views of Overseas Chinese Students and Scholars in the 1990s*. Berkeley, CA: Institute of East Asian Studies, University of California, 1995.

Index

211 Program, 45, 50, 116
 doctoral students, 142
 funding, 117–18
 key (*zhongdian*) institutions, 121
985 Program, 45, 50, 116, 117–18, 121

adult higher education, 129–30
advanced technology, 285
aircraft and spacecraft manufacturing, 296
Alibaba, 184–5
"amphibians", 245
Anhui, 340
Annual Report of the State Programs of Science and Technology Development, 355–6
Anti-Bourgeois-Liberalization Campaign, 172
Anti-Rightist Campaign (1957), 24
Asian financial crisis, 76
awards, 181–2

Bai Chunli, 29, 30, 225
Baidu, 184–5, 237
banking professionals, 237, 321–2
Barnes, Jeff, 323
Barro, Robert, 6–7
Becker, Gary, 3–4, 5–6, 158–9
Beijing, 89, 204, 295–6, 296
Beijing Geological College, 121
Beijing University
 as comprehensive (*zonghe*) institution, 121
 as source of US doctorates, 126
 establishment of, 111
 funding, 117–18
 Guanghua School of Management, 324
 history, 112
 place in hierarchy of Chinese higher education, 122

reliance on foreign experts for teaching ICT, 305
 world ranking, 159
Benhabib, Jess, 7
benke (bachelor's degree), 126
Binhai New Development Zone 319–20
biotechnology, 315–19
blue Book series, 371
Boxer Indemnity Scholarship Fund, 214
brain circulation, 212–13
brain drain
 at high level, 230–4
 challenge presented by, 30–3
 data problems, 221–30
 rate of return as measure of, 225–33
 seriousness of, 233–4
 software industry, 299–300
brain gain, xviii, 3, 213, 251, 253, 277
Bt-cotton, 316

cadre (*ganbu*), 65
CAE (Chinese Academy of Engineering), 77
Campaign Against Spiritual Pollution, 172–5
Canberra Manual, 58, 64
capitalist roaders (*zouzipai*), 23
CAS (Chinese Academy of Sciences)
 correlation to official hierarchy, 169–70
 doctorate requirement for new hires, 178–9
 flow of postgraduates, 158
 help from overseas Chinese academics, 246
 One-Hundred Talent Program (elite membership), 50, 53, 236
 S&T personnel, 78–82, 92, 95–8
 yuanshi, 77

CAS (Chinese Academy of
 Sciences) (cont.)
yuanshi stipend from the state
 204–7. *See also* One-Hundred
 Talent Program
CEIBS (China Europe International
 Business School), 324
Center for S&T Statistics and Analysis,
 359
Center for S&T Statistics and
 Information (Huazhong
 University of Science and
 Technology), 359
Chang, Iris, *Thread of the Silkworm*,
 xxii
Chen Chunxian, 183
Chen Jin, 249–50
Chen Yi, 172
Chen Zhu, 239, 344
Chengdu, 293
Cheung Kong Graduate School of
 Business, 324
Cheung Kong Scholars Program
 45–50, 50, 116
 financial awards, 194
 interest in appointing social
  scientists, 243
 key (*zhongdian*) institutions, 122
 with aim of attracting overseas
  Chinese students, 234, 235
 yuanshi numbers, 76–7
China
 aging population, 38–9, 119,
  339–40
 as global technological power, 334–7
 HRST growth, 71–7
 talent challenges
  and China's political development,
   342–4
  brain drain, 30–3, 221–30,
   225–33, 230–4, 233–4,
   299–300
  Great Proletarian Cultural
   Revolution, 16–17, 23–30, 40
  leadership actions to address,
   39–55
  MOEd Programs, 50
  overview, 22–3, 55–6, 337–42
  quality problems, 33–8
 talent pool future, 344–6

*China Education and Human Resource
 Development Report 2005–2006*,
 xxi–xxii
China Educational Yearbook, 364
China High Technology Industry Data,
 364
China Labor Statistical Yearbook,
 359–64
China Population Statistical Yearbook,
 359–64
*China Science and Technology
 Indicators*, 64, 359, 364
*China Science and Technology
 Statistical Data*, 364
China Statistical Yearbook, 351,
 359–64
*China Statistical Yearbook on
 Education*, 359–64, 367
*China Statistical Yearbook on
 Education Expenditure*, 359–64
*China Statistical Yearbook on High-
 Technology Industry*, 359–64,
 364
*China Statistical Yearbook on Science
 and Technology*, 353, 359–64
China Talent Report, 371
Chinese official statistics
 finding and recognizing discrepancy,
  372–5
 history of collection apparatus
  349–52
 multiplicity of sources, 370–2
 overview, 347–8
 reliability, 348–9
 S&T statistics
  evolution, 352–6
  major centers, 358–9
  major publications, 359–65
  problems, 365–9
  system, 356–8
  using, 369–75
  understanding Chinese definitions,
   369–70
Chinese Student Protection Act (US
 1992), 218, 229
Chow, Gregory, 349
Chunhui Program (*chunhui jihua*),
 235–6
chushi (specialty examinations), 128
civil service, salaries, 204

Compilation of China Statistical Materials on Science and Technology, 364
comprehensive (*zonghe*) institutions, 121
computer software studies, 133
Cross-Century Outstanding Personnel Training Program, 235
Cultural Revolution. *See* Great Proletarian Cultural Revolution
curriculum issues, 36–8

Dalian, 306–9
danwei (China's state-owned enterprises and institutions)
professionals in, 72, 92, 95
R&D personnel, 99
S&T workers in, 74
danwei gongpai (institutionally sponsored) overseas students, 217
data sources for this book, xxvi–xxviii, 269–70. *See also* Chinese official statistics
data unavailability, 53–4, 367–8
demographic dividend, 38–9. *See also* China; aging population
Deng Xiaoping, 170–1
comment on Brain Drain, 217, 219
respecting knowledge and talent 17, 41
Deng Xingwang, 245
Department of Organization of the CCP Central Committee, 65
Document, 18, 47, 300–1
Drucker, Peter, 11
"dumbbell" model, 245

economics (study subject), 133–8
Education Act (1996), 116
Education Revitalization Action Plan, 116, 118
education, individual economic returns from, 5–6, 16–17
educational spending, 263
Electronics Street (*Dianzi Yitiaojie*), 183–4
engineering graduates, xviii, xxiii–xxiv
engineering studies, 138, 142
engineers, definitions, 62

English literature studies, 133
erji xueke, 127
examinations, 128–9
experience, lack of, 22

Fang Yi, 217
FDI (foreign direct investment)
as driver of demand for scientists and engineers, 256–9
changing nature of, 336–7
fei zhongdian (non-key) institutions, 121, 159–60
fenpei (job assignment) system, 115, 175–82
fields of study (*xueke menlei*), 127
FIEs (foreign-invested enterprises)
migration to second-tier cities, 296
S&T workforce, 83
high-technology industries, 289–292
finance professionals, 237, 321–2
Florida, Richard, 11
Ford (American company), 293
foreign investment, growth in, xix
Founder, 183
"four modernizations", 41, 163, 171, 191, 216
Frascati Manual, 62–3
FTE (full-time equivalent), 68
Fu Xinyuan, 247
Fudan University, 121
Fujian, 89
Furong Scholar Program, 50
fushi examinations, 128

ganbu (cadre). *See* cadre (*ganbu*)
gang guan rencai (party administer's cadre) principle, 42
gaoji zhishi fenzi (high-ranking intellectuals), 168, 190
genome sciences, 315
getihu (private entrepreneurs), 191
GM technology, 316
gongnongbing xueyuan (worker-peasant-soldier students), 28, 29–30, 191
gongpai (government/institutionally sponsored) students, 218
government sponsored (*guojia gongpai*) students, 217

graduates
  numbers, xviii
  unemployment, 267. *See also*
    engineering graduates;
    postgraduates
Great Proletarian Cultural Revolution,
    16–17, 23–30, 40
Great Wall Program, 302–4
guanbenwei (official-centeredness), 169
Guangdong, 89, 204, 293, 295, 296
guanxi, importance of, 242, 346
Guidelines of Chinese Education Reform
    and Development (1993), 116
Guizhou, 296
guojia gongpai (government sponsored)
    students, 217
GVIO-IT (gross value of industrial
    output from IT), 260

haigui (returned Chinese students and
    scholars)
  characteristics of, 236–41
  overview, 212
  problems emerging, 247–8
Hainan, 89
Hebei, 340
Heckman, James J., 19
Heilongjiang, 296
high-end S&T talent, 76–7
higher education
  admissions processes, 126–30
  development of, 111–16
  enrollment rate, 110
  enrollments, 130
  financial cost to individuals, 115–16
  hierarchy of, 121–6
  initiatives since 1990s, 116–20
  interest in, 110
  quality of, 158–63
  upward mobility, 114–15. *See also*
    tertiary education
High-Level Innovative Talent
    Development Program, 50
high-ranking intellectuals (*gaoji zhishi
    fenzi*), 168, 190
high-technology entrepreneurship,
    182–6
high-technology exports, 263–4
high-technology industries
  definitions, 285–6

  overview, 286–92
  regional distribution of talent, 292–9
  S&T workforce. *See also*
    biotechnology; nanotechnology;
    software industry
  in foreign-invested enterprises
    (FIEs), 289–92
  quality, 289
  size, 286
high-technology parks, 292
hongyanbing (red eye disease), 244
HRST (human resources in science and
    technology)
  as metric of potential technological
    strength, 1
  definitions
    Canberra Manual, 58–9
    education, 59–61
    in Chinese context, 64–71
    operational, 62–4
    stocks and flows, 61
  flow of, 145–58
  limitations of formal statistics, 54
HRST/population ratio, definitions,
    61–2
HRST/workforce ratio, definitions, 62
HRSTC (HRST core), definitions, 59
HRSTE (HRST education), definitions,
    59
HRSTO (HRST occupation),
    definitions, 59
HRSTU (HRST unemployed),
    definitions, 61
Hu Jintao, 18, 43, 210
Huazhong University of Science and
    Technology, 117
human capital, 3, 3–5, 58. *See also*
    human resources
Human Capital (Becker), 4
human genome, 315
human resources
  and economic growth, 1–2, 3–8
  and globalization, 2–3, 11–16
  and innovation, 2, 8–11
  strategic importance in China's
    development, 16–19
Hunan, 89

ICT (information and communications
    tech) sector, 296

IDC, 185
information sector
  inclusion in official statistics, 200
  incomes, 204
  wages, 265
institutionally sponsored (*danwei gongpai*) students, 217
Intel (American company), 185, 293, 296–9
intellectuals (*zhishi fenzi*)
  Cultural Revolution, 25
  definitions, 65, 168
  income, 195, 201–3. *See also* S&T workforce; income
  Party policy, 170–5. *See also* Anti-Rightist Campaign (1957)
international certification, software industry, 309–12
International Standard Classification of Education (ISCED), 59–61
Internet, 260
internships, 162
IPR (Intellectual Property Rights), recent attention to, 237, 265
ISCO 88 (International Standard Classification of Occupations), 63 4

Jiang Zemin, 45, 171
  comment on brain drain, 220
Jiangsu, 89, 204, 293, 295, 296
Jiangxi, 89, 296
Jiaotong University, 111
jibie, 168–9
Jilin University, 121
job assignment (*fenpei*), 175–7, 178
job mobility, 177–8, 180
job security, 179–80

keji gongzuozhe (S&T workers), 68, 74
keji huodong renyuan (S&T personnel)
  definitions, 67–8
  demand
    drivers of, 255–66
    forecast, 271
    modeling, 268–71
  Diaspora, 277
  growth in, 74, 76
  institutional distribution, 78
  shortage

possibility of, 276–7
reasons for, 278–82
software industry, 306–9
supply. *See also* high-end S&T talent
  drivers of, 266–8
  forecast, 274–5
  modeling, 268–71
keju kaoshi (imperial civil service examination), 167
key (*zhongdian*) institutions, 121, 159–60
knowledge workers, 11

Lee, Kai-fu, 282
Lenovo, 183, 330, 337
Level 5 education, 59–61
Level 6 education, 59–61
Li Kai-shing, 324
Li Tieying, 219
liangdan yixing (strategic weapons programs), 103, 215
Liaoning, 340
ligongke (polytechnic) universities, 121
ligongke (science and technology), enrollments, 130–3
literature studies, 133
liuxuesheng (overseas Chinese students and scholars)
  as significant asset, 244–6
  definitions, 370
  history of overseas study movement, 213–16
  measures to facilitate return, 230–1
  overview, 212–13
  policy post-1978, 216–21
  problems emerging, 246–50
  programs to encourage return to China, 234–6
  reasons for non-return to China, 242–4
Lucas, Robert, 4–5

management (study subject), 127, 133
managers
  education, 323–9
  shortage of, 321–3
  utilization, 329–31
mandatory subjects, 127, 162
manpower planning, 175–6

*Manual for Statistics on Scientific and
    Technological Activities*
    (UNESCO), 353
Mao Zedong
  and Cultural Revolution, 23
  and intellectuals, 17. *See also* Great
    Proletarian Cultural Revolution
MBAs (Masters of Business
    Administration), 323–4. *See also*
    managers; education
McKinsey Global Institute, 22
medical equipment sector, 296
medicine, postgraduate admissions, 142
Medium to Long-Term Plan for the
    Development of Science and
    Technology 2006–2020 (MLP),
    xix, xxiv–xxv, 43–4, 317
Microsoft, 302–4, 336
Mincer, Jacob, 3–4
misconduct in research, 208, 243.
    See also Chen Jin; Xu Xiping
MOEd (Ministry of Education)
  data collection, 54, 221–2
  initiatives, 116–17. *See also* 211
    Program; 985 Program; Cheung
    Kong Scholars Program; Cross-
    Century Outstanding Personnel
    Training Program; High-Level
    Innovative Talent Development
    Program
MOLSS (Ministry of Labor and Social
    Security), data collection, 54
MOP (Ministry of Personnel)
  data collection, 53–4. *See also*
    Hundreds; Thousands; and Ten
    Thousands of Talent Program
MOST (Ministry of Science and
    Technology), data collection, 54
Motorola (American company), 293

Nanjing University, 121
Nankai University, 121
nanotechnology, 319–21
National Natural Science Foundation
    of China (NSFC), 44, 186
National Research Center for Science
    and Technology for Development,
    356
National Science Fund for
    Distinguished Young Scholars
    Program, 51–2, 76–7, 234

National Statistics Law, 351
Natural Science Award, 182
NBS (National Bureau of Statistics)
  data collection, 54
  history, 349–51
  role, 357–8
NDRC (National Development and
    Reform Commission), data
    collection, 54
Netease, 184–5
New Century Outstanding Personnel
    Support Program, 235
New Technology Company
    (predecessor of Lenovo), 183
Nie Rongzhen, 174
Nilekani, Nandan, 322
Ningxia, 204, 292
Nobel Prizes, 103
non-ethnic-Chinese scholars, 158–9
non-key *(fei zhongdian)* institutions,
    121, 159–60

objectives of this book, xxiv–xxv
one-child policy, 116, 163, 267,
    323
One Hundred, One Thousand, and Ten
    Thousands of Talent Program
    52–3, 77, 234
One-Hundred Talent Program
  aim of attracting overseas Chinese
    students, 234
  description, 50–1
  financial awards, 194
  foreign doctorates, 239
  requirement to work full-time in
    China, 249
  yuanshi, 76–7
online gaming, software development,
    312–14
Orleans, Leo, xxi, 221, 338
overseas Chinese students and scholars.
    See liuxuesheng

pharmaceuticals sector, 296
political studies, 162
polytechnic *(ligongke)* universities
    121
population census, 351
postgraduates
  admissions procedures, 126–9
  career prospects, 186–90

enrollments, 142–5
flow of, 152–8
program types, 126
quality, 160
professionals (*zhuanye jishu renyuan*)
growth in, 72
replacing category of intellectuals,
65–6
programs for promoting talent
211 Program, 45, 50, 116, 117–18,
121, 142
985 Program, 45, 50, 116, 117–18, 121
Cheung Kong Scholars Program
45–50, 76–7, 116, 122, 194,
234, 235, 243
High-Level Innovative Talent
Development Program, 50
One Hundred, One Thousand, and
Ten Thousands of Talent
Program, 52–3, 77, 234
One-Hundred Talent Program, 50–1,
76–7, 194, 234, 239, 249
problems implementing, 53–5

Qian Changzhao, 168
Qian Xuesen, xxii, 182
Qian Yingyi, 158, 246
Qianjiang Scholar Program, 50
Qinghai, 204, 292
Qinghua University
armed conflict during Cultural
Revolution, 25
as *ligongke* (polytechnic) university,
121
as source of US doctorates, 126
China-foreign cooperative MBA
program, 325
elitist status, 122
funding, 117–18
help from overseas Chinese
academics, 246
quality of education, 158
restructure to become multidisciplinary polytechnic
university, 112
School of Economics and
Management, 158, 246, 324
special stipend to faculty members,
193
world ranking, 159

R&D (research and development)
definitions, 62–3, 64
foreign corporate centers, 32–3
official statistics collection, 353–5
personnel, 78, 92
spending, xviii, 261, 262–3
R&D personnel (*yanjiu kaifa renyuan*)
definitions, 68
educational attainment, 99
forecasting problems, 274–5
growth in, 76
institutional distribution, 78
per capita, 339
Rao, Yi, 240, 245–6
Rawski, Thomas, 349
red eye disease (*hongyanbing*), 244
redness, 173–5
rencai, xix–xx, 66–7
Report on China's Talent 2005
(Chinese Academy of Personnel
Science 2005), xxi–xxii
*Report on the Development of Chinese
Talent*, xxi–xxii, 371
researchers, definitions, 62–3
Resolution on Education Reform
(1985), 116
returnees. *See haigui* (returned Chinese
students and scholars)
Romer, Paul, 5, 10
Rong Hong (Yung Wing), 213
round-tripping, 256

S&T (science and technology),
spending growth, xviii, 261–2
S&T activity, definitions, 69–71
S&T personnel (*keji huodong renyuan*)
definitions, 67–8
demand
drivers of, 255–66
forecast, 271
modeling, 268–71
Diaspora, 277
growth in, 74, 76
institutional distribution, 78
shortage
possibility of, 276–7
reasons for, 278–82
software industry, 306–9
supply. *See also* high-end S&T talent
drivers of, 266–8

S&T personnel (*keji huodong renyuan*) (cont.)
   forecast, 274–5
   modeling, 268–71
S&T workers (*keji gongzuozhe*), 68, 74
S&T workforce
   age and professional rank, 92–3
   career prospects, 186–90
   comparative perspective, 105–7
   definitions, 71
   educational attainment, 95–100
   female proportion, 90–1
   geographical distribution, 83–90
   high-technology industries
      in foreign-invested enterprises (FIEs), 289–92
      quality, 289
      size, 286
   income, 195–207
   institutional distribution, 77–83
   job assignment, promotion, mobility, and reward, 175–82
   numbers employed, 180–1
   quality assessment, 101–5
   satisfaction, 207–8
Salvendy, Gavriel, 158
Saturday engineers, 192, 193
scholar-officials, 167–8
Science Citation Index, 101, 207, 318, 335
scientific papers, xviii–xix, 101–3, 318, 335
scientists, definitions, 62–3
SEC (State Education Commission), 116–17
Shaanxi, 89, 293, 295, 296, 340
Shanda, 184–5
Shandong, 340
Shanghai
   concentration of scientists and engineers, 293, 295, 296
   incomes, 204
   medical equipment sector, 296
   S&T workforce numbers, 89.
      See also Training Program of Scarce S&T Talent for Nanotechnology
Shanghai Jiaotong University, 117, 121
Shanghai Medical University, 121
Shanghai University of Finance and Economics, 324

Shanxi, 89
Shen Tong, 247
Shi, Yigong, 231–2
Schultz, Theodore, 3–4, 9, 16
Sichuan, 293, 296, 340
Sina, 184–5
Sitong (Stone), 184
software colleges, 54
software industry
   brain drain, 299–300
   characteristics of software professionals, 312
   exports, 311–12
   international certification, 309–12
   overview, 299–302
   shortages in specific areas, 306–9, 312–15
   training, 302–9
Sohu, 184–5, 237
Solow, Robert, 4
Southwest Associated University (*Xinan Lianda*), 111
specialty institutions, 121
Spigel, Mark, 7
Statistical Materials on Science and Technology, 353
stem cell research, 241
Stiglitz, Joseph, 158–9
"stinking number nine" (*chou laojiu*), 25, 172
Stone (*Sitong*), 184
strategic weapons programs (*liangdan yixing*), 103, 215
Stride from a Country of Tremendous Population to a Country of Profound Human Resources, xxi–xxii
student admissions, 34–5
subject choices, 126–8
Sun Yatsen, 214
Sun Yueqi, 168
Suntech Power, 237

Taiwan, *liuxuesheng* return rate, 250
talent, 20. *See also* human resources; *rencai*
talent wars, 15, 283, 290–2
Ten Great Years (NBS), 349–50
Tenth Five-Year Plan for Education Development, 119

tertiary education, 59–61, 339
Thread of the Silkworm, xxii
"Three Represents" theory, 171
Tiananmen Square incident, 173, 184,
    218, 227, 235, 325, 342
Tianjin, 89, 204
Tianjin University, 111
Tibet, 89, 204, 292
tolerance, 11
tongyi fenpei, 177
tongzilou, 194
Torch Program, 312, 355–6
training, 180
Training Program of Scarce S&T
    Talent for Nanotechnology, 320–1
tubie (domestically trained academics),
    247

undergraduates
    admissions procedures, 126–8
    enrollments, 130–8
    flow of, 145–52
    program types, 126
UNESCO (United Nations
    Educational, Scientific, and
    Cultural Organization)
    HRST definitions, 59–61, 62.
        *See also Manual for Statistics on
        Scientific and Technological
        Activities* (UNESCO)
universities
    ability to absorb admissions increase,
        35–6
    admissions hike, 120
    curriculum issues, 36–8
    funding, 36
    geographical distribution, 122
University of Electronic Science and
    Technology, 122
US
    Chinese PhDs, 31, 231–2
    immigration policies towards
        international students, 251–2
    scholarships for Chinese students,
        214–15
    venture capital, 185

wage rates, 179, 184–5. *See also*
    awards
Wan Gang, 29–30, 239, 344

Wan Runnan, 184
Wang Xiaodong, 244, 245
Wen Jiabao, 18, 210
Weng Wenhao, 168
whiteness, 173–5
working week, 208
Wu Yishan, 101
Wuhan University, 121

Xi'an Jiaotong University, 121
xiafang policies, 176
Xidian University, 122
Xie Xide, 218
Xin, William (Xin Weirong), 247
Xinan Lianda (Southwest Associated
    University), 111
Xu Xiping, 249
xueke menlei (fields of study), 127

Yan Yonghong, 238
Yangtze River Delta, 293
yanjiu kaifa renyuan (R&D personnel)
    definitions, 68
    educational attainment, 99
    forecasting problems, 274–5
    growth in, 76
    institutional distribution, 78
    per capita, 339
yiji xueke, 127
Yung Wing (Rong Hong), 213

Zhang Tiesheng, 28
Zhao Ziyang, 184, 217
Zhejiang, 84–9, 204, 293, 295, 296
Zhejiang University, 117, 121
zhicheng (professional standing), 69
zhishi fenzi (intellectuals)
    Cultural Revolution, 25
    definitions, 65, 168
    income, 195, 201–3. *See also* S&T
        workforce; income
    Party policy, 170–5. *See also*
        Anti-Rightist Campaign (1957)
zhongdian (key) institutions, 121,
    159–60
Zhongguancun Science Park, 182–4,
    236
Zhou Enlai, 170, 172
Zhou Peiyuan, 217
Zhu Rongji, 51, 237, 349

zhuangyuan, 122, 127

zhuanke programs, 126, 130–3, 138, 152, 160

zhuanye, 127

zhuanye jishu renyuan (professionals) growth in, 72

replacing category of intellectuals, 65–6

zifei (self-sponsored) overseas study, 217, 222

zonghe (comprehensive) institutions, 121